Migration and Diversity in Asian Contexts

The **Institute of Southeast Asian Studies (ISEAS)** was established as an autonomous organization in 1968. It is a regional centre dedicated to the study of socio-political, security and economic trends and developments in Southeast Asia and its wider geostrategic and economic environment. The Institute's research programmes are the Regional Economic Studies (RES, including ASEAN and APEC), Regional Strategic and Political Studies (RSPS), and Regional Social and Cultural Studies (RSCS).

ISEAS Publishing, an established academic press, has issued more than 2,000 books and journals. It is the largest scholarly publisher of research about Southeast Asia from within the region. ISEAS Publishing works with many other academic and trade publishers and distributors to disseminate important research and analyses from and about Southeast Asia to the rest of the world.

Migration and Diversity in Asian Contexts

Edited by **Lai Ah Eng**, **Francis L. Collins** and **Brenda S.A. Yeoh**

INSTITUTE OF SOUTHEAST ASIAN STUDIES
Singapore

First published in Singapore in 2013 by
ISEAS Publishing
Institute of Southeast Asian Studies
30 Heng Mui Keng Terrace
Pasir Panjang
Singapore 119614

E-mail: publish@iseas.edu.sg
Website: http://bookshop.iseas.edu.sg

All rights reserved. No part of this publication may be reproduced, stored in a retrieval system, or transmitted in any form or by any means, electronic, mechanical, photocopying, recording or otherwise, without the prior permission of the Institute of Southeast Asian Studies.

© 2013 Institute of Southeast Asian Studies, Singapore

The responsibility for facts and opinions in this publication rests exclusively with the authors and their interpretations do not necessarily reflect the views or the policy of the publisher or their supporters.

ISEAS Library Cataloguing-in-Publication Data

Migration and diversity in Asian contexts / edited by Lai Ah Eng, Francis L. Collins and Brenda S.A. Yeoh.
1. Asia—Emigration and immigration.
2. Multiculturalism—Asia.
3. Ethnicity--Asia.
I. Lai, Ah Eng.
II. Collins, Francis L.
III. Yeoh, Brenda S.A.
JV8490 M631   2013

ISBN 978-981-4380-47-8 (soft cover)
ISBN 978-981-4380-46-1 (e-book, PDF)

Typeset by Superskill Graphics Pte Ltd
Printed in Singapore by Mainland Press Pte Ltd

CONTENTS

List of Contributors   vii

Acknowledgements   xii

Introduction: Approaching Migration and Diversity in Asian Contexts   1
Francis L. Collins, Lai Ah Eng and Brenda S.A. Yeoh

PART I: Migration, Multiculturalism and Governance in Asia

1. Multicultural Realities and Membership: States, Migrations and Citizenship in Asia   31
   Maruja M.B. Asis and Graziano Batistella

2. Multicultural Coexistence Policies of Local Governments in the Tokyo Metropolis: A Comparative Examination of Social Integration in Response to Growing Ethnic Diversity   56
   Stephen Robert Nagy

3. The Place of Migrant Workers in Singapore: Between State Multiracialism and Everyday (Un)Cosmopolitanisms   83
   Fred C.M. Ong and Brenda S.A. Yeoh

4. Selective State Response and Ethnic Minority Incorporation: The South Korean Case   107
   Nora Hui-Jung Kim

5. The Tug of War over Multiculturalism: Contestation between Governing and Empowering Immigrants in Taiwan — 130
Hsia Hsiao-Chuan

PART II: Identities

6. Mixed-ethnic Children Raised by Single Thai Mothers in Japan: A Choice of Ethnic Identity — 163
Kayoko Ishii

7. Being Indian in Post-colonial Metro Manila: Identities, Boundaries and the Media Practices — 182
Jozon A. Lorenzana

PART III: Practices

8. The *Kopitiam* in Singapore: An Evolving Story about Migration and Cultural Diversity — 209
Lai Ah Eng

9. Spatial Process and Cultural Territory of Islamic Food Restaurants in Itaewon, Seoul — 233
Doyoung Song

10. Competition and Constructedness: Sports, Migration and Diversity in Singapore — 254
Robbie B.H. Goh

Index — 277

LIST OF CONTRIBUTORS

Maruja M.B. ASIS is Director of Research and Publications at the Scalabrini Migration Center. She is a sociologist who has been working on migration issues in Asia. Her current research deals with the impact of government regulations on the protection of Filipino domestic workers, employment and migration of the Filipino youth, health and well-being of migrants' children in the Philippines (part of a four-country study in Southeast Asia), and capacity-building of migrants' associations and Philippine government institutions as development partners. She is Co-editor of the *Asian and Pacific Migration Journal* and *Asian Migration News*. She has published in journals/books and has participated in international conferences and expert group meetings.

Graziano BATTISTELLA is the director of the Scalabrini Migration Center, where he has returned after seven years as president of the Scalabrini International Migration Institute in Rome. He founded the *Asian and Pacific Migration Journal,* of which he is co-editor. His research interests are in the area of migration policies, the human rights of migrants, and ethical issues related to migration. He edited recently in Italian a dictionary on migration, titled *Migrazioni: Dizionario Socio-Pastorale*.

Francis L. COLLINS is a Lecturer in Urban Geography at the School of Environment, University of Auckland. Before joining the University of Auckland Francis held positions in the Asia Research Institute and Department of Geography at the National University of Singapore. His primary research interest is the intersection between migratory processes and experiences and the changing form of cities with a particular emphasis on the lives of temporary migrants. Currently, Francis' research focuses on the mobility of international students within Asia and the changing institutional structure of universities in the region; temporary migrants and emerging experiences of diversity in Seoul, South Korea; and questions of livability in cities within Asia. Francis has published on these topics in international journals within geography, migration and urban studies including recent publications in Geoforum, Urban Studies and Progress in Human Geography.

Robbie B.H. GOH is in the department of English Language and Literature, NUS, and Vice-Dean of the Faculty of Arts and Social Sciences. He works on Christianity in Asia, diasporic cultures and literatures, popular culture and nineteenth-century literature. Recent publications include *Contours of Culture: Space and Social Difference in Singapore* (2005); *Christianity in Southeast Asia* (2005); *Christian Ministry and the Asian Nation: the Metropolitan YMCA in Singapore* (2006); and articles in *Crossroads, Journal of Commonwealth Literature, Social Semiotics, International Journal of Urban and Regional Research*, and in other journals and edited volumes.

HSIA Hsiao-Chuan is Professor and Director at the Graduate Institute for Social Transformation Studies, Shih Hsin University, Taipei. As the first scholar studying marriage migration issues in Taiwan, her first well-known book is titled *Drifting Shoal* (流離尋岸): *the "Foreign Brides" Phenomenon in Capitalist Globalization* (in Chinese). Her other publications analyse issues of immigrants, migrant workers, citizenship, empowerment and social movement. Hsia is also an activist striving for the empowerment of immigrant women and the making of im/migrant movement in Taiwan. She initiated the Chinese programs for marriage migrants in 1995, leading to the establishment of TransAsia Sisters Association, Taiwan (TASAT). She is also the co-founder of the Alliance for the Human Rights Legislation for Immigrants and Migrants and serves as the board member of Asia Pacific Mission for Migrants, and a member of the International Coordinating Body of the International Migrants Alliance.

Kayoko ISHII, Ph.D., is a sociologist whose focus of research is on social change of minority/rural population in Thailand. Her current focus is on Thai migrant women and their children in Japan. Amongst her recent publications are *Ethnicity and Citizenship: From the Case of Multicultural Community* (2007), "Social Network among Foreign Residents in Japan: the Case of Thai Migrants in Tokai Area", *NUCB Journal of Economics and*

Information Science 50, no. 2, and *Comparative Study on Networks among Foreign Residents in Japan: Comparative Study on Philippine, Chinese and Thai migrant* (2007, edited by K. Ishii, final report for research project of Ichihara International foundation). She is currently an associate professor in the Faculty of Economics, Nagoya University of Commerce and Business.

Nora KIM is an assistant professor of sociology at University of Mary Washington, Fredericksburg, Virginia, U.S.A. Her research interests include international immigration, multiculturalism, race and ethnicity, nationalism, citizenship, and East Asia. She has published in the *International Migration Review*, *Nations and Nationalism*, and *Citizenship Studies*.

LAI Ah Eng is senior research fellow, Asia Research Institute and teaching fellow, University Scholars Programme, National University of Singapore. She has worked in various research capacities at the Consumers' association of Penang, Housing Development Board (Singapore), the National Archives of Singapore, Institute of Southeast Asian Studies (Singapore) and Institute of Policy Studies (Singapore), and lectured at the Departments of Sociology and Social Work, National University of Singapore. Her research areas include multiculturalism, migration, family and heritage. Her major publications include *Meanings of Multiethnicity: A Case Study of Ethnicity and Ethnic Relations in Singapore* (1995), *Beyond Rituals and Riots: Ethnic Pluralism and Social Cohesion in Singapore (2004)*, *Secularism and Spirituality: Striving for Integrated Knowledge and Success in Madrasah Education in Singapore* (co-edited) (2005), and *Religious Diversity in Singapore* (2008). She has also written articles on ethnicity, religion, gender and family.

Jozon A. LORENZANA is a Ph.D. student in social anthropology at the University of Western Australia. He is also instructor in the Department of Communication, School of Social Sciences at the Ateneo de Manila University. His research interests include migrant cultures and relations in India and the Philippines; practices of class; senses and emotions; gendered and mediated relations; masculinity in Australia.

Stephen R. NAGY is currently an Assistant Professor at the Chinese University of Hong Kong's Department of Japanese Studies. He obtained his Ph.D. from Waseda University in International Studies in December 2008 for his dissertation entitled "Analysis of the Multicultural Coexistence

Ideas and the Practices of Local Governments in the Tokyo Metropolis". His current funded research projects are "Human Security Paradigm in Japan: Exploring the Challenges and Possibilities of International Cooperation in Northeast Asia" and "Investigating the Role of Local Governments Immigration and Migrant Policies in Hong Kong and Tokyo". His research interests include migration, human security, Asian regional integration and regionalism in Asia. In conjunction with his research focus on Asian regional integration he was appointed a Senior Fellow with the Global Institute of Asian Regional Integration (GIARI), Waseda University.

Fred C.M. ONG is currently a full-time teacher at National Junior College and a part-time Masters candidate in Social Science (Geography) at the National University of Singapore (NUS). He was a recipient of the Singapore Journal of Tropical Geography Book Prize in 2007, and a research scholar from 2008–10 He is interested in a wide array of topics including the politics of space, migration in Asian cities, cosmopolitan urbanism, issues of ethnicity and nationality and tourism geographies. His current research focuses on debates on public space, low-skilled migrant workers and cosmopolitan urbanism. More specifically he is investigating the attitudes and competencies of Singaporeans towards male migrant workers congregating within public spaces that have not been traditionally regarded as gathering places for these workers, and examining how these spatial perspectives relate to developments within cosmopolitanism studies.

Doyoung SONG is a professor at the Department of Cultural Anthropology, Hanyang University, Korea. His main research focus is on the spatial process and culture in urban context. After his doctorate thesis on Tunisian migrant-merchants in France (1993, Ecole des Hautes Etudes en Sciences Sociales, Paris), he continued his research on the relationship between urban space and culture of diversity in Islamic cities of Mediterranean Region. Working at Seoul Development Institute (1994–95) and the University of Seoul, Deparment. of Urban Sociology (1996–2007), he also did several case studies on the districts of Seoul, Paris, and some Moroccan cities concerning cultural policy of urban space and cultural diversity. Currently, he is preparing a comparative study of Muslim communities in Korean cities and in some Mediterranean cities.

Brenda S.A. YEOH (D. Phil. Oxford) is Professor, Department of Geography as well as Dean of the Faculty of Arts and Social Sciences. She is Research Leader of the Asian Migration Research Cluster and her research interests include the politics of space in colonial and post-colonial cities; gender; migration and transnational communities. Her first book was *Contesting Space: Power Relations and the Urban Built Environment in Colonial Singapore* (1996; reissued 2003). She has also published more recently *State/Nation/Transnation: Perspectives on Transnationalism in the Asia-Pacific* (2004, with Katie Willis), *Migration and Health in Asia* (2005, with Santosh Jatrana and Mika Toyota), *Asian Women as Transnational Domestic Workers* (2005, with Shirlena Huang and Noor Abdul Rahman), *Working and Mothering in Asia* (2007, with Theresa Devasahayam) and *Over Singapore 50 Years Ago* (with Theresa Wong).

ACKNOWLEDGEMENTS

The editors wish to thank Ms Li Hongyan for her careful copyediting services in this book project.

INTRODUCTION
Approaching Migration and Diversity in Asian Contexts

Francis L. COLLINS, LAI Ah Eng and
Brenda S.A. YEOH

Migration and the human diversity that necessarily accompanies it present multifarious challenges and opportunities within the varied social and cultural landscapes of Asia. The contributions in this volume set out to interrogate some of these challenges and opportunities and to discuss emergent governance regimes, identities and practices across and within the nations, cities, neighbourhoods, communities and families of East and Southeast Asia. This simultaneously varied and integrative approach to the subject matter speaks to the wide-ranging temporal and spatial dimensions of migration and diversity in Asia. In some parts of the region, contemporary migration and diversity symbolize a historically significant rupturing of long-held self-representations of ethnically homogeneous nations and communities (such as in Japan and Korea). Elsewhere, migration as both historical memory and contemporary experience serves as a foundational basis to the imagining of a multicultural nation and community (as is the case in Malaysia and Singapore). Within such polarities of collective belonging, diversity is also negotiated on an everyday basis in the homes of multiethnic families, in the lives and identities of minorities and individuals, and in the always challenging encounters with others in social spaces such as workplaces, public spaces, restaurants and sports fields.

This introduction serves as an entry point into the themes addressed in this volume, situating the more detailed chapters that follow within extant scholarship on migration and diversity in Asia. In reviewing the current treatment of migration and diversity in Asia, it is clear that while both "migration" and "diversity" as phenomena are of increasing interest to scholars within and beyond the region, there are very few examples of scholarship that have focused on how they relate to each other. Rather, most academic work has been concerned *either* with increasing mobility within the region *or* with the already diverse social and cultural landscapes of certain parts of the region, instead of the ways in which mobility feeds into changing experiences of diversity (and vice versa), both historically and in the contemporary era. This volume, then, offers a first step in the effort to understand the increasingly important question of human mobility and its subsequent effects on population diversity in a region that is becoming ever more open and central to the processes of globalization. The chapters are primarily and necessarily empirical, with a focus on grounded understandings of migration and diversity issues. At the same time, we conclude this introductory chapter by pointing to the potential for new directions in theory building that are cognizant of the region's contextual specificities and the rich evidence they provide.

THE STUDY OF MIGRATION IN ASIA

Migration from, to and within the Asian region is certainly not new (Castles and Miller 2008). Until the eighteenth century, Asia, particularly in China, India, and emerging empires and regional centres, was a site of tremendous economic expansion of trade and commercial ties based on overland and sea routes which facilitated the movements of traders, missionaries, adventurers and fortune-seekers. During distinct colonial periods, the mass movements of labourers and traders as well as colonial settlers, missionaries and others also played significant roles in the development of European colonies, often providing the basis for the heterogeneous societies (Kymlicka and He 2005) and significant diasporic communities (Lal, Reeves, and Rai 2006; Pan 1999) that now characterize parts of the region. Emigration out of the region was also a key characteristic of the late nineteenth and early twentieth centuries, as considerable numbers of Chinese and Japanese migrants made their way to Southeast Asia, the United States, Canada and Australia before restrictive policies came into place. Other examples of historical migration include internal migrations within China and Manchuria in the late nineteenth and early twentieth centuries, the movement of Koreans under Japanese colonialism, mass population displacements following the partition of the Indian subcontinent (Castles and Miller 2008), and migrations within Southeast Asia and the Malay Archipelago.

While these major histories of migration certainly have their particular systems of movement and mobility, recent scholarship has tended to focus on identifying and delineating the systems of migration embedded within contemporary global processes since the 1970s (Massey et al. 1998). Writing in the late 1990s as this system was becoming increasingly coherent, Massey et al. (1998) identify four key contributing factors in their focus on the "Asia-Pacific": shifting national origins of migrants into Japan and Australia; net-migration losses in New Zealand; the rapid economic development of some countries in the region including Hong Kong, Korea, Taiwan, Malaysia and Singapore; and the growth of refugees in Southeast Asia following the conflicts of the 1960s and 1970s. Shifting from a focus on Western receiving nations (as reflected in Massey et al.'s perspective), it is also necessary to identify large-scale labour migration (both independent and government arranged) since the 1970s from countries throughout Asia to the Middle East, a pattern that served as the leading edge of Asian migratory trends in the 1970s and which continues to the present. Overall, these factors have led to considerable increases in emigration of skilled migrants from the region into Australasia as well as North America and Europe; increased movement of migrant labour from the poorer Asian countries to the rapidly developing economies of East and Southeast Asia as well as to the Middle East; and considerable issues surrounding the presence and rights of displaced populations and undocumented migrants.

From the 1980s, a feminization of Asian migration became increasingly apparent, particularly to meet the growing demand in the gender-segmented markets of domestic work, entertainment and sexual services. Initially, it was mainly non-governmental organizations (NGOs) providing direct advocacy and welfare services which tracked these flows and first raised serious (and public) attention on the work and living conditions of Filipino mail-order brides in Europe (1980s); Filipino and Thai entertainers and sex workers in Japan; and Filipino, Thai and Indonesian domestic workers in Singapore, Malaysia and the Middle East (1980s and 1990s).

Some of these trends have become even clearer since the late 1990s, coupled with the increasing prevalence of female migration from the Philippines, Vietnam and Indonesia to Japan, Korea, Taiwan, Malaysia and Singapore for marriage and marriage-cum-work. The emergence of migration agents or brokers as key players in population mobility and the broader development of a "migration industry" that fills the void left by receiving states that are less than willing to make bilateral arrangements for labour supply with countries of origin is another significant aspect (Castles and Miller 2008; Xiang 2007), while another emerging trend is the mobility into, within, and out of Asia of highly skilled migrants (Yeoh and Lai 2008), students (Mok 2006) and returnees (Tsuda 2009). In contrast to these increasing trends, the Asian region has experienced a relative decline in the number of refugees at 3.4 million in 2004 compared to 5.4 million in 2000 — a fact that Castles and Miller (2008) put down to political stability and fewer internal or international conflicts — although the continued flight of the Rohingyas and other ethnic minorities from Burma reminds us that this remains an ongoing issue in Asia.

The new population movements in Asia have begun to attract significant attention from scholars at the same time that they have also become an increasingly central concern for states within the region (Asis and Piper 2008). The bulk of research on migration in Asia has been focused on labour migration as regional labour markets have gradually become more integrated and as states have become increasingly aware of their reliance on imported labour power. In 2010, Asia accounted for about one quarter or 30.7 million of the 105.5 million migrant workers globally, an increase from 25.6 per cent to 29 per cent of the global stock since 2004 (International Labour Office 2010). Labour migration in Asian countries is largely intra-regional, with large numbers of migrants originating from particular countries within the region such as the Philippines and Indonesia in Southeast Asia; India, Pakistan and Bangladesh in South Asia; and, more recently, China and Vietnam. Equally, there is a small group of newly industrialized countries within the region which dominate as the destinations of labour migrants: Hong Kong, Japan, Singapore, South Korea and Taiwan. Other nations such as Malaysia and Thailand act as both origins of considerable numbers of labour migrants while also hosting imported labour from neighbouring countries, mainly Indonesia and Burma (Asis and Piper 2008).

Labour migration in Asia primarily revolves around low-skilled workers in two highly gendered categories: low-skill (often male) workers in industries like manufacturing and construction, and female migrants working in domestic service, entertainment or the service industry (Hewison and Young 2006). There is also important, if numerically less significant, high-skilled migration into many of the same major destination countries (Iredale 2003). Often, such workers are professionals in in-demand sectors like information technology, engineering, finance and health, and receiving countries and companies have developed policies that actively seek to attract these workers with offers of attractive packages and permanent residence. A final significant group in terms of migratory flows in the region are female marriage migrants from developing countries who have become an increasingly notable presence in Japan, Singapore, South Korea and Taiwan in recent years (Piper and Roces 2003).

Recent research on the growth of labour migration systems has generally focused on either building up empirical data on the flows of migrants or on the development of policy regimes for sending or receiving migrants in various parts of the Asian region (Asis and Piper 2008). This has included considerable research into the political, economic and population influences on changing migration patterns in Asia, in particular the emergence of labour shortages in low and unskilled manufacturing areas in newly industrialized economies since the 1980s (Hugo 1998). In all of these locations, migrant workers are almost completely concentrated in sectors that are characterized by "3D" jobs that are dirty, dangerous and difficult and that attract the very minimum of wages; effectively parts of the economy that can no longer attract and retain members of the local population (Stahl 1999). Policy regimes governing the arrival and presence of migrant workers operate in a manner that further enhances their unstable position, maintaining strict restrictions through "use-and-discard" contract labour systems (Yeoh 2006) which encourage transience, discourage settlement, and provide states with the capacity to rapidly reduce their foreign labour force in times of economic downturn (Ahmed 1998).

Within this broader effort to map the flows and responses to international migration has been a particular focus on the feminization of human mobility within Asia over the last two decades (Heyzer 2007; Oishi 2005). Early scholarship in this area focused on the emergence of "mail-order-bride" phenomena with an emphasis on the systems of migration (Chun 1996; Tolentino 1996), the legal responses of sending and receiving states (Meng 1994), and the experience of women themselves (Robinson 1996; Ordoñez 1997). Other earlier research investigated female migration to work as entertainers, often involving migrants from the Philippines and

Thailand working in the developed economies of East Asia in employment that is closely associated with the sex industry (Tyner 1997; Yea 2004), or alternatively the circulation of sex tourists in the converse direction (Truong 1983).

More recent work on the feminization of migration in the region has paid particular attention to two forms of mobility that involve women who not only cross international borders but also fulfill key roles in the making of households as domestic workers and international marriage migrants. The former involves the movement of large numbers of women from countries like the Philippines, Indonesia and Sri Lanka as early as the late 1970s to the Middle East, and more recently to Singapore, Hong Kong and Taiwan (Huang, Yeoh and Rahman 2005; Yamanaka and Piper 2005; Wong 1996). Research here has focused on negotiations of complex spaces between labouring abroad and mothering at home (Yeoh and Huang 1999), the framing of positionalities within international divisions of labour cut across by gender, class, race and nationality (Parreñas 2000), and new movements supporting the rights of domestic workers (Lyons 2005; Piper 2005).

Furthermore, asking questions about the gendering of migration, rather than simply the different migrations of men and women, is an emergent literature on international marriage migrations in the region. Although clearly related to earlier mail-order-bride systems, contemporary modes of international marriage migration have moved from a marginal status to a significant mode of social reproduction in Singapore, Taiwan, South Korea and Japan (Piper and Roces 2003). In the process, women from China, Vietnam, Thailand, the Philippines and other developing countries have become embedded within projects of nation building, such as population replacement due to mass ageing and lower fertility rates, that raise serious questions about diversity, cultural maintenance and integration (Kim 2007; Wang and Bélanger 2008); the role of brokerage agencies (Lu 2008); associations with trafficking (Jones and Shen 2008), and the lives of a generation of mixed-ethnicity children in previously homogeneous societies (Ishii *this volume*).

While much migration in Asia is taking place amongst those perceived to be low-skilled labourers or potential mothers of the next generation, there are also emerging trends of mobility amongst more skilled migrants into and within the region. Indeed, a number of Asian nations are now actively recruiting skilled professionals and are developing policies that provide pathways to residence and even naturalization for migrants with significant financial resources or human capital (Castles and Miller 2008). These flows of migrants include professionals working in sectors long associated with skilled migration elsewhere, such as Information Technology, but also includes "foreign talent" (Yeoh 2006) in areas as diverse as sports (Goh *this volume*) and various mobilities associated with health and care-work (Connell 2008). Scholars have also identified two key state strategies within these policies. On the one hand, there is evidence that sending countries with large populations of professionals or students abroad are seeking to attract them back through incentive programmes or encouraging a sense of attachment to place and an obligation to national development (Skrentny et al. 2007). India's recent changes to its citizenship laws offer a useful example in which "people of Indian origin" of certain nationalities could be granted visa-free travel, investment opportunities, and access to educational institutions (Dickinson and Bailey 2007). At the same time, researchers have identified a new focus by receiving countries on attracting international students as potential contributors to future skilled populations, and in particular a shift from Asian countries simply sending students abroad to the West towards new efforts to attract overseas students to China, Taiwan, Japan, South Korea, Singapore and Hong Kong (Mok 2006).

Outside of scholarship that focuses specifically on these dominant state-sanctioned forms of international mobility, three other issues have featured significantly in scholarship in and on Asia which are beyond the scope of this volume but nonetheless do warrant some brief mention here. The first is the rather tricky issue of internal migration, often not considered within key migration textbooks (Massey et al. 1998; Castles and Miller 2008) because it does not include the crossing of national borders but which may involve major dimensions of diversity and crossings of cultures. The sheer scale and intensity of internal migratory trends and the quite distinct challenges it raises for states, communities and migrants mean that this focus is beyond the scope of what can be accomplished here. There is, however, no doubting the significance of internal migration in the Asian context. Large countries like China, India and Indonesia have huge populations of internal migrants who leave rural areas in search of work in major cities and emerging agricultural and industrial regions (Liang and Ma 2004; Deshingkar 2009; Tirtosudarmo 1997). Indeed, China's "floating population" of internal migrants at 120 million is numerically more significant than all international mobility in the region combined (Zhu 2006). Also, there are no doubt important inter-linkages between international and internal migration in Asia, either in terms of graduation from internal to international migration, the role of social networks and agencies across both modes, and the labour market influences that each migration appears to have on the other (Skeldon 2006). Yet, as the different contributions to this volume illustrate, despite these connections the role of borders and their management in the facilitation, limitation and regulation of mobility, particularly in Asian contexts, require specific attention as do the particular kinds of diversity that result from international movements.

A second characteristic of mobility that is significant within the Asian region and that has been the subject of some scholarly work, although beyond the purview of this volume, is the mobility, rights and experiences of undocumented and irregular migrants. The presence of this category of migrants varies considerably in the region, with numbers estimated to be approaching nearly 1 million in Thailand (Chalamwong 2004), constituting two-thirds of the total foreign workforce in the late 1990s in South Korea (Seol 2000), and negligible numbers in Singapore (Abella 2006). Scholars working in this area have focused on the causes of irregular migration (Asis 2004), its connections with documented flows, and practices of the state in seeking to control, expel or at times turn a blind eye to the presence of undocumented migrants (Ghosh 1998). There have also been efforts to focus on the rights of undocumented workers whose legal status makes them extraordinarily vulnerable, subject to potential injury or even death without recourse to the law (Piper and Uhlin 2002).

Human trafficking and people smuggling also remains a significant feature of migration within the Asian region. Although Southeast Asia and the Greater Mekong Subregion in particular are considered the epicentre of trafficking that involves both labour and sexual exploitation, there is growing evidence of a trafficking trade linking Nepal and Bangladesh as source countries with India and Pakistan as destination countries, as well as sex-trafficking into more developed Asia-Pacific countries such as Australia, Hong Kong, Japan and South Korea (Human Rights Watch 1995; International Organization for Migration 2000; Okubo and Shelley 2011). There are multiple dimensions to this phenomenon, not least the problematic overlaps between labour migration, marriage migration and forms of human trafficking (Yea 2011). There is also growing interest amongst scholars, particularly since the enactment of the UN Trafficking

Protocol in 2003 and the growing prominence of the US State Department's annual TIP report since 2001. Unsurprisingly, given the way trafficking is represented in popular and policy discourses as victimization, much scholarship has pointed to the ways in which vulnerability is produced (Kojma 2011): in home country social relations (Yea 2005), through the work of agents and other intermediaries (Simkhada 2008), and through forms of unilateral, bilateral and multilateral government regulation (Okubo and Shelley 2011).

The issue of vulnerable populations and exploitation through migration points to another prominent issue: the limited rights of most migrants in Asia (Piper 2004; Yeoh 2006) and the emergence of national and transnational human rights movements in Asia, and in particular NGOs' advocacy work on migrant rights (Piper and Uhlin 2002). This has been a particular feature of debates in Northeast Asia where NGO movements have been successful in achieving important concessions (Lim 2003). Such movements also play an important role in incorporating even temporary migrants into local political contexts (Tsuda 2006) but also more generally contribute to new vibrant forms of democratic multiculturalism (Shipper 2008). Looking to the future, these debates have also raised important questions about the citizenship and residence status of temporary migrants, especially in countries where migrant workers now form an indispensible part of the economy (Kim 2009). The recent (2009) setup of a human rights mechanism among ASEAN countries suggests the new potential to address similar "rights" issues faced by undocumented and other vulnerable migrants is also emerging in Southeast Asia.

As this summary suggests, there is now a considerable amount of research on migration within the Asian region that reveals increasing and diversifying levels of mobility and an increasing attention paid to the phenomenon by the region's states. It is also clear that the bulk of this work has tended to focus on analysing what Massey et al. (1998) identified in the late 1990s as the emerging "migration system" within the region. However, as Asis and Piper (2008, p. 427) have identified in their recent overview of labour migration in Asia, this focus on gathering "information for practical purposes" and a tendency to operate as a "running commentary of a phenomenon in progress" has limited the extent to which studies of migration have been able to engage with conceptual questions or with the wider diversity of migration-related issues that have been common elsewhere. Indeed, there has been much less study of the formation of transnational communities in Asia, the identities of migrants abroad or the interaction that migrants have with local populations. These are important questions for a more mature state of migration research in the region. They also raise significant issues for understanding the complex issues that are now emerging as migration becomes a more permanent feature of lives in Asia. Not least amongst these issues are the new forms of social and cultural diversity that are emerging as the presence of migrants becomes a central feature of everyday lives throughout Asia.

THE STUDY OF DIVERSITY IN ASIA

While the literature on international migration in Asia is clearly well established and increasingly varied, equivalent scholarly inquiry into emergent diversity is much less apparent. Moreover, where the former has largely focused on contemporary mobility associated with work and marriage, scholarship on diversity in Asia has tended to approach this issue as a historically constituted reality. As such, the focus has been mainly on those countries where diversity is a foundational part of nation-building or on other contexts where internal or cross-border minorities have been a significant presence (Hefner 2001; Goh et al. 2009; Kumar and Siddique 2008; Kymlicka and He 2005). In this regard, more attention has been paid to issues within South and Southeast Asia where diversity and the presence of minorities have long prevailed and much less so in Northeast Asia where diversity, if recognized at all, is seen as a temporary rupture of long-established homogeneity.

In Western European contexts such as the United Kingdom, Germany, France, Denmark and Holland (Madood and Werbner 1997) and "immigration countries" such as Canada, Australia and New Zealand (Pearson 2001), the concerns and debates on diversity variously focus around the discourses and practices of "multiculturalism", "integration", "rights and responsibilities", "social cohesion", "social inclusion", "cosmopolitanism" and "unity in diversity" and, in the post-September 11 environment, much attention has been paid to Muslim minorities. In contrast, there has been relatively little attention given to the growing diversity in Asia in contemporary times. While debates are also emerging over diversity issues in some Asian settings, there has not been a similar level of attention given to the processes, meanings and significances embedded in these issues as compared to the prominence evident in European contexts; neither has there been sufficient attempts to understand diversity issues within the contexts of highly distinct and varied postcolonial histories, cultures, geographies, and political economies specific to Asia. Rather, questions of diversity in Asia have been addressed within the larger corpus of work on the history of migration in colonial societies and the processes and tensions within nation-building, particularly in the context of the heterogeneous societies of Indonesia, Malaysia and Singapore.

During the colonial era, the heterogeneity of populations, mostly arising from labour recruitment and migration systems, did not escape the notice of scholars and colonial administrators. This gave rise to important conceptualizing work such as the plural society thesis of Furnivall (1967) which became the dominant theoretical framework for studying colonial and heterogeneous societies. Studies on specific immigrant populations, such as the Chinese in Southeast Asia (Purcell 1965), as well as anthropological studies of specific cultural/ethnic groups also made important contributions to understanding diversity and the constitution of racial/ethnic categorizations under colonial administration in Malaya and Singapore. With the imminence and then achievement of independence, concern shifted to building viable and cohesive nation-states out of these heterogeneous societies, and scholarship from the 1950s onwards primarily focused on migration histories, demographics, citizenship and identities of settlers and minorities (Wang 1988, 1989; Yen 1986; Sandhu 1969; Arasaratnam 1979; Sandhu and Mani 1993). This included accounts of political movements in which immigrants played pivotal roles, such as the Chinese in the anti-colonial Communist movement in Malaya, and the political and cultural issues of post-colonial nation-building (Emerson 1960; Bell 1976; Bell and Freeman 1974; Horowitz 1985). Many from the first and second generations of local scholars focused on specific communities or aspects within the nation-building project and processes specific to new nation-states, such as communalism and political accommodation in Malaysia (Ratnam 1965; Muzaffar 1974). More focused studies also engaged with the potentially divisive issues of language, culture and religion in Singapore and Malaysia (Tham 1971; Chiew 1983; Chan 1984; Puru Shotam 1989), the effects of race-based colonial policies on immigrant as well as indigenous populations in Malaysia (Lim 1977; Shamsul A. B. 1986) and the role of immigrants in nation-building (Suryadinata 1997).

Nation-state building continues to dominate research and writing in the postcolonial societies of Southeast Asia, in part because their relatively new nation-state building projects are still works-in-progress. Thus, where issues of ethnicity, language, culture and religion first emerged as potentially divisive in the newly independent nation-state, as was the case in Malaysia, they have now re-emerged to hinder projects of nation-building, ethnic integration and social cohesion in ways that are influenced by a complex interplay of policy and social forces (Mandal 2001; Shamsul 2001; Lim, Gomes, and Raham 2009). In the Malaysian case, those from second and subsequent generations of Chinese and Indian descent who are full-fledged citizens are still viewed as immigrants by some Malays who consider themselves indigenous and *bumiputra* (sons of the soil), and minority issues on language, culture and religion remain hotly contested. In the context of recent Islamization among Malays and growing religiosity among others, issues of religious practice and conversion in particular have become controversial and divisive among Malaysia's diverse and overlapping ethnic and religious populations (Mohamad 2009, Whiting 2008).

In Singapore, the CMIO (Chinese, Malay, Indian and Others) model of multiculturalism that continues the racial categories employed by British colonial administrators was first laid as a foundation for the newly independent nation-state in the 1960s (Benjamin 1976). To this day it continues to be under scrutiny and contestation for its underlying assumptions about the fixedness of ethnic culture and its perpetuation of differentiation and separation by ethnicity (Siddique 1989; Chua and Kwok 2001). Also, language issues around the use of English (inherited from the British), Singlish (a local version of English influenced by various Chinese dialects, Malay and Indian) and Mandarin (dominant language of the Chinese majority population and new Chinese immigrants) continue to be debated in terms of their relative cultural and economic values. The arrival of recent immigrants adds yet another layer of complexity and challenge to CMIO multiculturalism, such as the (mis)fit of immigrants into the CMIO schema, the "rightful" place and use of English by immigrants, and local-immigrant interaction and integration issues (Yeoh 2005). What is of significance here is that always underlying nation-building are issues pertaining to social and cultural diversity and the challenges of negotiating them, however diversity and multiculturalism may be defined within national and local contexts.

Where recent research has started to address questions of diversity in Asia, it has often looked at applicability of Western approaches to multiculturalism within Asian contexts. Kymlicka (2005), for example, notes that the particularities of cultural diversity in Asia, where long-established minority groups are equal citizens and/or key contributors to the nation-state even as they desire neither independence nor assimilation, means that Western models of integration or minority rights are not easily applied. Yet, at the same time, the absence of large-scale debates about minority rights and integration that follow European models does not mean that diversity is not a key dynamic in the region. On the contrary, research has found that diversity is often viewed as a part of everyday life in countries like Indonesia, Malaysia and Singapore (Hefner 2001; Lai 1995; Gomes, Kaartinen, and Kortteinen 2007; Goh et al. 2009; Wise and Velayutham 2009). This is not to suggest that conflict around differences in ethnicity, culture, language and religion do not take place; they certainly do, as research around experiences of racism and issues of cosmopolitanism in places like Singapore make clear (Gomez 2010; Ong and Yeoh *this volume*; Velayutham 2009). It is to point out that the negotiation of such differences is often treated as part and parcel of community and everyday life (Lai 1995; Lai *this volume*).

A less notable presence within the study of diversity in Asia has been the impact of more recent migratory waves on the cultural constitution of communities and nations. Certainly, some of the forms of migration discussed in the previous section raise important questions about diversity — particularly the question of new transnational marriages in changing the ethnic/cultural make-up of both present and future generations of families. Yet, even here, there appears to be little effort to connect debates around the processes of migration with the emergence of new forms of diversity, but rather a more descriptive focus on policy responses. In the case of labour migrants, the assumed transience of these subjects in state policy and rhetoric has meant that little discussion of diversity has emerged.

Clearly, contemporary forms of migration do present significant challenges for scholarly understandings of diversity in the region. In some cases, this needs to be understood within the contexts of already pluralistic societies, such as Indonesia, Malaysia and Singapore, where new forms of migration are both extending and expanding the diversity of populations. Some of these societies have also historically encountered conflicts and tensions between ethnic groups, but this means they have also accumulated accommodation and integration experiences, efforts and processes that present contexts and possibilities for newer migrants to find openings in the fabric of communities. In other cases, contemporary forms of migration are occurring in relatively homogeneous societies such as Japan, South Korea and Taiwan, and diversity poses a new challenge to policy-makers, the public and immigrants themselves. In general, for members of host societies, the tremendous speed and scale of immigration and the variety of immigrants' backgrounds pose adjustment problems of perception and acceptance of immigrants and of changes to their existing social orders, cultures and identities.

APPROACHING MIGRATION AND DIVERSITY IN ASIA

This volume takes as its object of enquiry the intersection between processes of migration and experiences of diversity in Asia. Our geographical focus is in East and Southeast Asia, parts of Asia that are presently subject to considerable international migratory flows. This also means that there are important gaps that have not been addressed here, most notably the internal and international migration systems of China and South Asia, as well as the cross-border flows that characterize central Asian nations. Nevertheless, the chapters here represent an initial effort to draw together these debates around migration and diversity that have largely remained independent in scholarly literature in Asia but that are intricately intertwined not only in the lives of migrants but also in the goals of policy and discourses in the public domain. Indeed, unlike Western European, North American and Australasian contexts where notions of integration and assimilation draw these issues together — our review of scholarship in and on Asia has illustrated a tendency to focus on the distinct role of recent migration as a solution to labour shortages and changing family arrangements, and diversity as an already existing feature of some national polities or non-existent in others. In this regard, research on migration and diversity in Asia remains either under-theorized or overly reliant on conceptual frameworks developed in other empirical contexts (Parreñas 2010). Indeed, as Asis and Piper (2008, p. 425) aptly put it: "what is lacking is theory building", particularly in terms of the contextual specificities of Asia. While we do not endeavour to provide an overarching conceptual approach to studying migration and diversity in Asia within this introduction, not least because of the range and differences in experiences in the region, we do seek here to highlight some key issues within Asia that suggest the need for thinking differently about processes of migration and their relationship with diversity.

At the core of a more relevant approach to studying migration and diversity in Asian contexts is the pressing need to delineate and differentiate territorial configurations of Asia and the West. Indeed, Asian migratory systems and diversity experiences are markedly different from both the European model of supposedly homogeneous and insular states, and the North American and Australasian settler colonies which, whilst founded on migration, appear locked into models of multiculturalism that privilege the European/White/Caucasian subject as the core of the nation. Southeast Asia (and indeed Asia more broadly) fits uncomfortably within these models. In Southeast Asian nations, migratory processes and the diversification of populations neither marked the establishment of a nation-state in spite of indigenous populations (à la the white settler colonies), nor have they only occurred subsequent to consolidation of national territories and imaginaries (as in the mode of Western Europe). Instead, migration can be understood as *foundational* to the formation of the nation-state in Southeast Asia (particularly in Indonesia, Malaysia and Singapore), taking place both prior to and during the colonial period and then becoming entrenched in a post-colonial moment of independence and nation-state formation based on an *already existing* plurality.

Even in East Asia, where narratives of long-standing homogeneity have often been even more forceful than those in Western Europe, we need to understand contemporary approaches to migration and responses to diversity in Japan (Nagy *this volume*), South Korea (Kim *this volume*) and Taiwan (Hsia *this volume*) through the particularities of nation-state building and regional geopolitics. Korea's obsession with its own ethnic homogeneity, for example, would appear to be based in part at least on experiences of and resistance to Japanese colonialism, even as this homogeneity shrouds the historical presence of non-Koreans within the nation-state (Kim *this volume*) and historically entrenched modes of incorporating diversity in pre-colonial eras (Han 2007). As both Hsia and Nagy illustrate in their respective chapters, migratory movements and diverse populations are also not absent in the territorial configurations of the Japanese and Taiwanese nation-states but, unlike Southeast Asian states, diversity has often been denied through articulations of homogenisation that desire coherence between racial and national communities (see also Wang 1997).

Contemporary patterns of migration and approaches to citizenship outlined by Asis and Batistella in their chapter clearly build upon historical experiences of migration, constructions of nationhood, and already existing (or denials of) diversity. At the same time, they also suggest further fertile terrain for reconceptualizing migration and diversity in ways that build up from contextual specificities in and across Asia. Clearly, central amongst these specificities is the prevalence of migratory regimes that enforce transience on contemporary populations of labour migrants, particularly those considered unskilled and undesirable (Collins 2011). Each of the major receiving states within Asia (Hong Kong, Japan, Singapore, South Korea and Taiwan) is stringent in its maintenance of this distinction between temporary residents and permanent citizens, creating a context where encounters across this form of diversity are structurally problematic (Ong and Yeoh *this volume*). At the same time, however, each of these states has sought to incorporate other migrant subjects in different ways. Marriage migration is another common trend across these states. This is an arena where the migration of women leads into the very homes of the nation and the making of families and the next generation. As both Hsia (*this volume*) and Ishii (*this volume*) illustrate, the migration of women for marriage and an emerging generation of children with multi-ethnic identities serve as incipient diversities that problematize state-centred cultural and citizenship models and present opportunities for new sorts of connections between groups.

These varied moments of nation-state formation and consolidation through migration appear then as fundamental to ensuing experiences of diversity, constituting an ideological denial or acceptance of difference that sets the parameters for how diversity is played out in the always complex processes of nation-building. Hence the "separate but equal" and "unequal" models of multiculturalism espoused in Singapore and Malaysia respectively, the acceptance of Chinese diasporic presence in Thailand, the "unity in diversity" of Indonesia, but also the ongoing ideological homogenization of South Korea and Japan, and the ethnically-centred nationalism of Taiwan. Contemporary migration policies and approaches to diversity are necessarily developed in relation to these already existing cultural dynamics. At the same time, however, it is also clear that there is considerable feedback between evolving policy approaches, emerging migratory processes and the changing aspirations of the state and those of its populace. Hence, the multicultural framework and arithmetic of Singapore is gradually being problematized and modified by the arrival of new populations who do not fit easily into existing categories (Ong and Yeoh *this volume*; Goh *this volume*). In East Asia too, the rigorous adherence to homogeneity is being broken down as nations face the challenge of incorporating marriage migrants and their children who are literally reconstituting what it means to be Taiwanese, Japanese and Korean (Hsia *this volume*; Ishii *this volume*; Kim *this volume*). Such examples do not suggest that the state is relinquishing its grip on migration, diversity and their implications for nation-building; quite the opposite, they illustrate the fluid and evolving nature of policy approaches particularly in an era of accelerated population mobility in Asia.

Policies and responses to diversity also cannot simply be read through a singular nation-state centred narrative. Rather, closer analysis of differential incorporation of migrant subjects, the active advocacy by civil society groups and alternative modes of incorporation at lower levels of the state also play a role in structuring the inclusion of migrant-subjects and nascent engagements with diversity. In South Korea, for example, the state has not completely excluded all migrant subjects, but rather is engaged in a selective incorporation of some migrants over time, most notably marriage migrants, mixed-race Koreans and also, to a lesser degree, a historically resident ethnic Chinese population (Kim *this volume*) and ethnic Korean migrants from China (Kim 2008). In doing so, the state has also selectively drawn upon rhetorics of multiculturalism and discourses of human rights to relocate the social and cultural borders of the nation, charting a course towards a new, more diverse, but still exclusionary national imaginary. Civil society groups are clearly an important part of shifts towards new spaces for migrants in South Korea (Lim 2003), and also in Japan (Shipper 2008) and Taiwan (Hsia *this volume*). In contexts like Taiwan where citizenship is often locked into associations with ethnicity and the nation-state, advocates for expanded migrant rights provide examples of how exclusionary citizenship regimes can be transformed into more inclusive models (Hsia *this volume*) through the introduction of new radical modes of citizenship that problematize the exclusion of some migrants. In other contexts, local governments contribute to different modes of incorporation which, while not presenting a direct challenge to the nation-state, do render certain spaces more open to difference. Adachi and Shinjuku urban wards in Tokyo offer a useful example, having developed policies of "multicultural coexistence" to "secure the rights of all residents" in a context where, at the national level, there are systemic legal, cultural and linguistic barriers to inclusion (Nagy *this volume*). However, as Nagy's analysis illustrates, these policies are not simply imported rhetorical approaches to diversity but draw on the historical and contemporary specificities of each area to construct new more diverse urban communities within a national framework that still espouses homogeneity.

Existing alongside and sometimes superseding or countering these policy approaches is also an assemblage of practices for and experiences of negotiating diversity that are grounded in long-standing local processes which reflect evolving modes of accommodation within many Asian contexts. These are apparent in and through sites like the *kopitiam* that are historically grounded manifestations of everyday practices of living together through diversity (Lai *this volume*) or the emergence of new cultural spaces that bring together new migrants and older residents (Song *this volume*). These readings do not suggest that the everyday negotiation of diversity is always easy or without conflict. Indeed, Ong and Yeoh's *(this volume)* discussion of (un)cosmopolitan behaviour and attitudes of Singaporeans towards transient male migrant workers, and even the somewhat problematic incorporation of foreign sporting talent outlined by Goh *(this volume)*, illustrate some of the very real difficulties that emerge around changing diversities. In particular, they illustrate the disjuncture between the "opening up" of the nation brought about by state policy and the friction that materializes around different practices, spaces and identities in everyday life. At the same time, these frictions do not foreclose all possibilities for contact and flexibility between groups. Certain sites, like the food and community spaces of the *kopitiam* in Singapore discussed by Lai *(this volume)* or the new *halal* eateries of Itaewon in Seoul discussed by Song *(this volume)*, suggest that there are already resources for diversity in many Asian contexts that can be scaled up to achieve a broader, more inclusive and civil negotiation of difference. These examples highlight that in contexts where migration and diversity have been *foundational* to the formation of larger communities and nations (as in Southeast Asia) or where new diversity is accompanied by more worldly outlooks (as in South Korea), individuals and groups have developed the capacities required to engage with "others" they live amongst. Indeed, the *kopitiam* is but one of several public and everyday sites of encounter within a larger multicultural public housing setting in the Singapore context in which 85 per cent of the population live (Lai 1995; Lai 2011). There is a departure in this case, then, from the sorts of disinterested "tolerance" and objectified exoticization that have been viewed by some scholars as the crux of Western multiculturalism (Mitchell 1993; Žižek 1997). There are also, however, potential synergies here with emerging research on everyday encounters and the negotiation of diversity in specific local contexts that seeks to respond to both conservative and progressive critiques of multiculturalism (Amin 2002; Sandercock 2003; Wise and Velayutham 2009).

These multiple modes of negotiating, including and advocating for different forms of diversity in Asian contexts raise important questions about the relationship between national diversity policy and the daily experience of difference. They suggest, for example, that even as the state retains a hegemonic control on ideologies and imaginaries of diversity within national territories, these are neither all encompassing nor completely impregnable to popular participation. At the same time, they also point to distinct departures from modes of understanding migration and managing diversity in Western contexts where a focus on rights and recognition within the nation or the promotion of diversity has often superseded any efforts to deal with the complexities of everyday living in diverse contexts. Whilst foundational and nascent engagements with diversity in these Asian contexts are by no means unproblematic, they do suggest different possibilities for reformulating and rethinking the politics of diversity more broadly. Indeed, at a time when existing modes of multiculturalism are being questioned in the West (Grillo 2007), these examples of negotiating diversity in Asia, as shared circumstance, present insights that might contribute to new efforts to rethink approaches to migration and diversity across different territories both within and beyond Asia (Amin 2002; Sandercock 2003; Wise and Velayutham 2009).

The different evolving approaches to migration and diversity in the various Asian contexts discussed in this volume also raise significant questions about the identities of migrants and the position of future generations in society. In part, the challenge of identity formation for newer migrants and communities is one that already characterizes settlement processes historically in parts of Asia, involving the transition from sojourner to settler and their necessary political socialization into citizenship of a new nation-state of first generation immigrants (Wang 1989; Sandhu and Mani 1993) and also of local-born second and subsequent generation members who are full-fledged citizens. The identities of first generation immigrants do shift during these processes, from close associations with distant homelands to identities that, while still community-based, are grounded more in the politics, practices and experiences of the new country and less with pre-migration affiliations. In this respect, identity formation needs to be understood relationally, particularly in an era of heightened global mobilities and communications. This would mean taking into account both dynamics internal to particular migrant subjects and their connections and disconnections with other parts of society and broader diasporic networks that extend beyond both homeland and hostland (Lorenzana *this volume*). Identity formation is always a fraught process then, reliant not simply on ethnic affiliations but also refracted through representations of gender and class as communities themselves evolve and become increasingly involved in the necessarily stratified social life of settlement. For the second generation, particularly those whose parents come from different backgrounds, such complexities are likely to be even more prominent as they negotiate identities through hierarchies of ethnicity, class and gender that always threaten to position them at the margins of society (Ishii *this volume*). Nonetheless, looking to the future, it is also the next generation, whether of one or mixed heritage, whose experiences of diversity position them as the vanguard of as yet unscripted engagements with and negotiations of diversity. They may not be the hybrid creolized subjects so valorized in the study of postcolonialism, but as young people who have grown up amongst or between different groups, they offer considerable insight and hope for Asian futures characterized by both diversity and opportunity.

This volume brings together these different debates and issues through a range of chapters that focus on the dynamic relationship between migratory processes and social and cultural diversity in East and Southeast Asian contexts. The contributors come from a range of humanities and social science disciplines including anthropology (Lai; Song), communication studies (Lorenzana), literary and cultural studies (Goh), geography (Ong and Yeoh), international studies (Nagy), and sociology (Asis and Batistella; Hsia; Ishii; Kim). Correspondingly, the volume also incorporates diverse research methods including grounded ethnographic studies (Lai; Song), more structured qualitative interviews and observations (Ong and Yeoh; Ishii), media (Goh; Lorenzana) and policy analysis (Asis and Battistella; Kim; Nagy) and action research (Hsia). This diversity of perspectives and approaches is important because it provides a more encompassing account of the different and complex dimensions of migration and diversity in the Asian region and the ways in which it articulates itself through politics and policies, media representations and everyday life.

Beyond this Introduction, the volume is divided into three sections. The first section addresses Migration, Multiculturalism and Governance in

Asia. It begins with an broad region-wide overview of these issues in the chapter by Asis and Battistella before we turn to investigate the specificities of four nations within the region — South Korea, Taiwan, Singapore and Japan — focusing in particular on contemporary migratory flows and state techniques of governing the movement and incorporation of migrant subjects in them. The second section focuses on more detailed case studies of settlement and the emergent identities of diverse populations over generations. Here authors address more specifically the lives of second and third generation migrants and the children of mixed marriages, highlighting issues of belonging, encounter and circulation which emerge as part of the dynamics through which identities are formed and plural conditions are negotiated. The third and final section focuses on practices and draws our attention to the everyday negotiation of difference and diversity through sites like the multicultural Singaporean *kopitiam*, new ethnic restaurants in Seoul and the increasingly "foreign talent"-filled sports fields of Singapore. In charting various trajectories in contexts and levels that range from nation to region, city, community, family and individual, these contributions illustrate the multifarious experiences of and responses to migratory flows and diversity taking place within Asia. In doing so, the authors also remind us that the outcomes of these processes are always in the making, tenuous in some circumstances but also always an arena open to new progressive developments built upon lives increasingly marked by mobility and difference.

References

Abella, M.I. "Social Issues in the Management of Migration in Asia and the Pacific". *Asia-Pacific Population Journal* 2, no. 3 (2006): 61–86.

Ahmed, S.N. "The Impact of the Asian Crisis on Migrant Workers: Bangladesh Perspectives". *Asian and Pacific Migration Journal* 7, no. 2–3 (1998): 369–93.

Amin, A. "Ethnicity and the Multicultural City: Living with Diversity". *Environment and Planning* 34, no. 6 (2002): 959–80.

Arasaratnam, S. *Indians in Malaysia and Singapore* (revised ed.). Kuala Lumpur: Oxford University Press, 1979.

Asis, M. "Borders, Globalization and Irregular Migration in Southeast Asia". In *International Migration in South East Asia*, edited by A. Ananta and N. Arifin, pp. 199–227. Singapore: Institute of Southeast Asian Studies, 2004.

—— and N. Piper. "Researching International Labor Migration in Asia". *The Sociological Quarterly* 49 (2008): 423–44.

Bell, W. "Ethnicity, Decisions of Nationhood and Images of the Future". In *Ethnicity and Nation Building*, edited by W. Bell and W. Freeman, pp. 283–300. Beverley Hills: Sage Publications, 1976.

——— and W. Freeman. "Introduction". In *Ethnicity and Nation Building*, edited by W. Bell and W. Freeman, pp. 1–18. Beverley Hills: Sage Publications, 1976.

Benjamin, G. "The cultural logic of Singapore's Multiculturalism". In *Singapore: Society in Transition*, edited by Riaz Hassan, pp. 115–33. Kuala Lumpur: Oxford University Press, 1976.

Castles, S. and M. Miller. *The Age of Migration: International Population Movements in the Modern World*. New York: Guilford Press, 2008.

Chalamwong, Y. "Government Policies on International Migration: Illegal Workers in Thailand". In *International Migration in South East Asia*, edited by A. Ananta and N. Arifin, pp. 352–73. Singapore: Institute of Southeast Asian Studies, 2004.

Chan, H.C. "Language and Culture in a Multi-Ethnic Society: A Singapore Strategy". *Ilmu Masyarakat* (Jan–Mar 1984).

Chiew, S.K. "Ethnicity and National Integration: The Evolution of a Multiethnic Society". In *Singapore: Development Patterns and Policies*, edited by P.S.J. Chen, pp. 29–64. Kuala Lumpur: Oxford University Press, 1983.

Chua, B.H. and K.W. Kwok. "Social Pluralism in Singapore". In *The Politics of Multiculturalism: Pluralism and Citizenship in Malaysia, Singapore and Indonesia*, edited by R.W. Hefner, pp. 86–118. Honolulu: University of Hawai'i Press, 2001.

Chun, C.S.Y. "The Mail-Order Bride Industry: The Perpetuation of Transnational Economic Inequalities and Stereotypes". *University of Pennsylvania Journal of International Law* 17, no. 4 (1996): 1155–207.

Collins, F.L. "Transnational Mobilities and Urban Spatialities: Notes from the Asia-Pacific". *Progress in Human Geography* 36, no. 3 (2011): 316–35.

Connell, J. *The International Migration of Health Workers*. New York: Routledge, 2008.

Deshingkar, P. "Internal Migration, Poverty and Development in Asia: Including the Excluded". *IDS Bulletin* 37, no. 3 (2009): 88–100.

Dickinson, J. and A. Bailey. "(Re)membering Diaspora: Uneven Geographies of Indian Dual Citizenship". *Political Geography* 26, no. 7 (2007): 757–74.

Emerson, R. *From Empire to Nation: The Rise to Self-Assertion of Asian and African Peoples*. Boston: Beacon Press, 1960.

Furnivall, J.S. *Netherlands India: A Study of Plural Economy*. Cambridge, Cambridge University Press, 1967.

Ghosh, B. *Huddled Masses and Uncertain Shores: Insights into Irregular Migration*. The Hague: Kluwer Law International, 1998.

Goh, D.P.S., M. Gabrielpillai, P. Holden, and G.C. Khoo. *Race and Multiculturalism in Malaysia and Singapore*. New York: Routledge, 2009.

Gomes, A., T. Kaartinen, and T. Kortteinen. "Introduction: Civility and Civil Relations in South and Southeast Asia". Special issue: Civility and Civil Relations in South and Southeast Asia. *Journal of the Finnish Anthropological Society* 32, no. 3 (2007): 4–11.

Gomez, J. "Politics and Ethnicity: Framing Racial Discrimination in Singapore". *The Copenhagen Journal of Asian Studies* 28, no. 2 (2010): 103–17.

Grillo, R. "An Excess of Alterity? Debating Difference in a Multicultural Society". *Ethnic and Racial Studies* 30, no. 6 (2007): 979–98.

Han, K.K. "The Archaeology of the Ethnically Homogeneous Nation-State and Multiculturalism in Korea". *Korea Journal* 47, no. 4 (2007): 8–31.

Hefner, R.W. *The Politics of Multiculturalism: Pluralism and Citizenship in Malaysia, Singapore and Indonesia.* Honolulu: University of Hawaii Press, 2001.

Hewison, K. and K. Young. *Transnational Migration and Work in Asia.* New York: Routledge, 2006.

Heyzer, N. *Labour Migration and Trafficking: A Gender and Human Rights Approach.* Manila: Asian Development Bank, 2007.

Horowitz, D. *Ethnic Groups in Conflict.* Berkeley: University of California Press, 1985.

Huang, S., B.S.A. Yeoh, and N.A. Rahman. *Asian Women as Transnational Domestic Workers.* Singapore: Marshall Cavendish, 2005.

Hugo, G. "The Demographic Underpinnings of Current and Future International Migration in Asia". *Asian and Pacific Migration Journal* 7, no. 1 (1998): 1–25.

Human Rights Watch. *Rape for Profit: Trafficking of Nepali Girls and Women to Indian Brothels.* New York: Human Rights Watch, 1995.

International Labour Office. *International Labour Migration: A Rights-Based Approach.* Geneva, Switzerland: International Labour Office, 2010.

International Organization for Migration. *Paths of Exploitation; Studies on the Trafficking of Women and Children between Cambodia, Thailand and Vietnam.* Geneva, Switzerland: International Organization for Migration, 2000.

Iredale, R. "The Growth of Skilled Migration in the Asia Pacific Region". In *Migration in the Asia Pacific: Population, Settlement and Citizenship Issues*, edited by R. Iredale, C. Hawksley, and S. Castles, pp. 121–40. Northampton: Edward Elgar Publishers, 2003.

Jones, G. and H.H. Shen. "International Marriage in East and Southeast Asia: Trends and Research Emphases". *Citizenship Studies* 12, no. 1 (2008): 9–25.

Kim, A.E. "Global Migration and South Korea: Foreign Workers, Foreign Brides and the Making of a Multicultural Society". *Ethnic and Racial Studies* 32, no. 1 (2009): 70–92.

Kim, H.M. "The State and Migrant Women: Diverging Hopes in the Making of 'Multicultural Families' in Contemporary Korea". *Korea Journal* 47, no. 4 (2007): 100–22.

Kojima, Y. "Migrant Women and Their Vulnerability in the Trafficking-Migration

Continuum: Evidence from Asia". *Transnational Migration and Human Security* 6, no. 3 (2011): 147–58.

Kumar, S. and S. Siddique. *Southeast Asia: The Diversity Dilemma*. Singapore: Select Books, 2008.

Kymlicka, W. "Models of Multicultural Citizenship: Comparing Asia and the West". In *Challenging Citizenship: Group Membership and Cultural Identity in a Global Age*, edited by S.H. Tan. Aldershot: Ashgate Publishing Limited, 2005.

——— and B. He. *Multiculturalism in Asia*. Oxford: Oxford University Press, 2005.

Lai, A.E. *Meanings of Multiethnicity: A Case Study of Ethnicity and Ethnic Relations in Singapore*. Kuala Lumpur: Oxford University Press, 1995.

———. "A Neighbourhood In Singapore: Ordinary People's Lives 'Downstairs'". In *Future Asian Space: Projecting the Urban Space of New Asia*, edited by L. Hee, B. Davisi *and* E. Viray. National University of Singapore Press, 2011.

Lal, B.V., P. Reeves, and R. Rai. *The Encyclopaedia of the Indian Diaspora*. Singapore: Editions Didier Millet, 2006.

Liang, Z. and Z. Ma. "China's Floating Population: New Evidence from the 2000 Census". *Population and Development Review* 30, no. 3 (2004): 467–88.

Lim, T.C. "Racing *from* the Bottom in South Korea? The Nexus between Civil Society and Transnational Migrants". *Asian Survey* 43, no. 3 (2003): 423–42.

Lim T.G. *Peasants and their Agricultural Economy in Colonial Malaya 1874–1941*. Kuala Lumpur and New York: Oxford University Press, 1977.

———, A. Gomes, and A. Rahman, eds. *Multiethnic Malaysia: Past, Present and Future*. Petaling Jaya, Malaysia: Strategic Information and Research Development Centre; Kuala Lumpur: MIDAS, UCSI University, 2009.

Lu, M.C.W. "Commercially Arranged Marriage Migration: Case Studies of Cross-Border Marriages in Taiwan". In *Marriage, Migration and Gender*, edited by R. Palriwala and P. Uberoi, pp. 125–51. London: Sage Publications, 2008.

Lyons, L. "Transient Workers Count Too? The Intersection of Citizenship and Gender in Singapore's Civil Society". *Sojourn* 20, no. 2 (2005): 208–48.

Madood, T. and P. Werbner. *The Politics of Multiculturalism in the New Europe: Racism, Identity, and Community*. London: Zed Books, 1997.

Mandal, S. "Boundaries and Beyond: Whither the Cultural Bases of Political Community in Malaysia?". In *The Politics of Multiculturalism: Pluralism and Citizenship in Malaysia, Singapore and Indonesia*, edited by R.W. Hefner, pp. 141–64. Honolulu: University of Hawai'i Press, 2001.

Massey, D., J. Arango, G. Hugo, A. Kouaoucci, A. Pellegrino, and J.E. Taylor. *Worlds in Motion: Understanding International Migration at the End of the Millennium*. Oxford: Oxford University Press, 1998.

Meng, E. "Mail-Order Brides: Gilded Prostitution and the Legal Response". *University of Michigan Journal of Law Reform* 28, no. 1 (1994): 197–248.

Mitchell, K. "Multiculturalism, or the United Colours of Capitalism?". *Antipode* 25, no. 4 (1993): 263–94.

Mohamad, M. "Politicisation of Islam in Indonesia and Malaysia: Women's Rights and Inter-Religious Relations". In *Gender Trends in Southeast Asia: Women Now, Women in the Future*, edited by T. Devasahayam, pp. 95–110. Singapore: Institute of Southeast Asian Studies, 2009.

Mok, K.H. *Education Reform and Education Policy in East Asia*. New York: Routledge, 2006.

Muzaffar, C. "Protection of the Malay Community: A Study of UMNO's Position and Opposition Attitudes". M.Sc Thesis, Universiti Sains Malaysia, microfilm, 1974.

Oishi, N. *Women in Motion: Globalization, State Policies, and Labor Migration in Asia*. Stanford: Stanford University Press, 2005.

Okubo, S. and L. Shelley. *Human Security, Transnational Crime and Human Trafficking: Asian and Western Perspectives*. Routledge: New York, 2011.

Ordoñez, R.Z. "Mail-Order Brides: An Emerging Community". In *Filipino Americans: Transformation and Identity*, edited by M.P.P. Root, pp. 121–42. Thousand Oaks, CA: SAGE Publications, 1997.

Pan, L. *The Encyclopaedia of the Chinese Overseas*. Singapore: Chinese Heritage Centre, 1999.

Parreñas, R.S. "Migrant Filipina Domestic Workers and the International Division of Reproductive Labour". *Gender and Society* 14, no. 4 (2000): 560–81.

———. "Homeward Bound: The Circular Migration of Entertainers between Japan and the Philippines". *Global Networks* 10, no. 3 (2010): 301–23.

Pearson, D. *The Politics of Ethnicity in Settler Societies: States of Unease*. Houndsmills: Palgrave, 2001.

Piper, N. "Rights of Foreign Workers and the Politics of Migration in South-East and East Asia". *International Migration* 42, no. 5 (2004): 71–97.

———. "Rights of Foreign Domestic Workers: Emergence of Transnational and Transregional Solidarity?". *Asian and Pacific Migration Journal* 14, no. 1–2 (2005): 97–119.

——— and M. Roces. *Wife or Worker? Asian Women and Migration*. Oxford: Rowman and Littlefield Publishers, 2003.

——— and A. Uhlin. "Transnational Advocacy Networks: Female Labour Migration in East and South-East Asia: A Gendered Analysis of Opportunities and Obstacles". *Asian and Pacific Migration Journal* 11, no. 2 (2002): 171–95.

Purcell, V. *The Chinese in Southeast Asia*. London: Oxford University Press, 1965.

Puru Shotam, N. "Language and Linguistic Policies". In *Management of Success: The Moulding of Modern Singapore*, edited by K.S. Sandhu and P. Wheatley. Singapore: Institute of Southeast Asian Studies, 1989.

Ratnam, K.J. *Communalism and the Political Process in Malaya.* Kuala Lumpur: University of Malaya Press, 1965.

Robinson, K. "Of Mail-Order Brides and 'Boys' Own' Tales: Representations of Asian-Australian Marriages". *Feminist Review* 52 (Spring 1996): 53–68.

Sandercock, L. *Cosmopolis II: Mongrel Cities of the 21st Century.* London: Continuum, 2003.

Sandhu, K.S. *Indians in Malaya: Some Aspects of their Immigration and Settlement (1786–1957).* Cambridge: Cambridge University Press, 1969.

────── and A. Mani, eds. *Indian Communities in Southeast Asia.* Singapore: Institute of Southeast Asian Studies and Times Academic Press, 1993.

Seol, D.H. "Past and Present of Foreign Workers in Korea 1987–2000". *Asia Solidarity Quarterly* 2 (2000): 6–31.

Shamsul A.B. *From British to Bumiputera Rule: Local Politics and Rural Development in Peninsular Malaysia.* Singapore: Institute of Southeast Asian Studies, 1986.

──────. "The Redefinition of Politics and the Transformation of Malaysian Pluralism". In *The Politics of Multiculturalism: Pluralism and Citizenship in Malaysia, Singapore and Indonesia,* edited by R.W. Hefner. Honolulu: University of Hawai'i Press, 2001.

Shipper, A. *Fighting for Foreigners: Immigration and its Impact on Japanese Democracy.* Ithaca: Cornell University Press, 2008.

Siddique, S. "Singaporean Identity". In *Management of Success: The Moulding of Modern Singapore,* edited by K.S. Sandhu and P. Wheatley, pp. 563–77. Singapore: Institute of Southeast Asian Studies, 1989.

Simkhada, P. "Life Histories and Survival Strategies amongst Sexually Trafficked Girls in Nepal". *Children and Society* 22, no. 3 (2008): 235–48.

Skeldon, R. "Interlinkages between Internal and International Migration and Development in the Asian Region". *Population, Space and Place* 12, no. 1 (2006): 15–30.

Skrentny, J.D., S. Chan, J. Fox, and D. Kim. "Defining Nations in Asia and Europe: A Comparative Analysis of Ethnic Return Migration Policy". *International Migration Review* 41, no. 4 (2007): 793–825.

Stahl, C.W. "Trade in Labour Services and Migrant Worker Protection with Special Reference to East Asia". *International Migration* 37, no. 3 (1999): 545–68.

Suryadinata, L. *Chinese and Nation-Building in Southeast Asia.* Singapore: Singapore Society of Asian Studies, 1997.

Tham, S.C. "Cultural Diversity and National Identity: Some Theoretical and Empirical Considerations with Special Reference to Singapore and Malaysia". *Review of Southeast Asian Studies* 1, no. 3 (1971): 3–19.

Tirtosudarmo, R. "Economic Development, Migration, and Ethnic Conflict in Indonesia: A Preliminary Observation". *Sojourn: Journal of Social Issues in Southeast Asia* 12, no. 2 (1997): 293–328.

Tolentino, R.B. "Bodies, Letters, Catalogs: Filipinas in Transnational Space". *Social Text* 14, no. 3 (1996): 49–76.

Thanh-Dam, T. "The Dynamics of Sex Tourism: The Case of Southeast Asia". *Development and Change* 14, no. 4 (1983): 533–53.

Tsuda, T. *Local Citizenship in Recent Countries of Immigration: Japan in Comparative Perspective*. Oxford: Lexington Books, 2006.

———. *Diasporic Homecomings: Ethnic Return Migration in Comparative Perspective*. Stanford: Stanford University Press, 2006.

Tyner, J. "Constructing Images, Constructing Policy: The Case of Filipina Migrant Performing Artists". *Gender Place and Culture* 1, no. 1 (1997): 19–36.

Velayutham, S. "Everyday Racism in Singapore". In *Everyday Multiculturalism*, edited by A. Wise and S. Velayutham, pp. 255–73. Houndsmills: Palgrave-Macmillan, 2009.

Wang, G. "The Study of Chinese Identities in Southeast Asia". In *Changing Identities of the Southeast Asian Chinese since World War II*, edited by J.W. Cushman and G. Wang, pp. 258–78. Hong Kong: Hong Kong University Press, 1988.

———. "The Chinese as Immigrants and Settlers". In *Management of Success: The Moulding of Modern Singapore*, edited by K.S. Sandhu and P. Wheatley. Singapore: Institute of Southeast Asian Studies, 1989.

———. "Migration History: Some Patterns Revisited". In *Global History and Migrations*, edited by G. Wang, pp. 1–22. Boulder, Colorado: Westview Press, 1997.

Wang, H.Z. and D. Bélanger. "Taiwanizing Female Immigrant Spouses and Materializing Differential Citizenship". *Citizenship Studies* 12, no. 1 (2008): 91–106.

Whiting, A. "Desecularizing Malaysian law?". In *Examining Practice, Interrogating Theory: Comparative Legal Studies in Asia*, edited by P. Nicholson and S. Biddulph, pp. 223–66. Leiden: Martinus Nijhoff, 2008.

Wise, A. and S. Velayutham. *Everyday Multiculturalism*. Houndsmills: Palgrave-Macmillan, 2009.

Wong, D. "Foreign Domestic Workers in Singapore". *Asian and Pacific Migration Journal* 5, no. 1 (1996): 117–38.

Xiang, B. *Global "Body Shopping": An Indian Labor System in the Information Technology Industry*. Princeton: Princeton University Press, 2007.

Yamanaka, K. and N. Piper. "Feminized Migration in East and Southeast Asia: Policies, Actions and Empowerment". Occasional Working Paper. United Nations Research Institute for Social Development, Geneva, 2005.

Yea, S. "Runaway Brides: Anxieties of Identity among Trafficked Filipina Entertainers in South Korea". *Singapore Journal of Tropical Geography* 25, no. 2 (2004): 180–97.

———. "'Shades of Grey': Spaces In and Beyond Trafficking for Thai Women involved in commercial sexual labour in Sydney and Singapore". *Gender, Place and Culture* 19, no. 1 (2012): 42–60.

Yen, C.H. *A Social History of the Chinese in Singapore and Malaya 1800–1911*. Singapore: Oxford University Press, 1986.

Yeoh, B.S.A. "The Global Cultural City? Spatial Imagineering and Politics in the (Multi)cultural Marketplaces of South-East Asia". *Urban Studies* 42, no. 5–6 (2005): 945–58.

———. "Bifurcated Labour: The Unequal Incorporation of Transmigrants in Singapore". *Tijdschrift voor Economische en Sociale Geografie* 97, no. 1 (2006): 26–37.

——— and S. Huang. "Singapore Women and Foreign Domestic Workers: Negotiating Domestic Work and Motherhood". In *Gender, Migration and Domestic Service*, edited by J.H. Momsen, pp. 277–300. London: Routledge, 1999.

——— and A.E. Lai. "'Talent' Migration in and out of Asia: Challenges for Policies and Places". *Asian Population Studies* 4, no. 3 (2008): 235–45.

Zhu, Y. "China's Floating Population and their Settlement Intention in the Cities: Beyond the Hukou Reform". *Habitat International* 31, no. 1 (2006): 65–76.

Žižek, S. "Multiculturalism, or, the Cultural Logic of Multinational Capitalism". *New Left Review* 225 (1997): 28–51.

I

Migration, Multiculturalism and Governance in Asia

1

MULTICULTURAL REALITIES AND MEMBERSHIP
States, Migrations and Citizenship in Asia

Maruja M.B. ASIS and Graziano BATTISTELLA

INTRODUCTION

Most of the discussion on the nexus between migration and citizenship has focused on trends and practices in Western countries. This chapter will examine some tendencies in selected Asian countries which have been affected by migration. This focus aims to contribute to the discussion on citizenship as Asia presents some specific realities. Firstly, unlike the historical linkage to the post-Westphalian idea of the nation-state, the long colonial legacy in Asia and the rise of the nation-state in the post-colonial period de-linked the development of citizenship from the long process of "forgetting" which was part of the evolution of the nation-state in the Western experience.[1] Many Asian countries were still in the process of consolidating the nation-state project when large-scale, organized labour migration started in the 1970s. Migration, thus, complicated questions concerning citizenship for countries of origin and destination, but especially so for the latter. Secondly, the specific migration system that developed in some Asian countries, which is premised on keeping migration temporary, rules out settlement, family reunification and long-term integration, including acquisition of citizenship, for less skilled migrants.[2]

Despite the insistence on temporary labour migration, some settlement is taking place in the receiving countries in the Asian region. Also, some states (especially among the origin countries) are extending the right to vote and of dual citizenship — partly upon the urging of transnational communities and in recognition of the benefits of engaging with these communities — to their nationals working and/or living in other countries. In the face of continuing migration and de facto settlement, the state in receiving countries has responded reluctantly to these processes or has introduced further restrictions. The state in origin countries, on the other hand, can be seen to be playing a more active role vis-à-vis their diaspora populations, although the role of transnational communities is also significant.

This chapter addresses three questions: (1) How is migration in Asia redefining state conceptions of citizenship? (2) How accessible is the acquisition of citizenship to migrants in Asian countries? (3) What alternative pathways are available in the Asian context for migrants' incorporation in countries of destination? A brief discussion of the debate on citizenship is necessary before turning to discussing these questions.

WHAT DOES CITIZENSHIP MEAN?

The United Nations Department of Economic and Social Affairs, Population Division (2009) estimated the world's stock of international migrants at 214 million in 2010, up from the 2005 estimate of 195 million. The migrant stock is based on the mid-year estimates of persons outside their countries of birth (which provide a measure of the foreign-born as opposed to the native-born or non-immigrant population). Not all countries collect information on place of birth, making it difficult to generate comparable statistics on international migration.[3] Where this is unavailable, the alternative is to use data on citizenship.[4] The data on citizenship, however, is not a satisfactory measure of the international migrant population because citizens may include people who were foreigners (or the foreign-born) who had been naturalized. In the contemporary context of intense cross-border movements and possibilities for multiple belonging, the boundaries between "citizens" (insiders) and "non-citizens" (outsiders) have been blurred, rendering the measurement of international migration more difficult. Beyond measurement issues, the meaning of citizenship has become more contested under conditions of globalization, unabated international migration and the emergence of transnational communities. These changes have challenged the presumed congruence between the nation-state, territoriality and population, which is fundamental to the concept of citizenship. This idea can be gathered from how citizenship is defined or described. Citizenship, according to Soysal (1994, p. 2), "defines bounded populations, with a specific set of rights and duties, excluding 'others' on the grounds of nationality". A similar understanding is provided by Brubaker (1992, p. 31, as cited in Sejersen 2008, p. 523), who described citizenship as "an international filing system, a mechanism for allocating persons to states".

It is not only recently that the idea of citizenship has gone through important mutations (Riesenberg 2002). For the Greeks, citizenship had a political connotation (the participation of citizens in the public affairs of the *polis*, while non-citizens were excluded from it). For the Romans, citizenship had a juridical character, a stratified membership which progressively expanded into a cosmopolitan dimension, losing at the same time its cultural and political strength. The liberal approach of the Enlightenment produced a passive notion of citizenship, where the individual freely renounced some of his freedoms through a tacit consensus (the social contract of John Locke) in exchange for the benefits of an orderly living provided by the State. In contrast with the passive citizenship of John Locke, an active citizenship was promoted by Jean Jacques Rousseau and exemplified by the Jacobin phase of the French Revolution. Through the distinction of passive and active citizenship, Brian Turner (1992) has suggested a typology to specify the differences between the French, British, German and American ideal-types of citizenship. However, in all cases citizenship remained a stratified entitlement, and only after World War II did it acquire the meaning of equality of rights and duties for the citizens of most countries. In that regard, T.H. Marshall (1950) contributed the notion of social-democratic citizenship, indicating that full citizenship implied also equality of social rights. In this theoretical evolution of the notion of citizenship, migration is now pointing to the last frontier, the equal enjoyment of cultural rights. This trend has to confront the changes and challenges that occur when moving from a national territory to another.

National territory is jealously guarded by states, as indicated by the wars and conflicts that have been waged over territorial disputes. When borders move, nation-states are redrawn, turning former citizens into non-citizens (migrants). When citizens of one country cross national borders, they become international migrants[5] whose rights are redrawn as non-citizens in the country of destination. The shift in status from citizen/national to non-citizen/non-national — and the corresponding loss of a set of rights — is one of the factors that makes international migration inherently risky (Bhabha 2005).

International migrants who reside in a state where they are not citizens have varying degrees of inclusion and exclusion in the receiving state. In general, temporary migrants (such as workers) have fewer rights in the receiving states compared with permanent migrants. Temporary migrants are allowed to reside *temporarily* in the receiving state for some purpose, after which they are expected to return to their countries of origin; permanent migrants are allowed the right to stay and work without a time limit on the length of their stay in the receiving state. Permanent residents may opt to acquire citizenship after fulfilling certain requirements of the receiving state. As will be discussed in a later section, in view of changes in how origin states view their overseas-based population, those who have become naturalized citizens now also often have the option to retain the citizenship of their origin country.

Different approaches or models of migrant incorporation define the place of migrants in receiving states. These approaches range from differential exclusion, which allows migrants to participate in certain spheres of national life but not in others (e.g., temporary migrant workers are allowed to participate in the economic sphere, but are otherwise excluded from the social, cultural and political life of the receiving society), to assimilation (which requires cultural assimilation of migrants), to multiculturalism (which provides latitude for cultural expression) (Castles 2000). In practice, other forms of citizenship have also emerged, such as "civic" citizenship or "residence" citizenship, which entails de facto recognition of membership, allowing members participation at the local level, including the right to vote in local or administrative elections.

In view of these changes, how can citizenship, which is wedded to the framework of the nation-state, be more responsive to the realities and conditions of a globalized world?[6] The states' claim to protect "national interests" in privileging their "nationals" over "foreigners" conflicts with the principle of human rights as universal. From a rights perspective, people on the move do not (and should not) lose their rights when they cross borders. From the standpoint of the nation-state, however, states have the right and the duty to protect national interests from "foreign" interests. To maintain the distinction, the traditional notion of citizenship is based on citizens who belong to just *one* nation-state.

In traditional countries of settlement, some reinterpretation of citizenship is underway, one that points to the diminishing relevance of citizenship in migrant integration, particularly at the individual level. Since most countries of immigration grant eligible migrants some citizenship rights ("social" citizenship), migrants are finding it less crucial to apply for naturalization in the host country. Except for the exercise of political rights, citizenship does not provide migrants more benefits than what they already enjoy as long-term residents. Moreover, the increasing possibility to be politically active in their country of origin compensates for their reduced political rights in the receiving country.[7]

The introduction of multicultural policies in several receiving countries has also contributed to the diminishing importance of citizenship in the integration of migrants. Although multiculturalism has been formally instituted as a national policy in a few countries (Canada, Australia, Sweden and the Netherlands, but with considerable rethinking in Sweden and the Netherlands in recent times), most liberal states which are committed to religious and cultural pluralism have adopted the idea informally. Even an assimilation-oriented country such as France has allowed cultural differences; it simply refused to give multiculturalism official status (Joppke and Morawska 2003).

Multiculturalism thrived between the 1960s and the 1990s. A retreat from multiculturalism has been noted *circa* 1990s (e.g., Joppke and Morawska 2003) and after several political leaders in Europe have spoken against it, scholars recently spoke of a multiculturalism backlash (Vertovec and Wessendorf 2009). In some respects, a uniformity of analysis on multiculturalism is impossible, as there have been several ways to understand it and to implement it as a policy. It is not surprising, therefore, that countries like Canada and Australia maintain their multicultural policy, while European countries are moving away from it. In Asia, multiculturalism has been a de facto reality in several countries with a complex ethnic composition, and the social cohesion of different ethnic groups has guided to some extent the leadership in Malaysia and Singapore. Regardless of the various contexts in different parts of the world, it is evident that the multicultural crisis has resulted in two discernible trends (Joppke and Morawska 2003): (1) the resurgence of citizenship as a key factor in defining membership in a national polity, which was partly a response to the crisis of the welfare state and concerns that migrants might abuse the welfare system; and (2) the tendency of migrants to rely on their networks in adapting to the host society and growing evidence of migrants engaging in transnational practices.

Since the 1990s, the literature on citizenship has grown considerably alongside the development of new scholarship focused on migrant transnationalism. A key theme in this scholarship is a reconsideration of the role of the nation-state. One strand of the debate posits the declining significance of national citizenship as a necessary condition to membership in a polity. Analysing the incorporation of guest workers in European host societies, Soysal (1994) concluded that the model of national citizenship dominant at the turn of the twentieth century is giving way to *postnational* membership, a new model of membership that is premised on universal, deterritorialized notions of person's rights. In this model, states which adhere to international human rights standards grant the full range of rights to citizens and non-citizens alike. Bauböck's (1994) concept of transnational citizenship posits citizenship membership beyond national and territorial borders, but with the state maintaining the power to grant citizenship rights. As discussed elsewhere in the chapter, quasi-citizenship, denizens, or local citizenship provide another lens with which to view the changing role of the nation-state as purveyor of rights to its members. Although international migration, among others, may have eroded the centrality of the nation-state on citizenship matters, it has not been rendered irrelevant — and the Asian landscape provides evidence on this account.

HOW IS MIGRATION REDEFINING CITIZENSHIP IN ASIAN COUNTRIES?

Increasing and unrelenting migration in Asia since the 1970s has raised questions about migrants' rights, which, when considered vis-à-vis the rights of nationals, inevitably touch on citizenship.[8] However, as the discussion below will show, migration has had a modest impact in modifying the legal framework of citizenship in *countries of destination* in the region. Despite the growing presence of migrants, countries of destination are adamant in restricting the entry and residence of less skilled migrant workers while welcoming and integrating highly skilled and professional migrants. This template has hardly changed since the 1970s. In contrast, origin countries have taken significant steps to expand the incorporation of their overseas-based population as part of the "nation".⁹

It is important to note that the citizenship/nationality laws of most Asian countries were drawn before the "age of migration" (Castles and Miller 2009). Despite their different histories, the citizenship/nationality laws of countries in the region share some common elements. A review of citizenship laws reveals similarities in provisions concerning citizenship by birth (in general, birth within the national territory does not automatically confer citizenship) and by descent (this generally derives from the father in most cases, where a child born to a mother will have his/her mother's citizenship only if the father is unknown or stateless; in the Philippines, such a qualification is not necessary). Rules concerning descent have changed in several countries. In June 1998, Korea changed its Nationality Law, recognizing descent deriving from the mother (Lee 2003). Also, as of 15 May 2004, Singapore amended its Constitution in 2004 to grant citizenship by descent to babies born overseas to Singaporean mothers, a right that was previously granted only to Singaporean fathers (Ho 2008, p. 157).¹⁰ Prior to the 2008 amendment in Japan's nationality law, a child born to a foreign woman and Japanese man can qualify for Japanese citizenship only if the father claimed the child before birth or married the mother before the child reached the age of twenty. In June 2008, the Supreme Court ruled in a case lodged by ten Japanese-Filipino children living in Japan that "it was unconstitutional to limit nationality to those whose parents were married" (Reuters 2008).

Requirements for naturalization vary across the countries. Origin countries such as India, Indonesia, the Philippines and Thailand all require a period of residence (at least five years in most cases); knowledge/familiarity with language and/or culture and being economically independent apply in most cases; renunciation of previous nationality is not required for all. For Bangladesh, naturalization is based on ability to bring in investments of US$5 million or its equivalent in an industrial or commercial project; application for permanent residence requires an investment of US$75,000. Countries of destination, such as Japan, South Korea and Singapore, also have residence requirements (from three years to ten years); other requirements include knowledge of the language and culture, economic capacity, of good moral character. No details were available for Malaysia, except for the note that it does not encourage naturalization.¹¹ On paper, the rules seem straightforward, but the reality is more complex. The different provisions regarding naturalization via marriage will be discussed in another section.

Although various types of migratory movement are present in Asia (permanent migration to other regions, particularly North America, Europe and Australia; marriage migration; temporary labour migration; student migration; refugee movements), the most prominent has been and continues to be temporary labour migration, most of which is intra-regional. Labour migration is organized as strictly temporary, mediated by recruiting agencies, with mandatory return to the country of origin at the end of the contract. For *less skilled migrants*, family reunification is not allowed. This results in the virtual impossibility to establish long-term settlement and to have access to citizenship. For the *highly skilled and professional migrants*, the rules are different; they are sought after by receiving countries and are given the welcome mat: family reunification is allowed, and permanent residence is encouraged. In other words, there is a two-tiered system in the treatment of migrants: the withholding of rights in the case of less skilled migrant workers, and the extension of rights to the highly skilled and professional migrants.

As in Western countries, exclusion from membership does not mean that migrants are deprived of all rights. In general, they benefit from labour rights and limited social guarantees, with significant differences from country to country. For instance, migrants can form trade unions in Japan, but they are discouraged from doing so in Malaysia. The lack of a strong human rights tradition in the Asian context does not favour the practical enjoyment of "social" citizenship. Widespread abuses against migrants — particularly for those in an irregular situation and for women migrants in domestic work — have prompted advocacy in protecting and promoting migrants' rights rather than the larger issue of citizenship.

Although the policy of temporary migration remains unchanged, there have been some steps towards better protection of migrants. Singapore, for example, has imposed stiffer sanctions against the abuse of domestic workers. In order to curb unauthorized migration, Taiwan has extended the maximum length of work contract from three to six years. South Korea implemented the Employment Permit System (EPS) in 2004, acknowledging the need for foreign workers and to provide them with conditions similar to local workers; the EPS is expected to reduce unauthorized migration. Thailand, another country dealing with high levels of unauthorized migration, carried out a registration of migrant workers and offered protection for migrant workers.[12]

On the whole, the piecemeal approach in extending rights to migrant workers results in providing some workers' rights rather than the full range of rights extended to nationals or citizens. Migrants' integration, thus, is still confined to economic integration (which is limited to a sector or particular employer) in the receiving countries, and migrants are eventually expected to return to their countries of origin.

As mentioned earlier, migration trends have led to some changes in the notion of citizenship in *countries of origin*. In part, this change may be due to the "permanence" of temporary migration. Another factor is the importance of the transnational dimensions in the development prospects of origin countries. The Philippines has gone the farthest in granting political rights to overseas Filipinos. It passed two laws in 2003, one which grants absentee voting rights and another which allows dual citizenship.[13] Qualified overseas Filipinos voted for the first time in the 2004 national elections.[14] The decision to grant dual citizenship is not without pragmatic concerns — the expectation to generate investments is one of the reasons for enacting such a law. India deliberated on the Citizenship (Amendment) Bill, 2003, which would apply only to persons of Indian origin from sixteen countries (because of concerns about the possible use of unauthorized migrants to obtain Indian citizenship).[15] To date, India has yet to pass a dual citizenship law; for the time being, it has introduced the Overseas Certificate of India (OCI), which grants visa-free travel to India and access to economic benefits, except political rights. Table 1.1 summarizes the formal ways in which selected origin countries in the region are reaching out to their diaspora populations.

A general trend that can be noted across countries (including countries of destination and their efforts to link with their own diaspora populations — e.g., Malaysia's brain gain scheme, Thailand's Reverse Brain Drain Project, among others) is a more positive regard for their overseas-based nationals. There was a time that migrants were seen as traitors or deserters; today, those labels have disappeared.[16] States, thus, have also gone "transnational" in their attempts to extend the nation beyond the national territory. Another interesting development in this regard is a change in the more voluntary (or other types) of return migration that some states are pursuing. Bangladesh and China, for example, no longer require their nationals to return home, although both are keen in encouraging "mission visits".

Granting dual nationality is becoming a global phenomenon, but the trend is generally slower in the Asian region. Based on analysis of the

TABLE 1.1
Approaches in Linking with Overseas Populations

Country	Has office(s) dealing with overseas population?	Grants absentee voting?	Grants dual citizenship?
Indonesia	Workers	Yes	Yes (Children of Indonesian and foreign parentage should decide to choose Indonesian or foreign citizenship by 18 years of age)
Philippines	Workers and Settlers	Yes	Yes
Vietnam	Workers and Settlers	No	Yes
Bangladesh	Workers	Yes	Yes
India	Workers and Settlers	Yes	(Overseas Citizenship of India [OCI])
Pakistan	Workers and Settlers	No	Pakistan Origin Card
Sri Lanka	Workers	No	Yes

Notes: The offices in charge of the overseas population are: the National Agency for Placement and Protection of Indonesian Overseas Workers or BNP2TKI in Indonesia; the Philippine Overseas Employment Administration and Overseas Workers Welfare Administration (for migrant workers) and the Commission on Filipinos Overseas (for permanent settlers, including marriage migrants) in the Philippines; the Ministry of Foreign Affairs for permanent settlers and the Ministry of Labour, War, Invalids and Social Affairs for migrant workers in Vietnam; the Ministry of Expatriates' Welfare and Overseas Employment in Bangladesh; the Ministry of Overseas Indian Affairs in India; the Ministry of Labour Manpower and Overseas Pakistanis in Pakistan; and the Sri Lanka Bureau of Foreign Employment in Sri Lanka.

dual citizenship legislation of thirty-nine Asian countries, 23 per cent allow dual citizenship, which is considerably lower compared to the Americas (63 per cent), Europe (61 per cent) and Oceania (50 per cent) (Sejersen 2008, p. 533; Castles and Miller 2009, p. 47). Considered the most appropriate approach to address the transnational dimension of belonging experienced by migrants (which, according to Faist [1999] is not addressed by national citizenship or multicultural citizenship which still maintains the host country as the territory of reference), it does not enjoy sufficient currency in destination countries because of concerns about allegiance, a sensitive issue in the region. Likewise, Asia does not have any form of established transnational citizenship, in the sense of a supranational authority providing citizenship rights, such as that of the European Union. Except for the Association of Southeast Asian Nations (ASEAN) which has a visa-free arrangement among its member-countries, other regional organizations in Asia have yet to consider freedom of movement across national borders for citizens of member states.[17]

HOW ACCESSIBLE IS CITIZENSHIP TO MIGRANTS IN ASIAN COUNTRIES?

There are two pathways by which migrants can obtain citizenship in Asia: (1) possession of skills/ talents or capital, and (2) marriage to nationals.

While citizenship is off limits to less skilled migrants, highly skilled and professional migrants are sought out and welcomed by receiving countries. These wanted migrants are offered permanent residence, are allowed family reunification, and they can apply for naturalization. Foremost examples are Japan and Singapore. Japan's migration policy provides for twenty-seven categories of entry and settlement for professionals, but none for unskilled migrants. Presently, Japan has some 600,000 permanent residents, including long-term Korean residents. Singapore, on the other hand, allows employment pass holders (i.e., professionals who earn more than S$2,500/month) and S-pass holders who earn more than S$1,800/month, the right to apply for permanent residence and the possibility for naturalization.[18] Singapore has about a million foreigners, accounting for about a quarter of the city-state's population.

Investors are welcome in several countries. In the case of Singapore, an investment of S$1.5 million with the Singapore government in a range of business activities approved by the Economic Development Board could pave the way for permanent residence.[19] The premium on skills or capital implies a preference for those who can make an economic contribution to the receiving country.

In all receiving countries, permanent residence ranging from five to ten years is one of the preconditions for naturalization. This requirement, however, is changing. Recently, Singapore relaxed the requirements for those seeking citizenship. Where permanent residents were previously allowed to be away from Singapore for up to six months, it has been extended to twelve months, providing applicants more time and freedom to travel.[20]

Marriage as a way of gaining permanent residence and citizenship has increased alongside the increase in labour migration in the region. Unlike past patterns, intermarriages in Asia in recent years have involved locals (mostly men) marrying Asian partners. Receiving countries which do not have policies against intermarriages between migrant workers and their nationals have seen an increase in such marriages (Singapore and Malaysia do not allow, or at least, do not encourage intermarriages between migrant workers and their nationals). This is true for Japan, Taiwan and South Korea. Intermarriages in Japan have grown since the 1980s, while the trend is of recent vintage in Taiwan and South Korea. Some 5 per cent of marriages registered in Japan are intermarriages, mostly between Japanese men and other Asian women. The rise in intermarriages in Taiwan has been dramatic and their share has been substantial (300,000 to date). As a pathway to residence and later on citizenship, receiving countries in Asia require a minimum number of years for couples to stay married (two years in Singapore, three years in Japan, six years for mainland-born spouses and four years for other nationalities in Taiwan), a requirement that may put women in difficult marriages in a vulnerable situation. The break-up or the dissolution of a marriage before the required length of stay is met could also create problems for the residency rights of women and their children.

Intermarriages not only provide a window for permanent residence in Asia, but they are also a precursor to multicultural policies (promoting language education for foreign wives, or the education of multiethnic children are some of the pressing issues) and the expansion of immigrants' rights. In South Korea (e.g., Kim 2008), Japan (e.g., Burgess 2008), and Taiwan (e.g., Hsia 2009), discussions about multiculturalism have been driven mainly by concerns over international marriage migrants and less so by concerns about labour migrants.[21] Recent trends in intermarriages are also chipping at long-standing gender biases in citizenship laws.[22] In Taiwan, discriminatory policies concerning mainland Chinese spouses were recently dismantled, thanks to sustained lobbying and advocacy by marriage migrants and their supporters. In June 2009, the eight-year waiting period for mainland spouses seeking residency in Taiwan has been reduced to six years. On 12 August 2009, further amendments, including allowing mainland spouses to work in Taiwan after successfully completing an interview with the National Immigration Agency (*Taiwan Today* 2009).

WHAT ALTERNATIVES TO CITIZENSHIP ARE AVAILABLE TO MIGRANTS FOR INCORPORATION IN ASIAN COUNTRIES?

Contrary to the intent of states, some migrant settlement is taking place in Asia. Non-nationals are staying longer and establishing residence, although official acknowledgement of such presence is not always forthcoming. Four modes can be noted: long-term unauthorized settlement (example: Malaysia); extended residence due to extension of work contracts (examples are Hong Kong, Singapore and Taiwan); long-term legal residence (example: Japan); and local government initiatives (example: Japan).[23]

Malaysia's long history of migration is reflected in its identity as a multiethnic society. Indonesians and Filipinos started coming to Malaysia in the 1970s in response to opportunities in various sectors — plantation, construction, services — which have been eschewed by the majority of the local population. By the time Malaysia put in place a labour migration policy, the workers were already in the country. Regularization programmes, border controls, deportations, and the institution of more stringent immigration laws (2002) have not stopped unauthorized migration. Indonesians have formed ethnic enclaves, which enable *migrant gelap* (shadow migrants) to survive the uncertainties faced by unauthorized migrants (see Wong and Teuku Anwar 2003). Filipinos in Sabah face a similar situation. The unresolved territorial claim that the Philippines has on Sabah complicates the situation of Filipinos in the state (see Battistella, Asis, and Abubakar 1997; UNDP 2000). However, although they cannot openly engage with Malaysia and they have no access to services and legal protection, the demand for workers and the presence of networks in Malaysia (not to mention the proximity) are factors that contribute to relatively permanent residence (or recurrent migrations) without authorized status.[24]

The extension of work contracts has resulted in the extended residence of legal migrant workers, which has led to the creation of minority communities in countries such as Hong Kong, Singapore and Taiwan.[25] However, their sheer presence, especially their visibility, has not always worked to their advantage — their weekly gatherings have invited some negative reactions from the local population. The migrant communities that have been formed are mostly along ethnic/national lines. Aside from providing social support, these communities are conduits of information, assistance and empowerment to migrants. In Singapore, although the state does not provide specific support to the development of such communities, a number of civil society groups,[26] and more recently the state-affiliated National Trades Union Congress (NTUC) Migrant Workers Forum have been involved in initiatives, such as the marking of International Migrants' Day with events and celebrations, that recognize the presence and value of foreign workers to the Singaporean nation. Although migrants only have authorization for temporary stay, the communities they have formed have become a structural part of the society. It is an example of incorporation which can be described as "permanent temporariness".

Japan's claim as a homogeneous society is belied by the long presence of non-Japanese, largely Koreans as well as some Chinese, who were conscripted for labour by the Japanese government in the early part of the twentieth century. In recent years, these oldcomers were joined by newcomers, including those from other national groups, thus increasing and diversifying the migrant communities in Japan. The Koreans and Chinese comprise the majority of some 330,000 foreigners who were naturalized between 1945 and 2000 (Kondo 2002, p. 422). Compared with OECD countries, Japan's naturalization rate is lower (Kondo 2002, p. 422).

For the older generation of Koreans in Japan, opting out of naturalization is an assertion of their identity as Koreans and also as a reminder of Japan's colonization of Korea — these also give them some leverage in their engagement with the state. Other perspectives on the question of citizenship are emerging among Koreans in Japan. Korean lawyer Kim Kyeung-duk noted that Japanese citizenship has a different meaning to different generations of Koreans: independence for the first-generation; anti-discrimination for the second-generation; and self-realization for the third-generation (as cited in Kondo 2002, p. 423). The importance of the role of migrants (non-citizens) in the articulation of the concept of citizenship is further elaborated by Chung (2003) who interprets the intentional act of non-naturalization by migrants (the refusal of citizenship) as a strategic choice to gain visibility in the struggle to further the democratic process in Japan. It is also, somewhat paradoxically, a tactic that reveals an engagement in the political life of the nation that might typically be associated with the exercise of citizenship. Based on recent works on Koreans in Japan, Hester (2008, p. 139) sees an emergent willingness to acquire Japanese nationality in order to resolve the instability of living as a *Zainichi* or as a foreign resident in Japan (Hester 2008, p. 139). He traces the shifts in the discourse among Koreans in Japan from the end of World War II through the present. From 1991, there has been an increase in the naturalization of Koreans as well as increasing intermarriages with Japanese nationals and the emergence of a Korean-Japanese identity. Less stigmatization for those opting for naturalization among Koreans and the emergent discourse of *kyosei* or living together in Japanese society are contributing to this trend (Hester 2008, p. 139).

Through various periods, Koreans in Japan have been at the forefront of citizenship reforms and the advancement of multicultural issues. The repeal of fingerprinting and the "Japanese only" names in applying for citizenship are successful examples of hard-earned advocacies. The initiatives of some local governments in Japan suggest another mode of incorporating migrants in the Asian setting, something which could approximate "residence" citizenship. In contrast with a restrictive national policy, some local governments in Japan have taken the lead of developing policies and programmes that promote the inclusion of migrants. Skilfully utilizing and redefining the internationalization programme that Japan initiated in the 1980s, they have provided services to immigrants; in part, the move was motivated to prevent conflicts with the local population. For example, Kawasaki City has instituted the Foreigners' Advisory Council in 1996, which coordinates with the Mayor and the City Council (Tegtmeyer Pak 2001; Kondo 2002). Non-governmental organizations (NGOs) also play a critical role in providing services to migrants in Japan, particularly to those in an unauthorized situation, as well as in advocating for migrants' rights (Tsuda 2008, p. 7). Although such a structure falls short of full participation in local governance, it has nevertheless deepened the relation of mutual rights and obligations which is included in the concept of citizenship and somehow introduced the idea of "residence" citizenship.[27] Tsuda (2008) refers to this pattern as "local citizenship", i.e., "the granting, by local governments and organizations, of basic sociopolitical rights and services to immigrants as legitimate members of these local communities".

In this regard, the experience of Japan seems rather similar to that of some other countries, where local initiatives to integrate migrants and to promote their participation have provided occasions to test national legislation or constitutional provisions.[28] The active involvement of organized migrant communities can be an effective catalyst of change. In the city of Kawasaki the long-standing battle of the Korean community against finger printing was instrumental in developing closer ties with the municipality and acceptance of a higher level of participation of migrants in city affairs (Tegtmeyer Pak 2001). The mobilization of Japanese-Brazilians has also resulted in programmes to address the education of children (Yamanaka 2003, 2004).

While local citizenship contributes to the welfare of immigrants in the absence of nation-state recognition, Tsuda (2008) also points to local variations in immigrant rights and low civic participation among foreign residents as serious limitations. As such, there is a need for the national government to step in to extend formal citizenship rights, provide programmes and services, and to promote migrant integration. However, national programmes may not be sensitive to the needs of specific immigrant groups or unauthorized migrants may be unable to access such services for fear of being apprehended. He concluded that "[i]n the end, any coherent and effective immigrant citizenship and social integration policy must strike a balance between national and local policy making and service delivery, and the role of NGOs in supporting immigrant rights" (Tsuda 2008).

CONCLUSION

This overview of the relationship between migration and citizenship in Asia has suggested that, as in other regions, the relationship is multifaceted. Most of the migratory flows in Asia are dominated by the movement of migrant workers, who are not expected by definition to be incorporated in the receiving country and to whom access of citizenship is not available. Even "social" citizenship is only partially granted to migrants, as the system is not known for providing strong protection of social and economic rights. Nevertheless, the situation is also not static in Asia, and changes in policies provide for longer working contracts, improvement in labour standards and better working and living conditions. The situation is rather different for highly skilled migrants and professionals, who are normally assured access to permanent residence and ultimately to citizenship. However, their number is rather limited.

Where migration is having the clearest impact is on the citizenship norms in countries of origin. Concerned with maximizing the benefits of their diaspora populations, some countries of origin are strengthening the ties with their expatriate population by ensuring that migrants who have settled permanently in foreign countries and acquired foreign citizenship need not lose their citizenship in the origin countries. Temporary migrants abroad, who normally do not enjoy political rights in the country of employment, are increasingly given the possibility to participate in national politics through absentee voting.

If the impact of migration on citizenship is limited, access to national citizenship also remains limited. As in other parts of the world, citizenship is normally granted through naturalization and marriage. Naturalization requires permanent residence, which is accessible in general to highly skilled migrants and professionals. Therefore, the rate of naturalization in Asian countries is not very high. Access to citizenship through marriage has expanded in some cases by opening the possibility for local women citizens to pass on citizenship to their spouses and/or children. Some countries, however, continue to discourage marriage between their nationals and unskilled migrants.

Under these conditions, what are the possibilities for the incorporation of migrants in the receiving countries? This is where practical situations indicate how the concept of citizenship, as a clear demarcation between those who belong and those who are excluded, reveals nuances and variations. For example, many unauthorized Indonesian and Filipino migrants have already formed communities in West Malaysia and Sabah (East Malaysia) respectively, which allow them tacit (though precarious) residence status. While such a status does not provide them state protection, as shown in 2002 and 2004 when massive repatriations were implemented by Malaysia, it paradoxically also affords them deeper level of incorporation than regular migrant workers. While the work and residence of regular migrant workers are subject to the terms of their work permits, unauthorized migrants have established communities and parallel institutions in the receiving society, transforming temporariness into de facto permanence. In the case of Koreans in Japan, they have given denizenship[29] a new twist, as they actively engage the Japanese state in improving the democratic process. Japan's interest in projecting a more international outlook and nascent indications of multiculturalism seem to have encouraged younger Koreans to consider naturalization, which may further the process of multiculturalism in Japanese society. The "residence" citizenship granted to migrants by some local governments in Japan also marks a departure from the exclusionary policies of the national government.

The overview of the situation in Asia indicates that the level of migrant incorporation determines the type of protection and opportunities migrants will enjoy. As such a country's concept of citizenship is clearly crucial. As suggested by Koopmans and Statham (2003), if a country has a very ethnic concept of citizenship, migrants are defined as foreigners; excluded from the receiving society, migrants will tend to cling to their roots and cultivate transnational practices. If a country is more inclusive, migrants will be considered minorities, and they will attempt to further rights connected to their minority status. In most cases, receiving countries in Asia are resisting incorporation and migrants remain as foreign residents. Residence is not an irrelevant status. It is a prerequisite to obtaining social, cultural, economic rights, and access to citizenship. By virtue of residence, migrants, including unauthorized migrants, can have some rights (emergency health care and education of children, for instance) (Oriol 2003). How to expand residence rights, particularly in states that do not facilitate naturalization, is an initiative currently pursued by civil society.

Will citizenship remain the ultimate criterion for inclusion and membership? In the conflict between national citizenship and transnational citizenship it appears that some combination of the two is occurring and that assimilation and transnationalism often coexist in the lives of immigrants and their offspring.[30] The case of Koreans in Japan seems to point in this direction. Perhaps a realistic prospect is offered by Aleinikoff (2003, p. 122). He speaks of a trend towards neither nationalism, requiring naturalization for membership and limiting other rights to migrants, nor towards post-nationalism. Rather, he sees "a thickening of relations between domestic and foreign populations (through immigration, dual nationality, freer trade and travel, the communications revolution) that will occur within the regime of nation-states". He calls it "inter-nationalism", where more linkages are established among government agencies across borders, and agreements among such agencies determine a new transgovernmental order, but still within the framework of nation-states. To date, the experience of migrants' incorporation in Asia lags behind that of other regions and many barriers need to be dismantled before migrants, particularly the less skilled ones, can be allowed full admission in their host societies. Until that happens, migrants will have to look to their home countries for membership while making a living elsewhere as temporary migrant workers.

Notes

1. The drafting of citizenship and nationality laws in Asian countries coincided with their independence, most of which happened after the conclusion of World War II. It is interesting to note that the "forgetting" of ethnic roots has not been completely successful, as indicated by the emergence of ethnostates and the redrawing of national boundaries along ethnic lines in many parts of the world.
2. Temporary labour migration is carried out by imposing work contracts and requiring migrant workers to return home or to renegotiate an extension of their contract. In general, migrant workers' work permit does not allow them to transfer to another sector or employer, other than those specified in the work permit. Note that these restrictions only apply to less skilled migrants.
3. A special issue on the migration information system in selected countries in East, Southeast and South Asian countries is featured in the *Asian and Pacific Migration Journal* 17, no. 3–4 (2008): 231–438.
4. Where information on place of birth and citizenship is not available, the UN uses a model to estimate the number of international migrants for a given country. Of the 221 (out of 230) countries which had at least one source of data on international migration, 179 (78 per cent) collected information on place of birth, 42 (18 per cent) collected information on citizenship, and the rest had no information. For details concerning the data sources and estimation of the 2008 revision see UN, DESA, Population Division (2009).
5. Unless otherwise specified, the term migrant as used in this paper refers to international migrants. Moreover, unless otherwise stated, the paper adopts the UN recommended definition of international migrant, i.e., as a person outside his or her country of birth or country of usual residence for at least a year.
6. Other than citizenship, issues such as the environment, poverty, AIDS and terrorism, are also finding "national" responses inadequate and calls for a more global approach are growing. The role of non-state actors — including civil society — is acknowledged as stakeholders in many global issues. These non-state actors which operate transnationally consider themselves as part of a larger polity that transcend national boundaries.
7. Pragmatic considerations also dictate the decision of some migrants to acquire the citizenship of their host country — to be able bring in other family members or to travel with greater ease (e.g., it is easier to travel using a U.S. passport than a Philippine passport). Aihwa Ong spoke of "flexible citizenship" to refer to the strategies of Asian elites in selecting different sites for investments, work and family relocation <http://cio.ceu.hu/Bilder/Pacific_shuttle.pdf>, accessed 12 August 2004.

8. For details about migration in Asia, see Asis (2005), UNESCAP (2008) and IOM (2008), among others.
9. This is not limited to countries of origin. Some "destination" countries, such as Singapore, for example, are as keen to maintain their links to their expatriate populations (Ho 2008).
10. Another amendment was allowing Singaporean citizens by descent (children born to Singaporean parents abroad) to pass on Singaporean citizenship to their children. According to Ho (2008, p. 157), both changes reflect "how the Singaporean state values the familial lineage of citizenship". Notwithstanding these liberalizing amendments, Singapore does not allow dual citizenship, which poses contradictions to Singapore's citizenship policies (Ho 2008, p. 164).
11. See <http://www.multiplecitizenship.com/worldsummary>, accessed 19 June 2004.
12. To date, Japan is the only receiving country that maintains a policy of not accepting less skilled migrant workers.
13. The change of opinion concerning citizenship is notable. Article IV, Section 5 of the 1987 Philippine Constitution states: "Dual allegiance of citizens is inimical to the national interest and shall be dealt with by law." The realities of globalization and the large-scale migration of Filipinos led to a reconsideration favouring dual citizenship.
14. In defending the constitutionality of granting suffrage to overseas Filipinos (the complaint rested on the minimum residence required of local voters), the Supreme Court ruled: "While millions of Filipinos reside abroad principally for economic reasons, and hence they contribute in no small measure to the economic uplift of our country, their voices are marginal insofar as the choice of the country's leaders is concerned." (Gorospe 2005, p. 212).
15. See <http://www.murthy.com/news/UDdualin.html>, accessed 11 June 2004.
16. This view applied more to permanent settlers; migrant workers were not seen negatively. In fact, in countries such as the Philippines and Indonesia, migrant workers are considered as heroes because of their economic contributions.
17. Travel within Asia is not easy. Hong Kong is about the only destination which has a visa-free arrangement with many countries. Nationals of member countries of the Association of Southeast Asian Nations (ASEAN) can travel to other member countries without a visa for *short-term visits*. In contrast, SAARC (South Asian Association for Regional Cooperation) citizens do not enjoy such arrangements. Citizens of the more developed countries enjoy visa-free arrangements with many countries. The rest have to comply with visa requirements.
18. Singapore's all-out campaign to recruit foreign talents has generated some resentment among the locals, who feel that the government is overly favouring foreigners over home-grown talents.

19. See <http://www.expatsingapore.com/getting /citizen.html>, accessed 10 August 2004.
20. See <http://ofw.balita/ph/html/public_html/article.php?story=2004051408 0142184&mode=print>, accessed 11 June 2004.
21. The extension of support and assistance to marriage migrants contrasts with the notable lack of similar response towards labour migrants. Kim (2008) argues that while marriage migrants may benefit from the assistance extended to them, they may have compromised their cultural citizenship (on account of expectations for them to be "Korean" wives and mothers) to achieve Korean citizenship.
22. Women's groups in Malaysia have been working at amending the assumption of the citizenship law that married women should go to their husband's country. Malaysia's citizenship by registration applies only to women who are married to Malaysian men, but not vice versa (Yap 2004, p. 6). In South Korea, NGOs and women's groups have successfully lobbied to allow all spouses of Korean nationals, regardless of gender, to secure "Resident (F-2)" visas, i.e., visas that would allow the foreign spouses to work. NGOs in Korea are also asking the government to provide a special consideration for foreign spouses whose husbands had died or whose marriages break up within the required two-year period of marriage (Lee 2003).
23. Another mode of incorporation might be that of ethnic repatriates, such as the (temporary) return of Japanese Brazilians (*nikkeijin*) to Japan (e.g., see Tsuda 2003).
24. This scenario also applies to Burmese migrants in Thailand (see Amarapibal, Beesey and Germershausen 2003). It would be interesting to observe the developments with Thailand's implementation of the work permit system beginning this year.
25. Taiwan has a single entry and a ceiling of nine years maximum stay. Despite the ceiling, migrant communities have carved niches in Taipei and other places which have a large migrant presence.
26. These civil society groups include the Humanitarian Organization for Migration Economics (HOME), Migrant Voices (MV) and Transient Workers Count Too (TWC2).
27. The concept of full participation at the local level has been introduced in European countries — an example is the body of adjunct councillors elected by the migrant community to represent the migrants in the City Council in Rome.
28. The Statutes of the City of Genoa includes a provision that allows the participation of long-term residents in local elections. It is contested by the national government, which argues that such a right cannot be granted by a municipality unless allowed by a national law. Scholars and politicians in

Italy are debating whether granting foreigners the right to participate in local elections requires modifying the Constitution.

29. The term was coined by Thomas Hammar (1990), from an old practice in England by which a foreigner could receive from the king a letter ensuring his right to stay, to refer to permanent residents who are in a semi-citizenship status.
30. Smith (2003) offers a view of migrant-membership as an instituted process, which is shaped by four institutions and processes: home state domestic politics, the home state's relationship to the world system, transnational civil society, and the context of migrants' reception in the receiving country. He used this approach in analysing Mexico's overtures to Mexicans in the United States and emerging transnational practices between migrants and the home state.

References

Aleinikoff, T.A. "Between National and Postnational: Membership in the United States". In *Toward Assimilation and Citizenship: Immigrants in Liberal Nation-States*, edited by C. Joppke and E. Morawska, pp. 110–30. New York, NY: Palgrave Macmillan, 2003.

Amarapibal, A, A. Beesey and A. Germershausen. "Irregular Immigration into Thailand". In *Unauthorized Migration in Southeast Asia*, edited by G. Battistella and M.M.B. Asis, pp. 229–94. Quezon City: Scalabrini Migration Center, 2003.

Asian and Pacific Migration Journal. Special Issue: International Migration and Data Sources in Asia 17, no. 3–4 (2008): 231–438.

Asis, M.M.B. "Recent Trends in International Migration in Asia and the Pacific". *Asia-Pacific Population Journal* 29, no. 3 (2005): 15–38.

Battistella, G. and M.M.B. Asis. *The Crisis and Migration in Asia*. Quezon City: Scalabrini Migration Center, 1998.

———, M.M.B. Asis, and C. Abubakar. "Migration from the Philippines to Malaysia: An Exploratory Study". Research report submitted to the International Organization for Migration. Quezon City: Scalabrini Migration Center, 1997.

Baubock, R. *Transnational Citizenship: Membership and Rights in International Migration*. Aldershot: Edward Elgar, 1994.

Bhabha, J. "Trafficking, Smuggling, and Human rights". *Migration Information Source*, 1 March 2005. <http://www.migrationinformation.org/Feature/display.cfm?id=294>. Accessed 20 July 2008.

Burgess, C. "(Re)constructing Boundaries: International Marriage Migrants in Yamagata as Agents of Multiculturalism". In *Multiculturalism in the New Japan*, edited by N.H.H. Graburn, J. Ertl, and R.K. Tierney. New York and Oxford: Berghahn Books, 2008.

Castles, S. "Globalization and Migration: Some Pressing Contradictions". In *Ethnicity and Globalization*, S. Castles, pp. 124–32. London: Sage Publications, 2000.

────── and M.J. Miller. *The Age of Migration: International Population Movements in the Modern World*. 4th ed. London: Palgrave Macmillan, 2009.

Chung, E.A. "Non Citizens, Voice and Identity: The Politics of Citizenship in Japan's Korean Community". Working Paper No. 80. University of California, San Diego: The Center for Comparative Immigration Studies, 2003.

Faist, T. "Internationalization in International Migration: Implications for the Study of Citizenship and Culture". WPTC-99-08. University of Bremen: Institute for Intercultural and International Studies, 1999.

Gorospe, R.B. "The Promissory Notes Voters: A Critique of Macalintal v. Commission on Elections". *UST Law Review* 49 (2005): 199–237.

Hammar, T. *Democracy and the Nation State: Aliens, Denizens and Citizens in a World of International Migration*. Aldershot, Hant, UK: Avebury, 1990.

Hester, J.T. "Datsu Zainichi-ron: An Emergent Discourse on Belonging among Ethnic Koreans in Japan". In *Multiculturalism in the New Japan: Crossing the Boundaries Within*, edited by N.H.H Graburn, J. Ertl, and R.K. Tierney. New York and Oxford: Berghahn Books, 2008.

Ho, E.L.E. "'Flexible Citizenship' or Familial Ties that Bind? Singaporean Transmigrants in London". *International Migration* 46, no. 4 (2008): 145–76.

Hsia, H.-C. "Foreign Brides, Multiple Citizenship and the Immigrant Movement in Taiwan". *Asian and Pacific Migration Journal* 18, no. 1 (2009): 17–48.

International Organization for Migration (IOM). *Situation Report on International Migration in East and South-East Asia*, Geneva, 2008.

Joppke, C. and E. Morawska. "Integrating Immigrants in Liberal Nation-states: Policies and Practices". In *Toward Assimilation and Citizenship: Immigrants in Liberal Nation-states*, edited by C. Joppke and E. Morawska. New York: Palgrave Macmillan, 2003.

Kim, M.-J. "Gender, Motherhood, and Citizenship of International Marriage Migrants: Maternal Citizenship of Filipinas in South Korea". Paper presented at the annual meeting of the American Sociological Association, Boston, 31 July 2008. <http://www.allacademic .com/meta/p243042.inex.html>. Accessed 6 August 2009.

Kondo, A. "The Development of Immigration Policy in Japan". *Asian and Pacific Migration Journal* 11, no. 4 (2002): 415–36.

Koopmans, R. and P. Statham. "How National Citizenship Shapes Transnationalism: Migrant and Minority Claims-making in Germany, Great Britain and the Netherlands". In *Toward Assimilation and Citizenship: Immigrants in Liberal Nation-states*, edited by C. Joppke and E. Morawska. New York: Palgrave Macmillan, 2003.

Lee, H.-K. "Gender, Migration and Civil Activism in Korea". *Asian and Pacific Migration Journal* 12, no. 1–2 (2003): 127–53.

Marshall, T.H. *Citizenship and Social Class and Other Essays*. Cambridge: Cambridge University Press, 1950.

Oriol, P. *Résidents, étrangers, citoyens! Plaidoyer pour une citoyenneté européenne de résidence*. Paris: Presse Pluriel, 2003.

Reuters. "Japan Opens Nationality to Kids Born Out of Wedlock". 5 December 2008, <http://www.reuters.com/article/worldNews/idUSTRE4B41MJ20081205>. Accessed 6 August 2009.

Riesenberg, P. *A History of Citizenship: Sparta to Washington*. Malabar, FL: Krieger Publishing Company, 2002.

Sejersen, T.B. "'I Vow to Thee My Countries': The Expansion of Dual Citizenship in the 21st Century". *International Migration Review* 42, no. 3 (2008): 533–49.

Smith, R.C. "Migrant Membership as an Instituted Process: Transnationalization, the State and Extra-Territorial Conduct of Mexican Politics". *International Migration Review* 37, no. 2 (2003): 297–343.

Soysal, Y.N. *Limits of Citizenship: Migrants and Postnational Membership in Europe*. Chicago: The University of Chicago Press, 1994.

Tegtmeyer Pak, K. "Towards Local Citizenship: Japanese Cities Respond to International Migration". Working Paper No. 30. University of California, San Diego: The Center for Comparative Immigration Studies, 2001.

"Act Eases Restrictions on Mainland Spouses", *Taiwan Today*, 13 August 2009. <http://www.taiwantoday.tw/ct.asp?xItem=58029&CtNode=413>. Accessed 1 September 2009.

Turner, B. "Outline of a Theory of Citizenship". In *Dimensions of Radical Democracy: Pluralism, Citizenship, Community*, edited by C. Mouffe, pp. 33–62. New York: Verso, 1992.

Tsuda, T. "Local Citizenship and Foreign Workers in Japan". *Japan Focus*, 26 May 2008, http://www.japanfocus.org/-Takeyuki-Tsuda=2762. Accessed 6 August 2009.

———. *Strangers in the Ethnic Homeland: Japanese Brazilian Return Migration in Transnational Perspective*. New York: Columbia University Press, 2003.

United Nations Development Programme (UNDP). *Assessing Population Movement and HIV Vulnerability: Brunei-Indonesia-Malaysia-Philippines Linkages in the East ASEAN Growth Area*. Prepared by the Scalabrini Migration Center. Bangkok: UNDP, 2000.

United Nations Department of Economic and Social Affairs, Population Division (UNDESA). "Trends in International Migration Stock: The 2008 Revision (UN data base, POP/DB/MIG/Stock/Rev.2008). New York: UNDESA, 2009. Also available at <http://esa.un.org/migration>. Accessed on 1 September 2009.

United Nations Economic and Social Commission for Asia and the Pacific (UNESCAP). *Looking into Pandora's Box: The Social Implications of International Migration in Asia*. New York: UNESCAP, 2008.

Vertovec, S. and S. Wessendorf. *The Multiculturalism Backlash: European Discourses, Policies and Practices*. London and New York: Routledge, 2009.

Wong, D. and T.A.T. Anwar. "Migran Gelap: Irregular Migrants in Malaysia's Shadow Economy". In *Unauthorized Migration in Southeast Asia*, edited by G. Battistella and M.M.B. Asis, pp. 169–227. Quezon City: Scalabrini Migration Center, 2003.

Yamanaka, K. "Feminized Migration, Community Activism and Grassroots Transnationalization in Japan". *Asian and Pacific Migration Journal* 12, no. 1–2 (2003): 155–87.

———. "Citizenship and Differential Exclusion of Immigrants in Japan". In *State/Nation/Transnation*, edited by B.S.A. Yeoh and K. Willis, pp. 67–92. London and New York: Routledge, 2004.

Yap, M.C. "Malaysia's Laws Tear Families Apart". *Asian Migration Trail* (June 2004): 6–7.

2

MULTICULTURAL COEXISTENCE POLICIES OF LOCAL GOVERNMENTS IN THE TOKYO METROPOLIS
A Comparative Examination of Social Integration in Response to Growing Ethnic Diversity

Stephen Robert NAGY

INTRODUCTION

Since the early 1980s, Japan has used foreign workers to compensate for labour shortages in blue collar industries and other forms of employment deemed dirty, dangerous, and difficult (the 3Ds). Economic structural dependence on foreign workers has contributed to Japan's foreign resident population increasing to 2,186,121 in 2009, or 1.71 per cent of the total population (Figure 2.1).

According to the MOJ (2007) in its 2007 Immigration Control Report, increased migration to Japan can be attributed to six factors: (1) availability

FIGURE 2.1
Changes in the Number of Foreign Nationals from 1950 to 2009 and Its Percentage of the Total Population in Japan

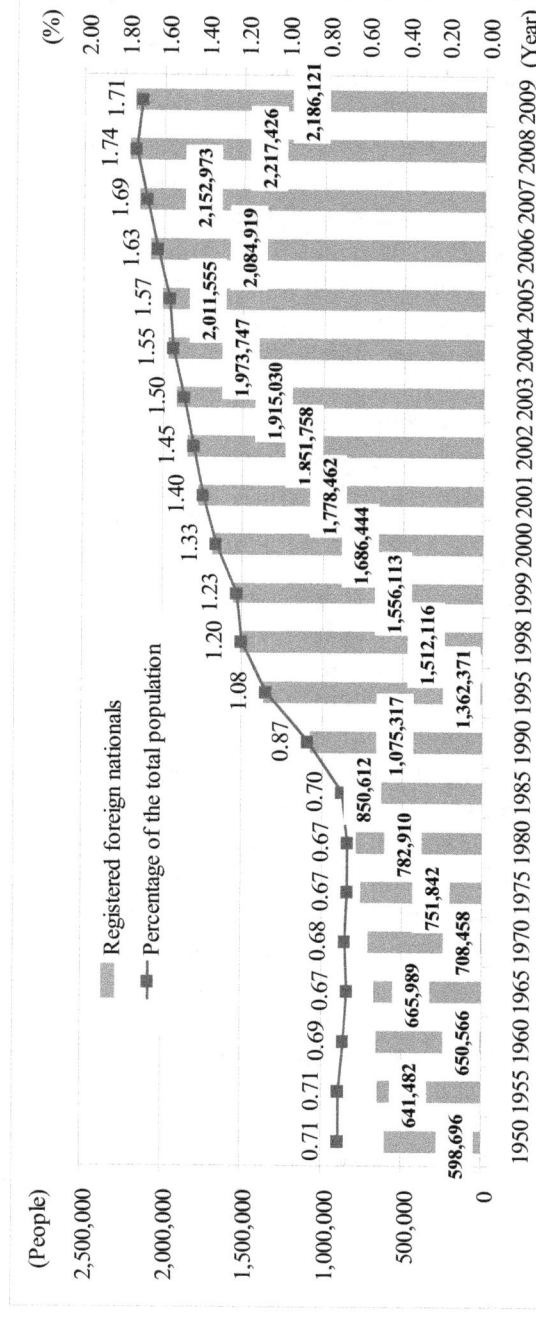

Notes: 1. "Number of registered foreign nationals" as of 31 December every year.
2. The "Percentage of the total population in Japan" is calculated based on the population as of 1 October every year from "Population Estimates" and "Population Census" of the Statistics Bureau, Ministry of Internal Affairs and Communications.
Source: Ministry of Justice (MOJ) 2010.

of Trainee Programmes; (2) special residency and opportunities for *Nikkeijin* (See Abella 1995, pp. 418–23; MOJ 1992, p. 12); (3) abundant jobs for foreign students and entertainers; (4) job opportunities for undocumented workers; (5) family reunion opportunities for those in international marriages; and (6) the ease with which foreigners can enter Japan and overstay their visas. This increase may be expected to continue as part of a comprehensive strategy to deal with the projected labour shortage (The National Institute of Population and Social Security Research 2006, p. 6). These state views on migration echo the views of neo-classical economic scholars that migration is a result of both macro-level pressures that compel or make migration possible, and the micro-level aspects of individual choice (Massey et al. 1993).

Employing the social integration metrics of structural integration, cultural integration, interactive integration and identificational integration, this chapter investigates the multicultural coexistence/social integration practices of two local governments in the Tokyo Metropolis (hereafter Tokyo): Shinjuku and Adachi. Its objective is to examine how local governments and ethnic communities contribute to the formation of local government-led social integration practices. Through understanding how ethnic communities influence social integration practices, local governments would be better able to mitigate the challenges of governing multiethnic municipalities, furthering the social integration of various ethnic groups while diminishing the inevitable frictions that arise when new ethnic groups settle in urban settings. Drawing on interviews with local government officials and primary documents collected during my doctoral studies in Tokyo (2004–08) and my tenure as the International Relations Coordinator in a local government in Tokyo (2001–04, 2005–06) this chapter investigates the different approaches that Adachi and Shinjuku take to the development of social integration policies. I argue that these differences are related to their respective foreign resident demographic profiles, past and projected changes in the number of foreign residents, and the particular settlement patterns which have formed in Adachi and Shinjuku.

This chapter is divided into three sections. The first section briefly examines discussions on the social integration of migrants; the second section, examines the social integration metrics of structural integration, cultural integration, interactive integration and identificational integration; and the third section analyses local government multicultural coexistence policies using social integration metrics.

Rationale for Choosing Tokyo Metropolis, Adachi Ward and Shinjuku Ward

Local governments in Tokyo were chosen for several reasons. First, municipalities in Tokyo are home to large numbers of foreign residents. To illustrate, the foreign population in Tokyo climbed to 418,116 in 2010 (Tokyo Metropolitan Government Statistics 2010*a*) — this number represents 3.22 per cent of the total metropolis population (Tokyo Metropolitan Government Statistics 2010*a*; 2010*b*). In some wards, foreign residents represent nearly 10 per cent of the total municipal population and are expected to rise in the coming years (Shinjuku Bunka Kokusai Kouryu Zaidan 2004, pp. 14–15). Hand-in-hand with the growing number of foreign residents residing in Tokyo is the disruption of the culturally homogeneous social fabric of Japan (Van Arsdol et al. 2005, pp. 35–39). This disruption is often articulated as *Gaikokujin Mondai* or "foreigner problem". Education, living conditions, discrimination, racism, housing, finding work, receiving and paying for social welfare programmes, parent-child linguistic and cultural gaps are but some of the dilemmas that have been associated with foreigners as early as 1984 (Kanagawa Kennai Zaiju Gaikokujin Jittai Chosa Iinkai 1985, pp. 1–6).

Second, by focusing on local governments in Tokyo and the effect of immigrants on policy development, we can better understand the challenges of multicultural coexistence and social integration faced by local governments that also encounter stark differences in terms of diversity and the proportion of foreigners. Some cities such as Osaka and Kawasaki City historically have larger numbers of foreigners who have resided in Japan prior to the end of World War II and who are known as old comers. The presence of these foreign residents or so-called old comers heavily influences how multicultural coexistence policy is planned and practised in the area (Noguchi 2007).

Third, Tokyo, because of its size, is a natural magnet for foreign workers and is therefore an ideal place to study their experiences. Cities such as Tokyo attract foreigners and alter their economic behaviour through overarching social relations, such as immigrant networks, immigrant niches, and enclave economics (Weber 1965/1922, pp. 88–115).

Lastly, the two municipalities of Adachi and Shinjuku in the Tokyo were chosen as case studies as they are the only cities in central Tokyo with detailed multicultural initiatives that can be examined.

SOCIAL INTEGRATION POLICIES

Scholarly views on social integration range from focusing on migrants' strategies to integration strategies by governments. For instance, the basic objective of social integration in the Program of Action of the World Summit for Social Development is to create a "society for all", in which every individual, each with rights and responsibilities, has an active role to play (Social Integration Branch, Division for Social Policy and Development (DSPD), United Nations Department of Economic and Social Affairs (UNDESA) 2008). Social integration, in Commitment 4 of the Copenhagen Declaration on Social Development, is defined as the process of:

> Fostering societies that are stable, safe and just and that are based on the promotion and protection of all human rights, as well as on non-discrimination, tolerance, respect for diversity, equality of opportunity, solidarity, security, and participation of all people, including disadvantaged and vulnerable groups and persons (Social Integration Branch, DSPD, UNDESA 2008).

Similarly, Cruz-Saco, describes social integration as follows:

> Social integration enables persons, regardless of their attributes, to enjoy equal opportunities, rights and services that are available to the so-called mainstream group... social integration eradicates stereotypes and ("mainstream") privilege; increase the voice of persons or groups that are vulnerable and have been marginalized; creates opportunities for their political participation; creates stable and decent job opportunities for traditionally underrepresented persons and groups, and promotes the development of capabilities among vulnerable populations so that they can overcome poverty and deprivation (Cruz-Saco 2008, pp. 2–3).

Scholars such as J.W. Berry (2006) consider multiculturalism to be one among several social integration strategies which include exclusion, separation and assimilation. Social integration from this perspective becomes more difficult to reconcile as there exists various groups that advocate different integration approaches, ranging from assimilation to multiculturalism developed to protect community rights (Chan-Kam, Griffith, and Leonard 2002, p. 4). Echoing Berry (2006), Trevor Phillips, current chair of the British Equality and Human Rights Commission, describes integration as a "two-way street" in which settled communities accept that new people will bring change with them and newcomers realize that they too have to change in order to move closer to an integrated society (Phillips 2005, p. 6).

From an assessment point of view, Esser (2000) classifies social integration into four basic dimensions: (1) acculturation; (2) placement;

(3) interaction; and (4) identification. These dimensions are further elaborated by Bosswick and Heckmann (2006, pp. 9–11) as: (1) structural integration (the acquisition of rights and the access to position and status in the core institutions of the host society), (2) cultural integration (or acculturation), (3) interactive integration (the acceptance and inclusion of immigrants in the primary relationships and social network of the host society) and (4) identificational integration (inclusion in a new society on the subjective level as indicated by feelings of belonging to and identification with the host society). Esser's social integration dimensions are used as metrics in this chapter as they provide useful ways to qualitatively measure integration.

MULTICULTURAL COEXISTENCE POLICIES IN ADACHI WARD AND SHINJUKU WARD

In 2006 and 2005, both Adachi and Shinjuku wards promulgated multicultural coexistence plans in response to the need to address intercultural frictions, to provide access to social welfare services in accordance with local government law as well as international conventions which require local governments and the national government to secure the rights of all residents. These plans have been formulated to balance and manage the following: current and future foreign resident and Japanese resident demographic profiles, each municipality's unique character, international marriage rates, visa composition of foreign residents, and associations with criminal activity by foreign residents.

Policies being implemented in Adachi and Shinjuku wards can be broadly categorized into four types of social integration (Table 2.1): (1) structural integration; (2) cultural integration; (3) interactive integration; and (4) identificational integration (Bosswick and Heckmann 2006, pp. 9–11). These measures aim to overcome systemic, cultural and language barriers in Japanese society by promoting more diverse social interactions, which in turn can contribute to the development of a more pluralistic society.

Structural Integration

Examining the Multicultural Coexistence Plans of Adachi and Shinjuku, we can glean distinct commonalities and differences in their respective focus and commitment vis-à-vis the four types of social integration listed above. Adachi's multicultural coexistence initiative is premised on forging a community that stresses "richness in difference" (Adachi Ku Kuminbu,

TABLE 2.1
Social Integration Types and Associated Specific Measures

	Contents of reform	Specific measures
Structural Integration	Structural changes within the local government that secure the removal of barriers to the economy and labour market, education system, local housing system, local welfare institutions and services, health system) and local political rights	(1) Labour market policies (2) Policies related to ethnic entrepreneurship and self-employment (3) Support for education (4) Support for vocational or professional training (5) Housing and health policies (6) Naturalisation policies (7) Promotion of civic and political participation
Cultural Integration	Policies that support and facilitate an individual's cognitive, behavioural and attitudinal change, which allow for acculturation in the host society (municipality)	(1) Language training (2) Support for foreign resident's culture (3) Support for secular or religious practices (4) Support for sporting activities
Interactive Integration	Policies that encourage the acceptance and inclusion of foreign residents in the municipality's social networks, voluntary organisations, PTAs, etc	(1) Provision of opportunities for Japanese and non-Japanese to interact as co-residents (2) Non-nationality based education (3) Non-nationality based housing (4) Japanese language training
Identificational Integration	Policies which encourage foreign residents to develop a feeling of belonging to the host society (municipality)	(1) Multicultural policies (2) Policies of recognition of foreigners' (immigrants') secular and religious organisations (3) Promotion of a culture of local citizenship ceremonies and events

Kokuminka 2006, pp. 16–19). Aiming to "create multicultural coexistence in Adachi with the cooperation of people with different mother tongues, culture and customs", Adachi's basic plan consists of four basic pillars:

(1) communication assistance; (2) lifestyle assistance; (3) the creation of a multicultural coexistent municipality, and (4) the setting up of multicultural coexistence initiatives (Adachi Ku Kuminbu, Kokuminka 2006, pp. 16–19).

Similarly, based on the report "Policies for foreigners: The plan for the promotion of the creation of a city of multicultural coexistence", Shinjuku's initial steps towards integrating their large and diverse foreign resident population are manifested as a plan that strives to promote the exchange between foreign and Japanese residents and foster mutual understanding of culture and history in order for them to live together harmoniously (Shinjuku Bunka Kokusai Kouryu Zaidan 2003, 2004). The key initiatives here are: (1) creating a municipality which is easy to live in; (2) deepening foreign residents' understanding of Japanese residents; and (3) creating a municipality in which foreign residents can live easily alongside their Japanese counterparts.[1]

Both municipalities include varying degrees of structural, cultural, interactive and identificational integration reforms into their initiatives (Table 2.2). Under the rubric of structural integration reform, they have committed to removing some of the structural barriers which prevent foreign residents from accessing social welfare programmes, enrolling in education programmes, residing in public housing, and fully mobilizing their resources when participating in the local labour market. Responses from two wards include the removal of nationality requirements for public housing, simplification of enrolment procedures for health care, hiring of non-Japanese nationals in health and welfare sections (when eligible), and the hiring of non-Japanese nationals in other administrative positions that deal directly with foreign residents such as International Exchange Sections.

Similarities aside, Adachi has developed three initiatives that set it apart from Shinjuku: (1) the establishment of a Centre for Business Creation; (2) the provision of non-nationality based start-up loans; and (3) the conduct of investigations regarding the inclusion of eligible foreign residents in the local referendum. Each initiative is an indicator of Adachi's commitment to the social integration of foreign residents. It also represents an attempt to come to terms with the changing ethnic diversity in the ward. The Centre of Business Creation forms a nexus in which foreign and Japanese residents can come together to engage in mutually beneficial business activities. Transactions are supported by the local government through introductions and the provision of venues for meetings, non-nationality based start-up

TABLE 2.2
List of Specific Measures Undertaken by Shinjuku and Adachi Wards vis-à-vis Integration

	Shinjuku Ward	Adachi Ward
Structural Integration	(1) Establishment of the Multicultural Coexistence Plaza (2) Simplification of enrolment procedures for health care, pension system (3) Establishment of a multilingual advisory and information centre (4) Non-nationality-based public housing scheme (5) Eligibility for public housing for special permanent residents, permanent residents, long-term residents and spouses of Japanese nationals (6) Hiring of non-Japanese in health and welfare sectors	(1) Establishment of Centre for Business Creation (2) Availability of non-nationality-based start-up loans (3) Establishment of Multicultural Coexistence Section (4) Non-nationality-based public housing scheme (5) Provision of multilingual services and information (6) Employing foreign staff (7) Support for collaboration between Japanese and non-Japanese businesses (8) All relevant administrative units involved in Multicultural Coexistence activities (9) Investigations on including eligible foreign residents in referendum
Cultural Integration	(1) Provision of multilingual information and advisory services (2) Online video providing information on living (3) Enrichment of Japanese language learning opportunities (4) Provision of multicultural awareness education with a focus on mutual respect and understanding (5) Strengthening current Japanese language training (6) Availability of advisory services (7) Availability of education subsidies for foreign children	(1) Japanese language classes (2) Intensive Japanese language studies for children (3) Multilingual information and advisory services (4) Living in Japan Seminar (5) Encouraging introduction of ethno-cultural background in festivals, schools (6) Fostering international understanding and human right education (7) Providing education for returnees (8) Interpretation and translation services (9) Guest teacher programme

Interactive Integration	(1) Provision of a multilingual disaster training (2) Recruitment of foreign residents for festivals, cultural exchange programmes (3) Encouraging participation in PTAs (4) Promotion of networking of foreign residents with other foreigners/Japanese residents	(1) Recruitment of foreign residents in PTAs, festivals, awareness programmes (2) Diversity training (3) Employing foreign staff (4) Non-nationality-based urban planning committees e.g. Multicultural Coexistence Promotion Committee (MCPC) (5) Expansion of opportunities for foreign residents to visit schools (6) Encouraging joint ventures between Japanese and non-Japanese businesses (7) Introductions to local Chamber of Commerce (8) Children's Assembly
Identificational Integration	(1) Establishment of multicultural coexistence plan (2) Promotion of mutual respect and understanding through cultural events	(1) Institutionalisation of Multicultural Coexistence Plan (2) Establishment of multinational MCPC (3) Offering multicultural coexistence education programmes (4) Future establishment of Foreign Advisory Council

loans, contractual information, legal guidance and the like. Investigations on how foreign residents can participate in local referenda are important indicators of steps towards residency status being disconnected from national-based citizenship towards local-based citizenship.

These changes have occurred in both wards owing to a number of factors. Pressures to adhere to international conventions related to the rights of migrants and international human rights standards have compelled local governments and created political space for them to remove obstacles for the employment of foreign residents in certain administrative sectors of local government. Being the immediate interface between foreign residents and the national government, local governments have also rationalized the provision of services to be on par with those offered to Japanese residents (Kashiwazaki 2000, p. 462; Menju 2003, pp. 34–38).

In the early 1980s, Adachi and Shinjuku, along with other municipalities in Japan with high concentrations of foreign residents, became aware that structural impediments such as housing restrictions for public housing and administrative services solely in the Japanese language hinder foreign residents, not only from successfully navigating through local community life, but also from thriving in local communities. Common problems included not receiving or understanding information related to school enrolment, vaccinations, enrolment in health care, pension systems and child subsidies. The removal of these barriers served two purposes: first, it ensured that the local government would not be responsible for providing the cost of health care coverage to uninsured foreign residents; and second, it was part of an overall strategy promoted and recommended by the then Ministry of Home Affairs to internationalize from within, ensuring that each municipality was easy to live in for all residents.

Shinjuku: Financial Realities and Criminalization of Foreign Residents

Demographic realities in Adachi and Shinjuku ward, in particular the continued rapid and predicted rise in foreign resident population, have also played an important role in shaping the way in which structural integration reforms in both wards have occurred with some urgency. For example, Shinjuku ward, which has the largest and most diverse number of foreigners per capita within Tokyo, had a foreign population of 35,211 foreign residents, representing almost 11.08 per cent of its population in 2010, and this is expected to increase to 30 per cent in the coming years (Shinjuku Bunka Kokusai Kouryu Zaidan 2004, pp. 1–2; Tokyo Metropolitan Government Statistics 2010*b*). Putting the population growth in perspective, Shinjuku Ward's registered foreign population increased 87.1 per cent, from 18,815 in 1995 to 35,211 in 2010.[2] In contrast to other wards in Tokyo, Shinjuku has the largest concentration, population and diversity in terms of foreign population, surpassing its nearest rival Adachi ward by almost 12,000 foreign residents, Edogawa ward by 9,500 and Minato ward by 13,400 (Tokyo Metropolitan Government Statistics 2010*b*).

Several other important factors have also contributed to Shinjuku's limited commitment to comprehensive structural integration. These include the large, temporary component of its foreign resident population, its role as a transit and work hub, its reputation for being home to Tokyo's red light district, and the influence of nationalistic politicians. Collectively, these factors decrease the incentive for local representatives to promote and support integration policies.

Shinjuku's temporary foreign population includes international students, the ward being home to several large universities that host substantial numbers of students for one to four years. After living in the ward for the duration of their studies, they either return to their home countries or move to more affordable municipalities in the suburbs in outer Tokyo, instead of settling in Shinjuku. Shinjuku's role as a transit, work and education hub also makes it a nexus point where foreign residents come to work, study or transit, but not to settle. The reason for the latter is twofold: the high cost of living and limited housing availability. Shinjuku's centrality in Tokyo makes it an attractive location but is too expensive for low-income students and workers to settle in.

Another factor influencing integration initiatives in Shinjuku is its nationalistic politicians and their perceptions of crime. Shinjuku is home to the Tokyo Metropolitan Government and Governor Shintaro Ishihara. It also has Tokyo's notorious red light district of Kabukicho. Governor Ishihara, along with other nationalist politicians use the mantra of "foreigner-related crime" as a rallying call against non-Japanese residents, by portraying foreign residents, in particular those living in Shinjuku and the Kabukicho area, as violent criminals (Ellis and Hamai 2007; *Japan Times* 2007).[3]

This negative tone has made advocating more comprehensive integration programmes a non-starter for local politicians who represent Japanese constituents. It is also evidenced by the reticence of Shinjuku multicultural coexistence policy-makers to initiate integration strategies that encompass some form of voting rights and political representation.

Adachi: Managing International Marriages

Adachi has also seen a large increase in the number foreign residents, especially of Filipino and Chinese extraction (Adachi Ku Kuminbu, Kokuminka 2006, p. 2). In 1980, 95.6 per cent of the foreign population were ethnic Koreans who can trace their origins to the colonial era (Adachi Ku Kuminbu, Kokuminka 2006, p. 29). However, from 1980s onwards, newcomers, primarily from China and the Philippines, began to settle in Adachi and other parts of Tokyo because of its relatively low cost of living (Tajima 2000). Moreover, many women from the Philippines entered Japan in the 1980s as "entertainers" (see Ito 1992; Kashiwazaki 2003, p. 139). This trend has continued unabated, resulting in a dramatic alteration of the demographic distribution of foreign residents in Adachi. Compared to the early 1980s during which ethnic Koreans (oldcomers) were the representative majority of those who were labelled foreigners, today they represent only 37.5 per cent of the current foreign resident population (Adachi Ku Kuminbu, Kokuminka 2010, p. 7). By 2025, Adachi City's foreign population is predicted to rise to 40,000 or 6.7 per cent of the total municipal population and to 70,000 approximately 14.7 per cent of the municipal population by 2050 (Adachi Ku Kuminbu, Kokuminka 2006, p. 1). With this expected rise and, in particular, the prediction that the newcomers will be predominantly of Asian origin, Adachi ward foresees that problems associated with national health care, education and housing will occur (see Kanagawa Zainichi Gaikokujin Mondai Kenkyukai 1992, pp. 7–14).

The shift from an ethnically Korean-dominated foreign resident population to one that encompasses large numbers of Chinese and Filipinos has compelled Adachi to create more opportunities, through structural integration reform, to enable all foreign residents to participate in the local community. The reasons for this continued influx of foreigners into Adachi ward are several. Firstly, in recent years, it has witnessed an increasing number of marriages between Japanese nationals and foreigners. As of 2008, 8 per cent of marriages in Adachi were international marriages compared to 5.1 per cent nationwide (Adachi Ku Kuminbu, Kokuminka 2010, p. 7). Second, the growth of Adachi ward's foreign population is associated with its relative proximity to the central Tokyo area. This location, together with its low living costs, serves Adachi foreign residents well, allowing quick access to the employment hubs in central Tokyo while enabling workers to avoid marathon commutes from the edges of the Tokyo Metropolis (Tajima 2000; *Japan Times* 2008).

Associated with international marriages are issues of long-term and/or permanent residence, dual nationality children, and naturalization. Long-term and/or permanent residence demands that local government undertake integrative measures so that foreign residents are neither marginalized nor disadvantaged in terms of accessing social welfare programmes, finding work and raising their new families. Not providing for these residents could result in them becoming a burden on the municipality and fellow residents because of their inability to live as ordinary Adachi citizens.

Dual nationality children are, in many cases, synonymous with educational challenges. Among other reasons, this is because of their inability to complete their education at local schools, as compared to Japanese children. This difference is partly due to the fact that although primary and secondary school attendance is mandatory for Japanese citizens, foreign children face difficulties in school because their foreign parents may not have the necessary language and cultural skills to help their children cope with their studies. To combat this problem, Adachi has volunteer Japanese teachers as well as a total of six months supplementary Japanese language education to help foreign children learn Japanese. Shinjuku also has various programmes for foreign residents as well as Japanese language training for foreign children. Unfortunately, there is no data on the number of foreign children in Shinjuku who are not attending schools, making the planning and implementation of education programmes for them a challenge.

The naturalization of spouses of Japanese nationals is another reason for the adoption of inclusive multicultural coexistence initiatives such as the establishment of a multinational Multicultural Coexistence Promotion Committee and the conduct of investigations on the participation of permanent residents in future local referendum and the election of local representatives (Table 2.3). For Adachi, international marriage has resulted in the embedding of foreign residents into the fabric of Adachi society through the children, long-term or permanent residence, and naturalization. This creates an opportunity for Adachi to develop an inclusive multicultural coexistence policy. On the other hand, Shinjuku with its lower levels of international marriage, higher numbers of temporary foreign residents, high-profile xenophobic politicians and a red light district associated with foreigner-related crime, has had less incentive to develop inclusive policies. As a consequence, there is a resistance to engage in reforms, especially those that offer foreign residents political representation, or at least some kind of voice in shaping Shinjuku ward's community, for example, like that of Adachi's Foreigner Advisory Committee.

Cultural and Interactive Integration

Shinjuku and Adachi share numerous congruent approaches to cultural and interactive integration (Table 2.3). The increased numbers of newcomers who are linguistically and culturally disadvantaged has led Adachi and

TABLE 2.3
**Comparative Chart of Adachi and Shinjuku Wards'
Multicultural Coexistence Policies**

		Adachi Ward	Shinjuku Ward
1	Total population	64,0000 (2006)	300,000 (2004)
2	Foreign resident population	21,405 (2006)	28,271 (2006)
3	Foreign resident population in %	6.7% (2006)	9.72% (2006)
4	Predicted foreign resident population in 2025 and 2050	40,000 (6.7%) 2025 (low estimate) 70,000 (14.6%) 2050 (low estimate)	37,811 (12.24%) 2025 No data for 2050
5	Change in proportion of foreign residents by nationality	1980 – 95.6% Korean 2005 – 42.2% Korean	2000 – 41% Korean, 31% Chinese 2006 – 44.6% Korean, 29.1% Chinese
6	Percentage of international marriages	1990 – no data 2000 – 5.9% (597 cases) 2007 – 8.9% (677 cases)	No data
7	Multicultural Coexistence Budget (Annual) Proportion per resident	13,329,000 yen	93,934,000 yen
8	Multicultural Coexistence Plan	Yes	Yes
9	Multicultural Coexistence Statement	Multicultural coexistence refers to the acceptance of different cultures and ethnicities and the development of good community relations by working together	Multicultural coexistence refers to the promotion of mutual understanding between Japanese and foreign residents, the awareness of Japanese language, social expectations, culture and customs so that: (1) cultural friction can be avoided and (2) foreigners do not become a burden to Shinjuku society

10	Multicultural Coexistence Major pillars	(1) Communication Assistance (2) Lifestyle Assistance (3) Creation of a multicultural coexistence community (4) Instituting a multicultural coexistence promotion system	(1) Create a municipality which is easy to live in (2) Deepening foreign residents' understanding of Japanese residents (3) Create a municipality in which all foreign residents can live easily alongside their Japanese counterparts

Notes:
△ Currently 11 municipalities nation wide
▲ As of February 2005 only 10 local government allow voting rights
Source: Nagy (2009, p. 388).

Shinjuku to invest in multilingual information and services, language and culture courses, and foreign advisory services. Besides removing linguistic obstacles to accessing services and participating in the local community, such cultural integration reforms facilitate acculturation and serve as interpretation mechanisms to mediate pressing needs. Other activities such as support for Japanese language classes, multilingual advisory services, multicultural awareness education, intercultural and human rights education contribute to language proficiency, self-reliance and bi-directional acculturation. At the cognitive level, both Japanese and foreign residents are being sensitized to their mutual needs, concerns and anxieties regarding each other. At the behavioural and attitudinal levels, language and cultural tools are being provided such that Japanese and foreign residents can alter their behaviour so as to engage in relationships that are marked by communication, cooperation and awareness, instead of intercultural friction and misunderstanding.

Another similarity in the wards' approaches is the promotion and support of foreign residents' business activities through collaboration and exchanges with local Japanese business leaders. Yet another example involve initiatives to establish nursery school facilities that can accommodate foreign resident children, the enhanced training for nursery school staff, educational advisory services, disaster training, aid for foreigners interested in starting their own companies, and the creation of volunteer groups that can be dispatched to help foreign residents when they encounter difficulties. The cultural and interactive integration reforms not only integrate foreign residents into their respective wards linguistically but, more significantly, allow foreign residents to weave themselves into community tapestries through programmes that encourage them to participate in parent-teacher associations, children's organizations and Chambers of Commerce. By focusing on policies that support and facilitate cognitive, attitudinal and behavioural bi-directional acculturation, both wards are promoting inclusiveness and promoting broader participation of all residents in their respective municipality. They demonstrate a vision of a ward in which its residents, local and foreign, are contributors to the development of their areas (See Adachi Ku Kuminbu, Kokuminka 2006, p. 19).

Under the rubric of cultural and interactive integration, both Adachi and Shinjuku are shaping their multicultural coexistence initiatives to: (1) support and facilitate the cognitive, behavioural and attitudinal dissonance that foreign and Japanese residents feel vis-à-vis each other; and (2) encourage the acceptance and inclusion of foreign residents in their various community organizations.

The largely congruent approaches to cultural and interactive integration in the two wards largely stems from the fact that both wards built their multicultural coexistence plans based on the views of the foreign and Japanese residents derived from large-scale surveys conducted in their wards on foreign residents in 2004. Responses in each survey to questions related to challenges, problems and opinions on integration of foreigners largely centred on cultural and interactive barriers to integration such as language hurdles, cultural awareness, and a dearth in opportunities to meet with and develop various kinds of relationships, concerns about cultural awareness, and participation in local organizations.

Lastly, since these initiatives do not revolve around political rights or representation, they are politically vacuous policies in which the support and drive for the development and implementation of these policies can be easily acquired. They are acceptable to both municipal governments because they do not require amassing large-scale support for policies; they do not require changes in municipal laws related to foreign residents; they can, in many cases, be farmed out to local non-profit organizations (NPOs); and they benefit all residents.

Identificational Integration Reform

The fourth and perhaps most difficult form of integration advocated by both wards is identificational integration, centred around which are policies that encourage a feeling of belonging to the host society and community. In contrast to the shared ideas and initiatives in the cultural and interactive integration reforms in both municipalities, we see distinct differences between the wards in their identification integration approaches.

Adachi: Towards Belonging and Local Citizenship

Adachi has at least four initiatives in its identificational integration reform: (1) the institutionalization of its multicultural coexistence plan; (2) the establishment of its multicultural coexistence committee; (3) the creation of multicultural coexistence programmes; and (4) conception of plans for the future establishment of a Foreigner Advisory Committee that would directly liaise with the Adachi local government. These initiatives foment identification with Adachi through their promotion of multicultural coexistence, recognition of foreign resident organizations as meaningful actors in Adachi society, and promotion of a culture of local citizenship.

To illustrate, Adachi ward has established a Multicultural Promotion Committee which consists of fourteen members of whom seven are Japanese, two are Chinese, one South Korean, one North Korean, one Nepalese, one Brazilian and one Filipino,[4] and is legally recognized by the municipal government and mandated to promote multicultural coexistence in Adachi ward. Its international composition, legal status and the fact that it reports its findings and recommendations directly to the local government highlight Adachi's commitment to creating an inclusive municipality. As an organization with non-Japanese members, it is valued by local government for its perspectives and potential to contribute to the ward's multicultural development. As a consequence of this recognition, Adachi is promoting a sense of local citizenship and ownership in its ward.

Adachi's initiative to create a multicultural coexistent community also includes the establishment of a Foreign Resident Advisory Board to enable foreign residents to have a voice in ward administration (Adachi City 2007, pp. 19, 27–28). This demonstrates Adachi's commitment to political inclusion of foreign residents. It is also demonstrative of how structural integration reforms in the Adachi local government are creating opportunities for foreign residents to be more involved in Adachi. This includes potential access to the local assembly's regular meetings to enable them to share and contribute to solving the challenges faced by foreign residents and, in some cases, Japanese residents as well. Adachi Ward is also currently investigating how to incorporate permanent residents into local referenda (Adachi Ku Kuminbu, Kokuminka 2006, p. 27), and is presently conducting research on adopting new legislation that would grant voting privileges to permanent residents in local elections. This demonstrates the ward's commitment to at least some level of inclusion for foreign residents' civic rights (Adachi Ku Kuminbu, Kokuminka 2006, p. 27). If realized, voting privileges would complete the inclusion circle, granting eligible foreign residents political suffrage. Here again, we are seeing strong and concrete steps to enhance foreign residents' identification with Adachi by promoting a policy that advances their sense of local citizenship through their participation in local affairs and elections.

Finally, the establishment of a Multicultural Coexistence Promotion System institutionalizes Adachi's multicultural coexistence vision. This includes the creation of formal municipal ordinances for the promotion of multicultural coexistence, and the strengthening of networking activities with other municipalities, the Tokyo Metropolitan Government and other associations through broadening multicultural coexistence policy information (Adachi Ku Kuminbu, Kokuminka 2006, pp. 21–22). More importantly, it is an open commitment to the basic premises outlined in Adachi's multicultural coexistence plan — this commitment reinforces the confidence of foreign residents vis-à-vis the recognition of their needs and ability to contribute as local citizens in Adachi.

Similar to structural integration reforms, the momentum behind identificational integration reforms in Adachi stems from the large influx of foreign residents since the 1980s, the expected increase in the foreign population, and the large number of international marriages. With the increasing numbers of Adachi residents having some connection with foreign residents — whether through marriage, long-term residency, settlement, children, business or other kinds of networks — Adachi has been compelled to find ways to include the voices of non-Japanese nationals and the hyphenated Japanese nationals in its development.

Shinjuku: Towards Parallel Societies?

In contrast to Adachi, Shinjuku's initiatives in identificational integration are: (1) the establishment of a multicultural coexistence plan; and (2) the promotion of mutual respect and understanding and culture events. The first is an official commitment to the promotion of multicultural coexistence that gives foreign and Japanese residents an understanding of the type, style and degree of multicultural coexistence that will take place in Shinjuku. The second emphasizes the development of mutual cultural understanding and respect to reinforce feelings of belonging to the community.

Institutionalizing Shinjuku's multicultural coexistence plan ensures that Japanese language classes and cultural classes provide participating residents with the rudimentary skills they need to navigate the complexities of life in Japan as a foreign resident (Regional and Cultural Affairs Department 2006*a*). Other initiatives such as multilingual advisory services and publications ensure that all resident foreigners are aware of their rights and responsibilities as residents of Shinjuku ward (Regional and Cultural Affairs Department 2006*b*). In both cases, foreigners can develop a feeling of belonging, at least at a linguistic and informational level, by being more aware of events in Shinjuku, having information on the social welfare services that they are eligible for, and in general become part of the information loop in the municipality.

The rationale behind these initiatives is that if foreigners are kept abreast of their rights and responsibilities, and if they have the language and cultural skills of the local community, they will not cause intercultural friction or be a burden to the Shinjuku local government and community. This strategy includes contributing to and receiving, when necessary, social welfare, pensions, national health care, education subsidies and child subsidies among others. Language and culture training as well as multilingual services are meant to decrease the chances that minority workers are exploited and, at the same time, increase their ability and willingness to seek medical, legal and other kinds of services when needed. In short, these initiatives ensure that foreign residents can and are fulfilling their obligations and meeting their needs as residents.

Notwithstanding the attempt to develop a feeling of belonging in Shinjuku, we can see that Shinjuku's multicultural coexistence practices revolve around: (1) a strong focus on preventing intercultural friction between Japanese residents and foreign residents; and (2) a large investment in printed multilingual information and advisory services for foreign residents. The aim is to provide basic services to as many foreign residents as possible through information and access to facilities. With regard to its efforts in diffusing intercultural friction, Shinjuku's multicultural coexistence platform seeks to address Japanese residents' perceptions of foreign residents, such as a rising number of crimes committed by them and growing frictions that can result from increasing numbers of foreign residents. For foreign residents, coexistence means diminishing the amount of discrimination and racism that exists in Shinjuku and Japanese society at large (Shinjuku Ku Bunka Kokusai Kouryu Zaidan 2006, p. 2).

Shinjuku's multicultural coexistence plan remains committed to ensuring that the minorities do not become a burden to the municipal government and the Japanese residents of Shinjuku. According to the Managing Director of International Exchange at Shinjuku Foundation for Culture and International Exchange:

> Multicultural coexistence practices are not about creating a municipality that minorities want to come to; rather they are about maintaining the integrity of the Japanese community, ensuring that the foreigners that do settle temporarily or for the long-term do not disrupt the traditional patterns of Japanese life. Multicultural coexistence programmes provide foreign residents with knowledge about Japanese customs and manners so they can avoid causing problems with Japanese residents. Moreover, multicultural coexistence practices are not about voting rights for foreigners (interviewed 21 September 2006).

With an approach to multicultural coexistence that views foreign residents as a potential burden to avoid rather than a potential contributor to the Shinjuku community, identificational integration reforms in Shinjuku remain a distant and intangible objective for the current policy-makers.

For Shinjuku's policy-makers, its growing ethnic diversity, large fluctuating foreign resident population, comparatively low international marriage rates, and the continued association of foreign residents with crime and destabilizing Japanese society particularly by xenophobic politicians all make advocating reforms to further integrate foreign residents into the Shinjuku community a difficult challenge to overcome. It is politically difficult to get support from constituents for reforms that will further integrate foreign residents into the local community when foreigners are characterized as crime-prone, disruptive, illiterate, culturally insensitive and temporary residents. In short, Japanese residents do not see foreign residents as co-residents with a shared identity; rather they see them as a separate group or community that exists within the local community — they are different, alien and not a contributor to the community. Consequently, they are not seen as a part of the politician's political plans. From the point of view of Shinjuku's foreign residents, identification with Shinjuku remains a distant dream when they feel they are portrayed negatively. Identification remains a challenge when they see other wards and municipalities across Japan recognizing the important role and contributions foreign residents.

CONCLUSION

Adachi and Shinjuku wards have different approaches to the development of multicultural coexistence. These differences are related to their respective foreign resident demographic profiles, past and projected changes in the number of foreign residents and the particular settlement patterns which have formed in Adachi and Shinjuku. Originally, both had foreign resident profiles that were predominantly Korean in ethnicity. The influx of newcomers was first brought about by the decrease in the number of Japanese migrant workers who moved into the inner city and the consequent need to fill positions. Second, in connection with this decreasing number of Japanese workers, housing became easier to find (Tajima 2000, pp. 349–64; Okuda 2000, pp. 343–48). Third, since many foreign migrants worked in service industries, living in municipalities with high concentrations of these industries is natural and inevitable. A fourth and crucial factor is that earlier foreign residents were able to set up businesses, find work and learn what was necessary to survive and prosper in these wards, and this serves as a magnet to newer migrant foreign workers who could easily tap into this valuable economic and social capital.

More importantly, changes in the demographics of those communities have contributed to ethnic realities that have influenced the development and direction of multicultural coexistence policies. In the case of Shinjuku, diversity has contributed to a policy that addresses intercultural friction, the importance of mutual understanding and foreign residents' access to services. Adachi ward's policies, on the other hand, have been shaped by changes in its demographic make-up from a previously Korean-dominated foreign community to one that has large numbers of other nationalities. The large numbers of international marriages that continue to grow in Adachi ward have also shaped the multicultural coexistence policy to become more inclusive.

The social integration reform indicators of structural, cultural, interactive and identificational integration demonstrate that Shinjuku and Adachi emphasize different kinds of initiatives in their multicultural coexistence plans. There are many similarities in the areas of cultural and interactive integration reforms because of their apolitical nature. However, both wards also have many differences in their structural and identificational integration reforms, these primarily arising from political incentives and perspectives of foreign residents. These policies are based on at least three factors: (1) the demographic diversity of foreign population; (2) the number and proportion of foreign residents; and (3) the municipality's record and reputation for crime. The growing numbers of foreign residents holding visas that show "spouse of a Japanese national" is indicative of a significant embedding of foreign residents into a municipality. The marriage between a Japanese and a non-Japanese and their children create direct links between foreign residents, Japanese residents and the local government. This compels local governments to take more progressive stances on inclusion and pluralism.

The migrant policies' differences revealed in this chapter allow us to drawn important conclusions about urban diversity at the local government level, even in largely homogeneous societies such as Japan. The case studies of Shinjuku and Adachi demonstrate that we must look at the micro-level in urban areas to understand how local governments or metropolitan areas like Tokyo are accommodating diversity. Simply, diversity is not widespread or similar; rather, there are diversity hubs with different characteristics that require distinct approaches to meet each hub's needs. In the case of Shinjuku and Adachi, these characteristics included population size of migrants, the origins of migrants, changing demographic profiles of migrants, international marriage rates, children of international families and the reputation of migrants in each ward.

For areas beyond the Tokyo Metropolis such as Osaka, Kawasaki, Nagoya and Hamamatsu, we would need to consider the historical relationship certain diversity hubs within them have with their respective migrants and how policies manifest themselves differently. For example, in the case of Osaka and Kawasaki, they have large populations of long-term resident, fluent Japanese-speaking Zainichi Koreans who have different needs from newcomers to Japan. The diversity hubs of Nagoya and Hamamatsu, on the other hand, are home to large numbers of ethnic Japanese South Americans (Nikkeijin) with language and cultural hurdles that require migrant policies which concentrate on integrating migrants with these backgrounds. Ultimately, what this illustrates is that there is no panacea for accommodating migrants in largely homogeneous societies such as Japan, as diversity is found mostly at the micro-level in urban contexts.

Notes

1. Interview with the Managing Director of International Exchange at the Shinjuku Foundation for Culture and International Exchange on 21 September 2006. Also see Shinjuku Bunka Kokusai Kouryu Zaidan (2004).
2. Tokyo Metropolitan Government Statistics (2010*b*) for 2010's data.
3. In the Policy Speech by the Governor of Tokyo, Shintaro Ishihara, at the Third Regular Session of the Metropolitan Assembly, 2003, he states that "One of the biggest tasks in restoring public safety in Tokyo is to control crimes by non-Japanese residents. Some foreigners who have entered Japan illegally or overstayed their visas are setting up crime organizations and engaging in violent crimes, creating a major social threat." See Tokyo Metropolitan Government (2003).
4. For the entire list of participants, including names, associations and nationality see Adachi City (2007).

References

Abella, M.I. "Asian Migrant Contract Workers in the Middle East". In *The Cambridge Survey of World Migrations*, edited by R. Cohen, pp. 418–23. Cambridge: Cambridge University Press, 1995.

Adachi City. <http://www.city.adachi.tokyo.jp/001/pdf/d02500043_1.pdf>, 2007. Accessed 4 March 2007.

Adachi Ku Kuminbu, Kokuminka [Adachi Ward Citizens Department, Citizens Section]. *Tabunka Kyousei Suishin Kikaku: Ikiiki Wakuwaku "Tabunka Kyousei Toshi Adachi"* [Multicultural Coexistence Promotion Plan: Adachi, an exciting, enjoyable multicultural city]. Tokyo: Adachi Ku Kuminbu, Kokuminka [Adachi Ward Citizens Department, Citizens Section], 2006.

―――. Tabunka Kyosei Suishin Keikaku 2010 nendo~2012 nendo: Ikiiki Wakuwaku "Tabunka Kyosei" Toshi Adachi [Multicultural Coexistence Promotion Plan 2010–2012: Adachi, an exciting, enjoyable multicultural city]. Tokyo: Adachi Ku Kuminbu, Kokuminka, 2010. http://www.city.adachi.tokyo.jp/012/pdf/d02500006_1.pdf. Accessed 19 November 2010.

Berry, J.W. "Mutual Acceptance among Immigrants and Ethnocultural Groups in Canada". *International Journal of Intercultural Relations* 30, no. 6 (2006): 719–34.

Bosswick, W. and F. Heckmann. "Integration of Migrants: Contribution of Local and Regional Authorities". *European Foundation for the Improvement of Living and Working Conditions 2006*. Ireland: CLIP Network, Cities for Local Integration Policy, 2006.

Chan-Kam, S., P. Griffith, and M. Leonard. "Migration, Integration and Citizenship:

Lessons From Around the World". UK: The Foreign Policy Centre, 2002. <http://fpc.org.uk/fsblob/31.pdf>. Accessed 3 March 2011.

Cruz-Saco, M.A. "Promoting Social Integration: Economic, Social and Political Dimensions with a Focus on Latin America". Paper prepared for the United Nations, Department of Economic and Social Affairs, Division for Social Policy and Development in collaboration with the Government of Finland, Expert Group Meeting, "Promoting Social Integration," 8–10 July 2008, Helsinki, Finland <http://www.un.org/esa/socdev/social/meetings/egm6_social_integration/documents/Promoting_Social_Integration.pdf>, 2008. Accessed 16 August 2011.

Ellis, T. and K. Hamai. "Crime and Punishment in Japan: From Re-integrative Shaming to Popular Punitivism". *Japan Focus*. <http://japanfocus.org/-Tom-Ellis/2340>. Accessed 19 November 2007.

Esser, H. *Soziologie. Spezielle Grundlagen. Band 2: Die Konstruktion der Gesellschaft* [The construction of social relationships]. Frankfurt and New York: Campus, 2000.

Ito, R. "Japa Yuki San Genso [The origins of Japa yuki] Saiko: 80 Dai Nihon he no Ajia Jin Josei Ryunyu". In *Gaikokujin Rodosha Ron: Genjo kara Riron he* [Foreign workers: From the reality to future], edited by T. Kojita and T. Iyotani. Tokyo: Kobundo, 1990.

Japan Times. "The Zeitgeist: Upping the Fear Factor, There is a Disturbing Gap between Actual Crime in Japan and Public Worry over it". 20 February 2007.

———. "More Children Born with a Foreign Parent, Japan Needs to Deal with the Legal Ramifications, Experts Say". 4 August 2008.

Kanagawa Kennai Zaiju Gaikokujin Jittai Chosa Iinkai [Kanagawa Prefectural Committee Investigation on Foreign Residents in Kanagawa Prefecture]. *Kanagawa Kennai Zaiju Gaikokujin Jittai Chosa Hokusho: Kankokujin, Chosenjin, Chugokujin ni tsuite* [Report on the investigation of Kanagawa Prefecture foreign residents: Koreans, North Koreans and Chinese residents]. Kanagawa: Kanagawa Kennai Zaiju Gaikokujin Jittai Chosa Iinkai [Kanagawa Prefectural Committee Investigation on Foreign Residents in Kanagawa Prefecture], 1985.

Kanagawa Zainichi Gaikokujin Mondai Kenkyukai [Kanagawa Research Group on Foreign Resident' Issues in Kanagawa]. *Tabunka, Taminzoku Shakai no Shinko to Gaikokujin Ukeire no Genjou: Kanagawa Ken no Jirei ni Sokushite* [Promoting the Kanagawa example: The reality behind promoting a multicultural, multiethnic society with foreigners]. Kanagawa: Kanagawa Zainichi Gaikokujin Mondai Kenkyukai [Kanagawa Research Group on Foreign Resident' Issues in Kanagawa], 1992.

Kashiwazaki, C. "Citizenship in Japan: Legal Practice and Contemporary Development". In *From Migrants to Citizens: Membership in a Changing World*, edited by T.A. Aleinikoff and D. Klusmeyer. Washington, D.C.: Brooking Institution Press, 2000.

———. "Kokusai Kouryu Kokusai Kyouryoku Katsudo no Ryoiki [The scope of International exchange and cooperation activities]". In *Kokusai Koryu Kyoryoku Katsudo Nyumon I: Kusa no ne Kokusai Koryu to Kokusai Kyoryoku* [An introduction to International exchange and international cooperation activities (I)], edited by T. Menju, pp. 135–54. Tokyo: Akashi Shoten, 2003.

Massey, D.S. et al. "Theories of International Migration: A Review and Appraisal". *Population and Development Review* 19 (1993): 431–66.

Menju, T. "Kokusai Koryu to Kokusai Kyoryoku Katsudo to wa? [What are international exchange and cooperation activities?]". In *Kokusai Koryu Kyoryoku Katsudo Nyumon I: Kusa no ne Kokusai Koryu to Kokusai Kyoryoku* [An introduction to International exchange and international cooperation activities (I)], edited by M. Toshihiro, pp. 34–38. Tokyo: Akashi Shoten, 2003.

Ministry of Justice. *Shutsunyukoku Kanri Kihon Keikaku* [Immigration control basic plan]. Tokyo: Ministry of Justice, 1992.

———. *2007 Immigration Control*. Japan: Immigration Bureau, Ministry of Justice, 2007.

———. *2010 Immigration Control*. Japan: Immigration Bureau, Ministry of Justice, 2010.

Nagy, S.R. "Analysis of the Multicultural Coexistence Ideas and the Practices of Local Governments in the Tokyo Metropolis". PhD dissertation, Waseda University, 2009.

National Institute of Population and Social Security Research. <http://www.ipss.go.jp/pr-ad/e/ipss_english.pdf>. Tokyo: National Institute of Population and Social Security Research, 2006. Accessed 3 January 2009.

Noguchi, S. "Finding Home: Immigrant Life in Japan". *Japan Focus*. <http://japanfocus.org/products/details/2349>. Accessed 2 June 2007.

Okuda, M. "Asian Newcomers in Shinjuku and Ikebukuro Areas, 1988–1998: Reflections on a Decade of Research". *Asian and Pacific Migration Journal* 9, no. 3 (2000): 343–48.

Phillips, Trevor. "After 7/7: Sleepwalking to Segregation". Speech given at the Manchester Council for Community Relations. 22 September 2005. <http://www.humanities.manchester.ac.uk/socialchange/research/social-change/summer-workshops/documents/sleepwalking.pdf>. Accessed 16 August 2011.

Regional and Cultural Affairs Department. *Shinjuku ku Japanese Classes*. Shinjuku-ku: Regional and Cultural Affairs Department, 2006*a*.

———. *Shinjuku News*. Shinjuku-ku: Regional and Cultural Affairs Department, 25 September 2006, No. 6, 2006*b*.

Shinjuku Bunka Kokusai Kouryu Zaidan [Shinjuku Culture and International

Exchange Association]. *Shinjuku Ku ni Okeru Gaikokujin Jumin to no Kyousei ni Kan suru Chosa Hokokusho (Heisei 16 Nen 3 Gatsu)* [Report on the investigation concerning coexistence with Shinjuku Ward foreign residents]. Shinjuku Ku: Shinjuku Ku Bunka Kokusai Kouryu Zaidan [Shinjuku Culture and International Exchange Association], 2003.

———. *Tabunka Kyosei no Machi Dukuru (Gaikokujin Jissaku) no Suishin ni Tsuite* [About the promotion of the creation multicultural coexistence city (Foreign resident policies)]. Shinjuku Ku. Shinjuku Foundation for Culture and International Exchange, 2004.

Social Integration Branch, Division for Social Policy and Development (DSPD), United Nations Department of Economic and Social Affairs (UNDESA). "Mission Statement", 2008. <http://www.un.org/esa/socdev/sib/index.html>. Accessed 2 March 2011.

Tajima, J. "A Study of Asian Immigrants in Global City Tokyo". *Asian and Pacific Migration Journal* 9, no. 3 (2000): 349–64.

Tokyo Metropolitan Government. Policy Speech by the Governor of Tokyo, Shintaro Ishihara, at the Third Regular Session of the Metropolitan Assembly, 2003. <http://www.metro.tokyo.jp/ENGLISH/GOVERNOR/SPEECH/2003/0303/2.htm>. Accessed 3 March 2008.

Tokyo Metropolitan Government Statistics. Gaikokujin Touroku Jinkou [Population of registered foreigners], 2010*a*. <http://www.toukei.metro.tokyo.jp/gaikoku/2010/ga10010000.htm>. Accessed 25 May 2010.

———. Tokyo to no Jinkou Suikei [Tokyo's population], 2010*b*. <http://www.toukei.metro.tokyo.jp/jsuikei/js-index.htm>. Accessed 25 May 2010.

Van Arsdol, M.D., Jr., S. Lam, B. Ettkin, and G. Guarin. "Population Trends and Migration Patterns". In *Crossing National Borders: Human Rights Issues in Northeast Asia*, edited by T. Akaha and A. Vassilieva, pp. 11–44. Tokyo: United University Press, 2005.

Weber, M. *The Theory of Social and Economic Organisation*, translated by A.M. Henderson and T.P. Parsons, Part I. New York: Free Press: 1965/1922.

3

THE PLACE OF MIGRANT WORKERS IN SINGAPORE
Between State Multiracialism and Everyday (Un)Cosmopolitanisms

Fred C.M. ONG and Brenda S.A. YEOH

INTRODUCTION

Increasing flows of transnational migration have fuelled a new spatial order of interconnectivities among nations and cities, leading to a host of both anticipated and unanticipated human encounters between locals and migrants. These encounters and the subsequent possibilities for creative synergies, destructive tensions and missed opportunities have had a significant impact on the sociocultural texture of cities. In particular, this has resulted in "populations and social structures which have previously been rather more separate now increasingly imping[ing] physically and materially on one another's living conditions" (Hannerz 1996, p. 56). In this light, cosmopolitanism as a unifying vision for urban democracy and governance, signifying a culture of openness and acceptance and underpinned by the values of inclusion and tolerance of difference, is back in currency. Some scholars have even proclaimed the cosmopolitan city as "the hallmark of truly global cities" (Short 2006, p. 223) and a necessary response to the empirical reality of multicultural cities of today (Binnie et al. 2006). However, this idealized treatment of cosmopolitanism as a solution to the multifarious sociocultural and sociopolitical landscapes of contemporary cities needs further probing, especially in the manner in which it has neglected the importance of "diverse local agents, social forces and institutions" in actively participating and shaping the processes of global city formation (Brenner and Keil 2005, p. 12).

Singapore provides a useful example of an emergent global city where a state-engineered "cosmopolitanization" has been central to aspirations of top-tier global city status. It is also, however, a city where the experience and application of cosmopolitanism has been neither universal nor unproblematic (see Yeoh 2004). In this vein, this chapter attempts to unpack cosmopolitanism in Singapore by uncovering two possible arenas of tension and slippage — in the discursive field and in the realm of everyday practices — in response to the state's "cosmopolizing" efforts. It begins with a brief review of academic discussions of cosmopolitanism and how the notion has been appropriated by the Singapore state, before launching into an investigation of how such state-mandated cosmopolitanism complements/contradicts Singapore's founding ideology of multiracialism as well as sentiments towards male foreign workers in public spaces.

REVIEWING COSMOPOLITANISM

Cosmopolitanism as an ancient term can be traced back to the third century BC when the Stoics argued for inclusionary cosmopolitan societies whose citizens — cosmopolites, to be precise — extended their "love of self... to all of humanity" (Dharwadker 2000, p. 6). The concept of cosmopolitanism appears to have been derived from the Greek understanding of the "cosmopolis", referring to the links between *cosmos* — the order of nature, and *polis* — the nature of human society (Featherstone 2002). Recent intellectual discussions of cosmopolitanism have, however, centred mainly on the tradition emerging from the work of German philosopher Immanuel Kant who, some two centuries ago, argued for the replacement of the law of nations with a "genuinely morally binding international law" to achieve the utopian vision of a "peaceful cosmopolitan order" (Kant 1795; cited in Stevenson 2002). Such a philosophy of global citizenship has triggered debates within political theory and citizenship studies, with some regarding cosmopolitanism as fundamentally opposed to national patriotism because it negates the sense of obligation to a national sovereignty, espousing in its place a sense of "thinking and feeling beyond the nation" that frustrates the national experience (Cheah and Robbins 1998; see Rée 1998). Proponents of such arguments have called for a globally-oriented citizenship in place of a cosmopolitan one, which insists on national solidarity while maintaining an active interest, responsibility and commitment towards the well-being of others and the creation of a "just world order" (Parekh 2003). Others have continued to advocate for a cosmopolitan virtue upon which citizenship should be based in the face of global diversity (Turner 2002).

Kant's notion of a cosmopolitan democracy has provided alternative ways of engaging with issues of globalization, citizenship and nationalism in an increasingly mobile and transnational world. However, cosmopolitanism exists not only in its political form; it also encompasses what Delanty (2006) has termed as moral and cultural cosmopolitanisms. These strands of cosmopolitanisms, likewise, emanate from Kant's influential writings on the cosmopolitan condition as being able to instil in humans "the universal feeling of sympathy, and the ability to engage universally in very intimate communication" (Kant 1968; cited in Cheah 2006). Cosmopolitanism hence connotes an "orientation [and] willingness to engage with the Other" (Hannerz 1996, p. 103) and a "stance towards difference which involves openness to, and tolerance of, diversity" (Young, Diep, and Drabble 2006, p. 1710). This entails the cultivation of a "particular set of skills and attitudes towards diversity and difference" (Binnie et al. 2006, p. 13) which equips cosmopolitans with the capacity to both embrace and receive the culture of the other.

Drawing on variants of cosmopolitanism in selective and superficial ways, the term has also gained currency as a discourse in place-marketing strategies as part of inter-city competition. As cities become increasingly multicultural and multiethnic, they become sites where "social differences are gathered in ... at unique scales and levels of intensity" (Jacobs and Fincher 1998, p. 1). Consequently, urban theorists concerned with city-planning issues have written about cosmopolitanism as an ideology to bolster relations between different people and to foster better understandings of these emerging cities of difference (Sandercock 2003, 2006). In recent years, cosmopolitanism has thus become an urban strategy — a "commodity", in Beck's (2004) words — used by many urban governors-turned-entrepreneurs to attract new businesses and foreign talents (Binnie et al. 2006). These "branding" strategies, in order to emerge victorious amongst the "place wars" between cities (Evans 2003), often involve the manifestation of cosmopolitanism as an urban re-imaging effort, illustrated by Binnie and Skeggs' (2004) work on the production of gay space with reference to the Manchester Gay Village; and as an urban regeneration initiative, exemplified by Chan's (2006) research on the Birmingham City Council's peaceful management of cultural differences within the city. The "cosmopolitan city" has thus grown in its importance as a branding strategy, especially in light of the "inter-urban competition within globalization and increasing international capital mobility", with many urban entrepreneurs worldwide embarking on attempts to market their cities as cosmopolitan (Young, Diep, and Drabble 2006). We turn our attention to Singapore, a city-state which exemplifies the messy terrain in which overlapping variants of the cosmopolitan discourse are selectively interpreted and reshaped into a strategic urban template to forge a global future for Singapore in its race to the top of the global cities league table.

THE STATE'S COSMOPOLITAN INTENTIONS

The state's cosmopolitan project was first proposed by then Prime Minister Goh Chok Tong (currently Emeritus Senior Minister [ESM]) when he spoke of turning Singapore into "a cosmopolis — an attractive, efficient and vibrant city exuding confidence and charm, and a magnetic hub of people, minds, talents, ideas and knowledge" (Goh 1999) at the World Conference on Model Cities. Since then, allusions to cosmopolitanism have been recurrent within political ideologues. ESM Goh (2002) reiterated the idea of a cosmopolitan city when stressing the importance of promoting the arts and culture in Singapore, while Prime Minister Lee Hsien Loong (PM Lee) contended that the country should capitalize upon its strength as a "cosmopolitan and open society" during his 2005 National Day Rally (Lee 2005). In its bid for the Youth Olympic Games 2010, the Singapore National Olympic Council had described Singapore as "enterprising, optimistic, vibrant, cosmopolitan and culturally rich"; subsequent write-ups on its website had affirmed the nation's status as a "young and cosmopolitan" city (Singapore 2010, 2008).

Singapore's cosmopolitan propaganda is symptomatic of worldwide "branding strategies" of deploying cosmopolitanism by entrepreneurial forms of urban governance. The state's cosmopolitanism project embraces a "two pronged approach" (Yeoh 2004; Ho 2006) as encapsulated in the Singapore government's Internationalization Strategy and Foreign Talent Policy: the first involves inculcating among Singaporeans an international outlook so as to facilitate their navigation in a globalizing world and increase their comfort level with foreign talents, while the second includes efforts to re-engineer the city-state as a place for cosmopolitans in a bid to attract and retain foreign talents (Yeoh 2005). Yet, such "Singapore-style cosmopolitanism" (Tan and Yeoh 2006) as envisioned by the state has not been without contention. While there has been little disagreement with the promotion of a "cosmopolitan and creative" city as a key plank of the state's vision for twenty-first century Singapore, some of the specific strategies to "cosmopolize" both people and places in the city have been more controversial — the influx of foreign talents has resulted in the "polarization of 'local' and 'foreign'" (Yeoh and Chang 2001, p. 1040), with social integration between locals and foreign talents "remaining at a superficial level" (Yeoh and Huang 2003, p. 335). "Singapore-style cosmopolitanism" has also been critiqued to be "unidirectional" — Singaporeans should not sink roots elsewhere while foreign talents are encouraged to look upon Singapore as home (Ho 2006) — and exclusionary, where the "underbelly of low-skilled, low-status 'foreign workers'" that sustains the economy has been systematically forgotten (Yeoh 2004). More recently, the state's "cosmopolizing" endeavours have taken on new dimensions by adopting a "talent-centric" approach which involves the retaining of not only overseas but local talents as well (ESC 2010), and an "open" society concept which encourages all Singaporeans to remain open to foreigners including foreign talents, foreign-born citizens, permanent residents and foreign workers (*Straits Times*, 2 February 2010; see Lee 2010). Here, we subject the state-engineered "cosmopolizing" effort to further scrutiny by: firstly, juxtaposing the current state-vaunted cosmopolitanism with the nation-state's founding philosophy of multiracialism based on the Chinese-Malay-Indian-Others (CMIO) model; and secondly, exploring the extent and nature of the "gap" between state visions of cosmopolitanism and everyday encounters in public spaces in the Singapore "heartlands", or public housing estates where the vast majority of Singaporeans live, via a case study focused on the attitudes of Singaporeans towards the presence of increasing numbers of South Asian male migrant workers during weekends in these spaces.

MULTIRACIALISM PLUS COSMOPOLITANISM?: FROM "FOUR OVERLAPPING CIRCLES" TO "HYPHENATIONS"

From the late 1980s, many cities and states in Asia have embraced an entrepreneurial regime based on the discourses and logics of globalization as they become increasingly integrated into regional and global circuits (Yeoh 2005). Simultaneously, given the colonial context from which many Asian nation-states emerged just a few decades ago, the "postcolonial enterprise of cultivating national identity and promoting national pride" remains highly salient (Yeoh 2001, p. 458). The cultural production of national identity remains a major project of the capitalist developmentalist state even as it wrestles with the demands of globalization. Singapore provides an interesting urban crucible to examine the tensions between nation-building discourses and those that serve the city in competing in the global league.

Against the backdrop of a plural society with racialized categories hardened by colonial policy, the postcolonial ruling elite's project of welding individuals and groups within the geographical boundaries of the independent "nation" into "one people" has been premised upon an ideology of multiracialism by creating a "multiracial, non-communist, non-aligned, and democratic socialist state" (Chan 1991, p. 158). Given the geopolitical sensitivities of a numerically Chinese-dominated nation in "a region of an overwhelmingly Malay make-up", a multiracialism which "protects the 'Malays' and 'Indians' by formally denying the 'Chinese' dominant status" was an "astute" solution to counter the "combustibility of inter-racial animosity" (Pang 2003, p. 13).

This state-vaunted formulation designates four "official" races — Chinese, Malays, Indians and "Others" — viewed as separate but equal, and encourages acceptance of the coexistence of different religious practices, customs and traditions of the various communities "without discrimination for any particular community" (Chan and Evers 1978, p. 123).[1] To avoid racial chauvinism, communalist sentiments based on race, dialect, surname or regional affinity are broken down and replaced with social relationships which derived their meaning from the overarching "nation-state framework" (Benjamin 1988, p. 36). Singapore's project of multiracialism is thus based on "a binary between the component 'elements' and the master-national self", where the "national identity and values are

... seen as developing out of the component Malay, Chinese, Indian and Eurasian cultures" (Brown 1993; cited in Pang 2003, p. 15). This "CMIO quad-chotomy" (Pang 2003, p. 17) of essentialized categories has been articulated using different analogies over the years,[2] including then Prime Minister Goh's (2000, p. 16) vision of "building a multi-racial nation through integration", not of "mosaic pieces" but "four overlapping circles":

> My preferred imagery for building a multi-racial Singapore ... is not mosaic pieces, but four overlapping circles. Each circle represents one community. The area where the circles overlap is the common area where we live, play and work together and where we feel truly Singaporean with minimal consciousness of our ethnicity. This pragmatic arrangement of seeking integration through overlapping circles has underwritten the racial and religious harmony that Singaporeans enjoy today.

Yet such racial harmony has been critiqued to be "substantively empty" with the nation-state's version of multiracialism being likened to an instrument of social control (Chua 2003). Others have argued that Singapore's brand of multiculturalism is an "artificial" one produced by a disciplinary state and suffers from the heavy-handed strictures on what constitutes "multiracialism" dictated by the state:

> The real fragility of the remarkable society that has been created in this tiny island state ... is not its ethnic and cultural complexity per se. It is rather in the artificiality of the attempts to prune into a precarious order ... In both size and its artificiality Singapore does indeed remind one of the bonsai: nature miniaturized and bent. The problem is that the bonsai, when its cramps are removed and it is put in a bigger pot, grows with the natural exuberance of the rest of nature (Clammer 1998, p. 26).

> The goal of peaceful multi-racial living has to be downloaded from the main frames of government, into the hard drives of Singapore's increasingly autonomous citizens (George 2000, p. 169).

Like the bonsai which loses its "miniaturized and bent" form when placed in a larger pot, the careful and controlled racial arithmetic of the CMIO model will no longer "add up" as the multiracial nation becomes unbound in the face of globalization forces, transnational flows and the increasing autonomy of both citizens and non-citizens. Following the state's "cosmopolizing" efforts as delineated in the previous section, it is inevitable that ethnic relations among groups and individuals in Singapore will become more complex, since the foreigners streaming into the city-state are not only providers of labour, skill and talent, but also bearers of specific geographies and histories, carrying multiple identities along dimensions of ethnicity, culture, customs and the like. In short, nationality is oftentimes inflected by ethnicity, and both must be taken into account when examining relationships predicated on racial categories. The insertion of foreign/ethnic others into Singapore, even if temporary but more so if permanent, will change the complexion of society and give rise to, possibly, a "new pluralism" that reinforces "the old conjunction of race and class in the new globalized economy" (Goh 2008, p. 248).

Even as the kaleidoscopic "socioscape" unfolds, the complexly variegated terrain continues to bear the marks of a skills divide. The irony of what might be read as the privileging of the spectacularity of "global talent" invested in a few distinctive individuals over the localized nature of being part of the "habitus" exhibited by the ordinary person was brought to a head when the national newspaper published two articles in the same day: "Two made Singapore honorary citizens" under "Prime News", and "He was born here, did NS here, and will raise kids here. So why is this man stateless?" in the "Home" section of the *Straits Times*, (23 October 2003). In the former, it was announced that British Nobel laureate Sydney Brenner and Italian chief executive of ST Microelectronics Pasquale Pistorio have been conferred honorary Singapore citizenship, Brenner for contributions to kick-starting biomedical research in Singapore, and Pistorio for his past and future investments in Singapore's semiconductor industry. In contrast, the latter article told the story of Barnabas Lim Ah Huat who was born and bred in Singapore, performed national service and was about to marry and raise his children in Singapore but was stateless because he was born out of wedlock. His application for Singapore citizenship was turned down twice, possibly because of a previous record of drug addiction. The "disparate fortunes" (in the words of a contributor to the forum discussion) of Brenner and Pistorio on the one hand, and Lim on the other, was not only indicative of the high premium accorded to talent in deciding how people are positioned in the "stateless"-"R-pass holder"-"Q-pass holder"-"P-pass holder"-"permanent resident"-"citizen"-"honorary citizen" continuum, but also the way race-blindness operates at the upper-end of the continuum, and possibly at the lowest-end too.

"Race" however is a significant factor for the in-between categories in the spectrum, and the extent of permeability and transition between adjacent categories. Among P and Q-pass holders (i.e. higher skilled employment pass holders) as well as permanent residents, it has been found that Asian rather than white foreigners have tended to be more positive about putting down roots in Singapore (Yeoh and Huang 2003). Asian P- and Q-pass holders are more likely to want to apply for permanent residence while Asian permanent residents are more enthusiastic about the possibilities of Singapore citizenship. As such, despite its aspirations to become a cosmopolis of different nationalities, it should be noted that the city is in no danger of becoming less "Asian" in terms of its more permanent demographic profile. This, however, does not imply that social integration will be unproblematic, for divisive issues may well also arise from differences within the category of "race". As "race" becomes inflected by differences in "nationality" and "history", the politics of sameness and difference within each "race" become more complex. Not only will the already unsatisfactory term "Others" become even more problematic as a catch-all residual category, the staple categories "Chinese" or "Indian" will also become even less homogeneous. Among the "Chinese", for example, it has been reported that the total number of PRC-Chinese who have become citizens, permanent residents and are studying or working in Singapore since 1990 is now estimated to be close to one million (*Straits Times*, 22 November 2008),[3] of which a considerable number (figure unknown) have made, or are likely to make, the transition from expatriate workers or foreign students to permanent residents, and some would continue along the trajectory to becoming citizens. Thus, while these new citizens of the nation would be officially inscribed as "Chinese", whether they would be accepted on the ground and folded into the prescribed category presented by the CMIO model is contentious. The degree of animosity expressed by "Singaporean-Chinese" towards "PRC-Chinese" was indicated by the following letter to the press, collectively written by a group of Chinese, "probably Western educated 20-somethings" (cited in then Prime Minister Goh's 2001 National Day Rally Speech):

> We do not feel any affinity to the Chinese people ... The cheena[4] people are sucking away all the foreign investments and along with them, our jobs ... we really cannot imagine a world with the cheena people in charge. The cheena people working in Singapore are really such a crude lot.

The resentment against PRC-Chinese is often expressed against the women, reflecting deep-seated anxieties that "the other China woman" — seductive precisely because she is the "same" yet "different" — will erode the nation's family values. "China brides", for instance, sometimes known as *xiao long nu* or "Little Dragon Ladies", are viewed as "fraudsters who use matrimony as a step to permanent residency or running away with the man's money" (*Straits Times*, 19 February 2006) while *pei du ma ma* (PRC-Chinese "study mothers" who accompany their children to Singapore to enrol them in Singapore schools) have similarly been tarred with the same brush as "having questionable morals — women of the night, husband stealers and gold diggers" (*Straits Times*, 7 February 2005, see Huang and Yeoh 2005; Yeoh and Yap 2008; Yeoh and Huang 2010). The strong gendered overtones are evident in that PRC-Chinese men working in Singapore — also in large numbers — may not be subjected to similar moral pronouncements. In one case, when asked why he decided to return (albeit a fraction of) the $8.8 million that his grandson, remittance agent Lam Chen Fong, swindled from 1,153 PRC contract workers, 82-year-old Lam Yuan Siew "wrote on a piece of paper — *yan huang zi sun*" referring to the notion that Singaporean-Chinese and PRC-Chinese are all sons of "Emperors Yan and Huang", that is, of Chinese ancestry (*Straits Times*, 20 November 2003). The elder Lam elaborated, "We are all Chinese and I understand their feelings for what my grandson has done" (*Straits Times*, 20 November 2003), reflecting a level of racialized empathy quite absent from discussions about PRC-women in the public domain.

It has been argued that transnational migration is a transgressive force eroding the boundaries of the nation-state, while advancing alternative concepts such as cosmopolitan or hybrid identities as counterpoints to the nation-state (Pellerin 1996, p. 81). Such interpretations, however, ignore the rigidity and resilience of state-imposed disciplinary categories and their continuing effects on structuring society. In Singapore, the CMIO model is not likely to become immediately obsolete in the face of intense transnational flows into the nation, despite the apparent contradictions and developing ferment of "intra-race" politics of identity. There is little to suggest that the framework of state nationalism-cum-multiracial citizenship will wither away, or that transmigrant groups — especially those regarded as unskilled foreign/ethnic others — will be given the space for engaging in new forms of claims-making in the nation-state. The situation in Singapore is more akin to Sassen's (2003, p. 12) view that "the national is highly institutionalized and is marked by socio-cultural thickness", where the denationalization of the economic sphere is coupled with a renationalization of immigrant policies.

As the efforts to cosmopolize Singapore continue unabated, however, it is likely that ethnic categories under the weight of transnational pressures will begin to become less bounded, to allow for and recognize complex forms of identifications and more nuanced ascriptions. The complexities of social identification were overtly recognized (possibly for the first time in a national speech) in PM Lee's 2006 National Day Rally Speech where, in his appeal to Singaporeans to welcome "new immigrants", he not only argued for a recognition of difference ("A Chinese-Chinese is different from a Singapore-Chinese. An Indian-Indian is different from a Singapore Indian"), but proposed that this can be done by allowing for "hyphenated" national-racial identities at least for the first few generations:

> ... we will hyphenate, Australian-Singaporean, Chinese-Singaporeans, Chinese-Chinese Singaporeans. But make them one of us and if we meet one of them, let's be friendly, let's go out of our way to show them around, help them, make them feel at home.... So even if the first generation is not completely Singaporean, the second generation growing up here will be and will contribute to Singapore (Lee 2006).

While CMIO-multiracialism has not been abandoned as a disciplinary framework drawn upon systematically to govern race relations in Singapore, the city-state's cosmopolitan ambitions are beginning to move understandings of racial categorization beyond the fixity of four "homogeneous but overlapping" circles to an acceptance of hyphenated identities as legitimate, even as the hope remains that the "hyphens" are transient phenomena that will dissolve with subsequent generations.

(UN)COSMOPOLITAN DISPOSITIONS AND THE PLACE OF MIGRANT WORKERS

The cosmopolitanization of Singapore and the way it challenges (or conserves) current discourses on multiracialism provides a glimpse of possible ideological shifts in the constant remaking of Singapore to compete on the global stage. We turn our attention to the way cosmopolitan ideals are played out in practice at the micro-level, by examining the attitudes of Singaporeans towards the presence of increasing numbers of South Asian male migrant workers during weekends in public space.

Over the past two decades, there has been an explosion in the numbers of migrant workers in Singapore, from 248,000 in 1990 (*Straits Times*, 10 November 2007) — about 8 per cent of the state's population — to 856,000 in 2010 — approximately 17 per cent (*Straits Times*, 23 February 2010). Since 2006, there has been an avalanche of rejoinders from the public and media in response to the flurry of complaints addressed to Members of Parliament by Singaporeans with regard to the presence of male foreign workers[5] in neighbourhoods (*Straits Times*, 10 November 2007; 26 January 2008). These debates, although polarized into two main camps (Chin 2008), have been predominantly negative, largely centred on (potential) spatial conflicts in public places (*Straits Times*, 8 June 2006; 25 November 2007). These conflicts were especially highlighted in 2008 over the government's plans to convert the vacant Serangoon Gardens Technical School building into a hostel for migrant workers. The proposed hostel was viewed as a "disamenity", by some long time residents in the middle-class Serangoon Gardens residential area, and 1,400 out of its 7,000 resident households signed a petition against it (various issues of *Straits Times*, 3–7 September 2008). In the aftermath of such rising resentment towards foreign workers, the idea of an "open society" has been reiterated time and again, with the Prime Minister reminding Singaporeans to be more tolerant towards foreign workers on several occasions, including his National Day Rally 2010 (Lee 2010; see *Straits Times*, 15 January 2007; 10 September 2008; 23 March 2009).

Similar anxieties have also been expressed by Singaporeans living in the western part of Singapore. For instance, residents of Jurong West had voiced their displeasure — many were reported to have been "left seething" — over the gathering of male migrant workers in the vicinity (*Straits Times*, 25 November 2007), and the latter's boisterousness has been cited as a possible reason for the locals' objection to these workers' presence in their midst. Such a response is reminiscent of the landscape contestation between South Asian workers and local Chinese residents in Little India in the late 1990s, although unlike Little India which has been a historical enclave with a "reputation as a network of [Indian] community comfort" (Siddique and Purushotam 1990, p. 71) and a "magnet for Indian immigrants" (Chang 2000, p. 349), Jurong West was never meant to be an ethnic enclave for migrant workers but a residential and industrial area. The area therefore presents a compelling site of encounters for investigating the limits and possibilities in the cosmopolitan disposition of the Singaporean public as may be discerned from their perceptions of and attitudes towards South Asian male migrant workers congregating within the vicinity of the local shopping mall — Jurong Point Shopping Centre — and its adjacent Boon Lay Mass Rapid Transit (MRT) Station and Bus Interchange. As an "everyday, public accessible place" (Day, Stump, and Carreon 2003, p. 312), the area attracts large flows of human traffic particularly during peak hours as well as a significant congregation of migrant workers over the weekends. Insofar as the notion of public space embeds within itself the public sociability of the city (Germain and Radice 2006), focusing on the myriad encounters with difference in these spaces provides us with a barometer for cosmopolitan sensibilities at ground level (Young 1990; Watson 2006). This allows us to gauge the extent to which multiple perceptions and meanings emerging from these localized encounters translate into a repertoire of "cosmopolitanisms from below". While training the analytical lens on everyday encounters in public space tends to focus on the transitory and contingent, we affirm Vertovec's (2011) views that these encounters, however fleeting, serve to shape and sustain everyday forms of civility in a particular society.

Almost all the Singaporeans[6] approached were critical of and uncomfortable with the substantial gatherings of male migrant workers in public spaces in Jurong West — it was principally felt that these workers behaved in ways deemed unacceptable by locals. Some examples of the inappropriate behaviour which migrant workers exhibit include "speaking very loudly", "hugging each other" and leaving behind peanut shells and beer bottles after their gathering over the weekends. In the words of David,[7] a Chinese salesman in an electronics shop in Jurong Point, for example, they "talk loudly and behave as if it is their place". Singaporean interviewees felt that "foreign workers" wishing to use the space should conform to the "conditions for inclusion ... routinely imposed by dominant social groups and actors" (Laurenson and Collins 2006, p. 186) in the host country: "If they do it in India then ok, but you come to Singapore you must know what it is like here.... There is this phrase ... about Rome — when in Rome, do what the Romans do" (Justin, 26-year-old Chinese staying nearby).

Singaporean interviewees also explained their discomfort at what they perceived as being "out of place" — they felt that South Asian foreign workers already have a "legitimate" place of their own in the form of the weekend enclave in Little India, as exemplified in the comments of Chitra, a 63-year-old Indian resident: "Little India is for [the foreign workers] to go. Got a lot of *Banglas* and Indians also go there, easier to meet friends and relax. So better for them to go there." Nonetheless, Chitra's recommendation did not stem from feelings of hostility towards these migrants. Her position was one of empathy; she highlighted that most of these South Asian workers came from villages in rural India or Bangladesh, and related how life in the rural regions of India — where her own parents came from — were "very different" from cities like Singapore, and that Singaporeans should "try to understand them". Nearly all the interviewees claimed that they felt little sense of antagonism towards the foreign worker population when they encounter large numbers in Little India over the weekend, unlike the uneasy feelings of "displacement" and "out-of-placeness" (Cresswell 1996) they experienced when confronted with the presence of similar numbers of foreign workers in Jurong West. As Tom, a 59-year-old Chinese resident, explained: "I will feel uncomfortable when there are a lot of [foreign workers]. From a majority group in Singapore, I suddenly feel like a minority group. So I don't come on weekends to this place."

Cosmopolitan sensibilities (or the lack of) hence take shape in highly spatialized and grounded ways: here they are up against well-entrenched "normative geographies" (Cresswell 1996, p. 10) that render different groups of people "in" and "out" of place in different parts of the city. At the same time, spatial geographies of prejudice are also inextricably conflated with the colour of race. For example, there was a tendency for Chinese interviewees to equate the term "migrant workers" with dark-skinned migrants from either Bangladesh or India, whereas when referring to labourers from other countries like People's Republic of China (PRC), Thailand or Burma, the interviewees would prefix their nationalities or ethnicities (e.g. Chinese workers, Thai workers, Burmese workers). During fieldwork, when asking Tony — an Army regular who frequents the site about thrice per week — if he noticed the presence of foreign workers in the area, his immediate response was to clarify if the researcher was referring to "Banglas" (i.e. Bangladeshi workers). When the researcher tried to shift the focus away from Bangladeshi workers to foreign workers in general, Tony queried (as if the researcher's question was redundant) if there were others. Clearly, he felt that "foreign workers" could be equated with "Banglas", a position he later confirmed by emphasizing that he only "saw the black ones".

Skin colour — as a marker of "race" and nationality — was often used in everyday conversations to signify the "abject status" (Sibley 1995) of foreign workers and as a basis to advance sweeping characterizations:

> Tony: ...Actually sometimes they quite *guailan*[8] one ... like they will make stupid comments among themselves when sometimes people walk past. Make funny stupid comments and laugh.... Not all [the migrant workers] lah. Only the black ones — the Banglas and the Indians...

These characterizations were also often associated with "imagined crimes" (*Today*, 12 November 2007): "The *Banglas*, they more *ticko*[9] than the others.... Got this *Bangla*, he went to molest his colleague's daughter... ... The *Banglas* all like that..." [Peter, 57-year-old Chinese retired resident].

In some cases, racializing the crime obviated the need for any evidence:

> Jenny (Chinese resident in her early fifties): You know got one group of migrant workers, Indians I think — they steal clothes ah! Men's clothes, pants ah, shirts ah, they all steal. Even women's clothes they also steal...
>
> Interviewer: Have you witnessed them in action before? Like, you got see them steal?
>
> Jenny: No. But, last time don't have this kind of thing. Must be them, because only start occurring last year...
>
> Interviewer: Any of your neighbours saw with their own eyes?
>
> Jenny: No. But confirm is them, if not who else can it be? Normal people meh?

By ascribing "a particular identity to groups without further exploration of the complexity of identifications, or of subjects' multiple and often contradictory identities" (Ehrkamp 2008, p. 120), labelling based on skin colour gives rise to an alternative moral mapping which subverts the cosmopolitan position that assumes that "all human beings are morally equal" (Heater 2002, p. 73, cited in Nijman 2007, p. 183). This is reinforced when looking at Singaporeans' "negotiation[s] of difference" (or lack thereof) within "local micropublics of everyday interaction" (Amin 2002, p. 960). For some Singaporeans, adopting "principles of non-interaction" (Sennett 2002, p. 47) is the easiest means of dealing with the presence of migrant workers, as seen in the case of Elizabeth, a 41-year-old Chinese housewife who makes weekly trips to the area to visit her parents:

> I think no need [for daily encounters] lah. They are not staying next to me, they are not [within] my social circle, and it's not as if I am working with them now. Not much association with them ... so I don't see the point nor the need to interact with them now.

This is particularly so because the site in question is, concurrently, a space of transit that allows for little sustained and deeper contact between Singaporeans and foreign workers. With the large crowds of people walking around, it "doesn't seem the right place to talk to others, let alone interact" [Siti, a Malay woman in her thirties who visits her mother who lives near Jurong Point two to three times a week].

Some Singaporeans employ strategies of avoidance to steer clear of foreign workers in view of potential risks and dangers associated with them (Brownlow 2005) and to avoid possible conflicts:

> I stay out of their way, they stay out [of] my way. I think that is my philosophy [Brad, 21 year-old Chinese undergraduate student staying nearby].

> There is no need for interaction *la*, like what my brother said, the more interaction there is, the more difficulties, problems you will get. So best is don't interact with them [Rohani, a 21-year-old Malay woman who shops regularly at Jurong Point].

Field observations also show how some Singaporeans would skirt the outer perimeter of the open grass patches where foreign workers gather over the weekends, instead of taking the path in between the grass patches as they would on other days. Brad sums up the attitudes of many interviewees towards Jurong Point and its adjacent spaces:

> The appeal to come here is no longer that strong anymore ... [My friends] don't like to meet here.... It's the same reason why Singaporeans avoid Lucky Plaza on weekends.... I guess it feels pretty weird, if you ask me, to walk around with [the foreign workers]...

In short, the tendency is for Singaporeans to *navigate away from differences*, rather than to *negotiate differences* (Binnie et al. 2006). Instead of employing "strategies" to "bridge boundaries with people who are different from them" (Lamont and Aksartova 2002, p. 1), they employ strategies to *maintain* boundaries, thus implying the lack of "a connection with, and respect and space for the cultural other" (Sandercock 2003, p. 2). Having said that, it is interesting to note how most of the interviewees became contemplative towards the end of the interview conversations, especially if they had previously expressed discriminatory views towards male foreign workers. They realized that foreign workers should not be "reduced to one aspect of their identities" (Ehrkamp 2008, p. 120). As Lesley, a 22-year-old Chinese graduate student staying near Jurong Point put it:

> Perhaps the opportunity to get to know them better is simply not there. Maybe they are not as bad as how we make them out to be. Or how the media makes them out to be. We probably need time... Singaporeans also got good and bad. They also got good and bad one, just that sometimes we don't remember got good ones.

One interviewee even went on to suggest that there was no fundamental difference between Singaporeans and foreign workers:

> Sometimes I think we're all part of the same common humanity — be it Singaporean Malay, or Chinese or Indian or what the government calls the Other. Whether you are from China, or whether you are from India, or Thailand, or Myanmar, it doesn't matter. Whether you are working as a bank manager, or a road-sweeper, it doesn't matter. We're all the same species right? Humans [Marhaidah, Malay housewife in her early thirties].

To this end, although everyday perceptions and discussions of South Asian migrant workers appeared, on the surface, mired in innuendoes of negative sentiments, running contrary to cosmopolitan hopes of defeating "parochialism, narrow-mindedness, and ultimately xenophobia" (Nijman 2007, p. 183), instances wherein cosmopolitan ideals of tolerance and openness, as well as a commitment to humanity, have also been expressed, seem to suggest otherwise. The racialized mindsets that seem apparent among many interviewees do not necessarily translate into anti-foreign xenophobia, but is open to more complex, ambivalent, tolerant and even empathetic stances towards migrant workers, an indication of the wide-ranging diversity of viewpoints under construction in contemporary Singapore.

CONCLUSIONS

Cosmopolitan discourses have been taken on board in Singapore primarily as a strategy of reimaging the city as part of urban entrepreneurialism as well as to "open up" the nation-state to absorbing foreign labour needed to compete effectively in a globalized economy. Less skilled foreign workers are confronted with a revolving door policy regulating their presence in the city while in the case of transnational elites with talents and skills which the city-state wishes to root and retain, the revolving door is slowed down as much as possible. These policies are not racialized in an overt sense and foreign others entering Singapore are expected to fit within the CMIO model of multiracialism which has been the nation-state's foundational philosophy since independence.

CMIO-multiracialism hence remains prescriptive even in the face of the influx of large-scale labour immigration. This has meant that racialized discourses drawing on racial categories and assumptions are very common in everyday communication. It is no surprise that Singaporeans approach the question of migrant workers with racialized mindsets, drawing on stereotypical characterizations (colour, race, nationality, etc.) to describe the most abject category of foreigners in the globalizing city. As seen in the case of local-foreign perceptions with regard to South Asian foreign workers, racialized mindsets can very quickly produce and compound racist prejudices, which are in turn drawn upon in characterizing the presence of foreign "others" in public space as a threat to mainstream life and values (Pain 2001).

Looking ahead, a key question if Singapore is to become more open to cosmopolitan sensibilities is whether the recent move proposed by the PM to "hyphenate" would bring about more progressive thinking around "race". It needs to be remembered that for now, hyphenation as a means to accommodate foreign others — to allow for the interplay of sameness/difference and to recognize more complex identifications — does not apply to the case of foreign workers who are not permitted to root in Singapore. However, the hope is that more flexible ways of thinking about the multiracial self will in time liberate the mind from racialized straitjackets and provide alternatives to thinking "along the lines of stereotypes", as indicated in Amy's (22-year-old Chinese resident) reflections:

> Actually sometimes I will think and wonder if it is inherent biasness on our local [people's] side.... By inherent biasness, I mean like we tend to think in a certain way, we tend to think along the lines of those stereotypes that are linked to the construction workers. Maybe they are not what we think...

The ability to "delegitimize essentialist identities which are always group related" (Ossewaarde 2007, p. 384) and to recognise others based on their "value and integrity as human beings, quite independently of their national affiliations" (Mau, Mewes, and Zimmerman 2008, p. 5) would be a minimal requirement of cosmopolitanism. In the case of Singapore, the ultimate litmus test for the "cosmopolitan imagination" (Lamont and Aksartova 2002, p. 2) and the opportunity to strengthen people's capacity to live with difference lies in how abject members of the city are perceived and thought of in everyday life in heartland spaces.

Notes

1. In 2007, the ethnic distribution in Singapore stood at 75 per cent Chinese, 13.7 per cent Malays, 8.7 per cent Indians and 2.6 per cent "Others" (Department of Statistics 2008). This racial arithmetic has remained fairly consistent over the last few decades.

2. For current realities, an IPS survey showed that there was generally strong support for the concept of a multi-racial society in Singapore: Malays and Indians were more supportive (88 per cent and 83 per cent respectively) than the Chinese majority (78 per cent) (Ooi, Tan, and Soh 2003). The same survey also found that inter-ethnic relations (measured by participation in festive occasions of other races and views on inter-racial marriages) have strengthened. These findings, however, need to be interpreted with caution for they do not necessarily capture the true quality of the *experience* of multiracialism, which is far more complex and multidimensional. A survey among primary schoolchildren showed that children tended to choose their friends from within the same ethnic group and that racial mixing was stultified in schools (*Today*, 12 August 2003). Lai's (1995) ethnographic work on ethnic relations in a public housing estate demonstrates the cracks and crevices which characterize the negotiation of multiracial living.
3. As official figures of foreigners in Singapore are not provided by the government, we have resorted to estimates used in the national newspaper.
4. *Cheena* is a derogatory term for a Chinese, suggesting a lack of refinement.
5. It should be noted that the use of the term "foreign worker" is prevalent in media and state discourse. Nonetheless, we prefer the term "migrant worker" as it humanizes workers as agents undertaking migration, while "foreign worker" emphasizes their excluded status as not local. In the chapter we use "migrant worker" wherever possible, unless citing from sources which use the term "foreign worker".
6. Between January and March 2008, a total of sixteen locals and six male migrant workers were interviewed — they were all approached in the research site except for three local personal contacts residing in the area. Participant observation was also conducted and recorded in a field journal for further analysis.
7. All the names of interviewees have been replaced with pseudonyms to ensure anonymity.
8. Hokkien (a Chinese dialect) term which means "trying to be funny" (in a negative sense).
9. Hokkien term which means "lecherous".

References

Amin, A. "Ethnicity and the Multicultural City: Living with Diversity". *Environment & Planning A* 34, no. 6 (2002): 959–80.

Beck, U. "Cosmopolitical Realism: On the Distinction between Cosmopolitanism in Philosophy and the Social Sciences". *Global Networks* 4, no. 2 (2004): 131–56.

Benjamin, G. "The Unseen Presence: A Theory of the Nation-State and its

Mystifications". Working Paper No. 91. National University of Singapore, Department of Sociology, 1988.

Binnie, J. and B. Skeggs. "Cosmopolitan Knowledge and the Production and Consumption of Sexualized Space: Manchester's Gay Village". *Sociological Review* 52, no. 1 (2004): 39–61.

———, J.J. Holloway, S. Millington, and C. Young. *Cosmopolitan Urbanism*. London: Routledge, 2006.

Brenner, N. and R. Keil. *The Global Cities Reader*. New York: Routledge, 2005.

Brownlow, A. "A Geography of Men's Fear". *Geoforum* 36, no. 5 (2005): 581–92.

Chan, H.C. "Political Developments, 1965–1979". In *A History of Singapore*, edited by E.C.T. Chew and E. Lee, pp. 157–81. Singapore: Oxford University Press, 1991.

——— and H.D. Evers. "National Identity and Nation Building in Singapore". In *Studies in ASEAN Sociology: Urban Society and Social Change*, edited by P.S.J. Chen and H.D. Evers, pp. 117–29. Singapore: Chopmen Enterprises, 1978.

Chan, W.F. "Planning Birmingham as a Cosmopolitan City: Recovering the Depths of its Diversity?". In *Cosmopolitan Urbanism*, edited by J. Binnie, J.J. Holloway, S. Millington, and C. Young, pp. 204–19. London: Routledge, 2006.

Chang, T.C. "Singapore's Little India: A Tourist Attraction as a Contested Landscape". *Urban Studies* 37, no. 2 (2000): 343–66.

Cheah, P. "Cosmopolitanism". *Theory, Culture and Society* 23, no. 2–3 (2006): 486–96.

——— and B. Robbins. *Cosmopolitics: Thinking and Feeling beyond the Nation*. Minneapolis: University of Minnesota Press, 1998.

Chin, Y. "Foreign Workers in Singapore: Integrating or Segregating Them?" RSIS Commentaries. S. Rajaratnam School of International Studies: NTU, 2008. <http://www.idss.edu.sg/publications/Perspective/RSIS1092008.pdf>. Accessed 20 November 2008.

Chua, B.H. "Multiculturalism in Singapore: An Instrument of Social Control". *Race & Class* 44, no. 3 (2003): 58–77.

Clammer, J. *Race and State in Independent Singapore 1965–1990*. Aldershot: Ashgate, 1998.

Cresswell, T. *In Place/Out of Place: Geography, Ideology and Transgression*. Minneapolis: University of Minneapolis Press, 1996.

Day, K. "Constructing Masculinity and Women's Fear in Public Space in Irvine, California". *Gender, Place and Culture* 8, no. 2 (2001): 109–28.

———, C. Stump, and D. Carreon. "Confrontation and Loss of Control: Masculinity and Men's Fears in Public Space". *Journal of Environmental Psychology* 23, no. 3 (2003): 311–22.

Delanty, G. "The Cosmopolitan Imagination: Critical Cosmopolitanism and Social Theory". *The British Journal of Sociology* 57, no. 1 (2006): 25–47.

Department of Statistics. "Singapore in Figures, 2008". Singapore Government,

2008. <http://www.singstat.gov.sg/pubn/reference/sif2008.pdf>. Accessed 20 November 2008.

———. "Singapore Population: Census 2000". Singapore Government, 2000. <http://www.singstat.gov.sg/keystats/c2000/handbook.pdf>. Accessed 20 November 2008.

Dharwadker, V. *Cosmopolitan Geographies: New Locations in Literature and Culture*. London: Routledge, 2000.

Economic Strategies Committee. "Sub-Committee Report: Making Singapore a Leading Global City". 2010. Available from: <http://app.mof.gov.sg/esc.aspx>. Accessed 28 December 2010.

Ehrkamp, P. "Risking Publicity: Masculinities and the Racialization of Public Neighbourhood Space". *Social & Cultural Geography* 9, no. 2 (2008): 117–33.

Evans, G. "Hard-branding the Cultural City: From Prado to Prada". *International Journal of Urban and Regional Research* 27, no. 2 (2003): 417–40.

Featherstone, M. "Cosmopolis: An Introduction". *Theory, Culture & Society* 19, no. 1–2 (2002): 1–16.

George, C. *Singapore: The Air-Conditioned Nation*. Singapore: Landmark Books, 2000.

Germain, A. and M. Radice. "Cosmopolitanism by default: Public sociability in Montréal". In *Cosmopolitan Urbanism*, edited by J. Binnie, J.J. Holloway, S. Millington, and C. Young, pp. 112–29. London: Routledge, 2006.

Goh, C.T. "Address by Goh Chok Tong, Prime Minister, at the Dinner of the World Conference on Model Cities, The Collyer Room, Westin Stamford". 19 April 1999, National Archives of Singapore. <http://stars.nhb.gov.sg/stars/public/>. Accessed 20 September 2008.

———. "Building a Multi-Racial Nation through Integration". Speech delivered at the Second Convention of Singapore Malay/Muslim Professionals, 5 November 2000. In *Speeches: A Bimonthly Selection of Ministerial Speeches [November–December]*, pp. 13–21. Singapore: Ministry of Information and the Arts, 2000.

———. "Address by Goh Chok Tong, Prime Minister, at National Day Rally 2001, NUS University Cultural Centre". 19 August 2001. National Archives of Singapore. <http://stars.nhb.gov.sg/stars/public/>. Accessed 20 September 2008.

———. "Address by Goh Chok Tong, Prime Minister, at National Day Rally 2002, NUS University Cultural Centre". 18 August 2002. National Archives of Singapore. <http://stars.nhb.gov.sg/stars/public/>. Accessed 20 September 2008.

Goh, D.P.S. "From Colonial Pluralism to Postcolonial Multiculturalism: Race, State Formation and the Question of Cultural Diversity in Malaysia and Singapore". *Sociology Compass* 2, no. 1 (2008): 232–52.

Hannerz, U. *Transnational Connections: Culture, People, Places*. London: Routledge, 1996.
Ho, E.L.H. "Negotiating Belonging and Perceptions of Citizenship: Singapore, a Cosmopolis?". *Social and Cultural Geography* 7, no. 3 (2006): 385–401.
Huang, S. and. B.S.A Yeoh. "Transnational Families and their Children's Education: China's 'Study Mothers' in Singapore". *Global Networks* 5, no. 4 (2005): 379–400.
Jacobs, J.M. and R. Fincher. "Introduction". In *Cities of Difference*, edited by R. Fincher and J.M. Jacobs, pp. 1–25. New York: The Guilford Press, 1998.
Lai, A.E. *Meanings of Multi-Ethnicity: A Case Study of Ethnicity and Ethnic Relations in Singapore*. New York: Oxford University Press, 1995.
Lamont, M. and S. Aksartova. "Ordinary Cosmopolitanisms: Strategies for Bridging Racial Boundaries among Working-Class Men". *Theory, Culture and Society* 19, no. 4 (2002): 1–25.
Laurenson, P. and. D. Collins. "Towards Inclusion: Local Government, Public Space and Homelessness in New Zealand". *New Zealand Geographer* 62, no. 3 (2006): 185–95.
Lee, H.L. "Speech by Lee Hsien Loong, Prime Minister, at National Day Rally 2005, NUS University Cultural Centre". 21 August 2005. Prime Minister's Office. <http://www.pmo.gov.sg/content/pmosite/mediacentre/speechesninterviews.html>. Accessed 20 September 2008.
―――. "Speech by Lee Hsien Loong, Prime Minister, at National Day Rally 2006, NUS University Cultural Centre". 22 August 2006. Prime Minister's Office. <http://www.pmo.gov.sg/content/pmosite/mediacentre/speechesninterviews.html>. Accessed 20 September 2008.
―――. "Speech by Lee Hsien Loong, Prime Minister, at National Day Rally 2010, NUS University Cultural Centre". 29 August 2010. Prime Minister's Office. <http://www.pmo.gov.sg/content/pmosite/mediacentre/speechesninterviews.html>. Accessed 20 September 2011.
Mau, S., J. Mewes, and A. Zimmermann. "Cosmopolitan Attitudes Through Transnational Social Practices". *Global Networks* 8, no. 1 (2008): 1–24.
Nijman, J. "Locals, Exiles and Cosmopolitans: A Theoretical Argument about Identity and Place in Miami". *Tijdschrift voor Economische en Sociale Geografie* 98, no. 2 (2007): 176–87.
Ooi, G.L., E.S. Tan, and K.C. Soh. "The Study of Ethnicity, National Identity and Sense of Rootedness in Singapore". Institute of Policy Studies, 2002. <http://www.spp.nus.edu.sg/ips/paparts.aspx>. Accessed 28 July 2009.
Ossewaarde, M. "Cosmopolitanism and the Society of Strangers". *Current Sociology* 55, no. 3 (2007): 367–88.
Pain, R. "Gender, Race, Age and Fear in the City". *Urban Studies* 38, no. 5–6 (2001): 899–913.

Pang, K. *(Post-)Modern Reimaginations of the Nation and "Multiracialism" in Global Singapore*. Final Year Dissertation, School of Geography, University of Oxford, 2003.

Parekh, B. "Cosmopolitanism and Global Citizenship". *Review of International Studies* 29, no. 1 (2003): 3–17.

Pellerin, H. "Global Restructuring and International Migration: Consequences for the Globalization of Politics". In *Globalization: Theory and Practice*, edited by E. Kofman and G. Youngs, pp. 81–98. New York: Pinter, 1996.

Rée, J. "Cosmopolitanism and the Experience of Nationality". In *Cosmopolitics: Thinking and Feeling Beyond the Nation*, edited by P. Cheah and B. Robbins, pp. 77–90. Minneapolis: University of Minnesota Press, 1998.

Sandercock, L. *Cosmopolis II: Mongrel Cities of the 21st Century*. London: Continuum Books, 2003.

———. "Cosmopolitan Urbanism: A Love Song to our Mongrel Cities". In *Cosmopolitan Urbanism*, edited by J. Binnie, J.J. Holloway, S. Millington, and C. Young, pp. 37–52. London: Routledge, 2006.

Sassen, S. "Globalization or Denationalization?" *Review of International Political Economy* 10, no. 2 (2003): 1–22.

Sennett, R. "Cosmopolitanism and the Social Experience of Cities". In *Conceiving Cosmopolitanism: Theory, Context and Practice*, edited by S. Vertovec and R. Cohen, pp. 42–47. New York: Oxford University Press, 2002.

Short, J.R. *Urban Theory: A Critical Assessment*. New York: Palgrave Macmillan, 2006.

Sibley, D. *Geographies of Exclusion*. London: Routledge, 1995.

Siddique, S. and N. Purushotam. *Singapore's Little India: Past, Present and Future*. Singapore: Institute of Policy Studies, 1990.

Singapore 2010 "Singapore 2010: First Youth Olympic Games". Singapore National Olympic Council, 2008. <http://www.singapore2010.sg/day/index.htm>. Accessed 30 December 2008.

Stevenson, N. "Cosmopolitanism, Multiculturalism and Citizenship". *Sociological Research Online* 7, no. 1 (2002). <http://www.socresonline.org.uk/7/1/stevenson.html>. Accessed 15 Feb 2008.

Strait Times, various issues, Singapore: Singapore Press Holdings.

Sunday Times, various issues, Singapore: Singapore Press Holdings.

Tan, S. and B.S.A. Yeoh. "Negotiating Cosmopolitanism in Singapore's Fictional Landscape". In *Cosmopolitan Urbanism*, edited by J. Binnie, J.J. Holloway, S. Millington, and C. Young, pp. 146–68. London: Routledge, 2006.

Today, various issues, Singapore: Singapore Press Holdings.

Turner, B.S. "Cosmopolitan Virtue, Globalization and Patriotism". *Theory, Culture & Society* 19, no. 1–2 (2002): 45–63.

Vertovec, S. *Migration and New Diversities in Global Cities: Comparatively Conceiving,*

Observing and Visualizing Diversification in Urban Public Spaces, MMG Working Paper 11-08, Max Planck Institute for the Study of Religious and Ethnic Diversity, Göttingen, 2011.

Watson, S. *City Publics: The (Dis)Enchantments of Urban Encounters*. London: Routledge, 2006.

Yeoh, B.S.A. "Postcolonial Cities". *Progress in Human Geography* 25, no. 3 (2001): 456–68.

———. "Cosmopolitanism and its Exclusions in Singapore". *Urban Studies* 41, no. 12 (2004): 2431–45.

———. "The Global Cultural City: Spatial Imagineering and Politics in the (Multi)Cultural Marketplaces of South-east Asia". *Urban Studies* 42, no. 4–5 (2005): 945–58.

———. "Bifurcated Labour: The Unequal Incorporation of Transmigrants in Singapore". *Tijschrift Voor Economische En Sociale Geografie* 97, no. 1 (2006): 26–37.

——— and T.C. Chang. "Globalizing Singapore: Debating Transnational Flows in the City". *Urban Studies* 38, no. 7 (2001): 1025–44.

——— and S. Huang. "Foreign Talent" in our Midst: New Challenges to "Sense of Community" and Ethnic Relations in Singapore. In *Beyond Rituals and Riots: Ethnic Pluralism and Social Cohesion in Singapore*, edited by A.E. Lai, pp. 316–38. Singapore: Eastern Universities Press for Institute of Policy Studies, 2003.

——— and N. Yap. "'Gateway Singapore': Immigration Policies, Differential (Non)Incorporation and Identity Politics". In *Migrants to the Metropolis: The Rise of Immigrant Gateway Cities*, edited by M. Price and L. Benton-Short, pp. 177–202. Washington: Syracuse University Press, 2008.

——— and S. Huang "Sexualised Politics of Proximities among Female Transnational Migrants in Singapore". *Population, Space and Place* 16, no. 1 (2010): 37–49.

Young, I. *Justice and the Politics of Difference*. Princeton: Princeton University Press, 1990.

Young, C., M. Diep, and S. Drabble. "Living with Difference? The 'Cosmopolitan City' and Urban Reimaging in Manchester, UK". *Urban Studies* 43, no. 10 (2006): 1687–714.

4

SELECTIVE STATE RESPONSE AND ETHNIC MINORITY INCORPORATION
The South Korean Case

Nora Hui-Jung KIM

How do states manage ethnocultural diversity? States have always been eager to control their borders. However, only recently has the importance of states in facilitating or constraining immigrant incorporation drawn academic attention (see Bloemraad 2006; Castles 1995; Freeman 2004; Hagan 2006; James 2005; Jayasuriya 1996; Joppke 1998, 2001; Papademetriou, 2003; Penninx 2003). A state's immigrant incorporation policies — such as naturalization rules, the provision of administrative services in an immigrant's native language, and the official endorsement of multiculturalism — can significantly facilitate immigrant settlement processes (Bloemraad 2006; Freeman 2004). Indeed, as Favell aptly noticed, the task of incorporating immigrants is increasingly conceived as "all things a *state* can 'do'" (Favell 2005, p. 43). Favell's observation raises important research questions: Why do states decide to become involved in the business of incorporating ethnic minorities and immigrants? What are some consequences of such state intervention?

Comparing the concepts of incorporation, integration, and assimilation highlights the significance of state intervention in immigrant incorporation.

Incorporation and integration are similar concepts, which include the measures and policies that assist immigrants in settling in the host countries. The notion of assimilation, in contrast, indicates a particular mode of incorporation. Assimilation is characterized by the fact that immigrants are expected to adopt the cultural traits and values of the host countries. The well-being of immigrants is influenced by the state's decision about whether to intervene in the incorporation of immigrants, and also by whether the state requests that immigrants assimilate. In the following section, I discuss and compare different modes of incorporation and their impact on immigrant incorporation in more detail.

The questions raised above are important in various Asian contexts. There is an increasing volume of immigration to several Asian countries. The well-being of these immigrants depends largely on specific immigrant incorporation policies. South Korea is one of the states facing the challenge of incorporating ethnic minorities. Korea has often been considered one of the most ethnically homogeneous countries in the world. In recent years, however, the ethnic composition of Korea's population has become more diverse than ever before — or more accurately, its ethnic diversity has finally been officially recognized. According to immigration statistics, the number of foreigners living in Korea doubled in the past five years, to about 2 per cent of the total population. This proportion is expected to triple in the next five years (Ministry of Justice 2006). The major sources of ethnic diversity include guestworkers and women migrants arriving via marriage arrangements (hereafter referred to as marriage migrants). Since the late 1980s, guestworkers from South and Southeast Asia have immigrated to Korea; by 2008, foreign workers comprised more than 10 per cent of the total labour force and 50 per cent of the entire foreign population in Korea. Although admitted as temporary contract workers, scholars suspect that more than half of such temporary guestworkers in Korea stay beyond their contract period and settle permanently. In addition to guestworkers, the number of marriage migrants is rapidly increasing (Lee 2008; Seol 2006). The number of marriages between a foreign woman and a Korean man as a percentage of total marriages increased from 0.2 per cent in the 1990s to 9.9 per cent in 2005. About 10 per cent of the total foreign population in Korea is composed of marriage migrants (Ministry of Justice 2006). Despite the Korean government's efforts or intentions, given the growing numbers of long-term guestworkers and marriage migrants, the increasing ethnocultural diversity of Korea seems inevitable.

Reflecting this trend, the Korean Government has been implementing various immigrant incorporation policies. Former South Korean President Noh, for example, declared that "the trend toward [a] multi-racial/multicultural society is irresistible" and therefore "it's high time to take measures to incorporate migrants and adopt multicultural policies" (Park and Park 2006). In terms of tangible policy changes, the South Korean Government passed two pieces of legislation regarding migrant incorporation on 26 April 2006: The Act on the Social Integration of Mixed-Race Koreans and Immigrants, and The Act on Marriage Migrant Integration; these two pieces of legislation provide the blueprint for immigrant incorporation policies. In addition, The Multicultural Family Support Act was introduced in 2007 (Lee 2008).

The South Korean state's recent involvement in immigrant incorporation raises some interesting questions. For instance, why did the Korean state introduce immigrant incorporation policies in the first place? Although increasing, a foreign population of 2 per cent is not particularly high compared to other immigrant-receiving countries. Historically, most Western European countries established immigrant incorporation policies when their ethnic minority population reached about 10 per cent of the entire population. Further, why does the Korean state equate the inflow of immigrants with Korea's transition to a "multicultural" society and frame immigrant incorporation policies as multiculturalism? Indeed, South Korea would seem to be one of the least likely Asian countries for the emergence of multicultural discourses. Singapore and Malaysia, for example, are both multiethnic states that officially embrace multiculturalism at the state level. Multiculturalism is not a foreign concept in Japan either, where there are significant numbers of ethnic minorities including the Ainu, Okinawans, and ethnic Koreans. Moreover, the Japanese state promoted a type of multicultural discourse during World War II (Lie 2001), in which the notion of the Greater East Asia Co-Prosperity Sphere envisioned Japan's incorporation of ethnic Koreans and Chinese as part of the Greater Japanese nation-state, although their status was inferior to the status of ethnic Japanese citizens.

In this chapter, I argue that South Korean immigrant incorporation policies are in large part the product of the Korean state's selective response to international and domestic pressures. This selective response results in the inclusion of certain groups of ethnic minorities and the exclusion of others. I demonstrate this point by comparing Korean state policies vis-à-vis four different groups: potential immigrants, guestworkers, ethnic Chinese settlers, and marriage migrants. Some guestworkers and marriage migrants are ethnic Koreans; although these guestworkers receive some preferential treatment (see Kim 2008), in general their ethnicity does not play a large role in the incorporation policies of the Korean state. Thus, I discuss guestworkers and marriage migrants without focusing on their ethnic backgrounds.

THE STATE AND IMMIGRANT INCORPORATION POLICIES

As the role of the state in immigrant incorporation has increased (Favell 2005; Hollifield 2000), the question of how "to bring the state in" has relied on two approaches. The first approach views the state as *constrained* by social and international actors. From this perspective, incorporation policies represent only the increasing rights of migrants (see Jacobson 1996; Kymlicka 1995, 2005; Soysal 1994). From the second perspective, the state uses incorporation policies as a governing strategy, that is, as a means to control the population and achieve its functional imperatives (see Bommes and Geddes 2000; Boswell 2007; Morris 2002, 2003).

Despite the centrality of these approaches, multiple factors (e.g., the interests of both social actors and the state) are necessary to explain the incorporation policies of a single state. First, immigrant incorporation policies, like other state policies, change over time and vary by target group. Indeed, no state exhibits a coherent immigration incorporation regime at a given time (Freeman 2004; Joppke and Morawska 2003). Rather, a state's immigrant policies are a "handful of loosely connected syndromes" (Freeman 2004, p. 945). Therefore, no single factor alone (either pressure from non-state actors or the state's own interests) can explain these varying, multifaceted immigrant incorporation policies.

The notion of selective response can be helpful in taking multiple factors into account. The state is pressured by domestic and international actors, but only selectively responds to such pressures based on its own interests and priorities. However, the interests and priorities of the state should not be treated as exogenous; the state's interest is itself culturally embedded and constructed (Brubaker 1992; Steinmetz 1999). Indeed, the particular cultural view of a nation-state can influence (and even constitute) the state's preference in terms of which immigrants to admit and how to incorporate them (Brubaker 1992).

The state's selective response will likely result in stratified and selective immigrant incorporation policies. More specifically, differential inclusion can be examined along four dimensions: (1) characteristics of immigrants, (2) spheres of incorporation, (3) modes of incorporation, and (4) rhetoric of incorporation.

Characteristics of Immigrants

The degree to which the state is involved in immigrant incorporation varies by the characteristics of immigrants, such as their legal status, skill level, and gender (Freeman 2004). For example, immigrants with permanent visas are distinctively privileged compared to those with temporary visas and undocumented immigrants (Freeman 2004). In most countries, political refugees receive more governmental assistance than other immigrants do. Another important factor is immigrants' educational characteristics or resources. Incorporating immigrants with particular skills and other needed resources fits the receiving state's interests. In contemporary Europe, Morris (2002) found a threefold stratification of rights status — national citizenship, citizenship in a European Union (EU) country, and citizenship in a Third World country.

However, focusing solely on immigrant characteristics fails to capture how the state defines and constructs these characteristics. The state does not randomly assign immigrants' visa statuses but, rather, exercises its symbolic power by labelling different types of immigrants (Bommes 2000). The state holds the symbolic and administrative capacity to differentiate between refugees, asylum seekers, illegal/legal migrants, guestworkers, and foreign talent. This differentiation is not simply a description of different groups of immigrants, but leads to and justifies differential incorporation measures for different groups (Morris 2002).

Spheres of Incorporation

Early studies of immigrant incorporation attempted to specify national immigration regimes. For example, Brubaker's seminal work in the area found that the different modes of immigrant incorporation in Germany and France (exclusion versus assimilation, respectively) led to different idioms of nationhood (ethnic versus civic) (Brubaker 1992). Identifying incorporation regimes led to the categorization of nation-states. For example, Soysal (1994) identified four membership models, using two variables: whether the state or society initiates immigrant incorporation, and whether the organizational configuration is centralized or decentralized.

However, the notion of an incorporation regime has been rightly criticized for its failure to capture the heterogeneity in immigrant policies within a single nation-state (see Favell 2005; Joppke and Morawska 2003), and because it presents a misleading picture of society itself. The concept equates the society with the nation-state (Chernilo 2006), and assumes the presence of a well-integrated national society (Freeman 2004; Joppke and Morawska 2003). Within the framework, immigrants are incorporated into this unquestioned "society". Contrary to the image of a well-integrated society, however, the ontological status of a modern nation-state can be better captured in terms of semi-autonomous fields or spheres, such as the economy, law, politics, education, health, and welfare (Luhmann 1982). Each individual in a nation-state is included in some spheres and excluded from others. From this perspective, a "non-integrated immigrant is a structural impossibility" (Joppke and Morawska 2003, p. 3). Every immigrant, as well as every citizen, is simultaneously included in certain spheres and excluded from others. Therefore, the unitary principle of inclusion/exclusion, on which the notion of incorporation regime relies, is invalid. The question of what kinds of immigrants are incorporated into which spheres is analytically more significant than whether or not immigrants are incorporated.

Modes of Incorporation

The simultaneous inclusion and exclusion of immigrants does not entirely nullify the analytical value of distinctive modes of incorporation. Rather, the modes of incorporation may differ by the spheres into which immigrants are incorporated, and by the characteristics of immigrants. In addition, multiple modes of incorporation may coexist within a nation-state.

Scholars have identified five major ideal types of incorporation regimes based on the experiences of Western states: total exclusion, differential exclusion, assimilation, pluralism, and multiculturalism (Castles 1995). Total exclusion, not admitting migrants at all, is not a viable option for most industrialized countries. Under differential exclusion, migrants are admitted solely as labourers and on a temporary basis. Guestworker systems are a typical example of differential exclusion, and are often adopted by states with a strong national ethnic character, such as Japan and Germany (Castles 1995). Assimilation, pluralism, and multiculturalism differ with respect to the extent to which immigrants are allowed to maintain and celebrate their own cultural traditions. In general, assimilation requires immigrants to abandon their own cultural traditions, pluralism allows immigrants to celebrate their own cultural traditions in private spheres only (e.g., in their homes), and the multi-cultural mode of incorporation welcomes and encourages immigrants to maintain and celebrate their cultural traditions in both private and public spheres. However, it is not always easy to distinguish between these modes of incorporation in practice. Some scholars consider multiculturalism a form of pluralism (see Oommen 2002), while others highlight the differences between the two (see Alexander 2006).

The Rhetoric of Incorporation

The rhetoric of incorporation is another important dimension of segmented incorporation. The ambiguity in the boundaries between the modes of incorporation mentioned above (i.e., assimilation, pluralism, and multiculturalism) is as much a result of representation and labelling as a matter of actual differences between the policies. The modes of incorporation are not necessarily identical to the rhetoric used to describe the modes. Representation is particularly important because incorporation modes always involve the normative assumptions of an ideal society. Thus, the labelling of an incorporation model is a matter of symbolic struggle. Analysing the rhetoric of incorporation can shed light on this symbolic political struggle between the state, domestic actors, and international actors.

To summarize, I examine the ways a state responds to different pressures and selectively incorporates immigrants. The individual effects of domestic, international, and cultural factors can vary within and among multiple dimensions of immigrant incorporation. One common result of a state's selective involvement in immigrant incorporation is a stratified, incoherent, loose web of modes of ethnic minority incorporation (Lockwood 1996; Menjívar 2006; Morris 2002, 2003). In the following sections, I examine the development of South Korean immigrant incorporation policies.

SOUTH KOREAN IMMIGRANT INCORPORATION POLICY DEVELOPMENT

South Korea is notorious for its strong ethnic definition of nationhood and its obsession with the purity of blood. For instance, in August 2003, an actress, the child of a Korean mother and a white father, was forced to hold a press conference to "confess" that she was not a "pure Korean". She cried from shame during the entire press conference. This incident illustrates the power of the notion of "ethnic purity" in Korea. The idea of ethnic homogeneity has been politically mobilized and reinforced since the Korean struggle for independence from Japanese imperialism during the early twentieth century. The idea of ethnic homogeneity was again employed and was further solidified as an efficient ideology for the mobilization and legitimization of economic development throughout the era of military dictatorship until the late 1980s (Hart-Landsberg 1993; Pai 1998; Shin 1998, 2006). The separation of the country into two Koreas left the Korean nation-building project unfinished, and this incompleteness is often used to justify the exclusion of other ethnic groups from Korea.

Against this backdrop, it may be surprising that the South Korean state has implemented a series of immigrant incorporation policies in the past few years. However, the type and the degree of the Korean state's involvement vary depending on the immigrant group. I have identified four modes of incorporation — total exclusion, differential exclusion, pluralism, and assimilation — in Korean immigrant incorporation policies. Total exclusion refers to territorial closure: there are "zero-immigration" policies. Differential exclusion denotes the denial of formal membership, in other words, the denial of access to citizenship or naturalization. Pluralism refers to the incorporation of immigrants without necessarily transforming the ethnic/cultural heritage of the immigrants. Assimilation, in contrast, refers to policies whose goals are to transform immigrants into "Koreans." Korean ethnic minority policies incorporate immigrants into three spheres: political, economic, and reproductive.

Total Exclusion: Potential Immigrants

The Korean state has yet to open its doors to potential immigrants despite a labour force shortage in certain sectors and a declining fertility rate. Korean scholars consider the myth of ethnic homogeneity one of the reasons the Korean Government remains reluctant to accept immigrants (Seol 2000). In addition to the myth of ethnic homogeneity, the division between the two Koreas is often cited as an excuse to keep the door closed. "No immigration" policies have been supported on the grounds that the North Korean population could provide ample labour force members once the two Koreas are reunited.

Differential Exclusion: Guestworkers

As explained in the previous section, the Korean state tries to totally exclude immigrants, especially low-skilled immigrants. To deal with acute labour shortages, however, the Korean Government has unofficially accepted labour migrants since the early 1990s under a guestworker scheme called the Industrial Trainee System (Kim 2008). As the name suggests, guestworkers have been treated as trainees and have not enjoyed any labour rights, such as workers' compensation or the right to organize (Park 2002). The Korean state also limited guestworker stays to three years and did not allow family reunification out of fear that guestworkers might settle in Korea (Seol 2000; Seol and Skrentny 2004). These measures clearly indicate the state's unwillingness to accept guestworkers as members of the Korean nation-state. Guestworkers have been treated as merely a convenient source of labour. As such, they have been incorporated into the Korean labour market, but excluded from all other spheres. Not unexpectedly, the maintenance of ethnic homogeneity is used as a rhetorical justification for the differential exclusion of guestworkers.

Recently, the Korean state amended guestworker policies to incorporate guestworkers more fully into the economy. For example, the state introduced the Employment Permit System (EPS), which replaced the Industrial Trainee System. EPS more fully incorporates guestworkers into the economy because it acknowledges them as labourers and accordingly grants them rights that are *almost* equivalent to those given to Korean workers (Lee and Park 2005).[1] In addition, other state measures indirectly incorporate guestworkers. For example, the Ministry of Labour funds NGO-run guestworker support centres in Korea. This governmental funding averages 30 per cent of the budgets of guestworker-advocacy NGOs (Shin et al. 2006). Despite these measures, guestworkers are still incorporated via differential exclusion. The scope of incorporation does not extend beyond the economic sphere; guestworkers are excluded from the political and reproductive spheres.

Pressure from Korean civil society actors was largely responsible for the changes in guestworker policies (Kim 2008; Lee and Park 2005). Koreans' activism on behalf of immigrants began in 1995 when thirteen Nepalese guestworkers publicly protested against inhumane treatment (Lim 2003, 2006). This incident provided some Koreans with a moral imperative to advocate for guestworkers. Since that time, Korean civil society groups have actively promoted the rights of guestworkers and have pressured the Korean state to adopt more liberal foreign labour policies. In addition to domestic pressures, international human rights norms have facilitated changes in Korean guestworker policies. Indeed, the Korean National Human Rights Commission (KNHAR), in alliance with guestworker advocacy NGOs, recommended that Korea should amend its foreign labour policies to meet international human rights standards (Cardenas 2002; Milly 2000). The effects of domestic and international pressure are most obvious in the rhetoric of the policy changes. The Korean state framed the adoption of EPS as an action that would "enhance the image of South Korea as a human rights-abiding country" (Korea Immigration Service 2006, p. 57).

However, the Korean state responded only *selectively* to domestic and international pressures. First, the Korean state differentiates between resource-rich foreign labourers and low-skilled labourers and more actively seeks to incorporate the former group. The state pursues "differentiated preferential treatment policies" regarding foreign labourers who might enhance "Korea's national competitiveness" (Ministry of Justice 2006, p. 57). Second, the Korean state considers some domestic actors legitimate but others invalid. Currently, political activism on behalf of guestworkers comes largely from three organizational actors: the Joint Committee of Foreign Migrant Workers in Korea (JCMK), the Network for Migrants' Rights (NMR), and the Migrants Trade Union (MTU). Korean activists run the first two NGOs, which maintain a close relationship with the Korean government. In contrast, the MTU is a guestworker trade union. The Korean state responds to "pressures" from JCMK and NMR, but does not even consider MTU a legitimate political partner. Indeed, the Ministry of Labour does not acknowledge MTU as a legal trade union because most of its members are illegal guestworkers.

From Differential Exclusion to Pluralism: Ethnic Chinese Settlers (Huaqiao)

Korea is well known for its exceptional ethnic homogeneity. Still, there are about 20,000 ethnically Chinese Korean residents (among a total population of 48 million South Koreans) permanently residing in Korea. While guestworkers were excluded from all aspects of the Korean nation-state except the economic sphere from the time they arrived in Korea, there were no state efforts to exclude ethnic Chinese settlers until after the 1949 communist revolution in China, after which the Korean state began to exclude ethnic Chinese. Scholars agree that the first group of Chinese who stayed in Korea for an extended period of time arrived during the 1882 Soldiers' Revolt under the Qing Empire (Cheong 2002). The ethnic Chinese population settled in Korea gradually, mainly due to the geographic proximity of mainland China and Korea. Starting in 1949, however, the Korean Government systematically excluded ethnic Chinese from the spheres of education, economy, and politics. The 1961 Alien's Land Act, for example, mandated that foreigners required permission to own land, so many ethnic Chinese were forced to sell their land. Although the restriction was relaxed in 1968, it continued to severely limit how much land a foreigner could possess until recently (Lee 2003, p. 121). In the political sphere, the ethnic Chinese had no rights to participate in politics or civil service.[2]

Recent policy changes now incorporate the ethnic Chinese population into spheres from which they were previously excluded. For instance, the 2002 Foreign Residents' Local Election Rights Act (FLEA) granted qualified foreign permanent residents (mostly ethnic Chinese) the right to vote in local elections, and thus signalled the incorporation of the ethnic Chinese population into the political sphere. Further, the 2002 Permanent Residence Act (PRA) finally acknowledged the ethnic Chinese as Korean residents, rather than visitors. This act incorporates the ethnic Chinese into the political sphere by according them the residential stability needed to vote under FLEA. Finally, PRA incorporates the ethnic Chinese into the economic sphere; permanent residents can "own, use and sell real estate" and participate in "unrestricted financial transactions" just as ethnic Koreans can. With these recent policy changes, ethnic Chinese residents have become fully incorporated into the economic sphere and partially incorporated into the political sphere.

As it was for guestworkers, the rhetoric of human rights has been employed to justify the incorporation measures applied to ethnic Chinese residents. Jung Dae Chol, the assemblyman who proposed the PRA, explained the rationale of the legislation:

> In the age of globalisation, this kind of treatment [not granting residential security] means we fall behind the times. Moreover, it flies in the face of an international standard that considers individuals the carriers of the rights

granted by international laws.... [Thus] by providing residence rights to long-term foreigners, this legislation will be a manifestation of our intent to promote human rights during the age of globalisation.[3]

As indicated above, the rhetoric of modifying ethnic Chinese incorporation policies resembles the rhetoric used to modify guestworker policies: enhancing Korea's reputation as a human-rights-promoting country in the international community. While guestworker-advocacy NGOs played an important role in facilitating guestworker policy changes, ethnic Chinese policy changes occurred in the absence of significant domestic pressure. For example, lobbying by the Chinese Residents Association (CRA) to relax the economic constraints imposed on foreigners has not been successful. Moreover, the CRA's agenda did not even include increased political participation. Thus, most ethnic Chinese were surprised at the passage of FLEA.

Based on the rhetoric of incorporation surrounding FLEA and PRA, and the absence of significant domestic pressure on this issue, it may seem that international pressures were the most important factor leading to changes in ethnic Chinese incorporation policies. However, the timing of these measures tells a different story. When former South Korean President and Nobel Peace Prize laureate Kim Dae Jung tried to persuade Japan to accord voting rights to Koreans permanently residing in Japan, the Japanese government used Korea's treatment of ethnic Chinese residents as an excuse not to change its policies. Thus, the Korean Government's decision to grant voting rights to its resident foreigners might be a strategic move meant to encourage similar policy changes in Japan (Lee 2003). Indeed, the National Election Commission claimed this motivation for FLEA: "[I]t is self-contradictory if we do not grant voting rights to foreigners when we have asked the Japanese government to accord voting rights to Koreans in Japan" (The National Election Commission Press Release).[4]

The Korean state's involvement in the incorporation of ethnic Chinese residents illustrates how the cultural understanding of the Korean nation affects the interests of the state. The ethnic notion of nationhood transcends the territorial boundaries of the Korean peninsula. As such, the well-being of Koreans in Japan became the business of the Korean state, requiring the state to make changes in its own treatment of residents of non-Korean descent. However, despite the expanded incorporation of ethnic Chinese residents, they may not have been included in the political sphere had such inclusion posed a serious political risk to the state. Only about 20,000 ethnic Chinese live in Korea (fewer yet are adults who can vote). In a population of nearly 50 million, their impact on elections is negligible.

Unlike guestworkers, who have been incorporated via differential inclusion, ethnic Chinese residents have access, though it is strongly restricted, to permanent residency or Korean citizenship. In the reproductive sphere, the Korean state has a *laissez-faire* attitude toward ethnic Chinese participation, which is demonstrated in the state's policies toward ethnic Chinese education. Most ethnic Chinese residents in Korea attend Chinese-only schools (funded by ethnic Chinese residents and the Taiwanese government) through high school. Ethnic Chinese schools face a dire situation due to decreasing financial support from the Taiwanese government. However, the Korean state refuses to address the issue. In this sense, pluralism is the mode of incorporation of ethnic Chinese residents in Korea. Pluralism does not mean a celebration or even accommodation of cultural differences. Rather, in the Korean context, it simply means that ethnic Chinese residents are free to practise and preserve their own culture as long as they do so via their own separate institutions.

From Non-intervention to Assimilation: Mixed-Race Koreans and Marriage Migrants

Marriage migrants and mixed-race Koreans are the two groups whose incorporation modes have changed most noticeably. International marriage is not an entirely new phenomenon in Korea. In the past, the Korean state did not intervene in the settlement of foreign spouses in Korea; incorporation was entirely up to individuals and their family members. However, this attitude of non-involvement has changed in recent years. In 2005, the Korean Immigration Bureau added the category of "marriage migrants" to its annual immigration report, which provided the Korean state with information critical for the implementation of policies specifically for marriage migrants. An analysis of news articles on migrant programs reveals that incorporation policies vis-à-vis marriage migrants primarily involve the reproductive sphere and follow the assimilation mode of incorporation.[5] The programmes provided to marriage migrants are spread across several categories: Korean language training (17 per cent), classes related to mothering and parenting (9 per cent), Korean culture and tradition classes (13 per cent), programmes on relationships (9 per cent), mentoring services (5 per cent), support for wedding ceremonies or visits to home countries (21 per cent), financial support or fund raising (9 per cent), and general training (16 per cent). Next, I provide some examples of programmes outlined in the articles. The following quotations describe the incorporation programmes and highlight the assimilative nature of the programmes aimed at marriage migrants, in which marriage migrants are expected to learn Korean culture and perform traditional roles of Korean wives, mothers and daughter-in-laws.

> The Gumcheon District [in Gyeonggido] has taken the role of a mother [to marriage migrants] by educating marriage migrants about making snacks and clothes for newborn infants, the timing for getting vaccinations, and nutritional facts. All of these are included in the special 12-week nursing classes. The District also has a plan to offer counselling about pediatrics in conjunction with the Center for Public Health (Yoo 2008).

> The Korean Women's Association's North Jeonra branch held an event entitled "Putting Multicultural Families on the Right Track" to help them better understand Korean culture and their expected roles in the community. The events covered traditional Korean etiquette and tea ceremonies. In addition, there were events such as rice-cake making that provided marriage migrants the opportunity to become familiar with Korean culture (Kim 2008).

The incorporation efforts also include mixed-race Koreans. For example, the Ministry of Education and Human Development (MOE&HD) announced its plans to include a section entitled "Overcoming Prejudice against Different Cultures" in civic education textbooks. New textbooks will acknowledge the multicultural tradition in Korean history, promote tolerance, and de-emphasize the purity of blood. Incorporation measures aimed at mixed-race Koreans are geared toward education, to prevent this group from forming an underclass when they enter the job market.

Until recently, being a mixed-race Korean was something to be ashamed of, as illustrated by the news conference mentioned above. Most mixed-race births in Korea involve a Korean woman and a U.S. soldier. The offspring of these couples are often referred to as "Amerasians", a term coined by Nobel Prize laureate Pearl S. Buck. The Korean Government has implemented only few indirect measures regarding mixed-race Koreans; for example, the Government contributes financially to the Pearl S. Buck Foundation, which provides mentoring and immigration services to Amerasian families. Amerasians have faced systematic discrimination, and most were forced to leave Korea. Because so many Amerasians emigrated to the United States, they do not directly benefit from recent incorporation measures. Rather, the primary beneficiaries of the recent measures are a different type of mixed-race Korean, "kosians". Kosian is a compound word (a combination of Korean and Asian) that is used to refer to the children of marriage migrants and Korean men. According to April 2006 MOE&HD statistics, about 13,400 kosians attended school in Korea (primary school through high school), a 68 per cent increase from the previous year.

The Korean state's involvement in the incorporation of marriage migrants and kosians was partially in response to domestic pressures. The Korean media and intellectuals criticized the state's lack of attention to mixed-race Koreans. Moreover, guestworker-advocacy NGOs have sought the Korean state's involvement, lest marriage migrants become victims of human trafficking or domestic violence. However, a closer examination of marriage migrant incorporation programmes clearly demonstrates that the state has responded only selectively to domestic pressures. While the NGOs' main requests were state intervention to prevent smuggling and domestic violence, most of the measures implemented focus on incorporating marriage migrants and kosians into the reproductive sphere.

Two important factors explain why the Korean state focuses on incorporating marriage migrants and mixed-race Koreans into the reproductive sphere. First, the Korean state realizes that marriage migrants and mixed-race Koreans can ease the burden of a shrinking population. Like most industrialized states, Korea faces the two-fold problem of declining birth rates and an ageing population. Korea's total fertility rate is 1.29,[6] the second lowest among OECD member states (only Hong Kong is lower). Marriage migrants can contribute to population growth in two ways. First, these women can become Koreans. To encourage marriage migrants to naturalize, the Korean state amended the Nationality Law in 2003 to ease citizenship acquisition requirements for marriage migrants.[7] Yet from the state's perspective, a far more important way that marriage migrants can improve population statistics is by bearing children — kosians. It is not surprising, then, that incorporation policies provide preferential treatment to marriage migrants with children. For instance, even before they acquire Korean citizenship, marriage migrants with children are eligible for social welfare services that are in principle limited to Korean nationals. In this sense, pressures from domestic actors resonate with the state's interest in ensuring population growth. This does not mean that the Korean state promotes imported brides as a solution for population decline. Rather, my argument addresses the timing of incorporation policies: barring a population problem, the Korean state might never have become involved in marriage migrant incorporation.[8] Similarly, incorporation policies might not have included marriage migrants if they did not provide solutions for the population problem.

The second reason incorporation policies for marriage migrants and mixed-race Koreans focus on the reproductive sphere is because these policies are based on a cultural understanding of gender roles. From this perspective, women serve as the biological reproducers of a nation by giving birth to and raising the future members of the nation-state (Yuval-Davis 1997, 1998). Korean marriage migrant incorporation policies certainly reflect such gender roles. In addition, these policies confirm the association between femininity and assimilability; women can presumably assimilate into a new culture more easily than their male counterparts. Further, wives tend to assimilate to their husbands' cultures. The gendered nature of incorporation policies is highlighted by the fact that very few incorporation policies address *male* marriage migrants. Although marriage between Korean women and male guestworkers is increasing, (though not as rapidly as marriages between Korean men and foreign women), the Korean state's policies are geared only towards female marriage migrants; male marriage migrant incorporation is left to the individual migrant and his family.

In terms of rhetoric, the Korean state uses "multiculturalism" to frame its marriage migrant and mixed-race Korean incorporation policies. For example, the preface of the Social Support Measures for Mixed-Race Koreans and Immigrants, which provided the blueprint for incorporation policies, reads "[These suggestions] will facilitate Korea's transition to an open, multicultural society where mixed-race Koreans and immigrants are not discriminated against, but are valued." The use of "multiculturalism" is curious, however, as the substantive mode of incorporation is much less multiculturalism and much more assimilation.

What explains this disparity between practice and discourse in Korean marriage migrant incorporation policies? The Korean state's selective response to international pressure is one reason for the disparity. Among Western states, "multiculturalism" has become the dominant mode of incorporating ethnic minorities and immigrants, and has replaced alternative modes of incorporation such as assimilation and pluralism (Kymlicka 2001). While some European states have returned to assimilation in practice (see Entzinger 2003), overt assimilation rhetoric has lost its legitimacy, as shown in the replacement of "assimilation" with "integration" or "incorporation." International organizations such as UNESCO have contributed to the institutionalization of multicultural modes of immigrant and ethnic minority incorporation. As a result, although the extent of the characterization may vary, "we are all multiculturalist now" (Glazer 2002). Multiculturalism is experiencing a quasi-monopoly status in the Western hemisphere and is now becoming predominant in Asian labour-importing nation-states as well (He and Kymlicka 2005). As a member of the international community of nation-states, Korea is expected to adhere to some international norms and standards. Indeed, the Korean state may be under greater pressure to conform to international norms because it is eager to increase its status in the international community (see Gurowitz 2006). However, the Korean state adapts only selectively, that is, at the level of discourse but not at the level of practice, to these international standards. In this sense, "the discourse of multiculturalism has penetrated more quickly than any actual practice of multiculturalism" (Kymlicka 2005, p. 54).

The Korean state incorporates immigrants differently because the Korean state considers marriage migrants settlers, but treats guestworkers and, to a lesser extent ethnic Chinese settlers, as sojourners. As mothers of Korean children and wives of Korean husbands, marriage migrants belong to *Korean families* and therefore to the *Korean nation*. This task of incorporating marriage migrants into the Korean nation cannot be accomplished without challenging the existing ethnic notion of nationhood or disrupting the purity of blood. The idea of multiculturalism — pursuing peaceful coexistence among different ethnocultural groups within a single nation-state — might become an attractive alternative to Korea's strong sense of ethnic nationhood. However, inclusion remains selective; those who have no "ethnic" ties to the Korean nation (i.e., ethnic Chinese settlers and guestworkers) are not included in the Korean nation. Notably, the rhetoric of "human rights" used to frame policies regarding ethnic Chinese settlers and guestworkers does not necessarily entail the notion of national membership; even guests can have rights. Contrary to human rights discourse, the discourse of multiculturalism is first and foremost about defining and envisioning a national community.

CONCLUSION

I have reviewed the Korean state's ethnic minority incorporation policies. The Korean state's selective responses to domestic and international pressures resulted in a set of modes of incorporation that treat groups of ethnic minorities differentially. Marriage migrants and mixed-race Koreans are incorporated into the sphere of reproduction, while ethnic Chinese residents are incorporated into the economic sphere and partially into the political sphere. Guestworkers are incorporated into only the economic sphere. Further, while the rhetoric of human rights is used to justify incorporation measures aimed at guestworkers and ethnic Chinese residents, the Korean state uses a discourse of "multiculturalism" to frame marriage migrant and mixed-race Korean incorporation policies.

The rather unexpected South Korean policy shift from non-intervention to active participation in incorporation provides a unique opportunity to probe the theoretical question of why and how liberal states become involved in the incorporation of ethnic minorities. Previous explanations tend to oscillate between state-centred and society-centred approaches that consider state intervention a result of either the state's own interest or pressure from non-state actors. In contrast, I have argued that immigrant incorporation policies can be better understood in terms of the state's selective response to domestic and international pressures. I have also argued that the state's selective response will most likely result in stratified and differentiated incorporation policies. This idiosyncracy of immigrant policies is a logical consequence of the state adopting different strategies simultaneously. I proposed four dimensions — characteristics of immigrants, sphere of incorporation, mode of incorporation, and rhetoric of incorporation — to analyse the stratified nature of immigrant incorporation policies. I believe these four dimensions provide a beneficial starting point for analysing immigrant incorporation policies in other countries.

Finally, the analysis of Korean immigrant incorporation policies reveals how culture, particularly the idioms of nationhood and gender roles, shapes the state's own interests. To maintain a desirable population size, the Korean state has drawn a new boundary by relaxing the previous ethnic purity requirement. With this relaxation, those who have familial ties to the Korean nation (marriage migrants and mixed-race Koreans) are now included in the Korean nation via their incorporation into the reproductive sphere. Other groups (guestworkers and ethnic Chinese residents) are still excluded. In this sense, Korea's incorporation policies are influenced by an ideology of ethnocentric nationhood; Korea grants preferential treatment to groups related by bloodlines. Although marriage migrants do not have direct ethnic ties to Korea, the Korean state views marriage migrants as members of the Korean nation because they are members of Korean families and bearers of future Korean citizens.

Notes

1. For example, guestworkers are now eligible for unemployment benefits and pensions, and may unionize.
2. Due to these exclusionary policies, the number of ethnic Chinese has decreased from more than 80,000 to around 21,000 over the past sixty years.
3. Korean National Assembly Minutes, No. 225: 18. <http://likms.assembly.go.kr/record/index.html>. Accessed 5 February 2007 (in Korean).
4. Kim Dae Jung's efforts to grant voting rights to foreigners may have helped him win the Nobel Peace Prize in 2000.
5. I used the news article search engine service provided by the Korean Press Foundation <http://www.kinds.or.kr>. This search engine's database includes 181 newspapers, both national and local. I limited my research to articles with "multicultural" in the headline, and identified those containing announcements of incorporation programmes and policies. In total, 1,240 articles mentioned policies and programmes, including fifteen entries from 1996 through 2005, forty-seven in 2006, 262 in 2007, and 917 in 2008.
6. The average number of children born alive to a woman (or group of women) during her lifetime if she were to pass through her childbearing years conforming to the age-specific fertility rates of a given year.
7. The general naturalization process requirements include five years of legal residency in Korea, and the ability to speak Korean and understand Korean culture as measured by naturalization tests. However, marriage migrants need to satisfy only one of two sets of less demanding requirements: (1) two years of legal residency in Korea with a Korean spouse, or (2) one year of legal residency in Korea after three years of marriage to a Korean national (Nationality Law, Article 6, Clause 2), and marriage migrants are exempt from taking naturalization tests.
8. Here the population problem refers only to the shrinking and ageing Korean population in general, which is different from the specific problem of rural bachelors. The latter predates the former and it was only when faced with increasing pressure to maintain a desirable population size that the Korean Government began to implement marriage migrant incorporation policies.

References

Alexander, J.C. *The Civil Sphere*. New York: Oxford University Press, 2006.
Bloemraad, I. *Becoming a Citizen: Incorporating Immigrants and Refugees in the United States and Canada*. Berkeley, Los Angeles and London: University of California Press, 2006.
Bommes, M. and A. Geddes. "Introduction: Immigration and the Welfare State". In *Immigration and Welfare*, edited by M. Bommes and A. Geddes, pp. 1–12. London and New York: Routledge, 2000.
Boswell, C. "Theorizing Migration Policy: Is There a Third Way?". *International Migration Review* 41 (2007): 75–100.
Brubaker, R. *Citizenship and Nationhood in France and Germany*. Cambridge, Massachusetts: Harvard University Press, 1992.
Cardenas, S. "National Human Rights Commissions in Asia". In *Sovereignty under Challenge: How Governments Respond*, edited by J.D. Montgomery and N. Glazer, pp. 55–82. New Brunswick (USA) and London (UK): Transaction Publishers, 2002.
Castles, S. "How Nation-States Respond to Immigration and Ethnic Diversity". *New Community* 21 (1995): 293–308.
Cheong, Y.R. "The Huaqiao Community in Korea: Its Rise, Demise, and Reemergence". *Journal of International and Area Studies* 9 (2002): 37–56.
Chernilo. D. "Social Theory's Methodological Nationalism". *European Journal of Social Theory* 9 (2006): 5–22.
Entzinger, H. "The Rise and Fall of Multiculturalism: The Case of the Netherlands". In *Toward Assimilation and Citizenship: Immigrants in Liberal Nation-States*, edited by C. Joppke and E. Morawska, pp. 59–86. New York, NY: Palgrave Macmillan, 2003.
Favell, A. "Integration Nations". In *International Migration Research: Constructions, Omissions and the Promises of Interdisciplinarity*, edited by M. Bommes and E. Morawska, pp. 41–67. Burlington, VT: Ashgate, 2006.
Freeman, G.P. "Immigrant Incorporation in Western Democracies". *International Migration Review* 38 (2004): 945–69.
Glazer, N. "We Are All Multiculturalists Now". In *Multiculturalism in Contemporary Societies: Perspectives on Difference and Transdifference*, edited by H. Breinig, J. Gebhardt, K. Lösch, pp. 37–51. Erlangen: Universitatsbund Erlangen, 2002.
Gurowitz, A. "The Diffusion of International Norms: Why Identity Matters". *International Politics* 43 (2006): 305–41.
Hagan, J. "Negotiating Social Membership in the Contemporary World". *Social Forces* 85 (2006): 631–42.
Hart-Landsberg, M. *The Rush to Development: Economic Change and Political Struggle in South Korea*. New York: Monthly Review Press, 1993.

He, B. and W. Kymlicka. "Introduction". In *Multiculturalism in Asia*, edited by W. Kymlicka and B. He, pp. 1–21. Oxford New York: Oxford University Press, 2005.

Hollifield, J.F. "The Politics of International Migration: How Can We 'Bring the State Back In?'". In *Migration Theory: Talking Across the Disciplines*, edited by C.B. Brettell and J. F. Hollifield, pp. 137–85. New York: Routledge, 2000.

Jacobson, D. *Rights across Borders: Immigration and the Decline of Citizenship*. Baltimore and London: Johns Hopkins University Press, 1996.

James, C.E. "Introduction: Perspective On Multiculturalism In Canada". In *Possibilities & Limitations: Multicultural Policies and Programs in Canada*, edited by C.E. James, pp. 12–20. Halifax: Fernwood Publishing, 2005.

Jayasuriya, L. "Immigration and Settlement in Australia: An Overview and Critique of Multiculturalism". In *Immigration and Integration in Post-Industrial Societies*, edited by N. Carmon, pp. 206–26. New York, N.Y.: St. Martin's Press, Inc, 1996.

Joppke, C. "Why Liberal States Accept Unwanted Immigration". *World Politic* 50 (1998): 266–93.

———. "Multicultural Citizenship: A Critique". *European Journal of Sociology* 42 (2001): 431–47.

——— and E. Morawska. "Integration Immigrants in Liberal Nation-States: Policies and practices". In *Toward Assimilation and Citizenship: Immigrants in Liberal Nation-States*, edited by C. Joppke and E. Morawska, pp. 1–36. New York: Palgrave Macmillan, 2003.

Kim, H.J. "Korean Women's Association, Putting Multicultural Family on the Right Track Event". *North Jeonra Daily*, 29 September 2008.

Kim, N.H.J. "Korean Immigration Policy Changes and the Political Liberals' Dilemma". *International Migration Review* 42 (2008): 576–96.

Kymlicka, W. *Multicultural Citizenship*. Oxford: Clarendon Press, 1995.

———. *Politics in the Vernacular*. Oxford: Oxford University Press, 2001.

———. "Liberal Multiculturalism: Western Models, Global Trends, and Asian Debates". In *Multiculturalism in Asia*, edited by W. Kymlicka and B. He, pp. 22–55. Oxford: Oxford University Press, 2005.

Lee, C. "'US' and 'THEM' in Korean Law". In *East Asian Law: Universal Norms and Local Cultures*, edited by A. Rosett, L. Cheng and M.Y.K. Woo, pp. 106–36. London and New York: RoutledgeCurzon, 2003.

Lee, H.-K. "International Marriage and the State in South Korea: Focusing on Governmental Policy". *Citizenship Studies* 12, no. 1 (2008): 107–23.

Lee, Y.W. and Park, H. "The Politics of Foreign Labor Policy in Korea and Japan". *Journal of Contemporary Asia* 35 (2005): 143–62.

Lie, J. *Multiethnic Japan*. Cambridge, Massachusetts: Harvard University Press. 2001.

Lim, T.C. "Racing From the Bottom in South Korea? The Nexus between Civil Society and Transnational Migrants". *Asian Survey* 43 (2003): 423–42.

———. "NGOs, Transnational Migrants, and the Promotion of Rights in South Korea". In *Local Citizenship in Recent Countries of Immigration*, edited by T. Tsuda, pp. 235–69. New York: Lexington Books, 2006.

Lockwood, D. "Civic Integration and Class Formation". *British Journal of Sociology* 47 (1996): 531–50.

Luhmann, N. *The Differentiation of Society*. New York: Columbia University Press, 1982.

Menjívar, C. "Minimal Legality: Salvadoran and Guatemalan Immigrants' Lives in the United States". *American Journal of Sociology* 111 (2006): 999–1037.

Milly, D.J. "The Rights of Foreign Migrants Workers in Asia: Contrasting Bases for Expanded Protections". In *Human Rights and Asian Values: Contesting National Identities and Cultural Representations in Asia*, edited by M. Jacobsen and O. Bruun, pp. 301–21. Richmond, Surrey: Curzon Press, 2000.

Ministry of Justice, Government of Korea. *Immigration Control Reform Plan* 2006. <http://www.moj.go.kr> (in Korean).

Ministry of Justice, Korea Immigration Service, "Immigration Policy Seminar Leaflet (Korean Title: Imming Jeongchack Seminar)". Seminar held on 8 June 2006 by Ministry of Justice, Korea Immigration Service.

Morris, L. *Managing Migration: Civic Stratification and Migrants' Rights*. London and New York: Routledge, 2002.

———. "Managing Contradictions: Civic Stratification and Migrants' Rights". *International Migration Review* 37 (2003): 74–100.

Oommen. T.K. *Citizenship and National Identity*. New Delhi and London: Thousands Oaks, 2002.

Pai, H.I. "The Colonial Origins of Korea's Collected Past". In *Nationalism and the Construction of Korean Identity*, edited by H.I. Pai and T.R. Tangerlini, pp. 13–32. Berkeley, California: University of California, 1998.

Papademetriou, D. *Policy Considerations for Immigrant Integration*. Washington, D.C.: Migration Policy Institute, 2003.

Park, H.G. and Park H.G. "Education Subsidy Available to Mixed-race Children (Korean title: Honhyul Adong Chuhak/Gyoyuk Jiwon)". *Seoul Simun*, 26 April 2006. <http://www.seoul.co.kr/news/newsView.php?code=seoul&id=200604 27002010&keyword=%B3%EB%B9%AB%C7%F6%20%B4%D9%B9%AE%C8% AD>. Accessed 21 Oct 2009.

Park, W.W. "The Unwilling Hosts: State, Society and the Control of Guest Workers in South Korea". In *Migrant Workers in Pacific Asia*, edited by D.A. Yaw, pp. 67–94. London: Frank Cass Publishers, 2002.

Penninx, R. *Integration: The Role of Communities, Institutions, and the State*. Washington, D.C.: Migration Policy Institute, 2003.

Seol, D.H. "Past and Present of Foreign Workers in Korea 1987–2000". *Asia Solidarity Quarterly* 2 (2000): 6–31.

———. "Women Marriage Migrants in Korea: Immigration Process and Adaptation". *Asia-Pacific Forum* 33 (2006): 32–59.

——— and J.D. Skrentny. "South Korea: Importing Undocumented Workers/Commentary". In *Controlling Immigration: A Global Perspective*, edited by W.A. Cornelius, T. Tsuda, P.L. Martin, and J.F. Hollifield, pp. 481–516. Stanford, California: Stanford University Press, 2004.

Shin, G.D., H.Y. Kim, I. Bong, Y. Kim, C. Park, K. Oh, and H.J. Kim. *Policy Research Report 2006–11: Residency Status of Foreign Workers and Their Needs for Administrative Services*. Gyeonging Research Institute (in Korean), 2006.

Shin, G.W. "Nation, History, and Politics". In *Nationalism and the Construction of Korean Identity*, edited by H.I. Pai and T.R. Tangerlini, pp. 148–65. Berkeley, California: University of California, 1998.

———. *Ethnic Nationalism in Korea*. Stanford, California: Stanford University Press, 2006.

Soysal, Y.N. *Limits of Citizenship*. Chicago: The University of Chicago Press, 1994.

Steinmetz, G. "Introduction: Culture and the State". In *State/Culture: State Formation After the Cultural Turn*, edited by G. Steinmetz, pp. 1–49. Ithaca and London: Cornell University Press, 1999.

Yoo, Y. "Helping Multicultural Families". *Seoul Newspaper*, 18 April 2008 (in Korean).

Yuval-Davis, N. *Gender and Nation*. London: Sage Publications, 1997.

———. Nationalism, Multiculturalism and Women. In *Multicultural Policies and the State: A Comparison of Two European Societies*, edited by M. Martiniello, pp. 63–74. The Netherlands: ERCMER, 1998.

5

THE TUG OF WAR OVER MULTICULTURALISM
Contestation between Governing and Empowering Immigrants in Taiwan

HSIA Hsiao-Chuan

MULTICULTURALISM: TOUCHING ON THE NERVES OF NATIONAL ANXIETY?

Shortly after the world was shocked by the attacks in Norway on 22 July 2011, the Taiwanese public was upset to learn that the self-confessed perpetrator and right-wing extremist, Anders Behring Breivik, made and posted a video on the Internet before going on his killing spree, in which he expresses his admiration for Taiwan, along with Japan and South Korea, as a "modern country that never adopted multiculturalism".

When this news spread across the Internet, many Taiwanese posted Web comments expressing their resentment and saying that Taiwan was not at all like how the Norwegian murderer had described it. Government Information Office Minister Philip Yang quickly issued a statement to the media stressing that Taiwanese society had always respected a plurality of cultures. Yang said that a democratic society should be a tolerant one in which different groups respect and appreciate one another, and that this was the kind of society that the international community generally took Taiwan to be. National Immigration Agency officials were also quick to assure the public that Breivik had never been to Taiwan. All this was supposedly to prove that Breivik's remarks about Taiwan were a baseless misinterpretation.

I expressed my opinions on this subject in an article published on 29 July in the Chinese-language *China Times*,[1] which had invited me to write bi-weekly commentaries for almost a year. In this article, I pointed out that although Taiwan has never seen a massacre of people of an ethnic minority or migrants by right-wing extremists, our laws, policies and systems are full of discrimination against immigrants and migrant workers. I pointed out that discriminatory attitudes are often seen in the words and actions of bureaucrats, while prejudice is pervasive in society at large. The article called upon Taiwanese who really want to refute Breivik's description of Taiwan as a monocultural society to say a resounding "no" to all words and actions that discriminate against immigrants and migrant workers. On 4 August, I subsequently received an anonymous letter containing a photocopy of a full-page report about Breivik that appeared on the Chinese-language *Apple Daily* on 25 July. The report includes a photograph of Breivik wearing a special forces diving suit and aiming a rifle at some imaginary adversary. In the blank space alongside the photograph, the anonymous letter-writer had scribbled the following shocking and hate-filled message:

> When will Taiwan get a brave man like this to kill all the mangy foreign workers and trashy foreign spouses who have crawled over from Southeast Asia and other backward regions to hang around in Taiwan, along with the shameless hypocrites who wave banners and yell slogans on their behalf in the bogus name of brotherly love — people like that bloody sow Hsia Hsiao-chuan? Because of this trash and because of you, our descendants will have to live in a trash heap!

This letter is not just an isolated, random incident. I have received several threatening letters over the past year, while other people and organizations that speak up for the rights of immigrants (particularly marriage migrants) and migrant workers have also received similar letters or have been harassed in various ways. I continue to receive threatening letters whenever the subjects of my commentaries are about issues of marriage migrants and migrant workers.

This anecdote reveals that the concept of "multiculturalism" in Taiwan is contested by many forces: non-Taiwanese (especially international communities whose perceptions about Taiwan that Taiwanese politicians and general public presume would affect Taiwan's status in international politics); the Taiwanese government; actors in the immigrant movement; and the Taiwanese people. On the one hand, both Taiwanese government and the general public consider "multiculturalism" as the norm, which is why they immediately denied Breivik's characterization of Taiwan and reassured the "international community" that Taiwan respects multiculturalism.

On the other hand, there are those who resent the existence of immigrants and migrants, particularly those from the less developed countries, and consequently are against advocacy and rhetoric promoting their rights. The fact that these people feel the need to send anonymous letters to threaten activists working for im/migrant rights reveals that the immigrant movement has had social impact, thus triggering their anxiety. Indeed, the invitation to me to write a bi-weekly column in a mainstream newspaper signals that issues and rights of im/migrants have been considered crucial by mainstream society.

In the following, I will examine how the meanings of the multiculturalism have been contested by two main forces: the actors of social movements and actors of the state. Rooted in the political development of nation-building in Taiwan since the 1980s, multiculturalism has gradually become a political rhetoric symbolizing the nationhood of Taiwan. By expanding the meaning of multiculturalism and other existent rhetoric, the immigrant movement has successfully challenged the governments' immigration policies and made the historically exclusionary model of citizenship in Taiwan more inclusive. At the same time, the Taiwan government has also struggled to maintain multiculturalism more as political rhetoric only, rather than granting more substantive and formal rights to immigrants.

CITIZENSHIP IN THE ERA OF GLOBALIZATION

Discussion of citizenship in the modern era has traditionally centred on the acquisition of rights and the exercise of obligations, and how rights serve to forge attachment to a particular nation-state which is traditionally conceptualized as culturally and morally homogeneous. As the world becomes increasingly globalized, recent writing has sought to decouple citizenship from its traditionally close association with the nation-state.

Several writers claim that national citizenship has lost its importance in the present era of globalization (Soysal 1994; Sassen 1996) and suggest that citizenship rights are irrelevant, and that labour rights and human rights should take precedence (Harris 1995; Soysal 1994). Soysal (1994, p. 1) argues that "a new and more universal concept of citizenship has unfolded in the post-war era, one whose organizing and legitimating principles are based on universal personhood rather than national belonging". Soysal's thesis for this transformation is based on the experience of "guest workers" in Europe, who live and work in a foreign country without acquiring citizenship status. Organizations representing guest workers have been able to mobilize support for the extension of basic social and civil rights, and thus the significance of citizenship has been reduced to the point where non-citizens' rights do not differ significantly from those of citizens (Soysal 1994, p. 119).

Soysal's thesis has been criticized for the following problems. First, while many guest workers might increasingly enjoy social and civic rights, they do not possess political rights. This problem of the lack of political rights is considered crucial since participation in the political realm is one of the major defining characteristics of "thick" citizenship (Faulks 2000). Without formal rights to vote or stand for office, immigrants can take little part in the formulation and implementation of policies that may impact negatively on their social entitlements and civil liberties. Faulks (2000) maintains that human rights by themselves do not ensure the development of participatory networks, which are necessary to sustain common institutions of governance and to build bridges between immigrant groups and the dominant culture within the polity. Since citizenship involves participation and responsibilities, Faulks believes that human rights cannot simply supersede citizenship, because enjoying rights without bearing responsibilities can only fuel hostility towards minorities who are perceived to benefit from public resources without playing their part in the community. For instance, in the study examining Ireland's 2004 Constitution Amendment which removes birthright citizenship from any future Irish-born children of immigrant parents, Tormey (2007) argues that one of the reasons why the amendment was passed is that migrant women are successfully constructed as "immoral citizen tourists" who have no loyalty or tangible connection to the nation and fail to fulfil the notion of reciprocity and repaying "Irish hospitality".

Critics have moreover argued that the guest worker's experience in Europe cannot be easily generalized into a widespread shift towards a post-national citizenship (e.g., Joppke 1998; Parreñas 2001; Piper and Roces 2003). The exclusionary practices of citizenship have been recognized as being ill-equipped to deal with an age of large-scale and heterogeneous migratory movements. The hope for post-national citizenship is that international human rights law would "provide a tool for sculpting a more inclusionary model of citizenship" (Lister 1997, p. 60) that would transcend nation-state boundaries. However, despite the proliferation of international conventions and human rights instruments, national citizenship, to a large extent, still determines the rights that different categories of migrants are able to exercise (Kofman et al. 2000; Castles and Davidson 2000). In practice, the international regime of rights is weak and non-existent outside of Europe (Ghai 1999). In the case of Taiwan, its exclusion from membership in the United Nations due to the one-China policy makes it a particular case where most international instruments of rights cannot apply.

Multicultural citizenship is an alternative proposed by scholars who recognize both the importance and limits of political citizenship, and is based on the idea that the nation-state contains a degree of plurality that allows migrants to retain their cultural identity provided they adhere to political norms. This pluralism does not negate the existence of a dominant culture but recognizes multiple cultures. In the political context of multiculturalism, Kymlicka (1995, p. 5) advances a theory of minority rights: "A comprehensive theory of justice in a multicultural state will include both universal rights, assigned to individuals regardless of their group membership, and certain group-differentiated rights or 'special status' for minority cultures," because all countries have a "societal culture" that places minority groups in a position of cultural inequality vis-à-vis the majority (Kymlicka 1995, 2001).

Multiculturalism, however, is not always an entirely positive development (Kofman et al. 2000). According to Faulks (2000), the first problem with a conception of citizenship centred on group rights is ascertaining which groups can legitimately claim to be special cases and where they deserve additional entitlements not available to other members of a polity, resulting in situations which may lead to tension between groups competing for special status. Multiculturalism may also encourage and fix essentialist and static views of migrant identities (Barry 2001; Bissoondath 1994). In Sweden for example, the government, which exerts considerable social control through the allocation of funds, tends to encourage organizations based on ethnicity at the local level, thus making it difficult to build bridges and migrant political alliances across ethnic differences. Alund and Schierup (1993, p. 140) thus speak of "prescribed multiculturalism" whereby immigrants and ethnic organizations are co-opted into the corporatist state and are politically marginalized.

Critics point out that an excessive emphasis on difference leads to a reduced focus on problems that are shared, and to a more combative anti-racist stance. For instance, the Netherlands Minorities Policy was altered in response to criticism of the government's emphasis on culture. Official rhetoric does not necessarily correspond to the reality of migrants' lives. Nor does it always correspond to any acceptance of these migrants by wider society. There has also been an increasingly vociferous critique of and disillusionment with Swedish multiculturalism, which has left migrants with unequal rights and segregated existences (Alund 1991, 1998).

Furthermore, to ask an individual to base their political position on a single fragment of their identity is a denial of their complex individuality. Multicultural citizenship thus runs the risk of essentializing and freezing as timeless cultural differences within the boundaries of homogeneous ethnic groups. Proponents of group-based citizenship tend to have a romanticized view of social groups, neglecting the fact that groups can themselves be oppressive to their members. National discourses are often used by elites to gloss over differences within the group and as an excuse for not tackling the roots of inequalities. The state and other institutions may accept cultural norms that communities have transplanted from their home society without any real considerations of the changes in their new economic and social environment. For instance, feminists have criticized the patriarchal nature of multicultural policies for not only reifying cultural differences within ethnic groups which are assumed to be homogeneous, but also supporting male leadership and the persistence of traditional values. These critics question who is really empowered to interpret and impose cultural norms in the framework of multicultural citizenship. Feminists also point out that multiculturalism may represent a more liberal tolerance of what goes on in the private sphere among different migrant groups; this can, however, still leave intact gender inequalities and repressive practices towards women. The case of domestic violence exemplifies the tolerance of practices in the private sphere on grounds of non-intervention in the customs of others (Kofman et al. 2000; Okin 1999; Yuval-Davis 1997).

As Bloemraad, Korteweg and Yurdakul (2008) point out, numerous Western countries appeared to embrace multiculturalism in 1990s, but by the end of the decade, observers noted governments' "retreat" from multiculturalism (Brubaker 2001; Joppke 2004). According to Joppke (2004), there have been changes by liberal states towards non-discriminatory immigration policies, liberalized citizenship rules and a general distancing from the old idea of assimilation. With the exception of language, the only explicit impositions on newcomers are liberal impositions, most notably a procedural commitment to liberal-democratic principles. The effect of this trend is to remove the case for programmes of multicultural "recognition", because "minority rights are compensation for states' strong nationalizing practices, and weakening of these nationalizing practices remove the case for (this type) of minority rights" (Joppke 2001, p. 437).

While Europe may have more liberalized policies and laws regarding immigrants as Joppke has contended,[2] the immigration policies and laws of the newly emerging immigrant-receiving countries in East Asia, including Taiwan, remain largely exclusionary. Consequently, multiculturalism and the case for minority rights arise in East Asia. Furthermore, as Bloemraad, Korteweg and Yurdakul (2008) point out, critiques of multiculturalism often presume that the meaning and content of multiculturalism are easily identifiable and universally the same. However, multiculturalism is not a unitary concept but is elastic enough to include different aspects which may shift over time (Kofman et al. 2000). Therefore, more research needs to be done to examine the meanings and practices of multiculturalism in different times and places. This chapter aims at providing a concrete case of Taiwan regarding how the meaning of multiculturalism has been formulated and transformed by forces of the state and social movements.

By detailing the development of the rhetoric of multiculturalism from the 1980s to the present, I illustrate how the meaning of multiculturalism is a battlefield of contestation, wherein both state actors and social movement actors actively engage themselves and each other to advance their agendas. In addition to documents of relevant laws, policies and programmes, much data is based on my praxis-oriented research and long-term involvement in the empowerment of Southeast Asian women immigrating to Taiwan through marriage (Hsia 2006, 2008) and the development of the immigrant movement in Taiwan (Hsia 2008).

My research on marriage migration began in May 1994 until the present time. In 1995, I initiated a Chinese literacy programme based on the theory of the "pedagogy of the oppressed" (Freire 1970) aiming at empowering marriage migrants. After several years and numerous experiences of trial and error, the marriage migrants empowered in the Chinese programmes collectively established a national organization, TransAsia Sisters Association in Taiwan (TASAT) in 2003. TASAT is a grassroots organization where marriage migrants are heavily involved in decision making, programme implementation and daily organizational operations. In 2003, I co-founded the Alliance for Human Rights Legislation for Immigrants and Migrants (AHRLIM) to spearhead a movement to promote the rights of migrant workers and immigrants in Taiwan, of which TASAT is one of the founding and active members. AHRLIM is the first alliance in Taiwan that focuses on the rights of both immigrants and migrants and has contributed much to the changes in major immigration laws and policies.

CITIZENSHIP AND IMMIGRATION POLICIES IN TAIWAN

Taiwan's policy of incorporation, as codified in its laws of citizenship, is based on the principle of *jus sanguinis*, inclusive of people who can claim a common ancestral origin, real or imagined, and somewhat exclusive of people who do not share that commonality. The coupling of national identity and the political unit that was established by Sun Yat-Sen, the founder of the Republic of China (ROC), reflects a traditional Chinese emphasis on lineage and ancestry (Cheng 2002).

Taiwan's economic growth and democratization in recent decades have, however, raised scepticism concerning its traditional nationalist ideology, and led to a variety of alternative conceptualizations vying for dominance in a new nation-state building project currently in progress (Cheng 2002). Despite recent changes in the immigration and nationality laws, however, it remains extremely difficult for those excluded from nationality to become citizens of Taiwan, except for spouses and children of Taiwanese citizens (Cheng 2002; Tseng 2004). Prior to the changes in the Nationality Act in 1999 (effective on 9 February 2000), foreigners could not be naturalized as Taiwanese citizens except for women married to Taiwanese men who qualify for naturalization because they are seen as being able to continue Taiwanese "blood lines" through their marriages.

The Taiwanese government did not have an explicit immigration policy[3] until the number of "foreign brides"[4] became significant in Taiwan.[5]

As a researcher working on marriage migration issues since 1994, I have observed how the government's attitudes suddenly changed in late 2002. Until mid-2002, government officials at both central and local government levels were of the view that the "foreign bride" phenomenon was a short-lived "fad" that fell outside their purview. In late 2002 however, two sets of statistics dramatically shifted the government's position. According to the statistics released in 2002 by the Directorate-General of Budget, one of every four new marriages in Taiwan was between a citizen and foreigner, and the majority of foreign spouses were the "foreign brides" and "mainland brides" of Taiwanese men. More importantly, at the end of 2002, the Ministry of Education released statistics indicating that one out of eight newborn babies was born to the family of a "foreign bride". On 21 February 2003, Premier Yu Shyi-kun chaired a meeting of Commission for Women's Rights and Welfare under the Executive Yuan (Taiwan's executive branch) to deliberate on the issue of "Assessment and Action Planning on Related Problems of Foreign and Mainland Spouses". This meeting concluded that from 2004, the government would allocate a specific budget targeting foreign and mainland spouses. Since then, every Ministry began to hold meetings to discuss issues surrounding "foreign brides" and potential policies and programmes for them.

In 2003, the Ministry of Interior (MOI), which was tasked with inter-ministry coordination of policies on "foreign brides", drafted the "Guidelines of Immigration Policy" and tried to rush through the establishment of the National Immigration Agency (NIA). In the first few versions of the draft guidelines, the focus was to create incentives for professional/managerial/skilled foreigners to immigrate to Taiwan, while stipulating that blue collar migrant workers were not allowed to apply for permanent residency and naturalization. The bill of Organic Act of the NIA proposed by MOI (2003a) in late 2003 showed that the main functions of NIA were to police, investigate and deport migrant workers and immigrants who are deemed by NIA officials to be illegal or dangerous, rather than to provide services for immigrants or protect their basic rights. Moreover, the legal grounds for deportation stipulated in the Immigration Act — such as "threatening national security" and "violating public interest" — were vague articulations which were potentially subject to manipulation. Under the framework of the proposed Organic Act of NIA, the human rights of immigrants and migrants were very vulnerable because this proposed agency did not provide any due process for prosecution or mechanism under which migrants and immigrants could appeal against deportation. In the same year, the MOI (2003b) also released the "Implementation Plan for Coaching Foreign Spouses for Adaptation" as the guiding plan for related programmes. Its declared objectives included: to improve the capacity of foreign spouses to adapt to Taiwan; to create a multicultural society; to build successful families with Taiwanese nationals; and to prevent all kinds of family and social problems resulting from ill-adaptation. The plan was primarily oriented towards "assimilation" and the main concern was to improve the adaptation of foreign spouses to Taiwanese society so as to ameliorate possible family and social problems.

As the number of marriage migrants from Southeast Asia and mainland China continued to increase, the worry about the "deterioration of the quality of the next generation" became a source of national anxiety. This anxiety was based on the assumption that since the marriage migrants are from developing countries, they must lack the skills necessary to educate their own children — an argument which clearly had sexist, racist and classist overtones (Hsia 2007). This national anxiety led the government to add more barriers to citizenship for marriage migrants (Hsia and Huang 2010). They had to meet several requirements including passing several medical inspections, staying in Taiwan for a certain period of time,[6] giving up their original nationality, submitting financial proof and passing Chinese proficiency examinations. The hurdle that troubled the marriage migrants and their families most was the financial proof requirement for the migrant's application for citizenship. Until November 2008 when the requirement was changed, each family was compelled to submit proof of financial security under very strict guidelines, including a bank statement or official receipts for income tax wherein the amount should be equal to 24 times the minimum wage (about NTD420,000 as of November 2008).

In short, citizenship in Taiwan for a long time was based on the tradition of *jus sanguinis* which also assumes homogeneity of its population. The Taiwanese government was forced to come up with immigration policies and related laws as a result of a large influx of marriage migrants. However, these immigration policies and laws were not inclusionary. Their main concerns were on ensuring effective measures to "govern" immigrants using selection principles to include "high quality" immigrants while excluding those deemed of "low quality"; the policing of immigrants as part of crime prevention; and the education of those "low quality" immigrants already living in Taiwan in order to assimilate them.

THE EMERGENCE OF THE CONCEPT OF MULTICULTURALISM IN TAIWAN

While the exclusionary model of incorporation is the tradition, a version of "multiculturalism" focused on the diverse ethnic background of citizens of Taiwan has evolved. In the 1980s, after decades of dictatorial rule by the KMT (Kuomintang or Chinese Nationalist Party), social movements aimed at toppling the KMT drew on controversies relating to the Indigenous Peoples to weaken the legitimacy of the KMT's rule. As a result of campaigns to amend the Constitution, provision for the rights of the Indigenous Peoples first appeared in 1994, declaring that the Indigenous Peoples' rights of political participation should be protected and their education, cultures, social welfare and economy improved (Lin 2000). In 1997, another Constitutional amendment resulting from political struggles led by the united front of the anti-KMT forces added more provisions declaring that "the nation recognizes *multi-cultures* and actively protects and promotes the languages and cultures of the Indigenous Peoples". One of the significant developments of this provision is the emergence of the concept of "multi-cultures". Although "multi-cultures" in this provision refer to the Indigenous Peoples (as opposed to the dominant Han people), the definition of Taiwan as a nation of "multi-cultures" provided a platform for the possibility of including diverse ethnicities (Chang 2002). According to Chang (2002), as a result of the "discursive formation" since the 1980s through various campaigns (along with the introduction of North American [especially Canadian] and Australian experiences of multiculturalism by some intellectuals and activists) "multiculturalism" gradually and unconsciously became Taiwan's basic national policy and the politically correct rhetoric.

Based on a survey of newspapers, Chang (2002) found that the word "multicultural" was almost non-existent prior to 1995. It was only from 1998 that the word appeared more frequently in the newspapers. However, it was still relatively underused at that time, considering that the concept already existed in the Constitution. After the presidential candidate of the Democratic Progressive Party (DPP), Chen Shui-Bien, won the election in 2000, symbols of the Indigenous Peoples and Hakka[7] cultures suddenly became more popularly used in the activities of both central and local governments. In 2001, during the founding ceremony of the Council for Hakka Affairs, Executive Yuan, President Chen stated that the "Republic of China is a multi-ethnic and multicultural nation. It is clearly stated in the

Constitution.... This is the basic national policy of our country..." (Chang 2002). In July 2004, the highest body for cultural policies, the Council for Cultural Affairs under the Executive Yuan, announced the "Declaration of Cultural Citizenship"[8] to emphasize the importance of multiculturalism. In October 2004, the Council organized the Conference on Ethnicities and Cultural Development and proposed its plan of action, in which new immigrants were included as one of the main "ethnic" groups[9] whose cultures should be respected and protected. In other words, at the level of national cultural policy, the cultural needs of new immigrants were already recognized by the central government in 2004, although they remained neglected in terms of actual programmes and implementation by the Council for Cultural Affairs (Wang 2006).

In short, the concept of "multiculturalism" in Taiwan emerged out of Taiwan's nation-building experiences and processes. It first appeared in Taiwan's political arena as the result of continuous campaigns and social movements since 1980s aimed at toppling the KMT regime. As the pro-independence movement became more prevalent, especially after DPP won the presidential election for the first time in 2000, the rhetoric of multiculturalism, along with human rights and democracy, have quickly become the politically and socially accepted values. They are also presumed to be the defining characteristics of Taiwan as an independent state, as distinct from the People's Republic of China (PRC). The rhetoric of democracy and human rights serves a political function in Taiwan's nation-building project (as opposed to the presumably dictatorial PRC), while the rhetoric of multiculturalism serves as a cultural function (as opposed to the presumably Han-dominant PRC).

The original notion of multiculturalism in this nation-building project originated from the anti-KMT regime did not, however, include immigrants and migrants. Indeed, most pro-DPP labour organizations were anti-migrant workers and many discriminatory policies and laws against marriage migrants and migrant workers were passed during DPP rule (from 2000 to 2008).

To counter the increasingly hostile sentiment and discriminatory policies and laws against migrant workers and marriage migrants, AHRLIM (Alliance for Human Rights Legislation for Immigrants and Migrants) and its member organizations have purposefully engaged themselves with the rhetoric of multiculturalism. Through this engagement, the concept of "multiculturalism" has been gradually broadened beyond indigenous peoples to also include marriage migrants and migrant workers. In the following section, I will illustrate how the traditionally exclusionary model of incorporation in Taiwan was gradually challenged and reformulated to become more inclusive.

MULTICULTURALISM AS STRATEGY TO DEVELOP THE IMMIGRANT MOVEMENT

Despite language and cultural differences posing major obstacles towards integration for new citizens, marriage migrants in Taiwan have demonstrated their active agency by participating in several protests against unfair treatment by various central governmental agencies.

One crucial challenge for the immigrant movement is to confront public concerns about the negative impacts of immigrants. Marriage migrants have faced enormous discrimination and are perceived as "social problems" and their increasingly significant presence has caused national anxiety in Taiwan (Hsia 2007; Hsia and Huang 2010). To gain the public's sympathy and support, the immigrant movement needs to debunk the pervasive negative images about immigrants. To this end, AHRLIM has adopted several strategies, including the radicalization of the existent values and rhetoric of multiculturalism, and the enhancement of immigrants' substantive citizenship through the marriage migrants' own subjectivity and agency (Hsia 2009). The following will discuss how the concept of multiculturalism has been incorporated as a strategy to expand the social and political spaces of im/migrants' participation, and consequently helped develop the immigrant movement's challenge of Taiwan's citizenship laws based on *jus sanguinis*.

Development of the Immigrant Movement in Taiwan

As mentioned earlier, the proposed framework of the NIA was very problematic because of its gaze on im/migrants as potential criminals and also because it did not provide a mechanism to protect their human rights. In order to promote their human rights, a group of concerned organizations joined together to form AHRLIM on 12 December 2003, becoming the first alliance to focus on immigrants' rights and related laws and policies.

AHRLIM's first action was to protest in front of the Legislative Yuan against the government's proposal to establish the above-mentioned NIA on 24 December 2003. Additionally, AHRLIM lobbied in the Legislative

Yuan to seek the support of legislators from different political parties. After intense rounds of lobbying and protesting, the proposal was defeated. When the government's plan to establish the NIA was temporarily halted, AHRLIM took the opportunity to examine the government's proposed amendments to the Immigration Act and drafted its own proposal for the establishment of acceptable norms for a comprehensive immigration policy. Toward this end, AHRLIM held a series of public forums as well as took to raising public awareness of issues related to immigrants and migrants by focusing attention on various cases of human rights violation and the problems with current immigration policies and regulations.

After intense and detailed discussions and debates, AHRLIM submitted to the Legislative Yuan in March 2005 its draft of proposed amendments to the Immigration Act, with endorsements from many legislators of all political parties. After another two years of struggle, the amendment was eventually passed on 30 November 2007. Important reforms in this newly passed amendment include anti-discrimination regulations, allowing marriage migrants who have been the victims of domestic violence to remain in Taiwan even if they are divorced, and ensuring rights for assembly and rally for im/migrants. The passing of the amendment of the Immigration Act in 2007 was the first major victory of the immigrant movement spearheaded by AHRLIM.

Another significant campaign led by AHRLIM was on the issue of the financial requirement for naturalization. On 9 September 2007, hundreds of immigrant women from Southeast Asia and mainland China joined a rally protesting against the financial requirements imposed on marriage migrants for obtaining citizenship. This rally attracted much media attention because it was the first time in Taiwan's history that hundreds of marriage migrants all over Taiwan participated in a street demonstration. As a result of continuous protests and lobbying, the financial requirement for applying for citizenship was changed in November 2008, in which applicants for citizenship only need to provide a statement declaring that the applicant or her spouse, parents or parents-in-law hold paid jobs and can provide her with financial support in Taiwan.

Radicalizing Existent Values and Rhetoric

In establishing a dialogue with the public, AHRLIM employed the strategy of gradually radicalizing existent values and rhetoric around multiculturalism along with those of human rights and democracy, so that im/migrants are perceived as equally entitled to, rather than excepted from, enjoying these values.

Since President Chen won the election in 2000 — the first time the opposition party won the presidential election over the long-ruling KMT — "nationhood based on human rights principles" has become a very popular rhetoric among politicians. AHRLIM's strategy was to draw upon and radicalize this rhetoric as seen in its first statement:

> The Government of Taiwan, which espouses a concept of nationhood based on human rights, is always touting its human rights record, yet has consistently ignored the rights of immigrants and migrants in its actual policies… As the media stirs up fear in Taiwanese society, the Government promotes policies that actively prevent new migrants and immigrants from enjoying the same rights and benefits allowed to other residents of Taiwan even as they work and make a positive contribution to Taiwanese society. In order to promote both the Human Rights of immigrants and migrants, as well as the development of a healthy, pluralist society, a group of non-governmental organisations concerned with Human Rights, immigration policy, foreign labour, and democracy have joined with lawyers and scholars bearing a long term interest on these issues to form The Alliance for Human Rights Legislation for Immigrants and Migrants (AHRLIM 2003).

Since the Republic of China is not recognized by most international institutions, one primary national anxiety is to prove to the world that Taiwan has achieved international standards in all spheres, in the hope that this will garner more support from the international community for Taiwan's claims to recognition as an independent state. AHRLIM has strategically played on this by using international conventions such as the Universal Declaration of Human Rights to push for a more inclusive immigration policy. Thus, in its first signature campaign its position was that:

> Every individual enjoys basic human rights, regardless of race, colour, gender, language, religion, political or other creed, nationality, social status, wealth, place of birth, or any other social distinction. We support plural social development and the promotion of social dialogue designed to eradicate discrimination (AHRLIM 2003).

In another example, AHRLIM protested against the Council of Labor Affairs' decision to increase medical check-ups for foreign teachers, and demanded that the government make good President Chen's promise at his inauguration speech for his second term, when he declared that "everyone is equal — whether you are from Tainan (his home county) or Vietnam, and should be protected for basic human rights".

In addition to human rights issues, "democracy" has been purposely constructed as an important aspect of national identity, especially since the DPP won their first victory in the presidential campaign in 2000 (in opposition to mainland China which is presumed to be lacking in democracy). Additionally, related concepts such as "citizenship" (or citizen's rights) and "civil participation" are also part of the common political rhetoric on the part of the government. Therefore, in one of AHRLIM's three demands in its protest against the government's proposal for the NIA, it framed the notion of "democracy" in terms of the active participation of the im/migrants, in line with the concept of multicultural citizenship as envisaged by Kymlicka (1995):

> Taiwan is a democratic country, where people have freedom and capacity to express their opinions about various issues. However, the government's policies and laws related to the human rights of im/migrants have never been publicly discussed, nor have they considered the rights of migrant workers, not to mention the importance of immigration policy for the prospects of Taiwan society (AHRLIM 2003).

AHRLIM argues that immigration policy is "a matter of the rights of im/migrants and their families, and what is embedded in immigration policy is what the society thinks of itself, and will influence Taiwanese people's image of 'citizens' and their identity". In this vein, it demands the expansion of "public discussions so that im/migrants and their families, and the general public can fully understand and participate" (AHRLIM 2003).

AHRLIM and affiliated organizations have also radicalized the meanings of multiculturalism to include im/migrants. As previously mentioned, ethnic issues had been critical catalysts for mobilization in the opposition movement and the DPP had successfully weakened the ruling KMT's legitimacy by criticizing, for example, its "national language policy" which detached non-Mandarin speaking people from their mother tongues. Since DPP gained power, ethnic issues have continued to be the focus. For example, the revitalization of ethnic languages has become a commonly accepted rhetoric, which in turn helps to popularize the concept of "multiculturalism". The DPP government has carefully employed the concept of multiculturalism to project a more democratic and progressive image, as seen in establishing the Council for Hakka Affairs, and two national TV stations for the Indigenous Peoples and Hakka Peoples, and the use of their "multicultural images" to promote international relations, such as by employing symbols of the Indigenous Peoples for publicity in international events.

These seemingly progressive values are however often exclusionary in practice. For example, the "mother tongues" of Southeast Asian marriage migrants have been ignored and devalued. AHRLIM and affiliated organizations have therefore seized every chance to radicalize the meanings of "multiculturalism" by appealing for the inclusion of new immigrants' languages and cultures as part of Taiwanese "multicultures". In celebrating Mother's Day in 2004, AHRLIM and affiliated organizations co-sponsored an activity titled "Mother's Name — Acknowledging New Immigrants and Migrants" with the purpose of "encouraging the public to acknowledge rich cultures the new immigrants have contributed to Taiwanese multiculturalism.... and striving to make Taiwan an island filled with rich cultures, respecting each other's cultures, different voices and faces".[10]

Demonstrating the Values of Multiculturalism

In addition to radicalizing existent values and rhetoric, active participation of immigrants themselves is crucial to enhancing the immigrant movement. In the first protest initiated by AHRLIM, marriage migrants organized by the TransAsia Sisters Association, Taiwan (TASAT) — the first grassroots organization for marriage migrants in Taiwan and one of the founding member organizations of AHRLIM — were at the front line, voicing their dissent by performing a skit. The members of TASAT have become significantly more active after their first protest, participating in most AHRLIM activities including internal discussions about issues and amendments to laws, and speaking at AHRLIM's protests or press conferences.

Marriage migrants organized by TASAT and other organizations have also been increasingly active in advocating for and protecting their own rights. On 6 July 2005, marriage migrants living in Taipei, accompanied by many women's, workers' and human rights groups, awaited marriage migrants from Southern Taiwan who took a midnight bus with their husbands, children and Taiwanese friends, to join the protest in front of the Executive Yuan against its decision to increase obstacles to obtaining citizenship. On 5 March 2004, dozens of marriage migrants from mainland China joined the rally organized by AHRLIM to protest against the new stipulation that spouses from mainland China should present proof of ownership of properties worth of NTD5 million. On 9 September 2007, to protest against the financial requirement in citizenship application, marriage migrants from both mainland China and Southeast Asia took to the streets to demand that the "financial requirement for citizenship" be scrapped.

The active participation of marriage migrants in advocacy and protest has gradually changed the public's perception of them. For example, a major newspaper gave significant space to reporting AHRLIM's protest on 6 July 2005, featuring a photograph of marriage migrants with steadfast looks on their faces despite a midnight bus trip with a vivid caption, "New Immigrants Fighting for Rights: To Appeal for Suspending Exams Newly Required for Naturalisation, A Group of Foreign Brides Marched to Executive Yuan with Traditional Straw Hats under Scorching Sun" (*China Times*, 2005). This scene is in sharp contrast with how "foreign brides" used to appear in the media, as helpless and shameful. This historic photograph was later widely disseminated and used in other newspaper accounts as well.

The empowerment for marriage migrants is a long process before they can actively participate in the immigrant movement, especially for those who do not speak Chinese. For marriage migrants from Southeast Asia, language barriers are the most immediate obstacles to their active participation in Taiwanese society. Looking to provide a means of increasing their participation in Taiwan societies and inspired by Freire's (1970) *Pedagogy of the Oppressed* and Boal's (1979) *Theater of the Oppressed*, I had initiated a Chinese Literacy Program for the "foreign brides" on 30 July 1995 to empower these marriage migrants (Hsia 2006). It was only eight years later that marriage migrants from these Chinese programmes themselves decided to form TASAT in December 2003, and in the same year it joined in the founding of AHRLIM.

In addition to protest action, AHRLIM and its member organizations have organized various activities for marriage migrants to demonstrate their native cultures to the public. For instance, in 2004, the Department of Civil Affairs of Taipei City Government requested that I recommended some professors to teach Southeast Asian languages to Taiwanese citizens in order to create a multicultural environment. This was pushed by the Committee of Women's Rights Promotion and Development, where several representatives of feminist organizations and I were invited to be members. I took this opportunity to convince the Taipei City Government to invite marriage migrants from Southeast Asia, rather than Taiwanese professors, to be the teachers for the Southeast Asian language programmes, arguing that these migrants are the real experts of Southeast Asian mother tongues and cultures. After a series of training sessions, marriage migrants organized by TASAT held three Southeast Asian Language programmes simultaneously, including Bahasa Indonesia, Vietnamese and Thai language courses, from 10 July to 20 September 2004. Based on this experience, TASAT initiated a semester-long course on Southeast Asian cultures which was open to the general public at the community college in Taipei County from March to July 2005. In 2005, the Council for Cultural Affairs asked me to conduct a study on how to promote Southeast Asian cultures in order to fulfil the policy objectives of promoting multiculturalism. In the policy recommendation report, I recommended that training should be available for marriage migrants who wish to become teachers for Southeast Asian languages and cultures. This recommendation was implemented and TASAT and other organizations were selected through a competitive process to receive grants to conduct training. Since then, TASAT has been actively training more marriage migrants from Southeast Asia to become teachers of their own languages and cultures. These marriage migrants have in turn been given opportunities for conducting lectures and courses in various settings.

Moreover, in September 2005, the first collection of writings, paintings and photographs by marriage migrants was published. Titled *Don't Call Me Foreign Bride*, the book caught public attention and the first print was sold out in less than a month. As this book's editor, I noticed that the most common response from readers was amazement over how talented marriage migrants were, as well as their greater appreciation of multiculturalism and awareness of their own prejudices. Additionally, marriage migrants organized by TASAT has formed a theatre group and completed a documentary film, while others have gone all over Taiwan to share their experiences and issues as marriage migrants in Taiwan via various cultural forms based on their native cultures.

In short, projecting the voices of marriage migrants into the public sphere has helped to subvert the public image of marriage migrants as submissive, problematic and incompetent. Through theatre plays, paintings, writings and other types of sharing at various forums and activities, marriage migrants have challenged Taiwanese stereotypes of them. As a result of TASAT's active involvement, several members of TASAT have received awards. For example, the former chairperson, who still maintains her Thai nationality, received the "Life Sustainable Award 2007" initiated by a private foundation for her achievement as "Cultural Ambassador for Southeast Asian Cultures". She also received the prestigious Extraordinary Award in 2008 by the National Youth Commission of Taiwan for her public participation, especially for her involvement in TASAT and AHRLIM, in advocating immigrants' rights. This is the first time that this national award has been given to a non-Taiwanese resident.

THE DIVERSIONARY TACTICS OF THE GOVERNMENT

While the discourse of multiculturalism has been used effectively to advocate for immigrant rights in Taiwan, it has also reached an impasse. Although the Taiwanese government cannot negate demands for multiculturalism, it adheres to a conservative notion of the concept. Through sponsoring various cultural activities such as "traditional" Southeast Asian dances and songs, the government aims to project itself as appreciative of multiculturalism. A few instances, however, indicate that it is less receptive of a more expanded and radical version of multiculturalism. In 2004, the Council for Cultural Affairs organized several multicultural activities alongside the previously mentioned Conference on Ethnicities and Cultural Development, and TASAT was invited to perform at one of these multicultural events. When I informed the Council that TASAT could sing a song and perform a play, they were very pleased. However, upon hearing that the song and the play would be about the lives and experiences of marriage migrants, including the isolation and discrimination they face in Taiwan, they immediately asked if TASAT could perform "traditional" songs and dances instead. The Council eventually decided not to include TASAT in the programme, because they found TASAT's presentation to be too critical. Similarly, TASAT was also refused funding when other governmental agencies and private enterprises found its programmes too radical. As Wang (2006) noted, the concept of cultural citizenship in Taiwan government's policy narrowly focuses only on traditional forms of arts, neglecting other aspects such as enhancing citizens' social and political capacities. This situation echoes what Alund and Schierup (1993) have pointed out: that governments tend to determine which immigrant organizations are worth funding as a form of social control, co-opting selected immigrant organizations into the corporatist state and in the process marginalizing them politically.

In 2003, the "Measures for Guidance of and Assistance for Foreign and Mainland Spouses" issued by MOI provided for eight priority areas: coaching for adaptation, medical and reproduction health, employment rights protection, education and culture, parenting, personal safety protection, establishing comprehensive laws and systems, and "implementing propaganda for correct concepts" (MOI 2003). These aim to serve as guidelines for programmes in the implementation of policies stipulated in the Implementation Plan for Coaching Foreign Spouses for Adaptation. Clearly, the policy orientation towards marriage migrants focuses on assimilation and accommodation — multiculturalism was not mentioned — in which marriage migrants are perceived as inferior in education and culture, thus requiring assistance in improving their parenting capabilities.[11] In the assessment report released in December 2003, the accomplishments under the category of "propaganda for correct concepts", "equality among ethnicities and mutual acceptance" were said to be promoted but "multiculturalism" was not mentioned (MOI 2003). Nor was the Council for Cultural Affairs included as part of the task force in the MOI measures before 2004.

"Multiculturalism" was only first incorporated in the assessment report by MOI released in May 2005. The reported accomplishments under the objective of "implementing propaganda for correct concepts" included projects "promoting positive attitudes towards different cultures and ethnicities, and providing multicultural information" through radio and TV programmes in foreign languages, which by and large means English-medium programmes such as CNN, BBC, Discovery, National Geographic, HBO, Cinemax and Disney. The project of "designing multicultural teaching materials, promoting multicultural development and positive acceptance of foreign and mainland spouses" was the only project directly dealing with issues of multiculturalism. In the assessment report by the NIA[12] (2007), among the total of 125 classes, the categories of programmes offered to immigrants included Classes for Coaching Adaptation (63 per cent), Classes for Motorcycle Licenses (12 per cent), Multicultural Participation (6 per cent), Language Learning (5 per cent), Multicultural-Sensitivity Training Workshops (for service providers, 5 per cent), Computer Classes (3 per cent), Interpreters' Training (2 per cent), Food and Cultures (3 per cent), and Parenting Education (1 per cent). Among these nine categories of programmes, seven were geared towards facilitating immigrants' adaptation to Taiwanese society. Two of the programmes that seemed multicultural-oriented were in fact accommodation-oriented in their actual contents. "Interpreters' Training" was focused on helping interpreters provide information (e.g., on reproductive health care) that would aid migrants in their adaptation, while "Food and Cultures" trained foreign spouses to open restaurants serving Southeast Asian cuisine as a means of livelihood. The only two programmes directly targeting "multiculturalism" are multicultural participation and multicultural-sensitivity training workshops. However, reality was very different from rhetoric. The report stated that 71,926 persons benefited from (i.e., participated in) the multicultural participation programmes. In reality, 70,000 of the "beneficiaries" were participants of a job-hunting fair, where both local employers and foreign spouses attended; 600 of them attended a New Year Walk; 700 attended forums on how foreign spouses should adapt to Taiwanese society; and another 341 attended certain field trips or exhibitions as part of adaptation. The only rationale for counting these figures as "multicultural participation" is that these activities were attended by both local citizens and foreign spouses. The only programme that could be justifiably counted as promoting "multiculturalism" was the training workshop for multicultural-sensitivity, which was held only once and was attended by only twenty-three service providers. In other words, "multiculturalism" is arguably largely rhetoric and government agencies sometimes make up reports by manipulating figures and reporting programmes as "multicultural" events even if they do not qualify as "multicultural".

In the conclusion of NIA's assessment report in 2007, three targeted directions for future programmes are: supporting programmes to promote the rights and welfare of new immigrants and their families; promoting advocacy-oriented services, and promoting multicultural societies. It is too early to judge these future programmes. However, it is noteworthy that while the main objective of the first target (i.e., "supporting programs to promote the rights and welfare of the new immigrants and their families") is to help immigrants "acquire the medium to speak out to ease their emotions in Taiwan", this is likely to mean "governing" the voices and emotions of immigrants rather than to "empower" immigrants to speak out and demand rights and welfare.

It is becoming clearer that the state (as well as private corporations) can only tolerate NGOs that advocate a version of multiculturalism that is unthreatening to the status quo. Organizations such as TASAT, which practises a form of contentious politics (Tarrow 2003) challenging existent structures (e.g. ideology and legal system), find it increasingly difficult to gain access to funding, without which the more radical organizations find it even more difficult to survive. Some NGOs are very aware of the danger of losing funds, and so are forced to comply with the demands of the state rendering issues of marriage migrants' empowerment and subjectivity somewhat secondary. The original objective to help marriage migrants has, in many cases, been replaced by the goal of obtaining funds. This can lead such organizations to consciously or unconsciously exoticize and marginalize marriage migrants. One indicator of this trend is that the NGOs most successful in raising funds in the name of helping marriage migrants have not joined AHRLIM despite having been invited to. More disturbingly, many NGOs manipulate the image of multiculturalism in order to acquire funding from governments and corporations. For instance, I once observed that, in order to convince a government agency to fund its organization, one NGO had its Taiwanese staff pretend to be Vietnamese by wearing traditional Vietnamese costumes at a proposal competition meeting at the Council for Cultural Affairs.

RETHINKING CITIZENSHIP FROM THE PERSPECTIVES OF SOCIAL MOVEMENTS

As cross-border migration increases, there is much discussion aimed at reformulating citizenship to transcend its close association with the nation-state. However, most theories of citizenship are too philosophical or ethical, and issues of *how* to transform the exclusionary regime of citizenship to a more inclusive regime have been neglected. From the perspectives of social movements, this chapter brings the issues of how to transform citizenship to the fore in Taiwan's history and context.

Unlike countries in Europe, North America and Australia, the influx of im/migrants into Taiwan is a relatively recent phenomenon. Consequently, the concept of multiculturalism may have different implications in Taiwan compared to countries with longer histories of immigration. For example, critics in Europe worry that multiculturalism aggravates social-economic and cultural distinctions, which potentially foster spatial segregation and hamper im/migrants' integration into labour markets and educational systems (Bloemraad, Korteweg and Yurdakul 2008). However, the great majority of im/migrants in Taiwan are marriage migrants who are embedded in the households of the Taiwanese citizens and many of whom become mothers of Taiwanese citizens. Therefore, promoting multiculturalism is unlikely to lead to spatial segregation.

Under the exclusionary and patriarchal model of incorporation, Taiwan's policy of immigration for a very long time only allowed wives and children of Taiwan citizens to be naturalized. This tradition of incorporation was meant to maintain Taiwanese people as the descendants of the Chinese. Marriage migrant women from Southeast Asia have been eligible for naturalization only because of their capacity to reproduce Taiwanese children, but which in turn creates the opportunity to challenge the long tradition of citizenship based on the principle of *jus sanguinis*. Marriage migrants being literally part of Taiwanese families and especially as mothers of Taiwanese citizens, the government cannot deny outright that they are entitled to the right of teaching their children "mother-tongues" as well as the right to practise democracy. If the government denies these rights, it runs the risk of confounding its legitimacy because it can be easily accused of violating human rights and being undemocratic. Therefore, by radicalizing the current rhetoric of multiculturalism, human rights and democracy, the immigrant movement has successfully shaken Taiwan's long tradition of exclusionary citizenship.

Compared to migrant workers, marriage migrants have an advantage in challenging the traditional exclusionary models of citizenship, because transnational marriages involving citizens from different nation-states and their children represent living challenges to the boundaries of nation-states. If the government denies outright the right of marriage migrants to become citizens, it is likely to face a legitimacy crisis. In short, the increasing trend of marriage migration provides an unparalleled opportunity to challenge the traditional concept of citizenship closely associated with the nation-state.

Moreover, compared to countries with longer histories of immigration, Taiwan, as an emerging recipient country, lacks infrastructure for immigrants, such as interpreters in public services and ethnic media. In his critique of multiculturalism, Joppke (2001) argues that it is not clear why the adoption of another language would deprive a person of a meaningful context of choice because, unlike religion, a person can speak several languages. This may be true in the old immigrant-receiving countries. In Taiwan, however, a non-Chinese speaking person not only finds it hard to find a decent job but also runs the risks of violating laws and being penalized unfairly, simply because most policies and regulations are only accessible to the Chinese-literate, and no proper interpretation is provided in most circumstances. Therefore, issues of languages for im/migrants in Taiwan are not just cultural, but also embedded in the basic legal, political, social and economic rights of im/migrants. By advocating multiculturalism and thus creating a social and political space where languages of the im/migrants are important, the basic rights of im/migrants can be better protected, and at the same time more job opportunities are created for them, such as those of interpreters and language teachers.

As Werbner and Yuval-Davis (1999) point out, multiculturalism is a double-edged sword. While recognizing the prospects of multicultural citizenship, we should also note that multiculturalism can, however, soon be co-opted without changing the substantive rights or even formal rights of citizenship for the immigrants. This chapter illustrates how the Taiwan Government employs various diversionary tactics, such as manipulating figures, so that the policy of multiculturalism only remains largely at the level of rhetoric rather than reality.

Despite the impasse of multiculturalism and multicultural citizenship, AHRLIM and affiliated organizations have deliberately employed the government's rhetoric to advance the immigrant movement. Furthermore, as Werbner and Yuval-Davis (1999) point out, the language of citizenship, despite its gendered history, provides women with a valuable weapon in the fight for human, democratic, civil and social rights. Moreover, community-level women's activism is not only a way of raising consciousness and self-confidence; it also opens up new spaces for women's voices to be heard. In other words, though the concept of multicultural citizenship can be co-opted, it is also part of a political field where the discourses of governing and empowering immigrants are constantly contested. What is crucial in this constant contestation is that it can serve as the pre-political base for social movements where immigrants and locals are politicized and gradually achieve the power to effect long-term changes in mainstream politics.

Notes

1. An English version of this ("Does Taiwan genuinely respect plurality?") translated by Julian Clegg) also appeared in the *Taipei Times*, 4 August 2011, p. 8. <http://www.taipeitimes.com/News/editorials/archives/2011/08/04/2003509871>.

2. But some researchers have pointed out that EU citizenship is also exclusionary. Parekh (2006) for example, points out that the status of EU citizenship is only open to citizens of EU member countries and cannot be given directly to immigrants from non-European countries.
3. Though the Entry, Exit and Immigration Act was passed in 1999, it mostly stipulated regulations regarding entering and exiting Taiwan.
4. The word "foreign bride" is common parlance in Taiwan and reflects the discrimination against Third World women. I use the term in quotes to remind readers that it is an ideologically charged term. The term "marriage migrant" has been used to combat discrimination, after the International Conference on Border Control and Empowerment of Immigrant Brides, held in Taipei, in 2007. See the Introduction of Hsia (2010).
5. From 1 January 1985 to 28 February 2011, there were 446,143 foreign spouses in Taiwan, including those who have been naturalized (29.3 per cent from Southeast Asia and 64.2 per cent from Mainland China). 93.1 per cent of these foreign spouses are women. Among the women from Southeast Asia, 66.2 per cent are from Vietnam, 20.9 per cent from Indonesia, 4.4 per cent from Thailand, 5.1 per cent from the Philippines, and 3.4 per cent from Cambodia (Ministry of Interior 2011).
6. For marriage migrants from mainland China, the required period was eight years, but which was changed to six years as of 3 July 2009. For marriage migrants from other foreign countries, the required period was three years.
7. Hakka people are one of the significant ethnic minorities in Taiwan, whose ancestors migrated from the southeastern provinces of mainland China.
8. To promote multiculturalism, the Council for Cultural Affairs pronounced this Declaration, which was then followed by the National Conference on Ethnicities and Cultural Development and Multicultural Festival.
9. The four main "ethnic" groups formerly used in public rhetoric in Taiwan are the Indigenous Peoples, Hakka, Holok and Mainlanders.
10. From a pamphlet regarding the "Mother's Name" activity.
11. In the programme for medical and reproduction health, marriage migrants are even encouraged to be sterilized.
12. NIA was formally established on 2 January 2007. Since its establishment, NIA has been the primary government agency that implements the immigration policy formulated by the central government, mostly by the Ministry of Interior.

References

Alliance for Human Rights Legislation for Immigrants and Migrants (AHRLIM). Petition of the Alliance for Human Rights Legislation for Immigrants and

Migrants, 2003. <http://tw.myblog.yahoo.com/migrants2006>. Accessed 1 October 2008 (in Chinese).

Alund, A. "The Power of Definitions: Immigrant Women and Problem Ideologies". In *Paradoxes of Multiculturalism: Essays on Swedish Society*, edited by A. Alund and C.-U. Schierup, pp. 47–68. Aldershot: Avebury, 1991.

———. "Swedish Multi-Cultural Society". *Soundings* 9 (1998): 176–80.

——— and C.-U. Schierup. "The Thorny Road to Europe: Swedish Immigrant Policy in Transition". In *Racism and Migration in Western Europe*, edited by J. Wrench and J. Solomos, pp. 99–114. Oxford: Berg, 1993.

Basch, L., N. Glick Schiller, and C. Szanton Blanc. *Nations Unbound: Transnational Projects, Postcolonial Predicaments and Deterritorialized Nation-States*. Langhorne, PA: Gordon and Breach, 1994.

Barry B. *Culture and Equality: An Egalitarian Critique of Multiculturalism*. Cambridge, MA: Harvard University Press, 2001.

Bissoondath N. *Selling Illusions: The Cult of Multiculturalism in Canada*. Toronto: Penguin, 1994.

Bloemraad, I. "Who Claims Dual Citizenship? The Limits of Postnationalism, the Possibilities of Transnationalism, and the Persistence of Traditional Citizenship". *International Migrant Review* 38, no. 2 (2004): 389–426.

———, A. Korteweg, and G. Yurdakul. "Citizenship and Immigration: Multiculturalism, Assimilation, and Challenges to the Nation-State". *Annual Review of Sociology* 34 (2008): 153–79.

Boal, A. *The Theatre of the Oppressed*. Adrian Jackson (Trans.). London: Pluto Press, 1979.

Brubaker, R. "The Return of Assimilation? Changing Perspectives on Immigration and its Sequel in France, Germany, and the United States". *Ethnic and Racial Studies* 24, no. 4 (2001): 531–48.

Castles, S. and A. Davidson. *Citizenship and Migration: Globalization and the Politics of Belonging*. Basingstoke: Macmillan, 2000.

Chang, M.-K. "On the Formation and Problems of the Discourses of 'Pluralism' and 'Multi-Culturalism' in Taiwan". In *The Future Taiwan*, edited by Xue Tiandong, pp. 223–75. Taipei: Huatai Pub, 2002 (in Chinese).

Cheng, L. "Transnational Labor, Citizenship and the Taiwan State". In *East Asian Law: Universal Norms and Local Cultures*, edited by A. Rosett, L. Cheng and M.Y.K. Woo, pp. 85–105. London and New York: RoutledgeCurzon, 2002.

China Times. "Nationalisation tests too harsh for foreign spouses". 7 July 2005 (in Chinese).

Faist, T. "Dual Citizenship as Overlapping Membership". *Willy Brandt Series of Working Papers in International Migration and Ethnic Relations* 3, no. 1 (2001): 1–41.

Faulks, K. *Citizenship*. London and New York: Routledge, 2000.

Freire, P. *Pedagogy of the Oppressed*. New York: Continuum, 1970.
Ghai, Y. "Rights, Social Justice, and Globalization in East Asia". In *The East Asian Challenge for Human Rights*, edited by J. Bauer and D. Bell, pp. 241–63. Cambridge: Cambridge University Press, 1999.
Harris, N. *The New Untouchables*. London: Penguin, 1995.
Heater, D. *Citizenship: The Civic Ideal in World History, Politics and Education*. London: Longman, 1990.
Hsia, H.-C. "Internationalization of Capital and Trade in Asian Women: The Case of 'Foreign Brides' in Taiwan". In *Women and Globalization*, edited by D. Aguilar and A. Lacsamana, pp. 181–229. Amherst, New York: Humanity Press, 2004.
———. "Empowering 'Foreign Brides' and Community through Praxis-Oriented Research". *Societies without Borders* 1 (2006): 89–108.
———. "Imaged and Imagined Threat to the Nation: The Media Construction of "Foreign Brides" Phenomenon as Social Problems in Taiwan". *Inter-Asia Cultural Studies* 8, no. 1 (2007): 55–85.
———. "The Development of Immigrant Movement in Taiwan: the Case of Alliance of Human Rights Legislation for Immigrants and Migrants". *Development and Society* 37, no. 2 (2008): 187–217.
———. "Foreign Brides, Multiple Citizenship and Immigrant Movement in Taiwan." *Asia and the Pacific Migration Journal* 18, no. 1 (2009): 17–46.
———. "For Better or For Worse: Comparative Research on Equity and Access for Marriage Migrants". Hong Kong: Asia Pacific Mission for Migrants, 2010.
——— and L.C.-H Huang. "Taiwan". In *For Better or For Worse: Comparative Research on Equity and Access for Marriage Migrants*, edited by H.-C. Hsia, pp. 27–73. Hong Kong: Asia Pacific Mission for Migrants, 2010.
Hsu, Y.-H. *Study on the Living Conditions of the Children of Foreign Spouses Families from Southeast Asia*. Research report funded by the Children's Bureau, Ministry of Interior, 2004 (in Chinese).
Joppke, C., ed. *Challenges to the Nation-State: Immigration in Western Europe and the United States*. Oxford: Oxford University Press, 1998.
———. "Multicultural Citizenship: A Critique". *European Journal of Sociology* 42, no. 2 (2001): 431–47.
———. "The Retreat of Multiculturalism in the Liberal State: Theory and Policy". *British Journal of Sociology* 55, no. 2 (2004): 237–57.
Kofman, E., A. Phizacklea, P. Raghuram, and R. Sales. *Gender and International Migration in Europe: Employment, Welfare and Politics*. London and New York: Routledge, 2000.
Kymlicka, W. *Multicultural Citizenship*. Oxford: Oxford University Press, 1995.
———. *Politics in the Vernacular: Nationalism, Multiculturalism and Citizenship*. Oxford: Oxford University Press, 2001.

Lin, S.-Y. *The First Nation: The Constitution Meanings of the Indigenous Peoples Movement in Taiwan*. Taipei: Chien-Wei, 2000 (in Chinese).
Lister, R. *Citizenship: Feminist Perspectives*. London: Macmillan, 1997.
Ministry of Interior. "Special Report on the Guidance and Education for Foreign and Mainland Spouses", 3 December 2003. <http://www.immigration.gov.tw/Outweb/Ch9/f9a-26.doc>. Accessed 3 March 2009 (in Chinese).
Ministry of Interior. "General Information of the Bill of Organic Act of National Immigration Agency", 2003a. <http://www.ey.gov.tw/public/Attachment/20031121162549653.doc>. Accessed 28 August 2009 (in Chinese).
———. "Implementation Plan for Coaching Foreign Brides for Adaptation", 2003b. <http://www.ris.gov.tw/ch9/f9a-12.html>. Accessed 5 March 2009 (in Chinese).
———. "Achievements of the Implementation of the Measures for Guidance and Assistance for Foreign and Mainland Spouses", 27 May 2005. <http://www.immigration.gov.tw/Outweb/ch9/0940601b.doc>. Accessed 3 March 2009 (in Chinese).
———. "Statistics on the Marriages between the Citizens and Foreigner", 2011. Available at <http://www.immigration.gov.tw/public/Attachment/13249411378.xls>. Accessed on 20 April 2011 (in Chinese).
National Immigration Agency (NIA). "Assessment Report of Year 2007 on Subsidising Local Governments for Coaching Foreign and Mainland Spouses for Adaptation", 2007. <http://www.immigration.gov.tw/Outweb/Ch9/b1234.doc>. Accessed 3 March 2009 (in Chinese).
Okin, S.M. *Is Multiculturalism Bad for Women?* Princeton, NJ: Princeton University Press, 1999.
Parekh, B. *Rethinking Multiculturalism: Cultural Diversity and Political Theory*. 2nd ed. New York: Palgrave Macmillan, 2006.
Parreñas, R.S. *Servants of Globalization: Women, Migration and Domestic Work*. Stanford, CA: Stanford University Press, 2001.
Piper, N. *Racism, Nationalism and Citizenship: Ethnic Minorities in Britain and Germany*. Sydney: Ashgate, 1998.
——— and M. Roces, eds. *Wife or Worker? Asian Women and Migration*. New York: Rowman and Littlefield, 2003.
Sassen, S. *Losing Control?* New York: Columbia University Press, 1996.
Soysal, Y.N. *Limits of Citizenship: Migrants and Post-National Membership in Europe*. London: University of Chicago Press, 1994.
Tarrow, S. *Power in Movement: Social Movements and Contentious Politics*. 2nd ed. Cambridge: Cambridge University Press, 2003.
Tormey, A. "'Everyone with Eyes Can See the Problem': Moral Citizens and the Space of Irish Nationhood". *International Migration* 45, no. 3 (2007): 69–100.
Tseng, Y.-F. "Politics of Importing Foreigners: Foreign Labor Policy in Taiwan".

In *Migration between States and Markets*, edited by H. Entzinger, M. Martiniello, and C.W. de Wenden, pp. 101–20. Sydney: Ashgate Publishing Limited, 2004.

Wang, L. "The Construction of Cultural Citizenship: The Development of Cultural Policy and the Practice of Citizenship". *Journal of Public Administration* 20 (2006): 129–59 (in Chinese).

Yuval-Davis N. "Citizenship and Difference". In *Gender and Nation*, pp. 68–88. London: Sage, 1997.

Werbner, P. and N. Yuval-Davis. "Women and the New Discourse of Citizenship. In *Women, Citizenship and Difference*, edited by N. Yuval-Davis and P. Werbner, pp. 1–38. London and New York: Zed Books, 1999.

II

Identities

6

MIXED-ETHNIC CHILDREN RAISED BY SINGLE THAI MOTHERS IN JAPAN
A Choice of Ethnic Identity

Kayoko ISHII

INTRODUCTION

This chapter investigates whether existing studies of the identity of mixed-ethnic children are adaptable to studies of such children in Japan, a country which was formerly predominantly mono-ethnic[1] where the mainstream ethnic group is *non-white*. While copious literature can be found concerning the identity of mixed-ethnic children, these studies have tended to draw from empirical data from white-dominated countries such as the United Kingdom or United States (Bratter 2007, p. 826; Eytan et al. 2007, p. 2; Patel 2009, p. 122). Thus, much of the literature concerns *whiteness* and its relation to mixed-ethnic populations, and empirical data on mixed-ethnic children from entirely or predominantly non-white societies remain scarce (Bratter 2007, p. 825). In this study, the identity of mixed-ethnic children will be examined on the basis of empirical data gathered in Japan. The results of this study will contribute to our understanding of how existing research frameworks might be adaptable to cases of diverse mixed-ethnic populations in Asia.

This study examines the following two issues relating to mixed-ethnic children in Japan: (1) whether mixed-ethnic children show a tendency to assimilate into the perceived mainstream and (2) whether mixed-ethnic children illustrate a *multi-ethnic identity*. The study analyses case studies of mixed-ethnic children in the target area of Nagoya City and its surroundings and pays particular attention to cases of children raised by single Thai mothers. First, I will provide an overview of current demographic shifts in Japan pertaining to the number of mixed-ethnic children and the rates of divorce among inter-ethnic couples. Second, I will analyse the choice of ethnic identity considered by mixed-ethnic children; essentially, whether to assimilate into the mainstream or not. Third, the *multi-ethnic identity* of mixed-ethnic children will be analysed. Finally, the mechanism that determines *multi-ethnic identity* will be examined through some case studies of mixed-ethnic children raised by single Thai mothers.

A Sociological Perspective on the Identity of Mixed-Ethnic Children

The concept of race as developed in both scientific and cultural discourses is a social product linked to notions of hierarchy within human beings (Patel 2009, pp. 1–2). The same can be said of the concept of ethnicity. Previous studies have indicated that the boundaries and identities of race and ethnicity are contextual and fluid (Bhugra 2004, p. 85; Wood 2009, p. 437). It is now understood that notions of race and ethnicity create boundaries and hierarchies among human beings (Patel 2009, p. 3), and that the individual possesses a self only in relation to the selves of the other members of his/her social group (Patel 2009, p. 12). In other words, racial/ethnic identities are not fixed but open to interpretation, modification, and interaction (Bratter 2007, p. 827; Patel 2009, p. 92). People choose their own racial identity, and in so doing, they settle on an identity best suited to a given context (Patel 2009, p. 120). Therefore, the chosen racial identity of mixed-ethnic children provides an important lens through which to understand race relations and racial differences (Bratter 2007, p. 827). Finally, we can perceive these identity[2] choices as reflective of the hegemonic stratification of social and economic spheres (Al-Hazza and Bucher 2008, p. 211; Chappell and Faltis 2006, p. 259).

Even as late as the early twentieth century, mixed-ethnic people were regarded in academic analysis as marginally human (Stonequist 1937). The assumption was that people raised between or among two cultural groups faced serious psychological difficulties as a result of being rejected by the dominant, lighter-skinned group and looked upon as different by the darker-skinned group (Patel 2009, p. 85). However, by the 1970s, empirical data began to accumulate and discussions of ethnic identity began to increase in number and complexity. The discussions tended towards two strands of thought. One strand said that racially stratified societies would place children of racially ambiguous parentage with that of the lower-status non-white parent (Bratter 2007, p. 824), and thus, all coloured or non-white people would be classified as "black" (Patel 2009, p. 86). Another strand said that racial mixing could result in the *whitening* of dark-skinned racial minorities by creating *white suburbs* viewed as culturally similar to the dominant group (Bonilla-Silva 2004, pp. 932–33; Bratter 2007, p. 824). Thus, certain racial minorities denied access to the *white suburbs* would remain at the bottom of the racial hierarchy (Bonilla-Silva 2004, pp. 932–33).

In contrast to such discussions, recent literature provides the aforementioned view of individual- and context-specificity, in which a person is understood to make the choice most suitable to his/her situation (Bratter 2007, p. 825). Modern literature argues that the ethnic identities of mixed-ethnic children are affected by many different factors, including class or societal status (Wood 2009, p. 436); national/cultural image or religion, physical features, gender, age, geographical location, and so on (Patel 2009, p. 15). Furthermore, recent literature suggests that some mixed-ethnic children create multi-layered, flexible, dynamic, and diverse identities constructed from established racial norms (Bratter 2007, p. 826; Eytan et al., 2007, p. 2; Patel 2009, p. 122). This is referred to as *multiethnic identity*. Unfortunately, almost all the empirical data in the existing literature pertains to white-dominated societies (Bonilla-Silva 2004, p. 931; Bratter 2007; Patel 2009; Wood 2009). Very few studies exist regarding the racial and ethnic identity of mixed-ethnic children in predominantly non-white societies, or even of mixed-ethnic children of non-white/non-white parentage (Bratter 2007, p. 825). This chapter examines this underdeveloped area of research using empirical data from mixed-ethnic children in Japan.

BACKGROUND

Intermarriage and Mixed-Ethnic Children in Japan

Since the 1980s, the number and percentage of inter-ethnic couples has been increasing in Japan and other countries in East Asia.[3] In 2005, one out of every twenty newly registered couples in Japan was a marriage between a Japanese citizen and a foreign national[4] (SID-MHLW[5] 2005). Until the 1970s, the term *intermarriage* in Japan usually referred to marriages between U.S. soldiers stationed in Japan and women from surrounding areas. However, since the 1980s, the number of inter-ethnic couples (excluding marriages to U.S. soldiers) has dramatically increased. The social image of inter-ethnic couples, as portrayed by the Japanese mass media, is that of Japanese women married to *Western*[6] husbands. However, presently, more than 80 per cent of inter-ethnic marriages in Japan are between Japanese and *non-Western* nationals (SID-MHCD 2005). As a result of the increase of inter-ethnic marriages, the number of mixed-ethnic children has also increased in Japan since the 1980s. Presently, one out of fifty newly registered babies is a mixed-ethnic child[7] (SID-MHLW 2005). As both the marriage rate and birth rate among Japanese-Japanese couples have decreased, the ratio of newborn mixed-ethnic babies has been increasing despite the fact that the overall total number of newborns has not increased since early 2000s (SID-MHLW 1987–2005). This phenomenon has rapidly expanded during the last twenty years. Thus, while mixed-ethnic persons are currently still uncommon among Japanese adults, the first generation of mass mixed-ethnic children are about to enter the Japanese job and marriage markets. Twenty years from now, the mixed-ethnic population will constitute one out of twenty Japanese adults and will play a key role in sustaining the Japanese economy and society. Even in these purely numerical dimensions, Japan is going through a dramatic transition, from a *mono-ethnic* country to that of a multiethnic country. However, compared to studies on countries with a white mainstream population (where mixed-ethnic discussions are common and have traditionally been controversial), there is relatively little research that has focused on multiethnic issues in Japan.

Divorce among Inter-Ethnic Couples

Existing sociological research scarcely discusses the issue of divorce among inter-ethnic couples and the condition of mixed-ethnic children of these divorced couples. As the number of inter-ethnic marriages has increased, so has the number of divorces among inter-ethnic couples (SID-MHLW 2005). As a result of this increase of such divorces, the number of mixed-ethnic children who experience parental divorce has also increased. In 2005, the parents of nearly 7,000 mixed-ethnic children were divorced.[8] The increasing rate of divorce amongst foreign wives and their Japanese husbands has been particularly notable since a case was made in 1996 that foreign wives (with a spouse visa) who are divorced may be entitled to a proper visa if they are fostering children who are Japanese nationals.[9]

Mixed-Ethnic Children Raised by Single Foreign Mothers

Presently, there are no formal statistics to ascertain the total number of mixed-ethnic children raised by single foreign mothers in Japan. Table 6.1 and Figure 6.1 shows (1) the number of newly inter-ethnic couples, (2) the number of divorced inter-ethnic couples, and (3) the number of newly registered mixed-ethnic children in Japan during the last twenty years. The numbers in the table are limited to inter-ethnic marriage between Japanese husbands and their foreign wives so as to focus on the discussion of single foreign mothers here.

There have been 427,537 mixed-ethnic couples (Japanese husband-foreign wife) married in Japan during the last twenty years, 227,318 children were born, and 123,116 couples were divorced. Put another way, the parents of 65,719 mixed-ethnic children were divorced. Empirically, *Western* mothers from North American countries and Western Europe tend to return to their countries with their children after their divorce. *Non-Western* mothers and mothers from East European countries and the former U.S.S.R. countries tend to remain in Japan even after the divorce.[10] In the case of mixed-ethnic children of Thai mothers, the divorce rate of Japanese husbands and their Thai wives in 2005 was estimated at almost 48 per cent among newly registered Japanese-Thai couples.[11] Although the precise number is not known, what is certain here is that the number of mixed-ethnic children raised by single foreign mothers has definitely increased. However, to date, there is no known research on either the situation or identity of mixed-ethnic children raised by single foreign mothers in Japan. This research focuses on such mixed-ethnic children, particularly from the standpoint of their identity.

TABLE 6.1
Estimated Number of Mixed Ethnic Children of Divorced Foreign Mothers and Related Numbers

Year	Marriage	Divorce (rate)	Mixed child	Expected numbers of mixed child of divorced foreign mother	Marriage	Divorce (rate)	No. of newborn mixed child	Expected numbers of mixed child of divorced foreign mother
1987	10,176	—	5,538	—	—	—	—	—
1988	12,267	—	6,615	—	—	—	—	—
1989	17,800	—	7,390	—	—	—	—	—
1990	20,026	—	8,695	—	—	—	—	—
1991	19,096	—	10,027	—	—	—	—	—
1992	19,423	6,174 (31.8%)	11,658	3,706	1,585	171 (10.8%)	473	51
1993	20,092	5,987 (29.8%)	12,412	3,699	1,926	186 (9.7%)	691	67
1994	19,216	5,996 (31.2%)	13,414	4,186	1,836	239 (13.0%)	748	97
1995	20,787	6,153 (29.6%)	13,371	3,958	1,915	315 (16.4%)	851	140
1996	21,162	6,171 (29.2%)	13,752	4,010	1,760	320 (18.2%)	827	150
1997	20,902	7,080 (33.9%)	13,580	4,600	1,688	362 (21.4%)	859	184
1998	22,159	7,867 (35.5%)	13,635	4,841	1,699	435 (25.6%)	852	218
1999	24,272	8,514 (35.1%)	13,004	4,561	2,024	540 (26.7%)	836	223
2000	28,326	9,807 (34.6%)	13,996	4,638	2,137	612 (28.6%)	736	211
2001	31,972	10,676 (33.4%)	13,177	4,400	1,840	682 (37.1%)	742	275
2002	27,957	12,087 (43.2%)	13,294	5,748	1,536	699 (45.5%)	670	305
2003	27,881	12,103 (43.4%)	12,690	5,509	1,445	678 (46.9%)	638	299
2004	30,907	12,071 (39.1%)	13,198	5,155	1,640	685 (41.8%)	579	242
2005	33,116	12,430 (37.5%)	17,872	6,708	1,637	782 (47.8%)	509	243
Total	427,537	123,116	227,318	65,719	24,668	6,706	10,011	2,705

Source: Vital Statistics of Japan (2005).

FIGURE 6.1
Estimated Number of Mixed-ethnic Children of Divorced Foreign Mothers

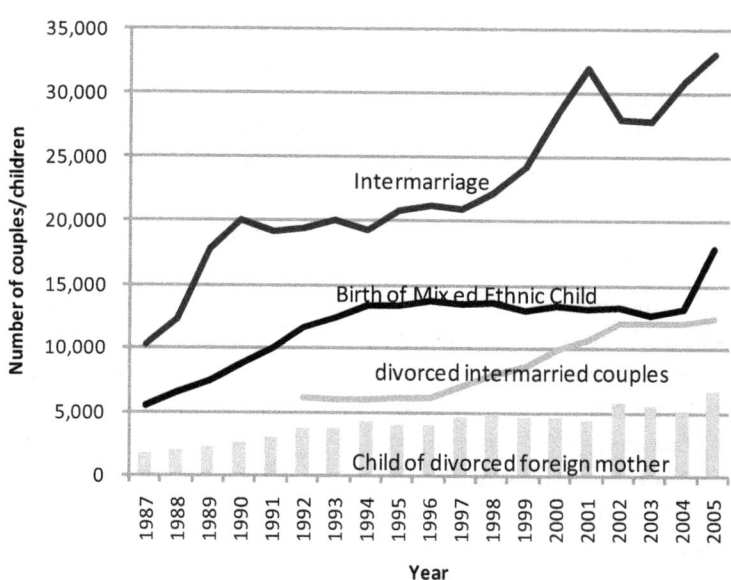

Source: Vital Statistics of Japan (2005).

RESEARCH OBJECTIVES

I conducted this study to test the following questions. First, do mixed-ethnic children show a tendency to assimilate into a mainstream ethnic group when it is not white? Second, under what circumstances would these mixed-ethnic children develop a *multi-ethnic identity?*

To my knowledge, this study represents the first attempt to examine the ethnic identity of mixed-ethnic children of divorced parents in Japan. This study adds another dimension to the prevailing academic views of the identity of such children through the following assumptions. First, the *choice* of ethnic identity for mixed-ethnic children is affected not only by the mainstream ethnicity but also by *ethnic power relations*. Second, *multi-ethnic identity* is found among mixed-ethnic children who *cannot* identify themselves with any advantageous ethnic groups within local ethnic power relations.

RESEARCH METHODOLOGIES

Data for this study was gathered using two types of research methodology: observation and interviews. Both observation and interviews were conducted between 2004 and 2008 in the target area of Nagoya City and its surroundings. Registered foreign residents comprise about 2.8 per cent of the target area's 2.2 million residents. Interviews were conducted in Japanese, English, or Thai, depending on interviewee preference.

In the observational part of the study, the following groups were observed: two mothers' groups,[12] which included approximately forty children; two NGOs supporting female migrants, which included more than fifty children; and twelve mixed-ethnic families (including both couples and children). The ages of the children observed ranged from eleven months to seventeen years. Data on mixed-ethnic children raised by single foreign mothers was gathered through the interview method. In addition, four cases were observed and in-depth interviews were conducted formally and informally between 2004 and 2008. The ages of the children interviewed ranged from six to twelve years.

The four in-depth case studies shared common characteristics. Japanese-Thai children were chosen as subjects because research on Japanese-Thai inter-ethnic couples and children is limited despite their comparatively high numbers (SID-HMLW 2005).[13] It must be noted that Thai mothers of mixed-ethnic children were understandably cautious and sensitive with regard to their children's identity; as a result, the sample size of the study was smaller than desired.

RESULTS

Choosing a Single Ethnicity

My investigation showed that the mixed-ethnic children tended to identify themselves with a single ethnic identity. Japanese-Western children tended to identify themselves with the *Western* ethnicity of their father or mother, rather than by their Japanese ethnicity. In contrast, Japanese-*non-Western* children tended to identify themselves with their Japanese ethnicity rather than by the ethnicity of their foreign mothers or fathers. The following comments are indicative:

> "Call me Michael; don't call me by a funny name" (10-year-old Japanese-English boy when called by his middle name which is a typical Japanese name.)

"I feel sorry for my mother because she is Thai" (8-year old Japanese-Thai boy.)

The boys were mixed-ethnic children of the same generation, living in the same area, and have never lived outside Japan. Both of them were attending local council schools. However, the Japanese-English boy identifies himself as English, whereas the Japanese-Thai boy identifies himself as Japanese. What does this mean? The Japanese-English boy's statement reveals a feeling of *racial advantage* over Japanese ethnicity by referring to a typical Japanese name as "funny". In contrast, the Japanese-Thai boy appears to have feelings of racial advantage over Thai ethnicity when he expresses his regret about his mother being Thai. In short, each boy chooses that single ethnic identity which is more *advantageous* to him from the choices available. This is confirmed by existing literature that points out that mixed-ethnic children choose an ethnicity that is more *advantageous* for them (Okun and Khait-Marelly 2008, p. 1376), but to date, scholars have not related this phenomenon to the effects of the mainstream-minority relationship and ethnic power relations.

Multi-Ethnic Identity of Children Raised by Single Foreign Mothers

Mixed-ethnic children raised by single Thai mothers often develop something resembling a *multi-ethnic identity*. For example, we have the case of K, a 7-year-old boy born to a Japanese father and Thai mother in the early 2000s in Japan. When K was asked which nation he belongs to (in Japanese, "who he is"), he replied, "I am not simply Japanese or Thai. I am partly Japanese, but partly Thai." This kind of reply was not common among the other Thai-Japanese mixed-ethnic children investigated in this research. Most Japanese-Thai children identify themselves with a single ethnic identity, that is, Japanese. K's parents divorced when he was four years old, and parental authority was formally bestowed on his Thai mother. After his parents' divorce, he and his mother stayed in an NGO shelter for a few months. His mother then found a job first at a municipal office, and then at a local company office a few years later. K's mother earns a monthly income that is sufficient to raise a child, and she does not maintain contact with her former Japanese husband and his family. She never told her family in Thailand about her situation because she did not want them to worry. As a result, she receives no support from K's grandparents on either side. K's mother also maintains a certain distance from people she calls "happy Thai madams", the Thai wives of Japanese men who are *happily* living in the area. Thus, K's mother also cannot expect to receive support from the other Thai women in the area.[14] Because K's mother has a proper visa and a regular position at a company, she receives public support granted for working mothers. She and K speak Japanese at home. All of K's friends at school are Japanese, and K seems to have assimilated into Japanese society.

ANALYSIS

Ethnic Power Relations Reflected in the Behaviour of Foreign Mothers

Both the advantages and disadvantages of ethnic identification by the children mentioned above seem to be reflections of local ethnic power relations. When I asked the foreign mothers of mixed-ethnic children whether or not they were able to perform the cultural/religious rituals of their native countries while in Japan, I found obvious differences between the responses of the Western and non-Western mothers. A typical response from a Western mother, a German mother in her mid-30s who is married to a Japanese man and has three children, is the following:

> We celebrate Easter and Christmas. Neighbours come to see what a *real* Christmas celebration is like, where we bake a whole turkey and set up a huge Christmas tree, which is a real fir tree that almost reaches the ceiling. The neighbours take photographs of themselves next to our Christmas tree.

In contrast, the following is a typical non-Western response, made by a Thai mother in her early 40s, married to a Japanese man, and raising three children:

> I am lucky because my Japanese mother-in-law is generous enough to allow me to participate in the *Songkram* festival (a Thai traditional cultural festival held for Thai migrants at a nearby park).

These comments seem to reflect differences in the ethnic power relations between foreign mothers and their families. Western mothers tend to take it for granted that major cultural/religious events from their native countries, such as Christmas or Easter, are accepted and even welcomed by Japanese families and neighbours. On the other hand, Thai mothers feel that they are *lucky* if their Japanese family allows them to *join in* the Thai cultural/religious events held in the park or community centre. Unlike their Western counterparts, Thai mothers do not celebrate any Thai cultural/religious events within their family homes. However, in a significant reversal, every Western mother interviewed was not happy with the mere acceptance by their Japanese family. The Western mothers often claimed that they were restricted in their ability to act as they normally would in their home countries; on the contrary, most Thai mothers claimed that they were managing well with their Japanese families.

Ethnic Power Relations Reflected in Choice of School

Another obvious demonstration of the abovementioned ethnic power relations is the voluntary segregation of mixed-ethnic children in the schools of the area. Most mixed-ethnic children attend local council schools, where school placement is officially determined on the basis of the residential district. However, four other schools are especially popular among parents who did not wish to place their children in local council schools:

(1) School A: an international school managed by a global international school group with its headquarters in Europe;
(2) School B: an international school managed by a local private school group;
(3) School C: a local private school that markets its *cosmopolitan* atmosphere; and
(4) School D: a local council school that many mixed-ethnic children attend.

For confidentiality reasons, none of these four schools revealed their actual number of mixed-ethnic students, but it is clear from interviews and observations that Japanese-Western children tend to attend schools A, B, and C, while Japanese-non-Western children tend to attend school D. Mothers who sent their children to schools A, B, and C made the following comments when explaining their choices:

> I did not want my child to experience the extreme academic competition that is prevalent in the Japanese school system. [American mother in her mid-40s, who has two mixed-ethnic children with her Japanese husband]

> I was afraid that my child would not become a bilingual speaker, since my husband decided to not return to the United States as initially planned. [Japanese mother in her mid-30s with an American husband and one mixed-ethnic child]

These mothers sent their children to international and private schools with a high ratio of mixed-ethnic children because they believed it to be advantageous for academic and social reasons. The following comments from mothers who sent their Japanese-*Western* children to local council schools seemed to confirm the first pair's view of private schooling:

> I would like to send my boy to an international school, but the cost is tremendously high. I have no choice but to send him to an ordinary local school. [Japanese mother in her mid-30s, married to an English man, and raising one mixed-ethnic child]

> I know it is better for my mixed-ethnic children to go to schools like school A, so that they can become *properly* bilingual and can be raised in a more cosmopolitan atmosphere. But it is too expensive for us. [Japanese mother in her late 20s with an Australian husband and two mixed-ethnic children]

Mothers of Japanese-*Western* mixed-ethnic children tended to view schools A, B, and C as preferable options, and sent their children to local council schools only if they could not afford the preferred schools.

The following is a comment from a Japanese mother in her early 40s with a Brazilian husband and two mixed-ethnic children who attend school D:

> I heard that it had quite a cosmopolitan atmosphere, so we moved to this area in order to send our children to this school.

On the surface, this mother's comment seems to be similar to that of mothers who send their mixed-ethnic children to schools A, B, and C. However, their situations are actually different; school D is an ordinary local council school, but most of the mixed-ethnic children are of Japanese-non-Western parents. One Japanese mother, in her late 30s, married to a Bangladeshi man and who has two mixed-ethnic children in school D, made the following comment:

> I used to send my girl to a local school nearby, but she would come home with a sallow face every day. She never said why, but I suspected that she was bullied at school. So, my husband and I decided to move to this area because we know that in this school, mixed-ethnic children are not unusual.

When I asked this mother why she did not send her children to schools A, B, or C, where there are also many mixed-ethnic children, she responded: "Because those are schools for white kids."

Most mixed-ethnic children, however, attend the nearest, cheapest, and most accessible local council school. The proportion of mixed-ethnic children who attend each of the abovementioned schools is not large. However, the point here is that for parents in search of *better educational circumstances* for their mixed-ethnic children, the choice seems to be different for those with Western parentage.

Effects of Ethnic Power Relations on Mixed-ethnic Children

The family is the primary institution through which ethnic power relations affect mixed-ethnic children. For instance, when, as an NGO delegate I attended a Thai festival held for migrants in the target area, I observed a Japanese woman who had brought her Japanese-Thai grandchild along. The Japanese grandmother did not even greet me as she mistook me for one of the Thai mothers. I said to the 8-year-old granddaughter "your grandma seems to be in a hurry this morning (that is why she forgot to greet me)". The girl replied "No, my grandma hates Thai people". This is likely to be an extreme case. However, such comments by the children reveal their exposure to ethnic bias and power relations at home.

Japanese fathers can also be agents in the conduct of ethnic power relations through their relationships with their wives. Although most fathers of Japanese-Thai children whom I contacted in this study claimed they accepted their Thai wives' culture, more subtle expressions of ethnic prejudice remained apparent. The following is a typical comment from a Japanese man in his late 40s, who had been married to a Thai woman for fifteen years:

> (Responding to the suggestion that he should send his wife to a free Japanese language course to learn Japanese writing) No, no. How can she master Japanese writing? She has to take care of the children. She won't be able to do that.

The husbands of the Thai mothers I met usually checked and wrote their wives' e-mails, ostensibly because their wives were unable to appropriately write/read in Japanese. Indeed, owing to motives that might be surmised, Japanese husbands sometimes preferred not to provide their Thai wives with the opportunity to improve their Japanese language skills. With rare exceptions, the illiteracy and powerlessness of Thai mothers is actively *preserved* in Japanese society. The following is a comment made by a Japanese man in his mid-30s who had recently married a Thai woman.

> My wife is just like a baby here. I worry about her all the time; so, since I married her, I go directly back home after work every day. I stopped drinking beer with my colleagues after work. If my wife were *not like this*, how could I be such a good husband? How else could I love my wife so deeply?

The thought processes of the men behind such comments suggest that they believe in and value the powerlessness in women. Moreover, this belief and value is not limited to husbands, but might also be ascribed to their mothers (Japanese mothers-in-law of Thai wives), as the following comment by a Thai wife in her early 30s signifies:

> When I first met my Japanese mother-in-law, she was happy and said, "I am a lucky old woman to not have an insolent, spoiled, and sophisticated young Japanese daughter-in-law. My son did a good job in choosing a young woman from a country like Thailand, where people still value thriftiness and patience."

Such a comment suggests that a Japanese mother-in-law might be happy not because of the individual character of her daughter-in-law, but because she is Thai. Such mothers-in-law often believe that Thai women are just like *traditional Japanese wives* — docile, obedient, patient, and unsophisticated — *simply because they are Thai.*

When compared to the experiences and position of Western mothers in relation to their Japanese family, this finding appears to correlate with extant literature on perceptions of "whiteness" and Japaneseness (Ashikari 2005). Such a reading associates whiteness as modernity and positions Japan and Japanese culture in a superior position to other nations and cultures in Asia, on par with even as it departs from the West (Bonnett 2002; Wagatsuma 1967). In this context, Thai mothers are viewed as less sophisticated but potentially more traditional and obedient wives and daughters-in-law — a positive representation in the eyes of family but one that nevertheless undermines their own agency within the family.

It is important to note that many Thai mothers themselves do not question or oppose such biased images, and might even unconsciously reproduce them when they try to be *good wives* or *good mothers*. In such a situation, Thai mothers tend to remain obedient, docile, and powerless, as expected by their Japanese family (though perhaps not explicitly). Under such circumstances, it is not surprising that Japanese-Thai children would say things like "I feel sorry for my mother because she is Thai." The more Thai mothers try to be the ideal mother by satisfying the expectations of their Japanese husbands or parents-in-law, the more they seem to be powerless. On the whole, this study reveals that Thai mothers are usually treated as foreigners by their Japanese family, including their children.

Why Mixed-Ethnic Children Raised by Single Thai Mothers Gain a Multiethnic Identity

Single mothers who are independent, socially mature, and who are the sole guardians of their children are a contrast to the "ideal Thai mothers" who live with their Japanese families. For the mixed-ethnic children of single Thai mothers, it is not easy to simply accept existing ethnic power relations. Furthermore, it is not easy for children of Thai single mothers to disconnect their identities from those of their mothers. Japanese-Thai children who are raised by single Thai mothers usually lose contact with their Japanese father and their father's Japanese family at a very young age. Also, they usually do not have any Japanese family members who might influence and support their ethnic identity construction. As a result, it seems difficult for them to gain an ethnic identity that is exclusively or predominantly Japanese.

At the same time, it is also not easy for Japanese-Thai children brought up by single Thai mothers, to identify themselves as exclusively or mainly Thai. For example, when a 10-year-old Japanese-Thai boy raised by a single Thai mother was asked what nation he belonged to, replied "...I'm not merely Japanese. But I'm not merely Thai either... I'm the son of my mother."

This mixed-ethnic child could not fully identify himself with the mainstream ethnic group (Japanese), but also found that it was not possible, or necessarily desirable, indeed *disadvantageous*, to identify himself strictly with the Thai ethnic group. Instead, he chose a *multi-ethnic identity* which was more flexible and diverse than any existing ethnic categories in the local society. It should be noted that only mixed-ethnic children raised by single mothers seemed to represent themselves through a multi-ethnic identity.

CONCLUSION

This study found that mixed-ethnic children living in the predominantly non-white society of Japan tended to identify themselves as either Western or Japanese. This could be analysed as a reflection of perceived hierarchical ethnic classifications. Those children who were able to identify themselves as Western almost always did so. Mixed-ethnic children who were unable to identify themselves as Western tended to identify themselves as Japanese, because non-Western foreign identities (e.g., other Asian or Latin American ethnicities) tended to be regarded as non-beneficial. A *multi-ethnic identity* was chosen only by children who were raised by foreign single mothers in Japan.

This result partly corresponds with previous studies that indicated that mixed-ethnic children negotiate their social environment and settle on the identity best suited to the given context (Patel 2009, p. 120). However, this study illustrates one point not mentioned by previous studies that have been conducted in predominantly white societies: that mainstream identity is not necessarily the most beneficial identity for mixed-ethnic children. As a result, in non-white societies such as Japan, the identity choices available to mixed-ethnic children are more diverse and complicated.

This study sheds new light on the extensive sociological literature concerning the ethnicity of mixed-ethnic children in former *mono-ethnic* countries. However, some issues require further examination. In this study, ethnicity was simplified into three categories: Western, Japanese, and non-Western. While the category "Western" is quite broad; it fails to include the notable difference between the term's definitions in Japan and other countries — a difference that suggests a varying value of *whiteness*. Similarly, the understanding of the non-Western category is likely to vary considerably across different contexts. The ambiguity therein highlights an interesting research dimension in ethnic identity studies from the sociological standpoint, namely, the variability of ethnic categories depending on social context. This point shall be investigated in future research.

Notes

This research was made possible by a grant for young researchers from the Japan Society for the Promotion of Science [Research number.18730343, Representative:

Kayoko Ishii]. An earlier version of the paper was presented at the "International Workshop on Migration & Diversity in Asian Context", 25–26 September 2008 at the Asia Research Institute, National University of Singapore. This research would not have been completed if not for the patient cooperation of all the mixed-ethnic families who generously responded to my interviews.

1. Oguma describes how the *myth of Japan* as a *homogeneous nation* has been thoroughly established, even though the country's ethnic background is in fact diverse (Oguma 1995). I have therefore italicized the term "mono-ethnic countries" in this chapter.
2. These are not cases of mixed-ethnic children but rather concern Latino migrant children in the United States (Chappell and Faltis 2007), and Arab American children (Al-Hazza and Bucher 2008); however, I believe that the arguments are relevant to this context.
3. An increase in the rate of intermarriage has also been reported in Korea (Kim 2009) and Taiwan (Wang and Chang 2002).
4. There were 714,265 newly registered marriages, of which 41,481 couples were the result of intermarriage with foreign nationals (SID-MHLW 2005).
5. SID-MHLW represents the "Statistics and Information Department, Minister's Secretariat, Ministry of Health, Labour and Welfare."
6. All *white*-looking persons are regarded as *Westerner* in Japan, even though, some of them would not be considered as mainstream *white* in their countries of origin. Therefore, I have intentionally italicised "Western" in this paper.
7. There were 1,062,530 newly registered babies, of which 21,873 were mixed-ethnic children (SID-MHLW 2005).
8. I calculated this number in the following manner: (number of divorced inter-ethnic couples ÷ number of newly married inter-ethnic couples) x number of newly registered mixed-ethnic children in that year.
9. Notice from the Immigration Bureau, Ministry of Justice dated 30 July 1996.
10. This information is collected from participant observation in the target area in between 2004 and 2008.
11. There were 1,637 newly registered Japanese husband-Thai wife couples, 579 newly born Japanese-Thai mixed ethnic children, and 782 divorces among Japanese husband-Thai wife couples in 2005 (SID-MHLW 2005).
12. Social groups for Japanese women who raise mixed-ethnic children.
13. According to SID-HMLW 2005, the four most common ethnicities of foreign mothers in Japan as of 2005 are Filipino (4,441 persons), Chinese (3,478), Koreans (2,583), and Thai (509).
14. See Ishii (2006) for details on the closed network of Thai female migrants in the target area.

References

Al-Hazza, T., and K.T. Bucher. "Building Arab Americans' Cultural Identity and Acceptance with Children's Literature". *The Reading Teacher* 62, no. 3 (November 2008): 210–19.

Ashikari, M. "Cultivating Japanese Whiteness: The Whitening Cosmetics Boom and the Japanese Identity". *Journal of Material Culture* 10, no. 1 (2005): 73–91.

Bhugra, D. "Migration and Mental Health". *Acta Psychiatrica Scandinavica* 109, no. 4 (2004): 243–58.

Bonilla-Silva, E. "From Bi-racial to Tri-racial: Towards a New System of Racial Stratification in the USA". *Ethnic and Racial Studies* 27, no. 6 (2004): 931–50.

Bonnett, A. "A White World? Whiteness and the Meaning of Modernity in Latin America and Japan". In *Working through Whiteness: International Perspectives*, edited by C. Levine-Rasky, pp. 69–106. Albany: State University of New York Press, 2002.

Bratter, J. "Will 'Multiracial' Survive to the Next Generation? The Racial Classification of Children of Multiracial Parents". *Social Forces* 86, no. 2 (2007): 821–49. Reprinted in *Racism in Post-Race America. New Theories, New Direction*, edited by Charles Gallagher, pp. 79–94, Social Forces Publishing 2008.

Chappell, S. and C. Faltis. "Spanglish, Bilingualism, Culture and Identity in Latino Children's Literature". *Children's Literature in Education* 38, no. 4 (2007): 253–62.

Eytan A, S. Durieux-Paillard, B. Whitaker-Clinch, L. Loutan, et al. "Transcultural Validity of a Structured Diagnostic Interview to Screen for Major Depression and Posttraumatic Stress Disorder among Refugees". *Journal of Nervous and Mental Disease* 195 (2007): 723–28.

Ishii, K. "Network within Thai Migrants in Japan: Case of Thai Migrants in Thokai Area" *NUCB Journal of Economics and Information Science* 50, no. 2 (2006): 249–66 (in Japanese).

Okun, B.S. and O. Khait-Marelly. "Demographic Behaviour of Adults of Mixed Ethnic Ancestry: Jews in Israel". *Ethnic and Racial Studies* 31, no. 8 (2008): 1357–80.

Patel, T.G. *Mixed-up Kids? Race, Identity and Social Order*. Dorset: Russell House, 2009.

SID-MHCD (Statistics and Information Department, Minister's Secretariat Ministry of Health, Labour and Welfare) *Vital Statistics of Japan* (2005), Statistics and Information Department, Minister's Secretariat Ministry of Health.

SID-MHLW (Statistics and Information Department, Minister's Secretariat, Ministry of Health, Labour and Welfare) (1987–2005). *Vital Statistics of Japan*, Welfare and Health and Welfare Statistics Association.

Stonequist, E. The *Marginal Man*. New York: Scribner's, 1937.

Wagatsuma, H. "The Social Perception of Skin Color in Japan". *Daedalus* 96, no. 2 (1967): 407–43.

Wang, H. and S. Chang. "The Commodification of International Marriages: Cross-Border Marriage Business in Taiwan and Viet Nam". *International Migration* 40, no. 6 (2002): 93–116.

Wood, M. "Mixed Ethnicity, Identity and Adoption: Research, Policy and Practice". *Child & Family Social Work* 14, no. 4 (2009): 431–39.

7
BEING INDIAN IN POST-COLONIAL METRO MANILA
Identities, Boundaries and the Media[1]

Jozon A. LORENZANA

INTRODUCTION

Contrary to the assumption that members of the Indian diaspora identify with a pan-Indian identity, current studies demonstrate that they have complex and plural identifications, constructed in gendered (Radhakrishnan 2008; Warikoo 2005), classed (Bhattacharya 2008), ethnic (Lock and Detaramani 2006) and "racialized" (Bhatia 2008) terms. These dimensions may overlap and are complicated by individual and migration histories, the diaspora's sense of belonging and identifications, and the specific cultures of the Indian diaspora in the host society. Recent scholarship on the Indian diaspora has explored the roles media play in the lives and identity formations of its members. On the one hand, consumption of media from the Indian homeland indicates a process of re-territorialization or how migrants "recraft a sense of community and cultural identity in new socio-geographic contexts" (Punathambekar 2005, p. 151). On the other hand, it suggests identification with the popular culture of the host society (Gillespie 1995). Analysing the role of the media in the diaspora, Roger Silverstone (2007, pp. 95–96) suggests that media offer diasporic groups various competing cultural spaces and alternative imaginaries. However, in relation to identity and community formations, media's influence is premature as identities by their nature are dynamic and changing (Silverstone 2007, p. 96). Ascertaining the roles of the media in identity productions of diasporas, without presuming its centrality, indeed needs further investigation. Warikoo (2005) finds that media, among other factors like school and family, affect ethnic identity choices among Indo-Caribbean youths in New York City. In similar vein, this chapter examines the role of the media in the identity formations of the Indian diaspora who are not in major cities of the global North where most studies in the field of Indian diaspora studies originate, but those in the global South, like Metro Manila in the Philippines. This study therefore attempts to represent the experiences of the Indian diaspora or peoples of Indian origin (PIOs) in lesser known destinations or host societies and consequently provides evidence for comparisons between experiences of the Indian diasporas in First World and Third World contexts.

I focus on the identity formations of young people or second/third generation members of the diaspora. What does it mean to be Indian in Metro Manila? How do the media contribute to the meanings of being Indian? Mindful of the debates about identity (more on this below), I used ethnic identity as a springboard to explore the complex identity formations and practices of this diasporic group. My interest in the role of the media here is not only an attempt to establish the conceptual link between media and identity but also as an empirical strategy to generate evidence for this sort of enquiry. Marie Gillespie's seminal work on television and youth culture among young Punjabi Londoners demonstrates how "common TV (or media) experiences supply referents and contexts for talk which is explicitly or implicitly about identities and identity positions" (Gillespie 1995, p. 25). This study builds on recent works on the Indian diaspora in the Philippines (Salazar 2008; Santarita 2008; Thapan 2002), which give little attention to young second/third generation members, including those with mixed parentage, i.e. Filipino-Indian unions. Instead of looking at consumption of media from the homeland, I turn to this generation's experiences with local and global entertainment media in the host society. During my initial queries and observations, I discovered that these youths were more engaged in either local (Filipino) or global (American) media and less engaged in Bollywood media culture. What enticed me was their constant reference to how Indians were represented in local entertainment media. I decided to take this direction as it presented an opportunity to probe into how Filipinos, at least in Metro Manila, imagine, represent and treat their immigrants. In so doing this study also provides a critique of Philippine society as "host" to diasporas and its orientations towards ethnic (among other axes of) difference.

I draw on studies (e.g., Ray 2001) that conceptualize identities as a positioning in context (Hall 1990/2003) and a process of defining boundaries (Barth 1969). Media contribute to this process by providing (symbolic) frameworks for inclusion and exclusion (Madianou 2005b; Silverstone and Georgiou 2005) that either weaken or reinforce boundaries. Following this framework, I analysed how second/third generation members of the Indian diaspora in the Philippines talked about their identities in autobiographical narratives, including experiences with the media. I argue that informants of the study claim multiple affiliations but tend to position themselves based on class and gender. Participants' ethnic affiliations intersect with class and gender positions. Commercial media influence the symbolic environment where these identities are formed. Local entertainment media reinforce stereotypical images of Indian men that promote distinctions between members of the diaspora. Global entertainment media events like beauty pageants provide alternative images that facilitate inclusion in Philippine society especially among females. How these young people positioned their identities could be traced to other contextual factors like class dynamics in the homeland and Philippine society, historical processes like colonization, the migration histories and trajectories of Indian immigrants and the classed/gendered culture of the Indian diaspora.

THE INDIAN DIASPORA IN METRO MANILA

Metro Manila is a megapolis comprised of thirteen cities and four municipalities, including the city of Manila, the capital of the Philippines, and Makati City, a central business district. It has an estimated population of 10 million that includes a majority of Catholic Christians from different Filipino ethnic groups and a minority of Filipino Chinese, Muslims, Indians and expatriate communities. The ethnic diversity of the city is masked by the common use of Filipino, the national language, in media and everyday talk, and the strong influence of Roman Catholicism in every aspect of life. Aside from ethnic affiliation, class is the most salient mode of differentiation in Manila or Philippine society as a whole. This could be partly explained by its historical trajectory.

Since independence from Spain in 1898 and the United States in 1946, Philippine governments have embarked on national development and modernizing projects through democracy and capitalism. Evolving from a state-regulated capitalist economy (1950s–70s) to a liberal market economy (late 1980s to present), the Philippines, however, remains a society where economic gains and opportunities are concentrated within and controlled by the economic and political elites, most of them based in the capital. The uneven sociopolitical development in the Philippines is, according to historian E. San Juan Jr. (2008), compounded by Americanization or the lingering influence of the United States in schooling, mass media, sports and music. Philippine sociologist Randy David observes that: "In hierarchical Philippine society, we measure a person's worth by his [sic] family background, his educational attainment, his profession, his connections and visible wealth" (David 2008). This is, in broad strokes, the "locality" and context in which the second/third generation Indians were born and brought up.

People from India have come to Philippine shores as traders in the pre-colonial era, as sepoys or soldiers of the British East India Company during the British occupation of Manila in the eighteenth century, and in the nineteenth and twentieth centuries as traders or migrants "in search of economic opportunities" (Santarita 2008). The small number of Indian migrants in Manila, compared to other countries in the Southeast Asia region, could be explained by the voluntary nature of such migration (Thapan 2001) and the historical circumstances of the Philippines during the turn of the century. Manila, then a Spanish colony, had limited contact with the British Empire which populated its colonies in the region (e.g., Singapore and Malaysia) and elsewhere with indentured Indian labourers. During this period a small number of Indian immigrants in Manila worked for branches of Indian or British trading firms.

Punjabis, Sindhis and Indian professionals working in multinational companies and multilateral organizations comprise the present Indian diaspora in Manila. According to the Philippine bureau of immigration, there are 20,215 registered Indians in the country (PCIJ 2007).[2] The Sindhis, who lost their homeland Sindh to Pakistan, have established themselves in cities across continents. Consistent with their occupational class in Sindh and like their counterparts elsewhere, Sindhis in the country are known as traders and urban dwellers. Early Sindhi immigrants worked for Indian and British trading firms in Manila and other cities of the islands and consequently put up their own businesses. In spite of the legal constraints imposed on foreign-owned entities in the Philippines, Sindhis have established a strong foothold in garments manufacturing, import and export.

The Punjabis, mostly Sikhs of rural backgrounds, are the biggest ethnic group in the diaspora. Driven by a desire to improve their economic situation, most of them have come to the Philippines to either engage in small-scale trading or money lending that usually caters to street or market vendors, working class Filipinos and small-scale businesses. Relatives of successful Punjabis would follow them to the Philippines and similarly establish their own business in the same or another area. Money lending has earned them a moniker among the locals, i.e., "five-six", a term used to describe the money-lending scheme of Punjabis where a borrowed amount earns 20 per cent interest per month. This job entails riding a motorbike and personally collecting debts in the heat of the day. While the terms are perceived as very usurious, Filipinos still resort to "five-six" because Punjabis do not demand any collateral and are often reliable (Olarte 2007). Unlike the majority of Sindhis who tend to live in gated communities in big cities, Punjabis are more integrated into local communities. The majority of Sindhis and Punjabis are residents but not citizens of the Philippines.

Aside from describing the origins and situation of the Indian diaspora in Metro Manila, we also need to think about their condition in conceptual terms to facilitate a critical and complex understanding of the group being investigated. I propose that they are simultaneously ethnic, diasporic and transnational. In relation to peoples in their locality, they are considered ethnic groups, defined by Richard Schermerhorn (1978, as cited in Cornell and Hartmann 1998/2001) as self-conscious populations who see themselves as distinct and have a common origin or symbol of their peoplehood. Based on my interviews, Indians see themselves as distinct from Filipino citizens and other ethnic groups like the Filipino Chinese and Muslims.

In its original sense, diaspora "had more to do with migration as colonisation rather than with uprooting and deterritorialisation" (Georgiou 2006, p. 47). The present understanding of diaspora not only emphasizes movement from a homeland but also grounding in a host society. According to James Clifford (1994, pp. 223–29), both displacement and dwelling constitute and characterize diaspora communities: for members of a diaspora "with varying degrees of urgency, they negotiate and resist the social realities of poverty, violence, policing, racism, and political and economic inequality". Clifford's definition not only acknowledges the immigrants' "grounding" in the host society but also paves the way to reflect on the conditions of diasporic groups.

With the increasing mobility of people, goods, capital and ideas through advancements in technologies of transport and communication, migrants and diasporas have become more connected to their places of origin. Thus, scholars like Safran, Sahoo, and Lal (2008, p. 1) have argued that "the transnational context is part and parcel of diaspora". It is indeed necessary to acknowledge the links or "social relations formed between the homeland and immigrants' adopted countries" (Glick Schiller, Basch, and Blanc-Szanton 1992, as cited in Bhattacharya 2008, p. 66) in analysing the conditions of the members of the Indian diaspora in Manila.

THEORETICAL APPROACHES AND RESEARCH QUESTIONS

My approach to identity assumes that it is plural and contextual. Individuals or groups can claim multiple affiliations (across ethnicity, class, gender, etc.). Although identities could be essentialized under certain circumstances (Madianou 2005*b*), they are dynamic, transforming through space and time. Stuart Hall's conception of identity is therefore useful for this study. First, Hall (1990/2003, p. 236) suggests that cultural identities are historical and therefore undergo constant transformation. They are subject to the continuous play of history, culture and power. Second, cultural identity is "not an essence but a positioning. Hence, there is always a politics of identity, a politics of position" (Hall 1990/2003, p. 237). This second definition recognizes the power relationships involved in the process of identification. Referring to the inherent diversity and heterogeneity of the diasporic experience, Hall argues that diasporic identities are "constantly producing and reproducing themselves anew through transformation and difference". Furthermore, they are "constituted not outside but within representation"[3] (Hall 1990/2003, pp. 244–45) or constructed through meanings and meaning systems. In this conception, identities are positioned and constituted in and through history, culture, power and representation.

Frederik Barth's (1969) theory of ethnic groups and boundaries becomes relevant here in expanding the meaning of identity positioning. This theory is consistent with the assumption that identities are flexible. According to Barth, ethnic groups define themselves through the maintenance of a boundary and "not the cultural stuff that it encloses" (Barth 1969, p. 15). He acknowledges that both cultural features that signal the boundary and the cultural characteristics of the members may change and may be transformed (Barth 1969, p. 14). Hence for Barth, boundary maintenance is a process of self-ascription and ascription by others. Ethnic groups maintain these "social boundaries" through interactions or relations with others in a process of "determining and signalling membership and exclusion" (Barth 1969, p. 15). Indeed, identities are not only positioned and claimed, but also maintained in relation to others.

And so I ask: How do young people from the Indian diaspora in Manila position themselves in autobiographical narratives? Following Taylor and Littleton (2006), I analysed autobiographical talk — in the context of an in-depth interview — of these young people to reveal ways they positioned their identities. I looked for self-ascriptions (Barth 1969) or informants' self-assertions (Warikoo 2005), and ascriptions by others or how they are labelled in the host society.

What do media have to do with identity positionings? The link could be established using Hall's proposition that identities are constructed within representation. Media is a practice of representation that uses image, text, symbol and sound. Silverstone and Georgiou's (2005) argument becomes relevant: the media are seen not to be determining identities, but contributing to the creation of symbolic communicative spaces in which identities can be constructed. Media influence this symbolic space through representations of minority or ethnic groups. Silverstone and Georgiou point out that minorities often do not appear in mainstream media. However, when they do appear, they are often represented in stereotypical and alienating images. According to Hall (1997, p. 258), stereotypes, a form of representation, "get hold of the few simple, vivid, memorable, easily grasped and widely recognised characteristics about a person, reduce everything about the person to those traits, exaggerate and simplify them, and fix them without change or development to eternity". Media spaces, where minority groups appear or not, become spaces where meanings about them are constructed. Such meanings "provide frameworks for inclusion and exclusion" (Silverstone and Georgiou 2005, p. 435). Indeed media contribute to the process of boundary maintenance through representations of minority groups that elicit either inclusion or exclusion (Madianou 2005*b*).

How groups are represented, whether in the media or everyday talk, relates to Barth's notion of ascription by others. Based on this assumption, I looked for threads about meanings, representations or stereotypes of being Indian and how the informants talked about these topics in their life and media experiences. Scholars (Gillespie 1995; Madianou 2005a) who have investigated the role of the media in diasporic groups have used talks about media content and experiences as a strategy to examine identities. This approach assumes that informants are treated as media audiences engaged in the consumption, reception and production of media.

Method

This study used a qualitative design to data gathering. The main method was in-depth interviews and it was supplemented by participant observation of events of the Indian community (Diwali celebration in 2006 and 2007), visits to temples (Sikh and Hindu) and to a Bollywood-themed club. As social networking sites and online journals are popular among young people in Manila, I also visited the pages of some informants for further biographical details.

Most of the informants were recruited through referrals by friends and by the research participants themselves. Ten (five females and five males) youths, between the ages nineteen to twenty-four, consented to participate in the study. The main criterion for their selection was that they were born of first generation Indian or Indian-Filipino parentage. The informants belonged to middle and upper middle class households, with occupations ranging from student, social worker, company executive to information technology professional. In terms of ethnic background, three were Punjabis, three were Sindhis and four had mixed parentage (Filipino mothers and Indian fathers) coming from different ethnic or religious backgrounds (Bengali, Konkan, Muslim). All of them knew and spoke Filipino and English. Only the Punjabis could speak the language of their parents. I also interviewed two officials of local Indian trade associations to provide context to the situation of Punjabis and Sindhis in Manila. They are: Gurpreet Sethi, a Punjabi and president of Indian Business of Bulacan; and Ram Sitaldas, a Sindhi and president of the Indian Chamber of Commerce. Table 7.1 provides some biographical details of the informants.

I identified themes from the interview narratives and interpreted these data based on the framework and related literature. Aside from the themes,

TABLE 7.1
Profile of Respondents

Pseudonym	Age	Occupation	Sex	Parentage	Citizenship
Usha	24	Manager	Female	Sindhi parents	Indian
Preity	19	Undergraduate student (psychology)	Female	Sindhi parents	Indian
Monika	19	Undergraduate student (management)	Female	Sindhi father and Filipino mother	Filipino
Deepa	26	TV writer	Female	Bengali father and Filipino mother	Filipino
Priyanka	22	Computer programmer	Female	Punjabi (Sikh) parents	Indian
Jeet	23	Social worker	Male	Indian father (from Karnataka), Filipino mother	Filipino
Sonny	18	Undergraduate student (integrated marketing communications)	Male	Punjabi (Sikh) parents	Indian
Ahmed	17	Fourth year high school student	Male (gay)	Indian (Muslim) father, Filipino mother	Filipino
Raja	24	Technology consultant	Male	Sindhi parents	Indian
Vikas	22	Sales executive	Male	Punjabi (Sikh) parents	Indian

I also paid attention to the affective dimension of their autobiographical narratives. In so doing, the narratives I gathered were also evidences of their lived experiences as young people of Indian origin in contemporary Manila. To protect their privacy, pseudonyms were used to refer to the informants' responses. As this work is limited to a specific locality, conclusions apply only to this purposive sample.

FINDINGS

Self Ascriptions: Class, Ethnic and Gender Identifications and Boundaries

Data suggest that informants consciously and unconsciously expressed multiple affiliations and claimed (contradictory) identity positions across dimensions of ethnicity, class, gender and religion. Class was a dominant theme that often intersected with ethnicity and gender. Caste, a relevant identity position in the Indian homeland, was mentioned only twice by two Punjabis. Most of them asserted their ethnicities (being Filipino, Indian, Punjabi, Sikh, etc.). However, during the introductory phase of the interviews other aspects of their identities like gender, personal traits and occupation were uttered before their ethnic identifications. Eight of ten claimed more than one ethnic affiliation as part of their ethnic background (e.g. half-Filipino, half-Indian, quarter Spanish) or as a matter of affinity. Informants tended to choose positions, categories or affiliations that have high symbolic power. While informants claimed positions and affiliations, they simultaneously drew classed and gendered boundaries between and within their ethnic groupings.

I observed that the informants' understanding of class was consistent with how the term is defined in the homeland, the Indian diasporas and host society. In India, "social class is often considered to be a combination of wealth and occupational status" (Bhattacharya 2008). For Hindu Punjabis in London, it is expressed through "commodities, housing, travel and preferences for occupation, leisure and lifestyle" (Raj 2003, as cited in Batnitzky, McDowell and Dyer 2008); and for Sindhis in Manila, Hong Kong and Jakarta, class is about "the value of one's wealth, occupational position and lifestyle" (Thapan 2002). According to Thapan (2002), education enhances one's class standing. For Filipinos, class could mean occupation (Kerkvliet 1990), family background, educational attainment, connections and visible wealth (David 2008), lifestyle, behaviour, consumption codes and practices, and ethnicity (Pinches 1999). From this review of definitions, Filipinos and Indians generally understand class in terms of occupation, wealth, lifestyle and consumption. Patterns in the personal narratives of informants reflected *combinations* of the meanings of class as: occupation, wealth, lifestyle, performance/behaviour, education or family background.

Sindhi informants tended to differentiate themselves from Punjabis whose common occupation, small-scale money lending or "five-six", has become a stereotype of Indians in Philippine society. Not only Sindhis, but the rest of the informants, pointed out that Filipinos readily assume that either they or their parents do "five-six" for a living. This assertion came out strongly when I asked them to talk about a locally-produced music video about a Punjabi hawker. Preity found the portrayal "funny ... (and) true, although it's degrading. When I saw it, I was really laughing out loud. I am not Punjabi." Usha and Raja claimed their class position by citing Sindhis' reputation in (large-scale) trading and manufacturing and their contribution to the Philippine economy. Being Sindhi has high symbolic value; becoming part of this community through wealth and lifestyle, as Jeet revealed, indicates a change in class position and social status:

> Jeet: When we first came to Manila, we weren't very well off. My parents really worked hard.... Only now we're doing pretty well financially. We moved to a village (a gated community) that has a lot of Indians. It's only now that we are able to connect with Sindhis.

Punjabi informants mutually distanced themselves from Sindhis not on the basis of occupation but in terms of lifestyle and gendered performance/behaviour.

> Priyanka: I was brought up in a very simple manner. My mother is simple and she had a hard life before. They were not rich, but they were not poor either.... I know Sindhis are rich. It's automatic. But if you talk about us, we're just simple folks.

> Sonny: I always tell my friends that I am different from them, "Don't ever make the mistake of associating me with Sindhis".... They speak English like girls do. We don't speak English at home...

Similarly on the aspect of behaviour, a female Sindhi informant commented that: "Punjabi guys are not civilised.... They ogle at you." These remarks suggest that class distinctions between these two ethnic groups also index meanings of femininity and masculinity. Certain classed behaviours which are construed in gendered terms are attributed to ethnic groups. In this configuration, Punjabi and Sindhi masculinities have both high and low symbolic value at the expense of being feminine ("speaking English like girls do"). While acknowledging that their parents are into money lending, Punjabi informants, however, were conscious of the fact that their generation has gone beyond this occupation and is now pursuing other interests. For example, Sonny is a marketing communications student in an Opus Dei-run university and Priyanka is an information technology professional.

Data also suggest that within Punjabi and Sindhi communities, distinctions were based on the presence/lack of education, wealth, lifestyle preference and behaviour. Sonny perceived newly arrived Punjabis as "not modernized, not conscious of their looks, and not aware of what the world really is because they were from rural villages". Senior members of the Indian community like Gurpreet Sethi, a Punjabi, and Ram Sitaldas, a Sindhi, attribute such behaviours to the lack of education among newly arrived immigrants. Indeed, for the Indian diaspora in the Philippines, education is used to distinguish themselves from each other and to counter the "five-six" stereotype. Priyanka's reaction "Are all Indians who have been educated here five-six?" demonstrates how second/third generation members assert their difference from other members of their ethnic group that still do money lending and trading. For Sindhis, boundaries are drawn based on a combination of value of wealth, lifestyle preferences and behaviour. Preity distinguished herself from those who "show-off" and "are not rich anymore but still have to maintain their lifestyle". For Sindhi informants, distinctions within their group are about the maintenance of status as signified by a certain level of wealth, lifestyle and consumption.

Informants from mixed parentage drew boundaries in relation to Sindhis and Punjabis and Indian citizens. Aside from the "five-six" label, they usually distinguished themselves from portrayals of Indians in foreign media. Images of poverty attached to Mother Teresa of Kolkata have strong resonance among Catholic Filipinos. Informants with one Indian parent, like Sushmita, pointed out that they have an upper class family background in India: "My grandfather belonged to a landed class ... all his life he just sat down and servants kept him cool."

Why would class matter among these second/third members of the Indian diaspora in Metro Manila? Punjabi and Sindhi informants, including those with one Indian parent like Monika, cited their community's preoccupation with status and reputation. Improving or maintaining one's (high) class position contributes to their standing (individually or as a family) in the community.

The tendency to draw class boundaries among members of the Indian diaspora is not uncommon. Bhattacharya (2008) observes that participants of her study were conscious of a social class system among Indians in New York City that replicated the one in India (Bhattacharya 2008, p. 76). I would like to suggest that this class differentiation is as much a reflection of the homeland as the host society's class hierarchy and relations. Based on their identity discourses, the occupational positions of ethnic groups in the Indian diaspora loosely correspond to lower/upper class positions in Philippine society. Being involved in trade for centuries, both in the Sindh and overseas, most Sindhis in the Philippines have set up successful businesses and consequently have identified with Filipino elites who reside in gated communities in Manila. To some extent, their historical context — losing their homeland Sindh during partition in 1947 — has also contributed to their establishment and settlement in the Philippines. On the other hand, Punjabis, by the nature of their occupation, are more in touch with the Filipino masses, their usual clients, and are indeed identified with them. However, the case of informants with Filipino and Indian parents challenges this suggested binary between Punjabis and Sindhis. Based on these informants' life stories, the class/ethnic backgrounds of both or one of the parents consigns them to the class hierarchy in India or the Philippines.

The migration histories and trajectories of these Punjabis, however, provide a way to think about their class beyond their identity positionings. Coming from rural farming backgrounds, first generation Punjabi immigrants in the Philippines become money lenders or traders. Since their goal is to achieve financial security they would scrimp and settle for what informants referred to as a "simple lifestyle". For those who have settled here, their second generation would acquire education and some job experience. According to Gurpreet Sheti, a senior figure in the Punjabi community in Manila, the Philippines is a transit point for Indian immigrants. For one, the immigration and citizenship laws of the country discourage foreigners from taking roots. This is evident not only in the citizenship by blood principle but also in the citizenship requirements for owning businesses and practising government regulated professions like medicine, law, accounting and engineering. For this reason, and the limited economic opportunities in the Philippines, educated children of first generation Indian immigrants tend to migrate to wealthier countries. A Punjabi informant, who is now in Australia, calls this an "upgrade". This observation reflects a similar trend called "twice migration" among Indians in countries like South Africa (Singh 2008). It also implies that Manila is just a stop en route to the final destination, a city in the global

North. Although Punjabis, in relation to Sindhis, have less symbolic value because of their group's reputation as money lenders and rural folks, their financial status — assuming their success in the business — in the Punjab or the Philippines earns them a measure of respect and adulation. Joefe Santarita (2008) finds that Punjabis in Western Visayas, central Philippines, for example, are treated as saviours by the locals more than their kin.

What came out in this study is the salience of class and its intersections with ethnicity and gender among the youth of the second/third generation Indian diaspora. In Metro Manila, it is not only class affiliation that is evident and important, but also the ethnic relations in the diaspora which somehow mirrors the relations between upper and lower classes in the host society and in the homeland. Ethnicity and class intersect to produce new identifications. Gender complicates this process through its relationships with classed performances. At the same time, the migration histories, contexts and trajectories provide a way to see the dynamic and fluid positions of the second/third generation members of the Indian diaspora. This is not to suggest that class alone is the primary mode of identification among the participants of the study; generational differences, caste and religion may also come into play. My focus on the theme of class and its intersections with ethnicity and gender is therefore a limitation of the study.

Ascriptions by Others: Race and the Media

In this section I focus on how Filipinos label Indians based on the personal and media experiences of the informants. I examine racialized representations of Indians in everyday talk and the media, and explain how they relate to the informants' positionings. In so doing I ascertain the roles media play in the identity formations of the second/third generation members of the Indian diaspora.

Racialized and Pathological Bodies

As discussed earlier, Indians are labelled based on the occupational stereotype "five-six", which has low symbolic value in a class and status-oriented society like the Philippines. Such stereotype contributes to boundary making along the axes of class, ethnicity and gender among informants. What this study finds equally interesting and revealing is the connotation of another stereotype, *bumbay*. This term is derived from the former name of the Indian city of Mumbai, Bombay. Anita Thapan (2002) suggests that early Indian immigrants during the American colonial period sailed from the port of Bombay and named their stores after the place. Early Filipinos identified these immigrants with their place of origin and shop's name. I argue that *bumbay* and its meanings suggest a "racialized" and "pathological" Indian body.

Informants understood their experiences in childhood and school as "racism" or "the display of contempt or aggressiveness toward other people on account of physical differences" (Todorov 1986, p. 370, as cited in Go 2004). Being physically different was a basis for exclusion (and inclusion) in Philippine society. Participants remembered being called *bumbay* or "five-six" by peers and strangers. Floya Anthias (1990/2001) labels such experiences as discursive racism: a set of representations embodied in daily language, texts, and practices. According to Avtar Brah (1996) racisms intersect with other axes of difference, primarily gender. Informants' experiences of racism support this claim.

Half of the informants experienced verbal and physical forms of abuse on the basis of the meanings of their bodies. Jeet observed that: "after 9/11 strangers assume I'm Arab and make terrorist-flavoured jokes". Priyanka disclosed that her schoolmates picked on her facial and body hair and called her ugly[4]: "For a girl this (being hairy) is not normal." Her understanding of how *her* body "ought" to be illustrates how gendered racism works: "... the female may be represented as embodying 'male qualities' which were thought to set them apart from the gentility of white womanhood" (Brah 1996, p. 156). This implies that Filipinos also expect female bodies in genteel form. Priyanka felt that people already pre-judged her character based on her physical attributes. She recalled being excluded from working groups in school. Similarly, strangers kept their distance from Jeet.

> Jeet: I ... was swimming in a public pool at around age eight and seeing a girl about my age drag her two brothers away from me while saying, in a voice dripping with revulsion, "*Wag tayo lalapit dyan, mga* bumbay *'yan, ang baho-baho*" (Let's not go near him, he's *bumbay*, he stinks).

This construction of an abnormal, pathological Indian body takes an overt expression in the experiences of Ahmed and Deepa. When Ahmed was in second grade at a Catholic school for boys his peers chased him over the field, pricked him with a pen and called him "AIDS virus". Looking back, he did not expect such behaviour and treatment from his schoolmates who come from affluent families. Deepa, who studied in an exclusive Catholic school for girls, had a similar incident:

> Deepa: I had this classmate in second grade. We had a letter writing exercise to a relative. I have been writing to my relatives in India ... to my *ima*, my grandmother, and so my letter was addressed to Mrs. Bakti George.[5] She grabbed it and said Bakti! Bakti! Bacteria! I was so mad!

Aside from this incident Deepa also got teased by her name which in Filipino means "not yet" (*di pa*):

> Deepa: People also make jokes about my name. Deepa! *Di pa naliligo, di pa kumakain, di pa nagtotooth brush* (Deepa! Haven't taken her bath, haven't eaten, haven't brushed her teeth). I still get it until now.... Not from people who are close to me.

Being called *bumbay*, bacteria, "AIDS virus" and ugly, and being bullied in school generated feelings of isolation, rejection and low self-worth among participants. However, in time they learned to deal with these taunts. Incidents of discrimination became rare as they attended the university or joined the workplace. Distance from the experience allowed Deepa to view teasing as a Filipino's way of establishing a connection: "I just know that Filipinos have these images of Indians. This is just what they know. Sometimes people just want to build a rapport with you. They'll just tease you like 'You're so fat!' It's just a form of that."

How do we account for these racial attitudes of Filipinos and their "pathological" representations of Indians? Avtar Brah (1997/2001) suggests that racisms have historical origins. Warwick Anderson's (2007) work on American colonial public health and medical practices in the Philippines is instructive in explaining such racial bias among Filipinos. It reveals a racialised and pathological construction of Filipino bodies, which was the basis for the U.S. colonial policy on public health and hygiene. By extension, I argue that Filipinos have internalized these attitudes and prejudices towards other "races" or peoples.

The colonizers who regarded themselves as "clean and ascetic" imagined and represented Filipino bodies as "dirty and infected, open and polluting". They institutionalized sanitation and hygiene by setting up sanitary commissions, instructing the local inhabitants in personal hygiene, home cleanliness and the care of the sick (Anderson 2007, p. 117). According to Anderson in order to become "self-governing subjects", Filipinos had to be clean and hygienic in their surroundings and their bodies (Anderson

2007, p. 109). The impact of this colonial project, Anderson notes, could be summarized in an observation by Victor Heiser, director of public health during the 1910s, "who found imitation ... wherever he went in the colonial Philippines" (Anderson 2007, p. 181).[6]

Filipinos' present preoccupation with hygiene and cleanliness (especially body odour) could be traced to this historical event. To be acknowledged as civilized, modern, Filipino citizen subjects, one has to demonstrate proper hygiene. The case of Preity exemplifies the prevalence and internalization of such attitude: "Some Indians say they are teased because they smell bad. Since my nanny is so particular about cleanliness, until now I have it in me: (I) brush my teeth after eating even small things, it's just imbibed (sic) in me." Preity mentioned that she had an easier time fitting in and befriending Filipino schoolmates compared to *other* Indian girls in school. This finding suggests that attitudes toward "race" or difference on the basis of the body and physical features could be influenced by colonisation. Filipinos' understanding and practice of hygiene, a colonial legacy, has become a means of inclusion and exclusion in society.

Media as Agents of Inclusion and Exclusion

Informants related to the classed and gendered representations of Indians in local and global media[7] in contradictory ways. In 2006, Michael V, a popular comedian and gag show host, came up with a compilation of his music videos that make fun of marginalized peoples in Philippine society. Produced by GMA Network, the second largest TV and news organization in the Philippines, each song from the album features Michael V spoofing gays, Indians, ugly people, etc. In the song *VJ Bumbay*, he mimics a male Sikh Punjabi by wearing a fake beard and wrapping a length of white cloth around his head to resemble a turban. Shot in black and white, and set in rap, the character of Michael V, a hawker, persuades the audience to buy his original but defective wares.

Most informants responded to *VJ Bumbay* as critical audiences. Male informants were particularly affected by this portrayal. However others did not say much about the video and were reflexive of its genre as an entertainment product: "it was funny and not to be taken seriously". Regardless of ethnic background, informants pointed out that the video stereotyped Indians as *bumbay*, referring to its classed and racialized meanings. Informants debunked this stereotypical image by asserting their class/occupation (owners of big businesses for Sindhis) and changing status (Punjabis taking other professions). They also cited the cultural heritage and achievements of Indians, especially the nation's recent economic performance. As discussed earlier this media representation has reinforced boundaries between Punjabis and Sindhis, and Indians and Filipinos.

Informants also criticized the media organization (GMA 7) for its treatment of ethnic minorities. Jeet deplored how the production, airing and marketing of the music video by a major media organization indicated an institutionalization of racial discrimination. Both Raja and Jeet observed that the music video reinforced the occupational stereotype, especially among the masses. Jeet, who works with street children, shared that they teased him with the song: "They pick up this message from the media which says that it's okay to make fun of people who are different." Indeed the music video has influenced the symbolic space that is Philippine entertainment media and has become a reference for imagining Indians.

If local entertainment media contributed to the exclusion of Indians, global media, to some extent, influenced the symbolic environment to their advantage. In the last two decades global media tend to represent India in favourable but gendered images. Smitha Radhakrishnan observes that Indian women, through gracing the covers of international magazines like *Time*, have symbolized "the progress of a nation" (Radhakrishnan 2008, p. 8). The visibility of Bollywood films and Indo-chic fashion is also part of this trend. Natasha Warikoo points out how American media have paid attention to Indian trends through the "fashion choices of celebrities like Madonna and Gwen Stefani". She finds that Indo-Caribbean girls in New York City draw from these cultural resources (Warikoo 2005, p. 819). The presence and performance of Indian beauty queens in televized international beauty contests have further created desirable images for India. The successive triumphs of Indian women in 1994 and 2000 in Miss Universe and Miss World pageants earned India a reputation for being a "new bonafide beauty superpower" (Bhatia 2000, p. B7, as cited in Parameswaran 2004, p. 347). In the Philippines, this trend has a considerable impact on the image of the Indian diaspora, especially for the women. The U.S.-based annual Miss Universe pageant, a media event taken seriously in Philippine society, in Thapan's (2002) observation, has helped boost the image of Indians locally.

The Miss Universe pageant held in Manila in 1994 demonstrated the importance of beauty contests in Philippine culture and society. In a bid to boost the tourism industry, the Philippine government hosted the event. No less than the President Fidel Ramos attended the coronation ceremony. Sushmita Sen, an 18-year old Bengali and Indian national, won the crown. The Miss Universe organization partnered with the Philippines' largest TV network, ABS-CBN, which gave full media coverage for three weeks in May, a time when most students are on vacation. McRonald Banderlipe (2003) claims that beauty contests, along with basketball, are Filipinos' favourite pastimes. He observes that beauty contests — Miss Universe being the most popular — provide standards against which Filipinos assess their body, image and womanhood. Sushmita Sen's victory meant that "Indians could be very good looking" (Thapan 2002, p. 144).

Female informants noted how this media event not only helped change Filipinos' perceptions of Indians, especially women, but also how they felt and looked at themselves as "Indians". They referred to this media experience when they talked about changes in ways they were treated by peers and even strangers. (Most of the female informants were either in their primary or high school years in 1994.) Deepa, who claimed to be half-Bengali, noticed that people were "remarking how smart they were at such a young age ... they were so eloquent, they sounded like philosophers". She felt proud and identified with the Miss Universe's Bengali identity:

> I remember feeling proud at that time. I have something in me. I have Bengali blood too...The resemblance was really striking! I really saw myself in them, especially the eyes. People remark at my eyes: pretty, *ang laki* (big)! My boyfriends tell me what they like most about me is my eyes. That really struck me...

Such positive representation of Indian women on global television generated feelings of high self-worth and awareness of one's Indian heritage, Bengali in particular. Deepa identified with being Indian through recognizing and confirming her physical appearance from mediated images that construct Bengali women as both beautiful and sensible. By emphasizing how others (including significant ones like her boyfriends) found her big "Bengali" eyes attractive, she suggested a connection between being Indian and being desirable.

Parameswaran (2004, p. 346) reveals that Indian print media's representations of global Indian beauty queens are classed and are constructed in the context of a nation that is renegotiating its marginal position in the global economy. The female informants' identification with

Indian beauty queens reflects not only an affiliation with an Indian identity but also a desire to be recognized as Indians in a privileged class position. The changing image of Indian women in Philippine society, however, was mediated by the symbolic power of a global media event that is owned and produced by an American media outfit. The sudden warmth experienced by Deepa and other female informants suggests that their symbolic inclusion in Philippine society is *still* enabled by American global media, which has the power to reward and create models of cosmopolitan (ethnic) identities. They promote, among others, upper class, English-speaking, achieving women — traits desired by modern Filipinos.

CONCLUSION

This study was premised on the need to investigate identity formations of young members of the Indian diaspora in cities of the global South like Metro Manila, and what media might have to do with this process. Data suggest that being Indian in this context is not so much about one's ethnic affiliation alone but a combination of class, gender and race. Boundaries among Indian ethnic groups are drawn along class and ethnicity; distinctions between Filipinos and Indians are based on racialized and classed representations. These identifications and distinctions are also gendered, resulting in contradictory experiences of difference.

The salience of class could be traced to the influence of the social organization of the host society, class hierarchy in the homeland and the status conscious culture of the local Indian communities. Racialized representations of Indians in popular discourse have historical origins that influence identity positionings and formations. The commercial orientation of local and global media exploits stereotypes and gives ethnic or national identities classed and gendered meanings. These media representations either reinforce or break boundaries within Indian ethnic groups and between Indians and Filipinos, influencing how identities of the second/third generation Indian diaspora are formed in the context of postcolonial Manila.

Safran, Sahoo and Lal (2008, p. 1) speak of the Indian diaspora developing "institutions, orientations and patterns of living specific to the institutional structures and socio-political contexts of the different hostlands". What this study finds is that there are more continuities than peculiarities in the experiences of young people of Indian origin in Metro

Manila, a city in the global South, in relation to other hostlands in the global North. Class identifications and distinctions have become significant among Indians in the United Kingdom and United States (Bhattacharya 2008; Radhakrishnan 2008; Raj 2003). Peoples of Indian origin, whether from the Caribbean or the subcontinent, are also subject to gendered and racialized experiences (Bhatia 2008; Warikoo 2005; Gillespie 1995) in these cities. In a study of Indo-Caribbean youths in New York City, Warikoo (2005) notices that females benefit from cosmopolitan representations of Indian women and males resist classed and racialized labels like being associated with taxi drivers and Arabs after 9/11.

Indeed my findings only strengthen James Clifford's (1994) argument that the diasporic condition is a classed, gendered and racialized phenomenon. Informants of the study who are second/third generation members of the Indian diaspora tend to experience contradictory attitudes towards ethnic difference that is constituted by class, gender and race. Such attitudes could be traced to a colonial past that imagined and treated people based on racial hierarchies that privileged white foreigners. On one hand, Filipinos have imbibed the racial prejudices of their American colonizers and have treated ethnic groups such as Indians in a similar manner, on the other, Filipinos tend to look up to "white" Americans and Europeans, according them preferential treatment. The members of the Indian diaspora are both beneficiaries of Filipinos' hospitality and victims of their prejudices. Indeed, the influence of colonization and the symbolic power of the colonizer linger on and inform the experiences of the Indian diaspora on Philippine shores.

Notes

1. An earlier version of this chapter titled "Being Indian in Post-Colonial Metro Manila: Ethnic Identities, Class, Race and the Media" was published in *Philippine Sociological Review* 56 (2008): 56–79. Reproduced with permission of the publisher.
2. Based on statistics of registered aliens (by nationality) with paper-based ACR (Alien Certificate of Registration) as of 18 June 2007.
3. Hall (1997, p. 61) defines representation as "the process by which members of a culture use language…to produce meaning".
4. The "ugly" and "beautiful" in Philippine society are relative. However, it is important to note that certain ethnic groupings have local terms that suggest a certain look and skin colour. *Mestizo* or *tisoy* refers to fair-skinned Filipinos who

have either Chinese or Caucasian heritage. *Chinito* refers to looking Chinese. *Arabo* not only signifies Arab-looking but also prominent facial features and body hair. *Negro* is for those with dark-skin, curly hair and flat nose. Finally the word *bumbayin* has emerged in contemporary vocabulary to suggest an Indian look that is characterized by prominent facial features and hairy skin. *Bumbayin* is often used to describe (good looking) men. This partly explains why people reacted negatively to Priyanka's body hair. None of the informants used the word *bumbayin*. Filipinos who are neither fair nor dark, describe themselves as *kayumanggi* (brown) or simply *Pinoy/Pinay* looking. How these local terms are used contextually suggests either positive or negative meanings. Moreover, the prominence of one's nose is also an index of desirability in Philippine society. Traditionally, being *mestizo* connotes "qualities of natural beauty and intelligence" and "worldliness, refinement, wealth and high culture" (Pinches 1999, p. 280).
5. I have changed the surname to protect the privacy of the participant.
6. This is not to suggest that Filipinos had no practices of hygiene during that period. Anderson (2007, pp. 192–93) notes that Filipino elites who also worked for the colonial health agencies thought that the "disease stigma more properly belonged not to race but to social class". Indeed, since the American colonial period class differences and boundaries were already in place.
7. Following a bottom-up approach, I limited my data and discussion on media representations of Indians in the Philippines and global media that my participants mentioned in their interviews. One of my informants also pointed out that if ever Indian nationals appear in local news they are portrayed as trivial i.e., achieving a Guinness Book World Record. When I was gathering data, I became aware of crime news involving Indian nationals (see Olarte 2007). Such news stories were not mentioned by my informants.

References

Anderson, W. *Colonial Pathologies: American Tropical Medicine, Race, and Hygiene in the Philippines*. Quezon City: Ateneo de Manila University Press, 2007.

Anthias, F. "Race and Class Revisited". In *Race and Ethnicity: Critical Concepts in Sociology* (vol. 1), edited by H. Goulbourne, pp. 193–212. London: Routledge, 1990/2001.

Banderlipe, M. "The Philippines and Beauty Pageants". In *Mabuhay To Beauty!: Profiles of Beauties and Essays on Pageants*, edited by W. Capili, et al., pp. 141–56. Quezon City: Milflores Publishing, 2003.

Barth, F. "Introduction". In *Ethnic Groups and Boundaries: The Social Organisation of Culture Difference*, edited by F. Barth, pp. 9–38. London: Allen and Unwin, 1969.

Batnitzky, A., L. McDowell, and S. Dyer. "A Middle Class Globality? The Working Lives of Indian Men in a West London Hotel". *Global Networks* 8, no. 1 (2008): 51–70.

Bhatia, S. "The New Beauty Superpower!". *Times of India*, 21 May 2000, pp. B7–B9.

———. "9/11 and the Indian Diaspora: Narratives of Race, Place, and Immigrant Identity". *Journal of Intercultural Studies* 29, no. 1 (2008): 21–39.

Bhattacharya, G. "The Indian Diaspora in Transnational Context: Social Relations and Cultural Identities of Immigrants to New York City". *Journal of Intercultural Studies* 29, no. 1 (2008): 65–80.

Brah, A. *Cartographies of Diaspora: Contesting Identities.* London: Routledge, 1996.

———. "Difference, Diversity, Differentiation". In *Race and Ethnicity: Critical Concepts in Sociology* (vol. 1), edited by H. Goulbourne, pp. 253–82. London: Routledge, 1997/2001.

Clifford, J. "Diasporas". *Cultural Anthropology*, 9, no. 3 (1994): 302–38.

Cornell, S. and D. Hartmann. "Mapping the Terrain: Definitions". In *Race and Ethnicity: Critical Concepts in Sociology* (vol. 1), edited by H. Goulbourne, pp. 76–99. London: Routledge, 1998/2001.

David, R. "Credit Culture". *Philippine Daily Inquirer*, 4 October 2008, p. A10.

Georgiou, M. *Diaspora, Identity and the Media: Diasporic Transnationalism and Mediated Spatialities.* New Jersey: Hampton Press, 2006.

Gillespie, M. *Television, Ethnicity and Cultural Change.* London: Routledge, 1995.

Glick Schiller, N., Basch, and C. Blanc-Szanton. "Transnationalism: A New Analytic Framework for Understanding Migration: A New Analytic Framework". In *Towards a Transnational Perspective on Migration: Race, Class, Ethnicity, and Nationalism Reconsidered*, edited by N. Glick Schiller, N. Basch, and N. Blanc-Szanton, pp. 1–24. New York: New York Academy of Sciences. *Annals of the New York Academy of Sciences* 645 (1992).

Go, J. "'Racism' and Colonialism: Meanings of Difference and Ruling Practices in America's Pacific Empire". *Qualitative Sociology* 27, no. 1 (2004): 35–58.

Hall, S. "Cultural Identity and Diaspora". In *Theorizing Diaspora: A Reader*, edited by J. Braziel and A. Mannur, pp. 233–46. Massachusetts: Blackwell, 1990/2003.

———, ed. *Representations: Cultural Representation and Signifying Practices.* London: Sage, 1997.

Kerkvliet, B. *Everyday Politics in the Philippines.* Berkeley: University of California Press, 1990.

Lock, G. and C. Detaramani. "Being Indian in Post-colonial Hong Kong: Models of Ethnicity, Culture and Language among Sindhis and Sikhs in Hong Kong". *Asian Ethnicity* 7, no. 3 (2006): 267–84.

Madianou, M. *Mediating the Nation: News, Audiences, and the Politics of Identity.* London: University College London Press, 2005a.

Madianou, M. "Contested Communicative Spaces: Rethinking Identities, Boundaries and the Role of the Media among Turkish Speakers in Greece". *Journal of Ethnic and Migration Studies* 31, no. 3 (2005b): 521–41.

Olarte, A. "Spate of Attacks Alarms Indian Community". *Philippine Star*, 7 August 2007. <http://www.abs-cbnnews.com/storypage.aspx?StoryId=87429>. Accessed 10 August 2009.

Parameswaran, R. "Global Queens, National Celebrities: Tales of Feminine Triumph in Post-Liberization India". *Critical Studies in Media Communication* 21, no. 4 (2004): 346–70.

Philippine Center for Investigative Journalism "Statistics of Registered Aliens by Nationality with paper-based ACR (Alien Certificate of Registration) as of June 18, 2007". June 2007. <http://pcij.org/blog/wp-docs/BI_aliens_by_immigration_status_june2007.pdf>. Accessed 10 August 2009.

Pinches, M. "Entrepreneurship, Consumption, Ethnicity and National Identity in the Making of the Philippines' New Rich". In *Culture and Privilege in Capitalist Asia*, edited by M. Pinches, pp. 275–301. London: Routledge, 1999.

Punathambekar, A. "Bollywood in the Indian-American Diaspora". *International Journal of Cultural Studies* 8, no. 2 (2005): 151–73.

Radhakrishnan, S. "Examining the "Global" Indian Middle Class: Gender and Culture in the Silicon Valley/Bangalore Circuit". *Journal of Intercultural Studies* 29, no. 1 (2008): 7–20.

Raj, D.S. *Where Are You From? Middle-Class Migrants in the Modern World*. Berkeley: University of California Press, 2003.

Ray, M. "Bollywood Down Under: Fiji Indian Cultural History and Popular Assertion". In *Floating Lives: The Media and Asian Diasporas*, edited by S. Cunningham and J. Sinclair, pp. 136–83. Lanham: Rowman and Littlefield, 2001.

Safran, W., A. Sahoo, and B. Lal. "The Indian Diaspora in Transnational Context: Introduction". *Journal of Intercultural Studies* 29, no. 1 (2008): 1–5.

Salazar, L. "The Indian Community in Metro Manila: Continuities, Changes and the Effects of Rising India. In *Rising India and Indian Communities in East Asia*, edited by K. Kevasapany, A. Mani, and P. Ramasamy, pp. 499–524. Singapore: Institute of Southeast Asian Studies, 2008.

San Juan Jr., E. *Balikbayan Sinta: An E. San Juan Reader*. Quezon City: Ateneo de Manila University Press, 2008.

Santarita, J. "Contemporary Indian Communities in Western Visayas". In *Rising India and Indian Communities in East Asia*, edited by K. Kevasapany, A. Mani, and P. Ramasamy, pp. 525–48. Singapore: Institute of Southeast Asian Studies, 2008.

Schermerhorn, R. *Comparative Ethnic Relations: A Framework for Theory and Research*. Chicago: University of Chicago Press, 1978.

Silverstone, R. *Media and Morality: On the Rise of the Mediapolis*. Cambridge: Polity, 2007.

———— and M. Georgiou. "Editorial Introduction: Media and Minorities in Multicultural Europe". *Journal of Ethnic and Migration Studies* 31, no. 3 (2005): 433–41.

Singh, A. "South African Indian Migration in the Twenty-First Century: Towards a Theory of Triple Identity". *Asian Ethnicity* 9, no. 1 (2008): 5–16.

Taylor, S. and K. Littleton. "Biographies in Talk: A Narrative-Discursive Approach". *Qualitative Sociology Review* 2, no. 1 (2006): 22–38.

Thapan, A. "Tradition, Change and Identity: Sindhi Immigrants in Manila". In *The Philippines as Home: Settlers and Sojourners in the Country*, edited by M.B. Asis, pp. 101–34. Quezon City: Philippine Migration Research Network and Philippine Social Science Council, 2001.

————. *Sindhi Diaspora in Manila, Hong Kong, and Jakarta*. Quezon City: Ateneo de Manila University Press, 2002.

Todorov, T. "'Race', Writing, and Culture". In *"Race," Writing, and Difference*, edited by H.L. Gates, Jr., pp. 370–80. Chicago and London: University of Chicago Press, 1986.

Warikoo, N. "Gender and Ethnic Identity among Second-Generation Indo-Caribbeans". *Ethnic and Racial Studies* 28, no. 5 (2005): 803–31.

III

Practices

8

THE *KOPITIAM* IN SINGAPORE
An Evolving Story about Migration and Cultural Diversity

LAI Ah Eng

INTRODUCTION

Hundreds of *kopitiam* (coffee shop in Chinese dialects) are found throughout Singapore, with the majority located in the HDB (Housing and Development Board) public housing estates in which 83 per cent of Singapore's population live. Often viewed as a quintessential feature of Singapore public culture and everyday life, the *kopitiam* is one among several institutions and spaces within which are embedded dynamic aspects and processes of migration and social-cultural diversity, set within the larger contexts of change and globalization throughout Singapore's history.

In origin a small-scale enterprise serving drinks and foods during the colonial period of mass immigration, the *kopitiam* has since evolved and experienced much change over several distinct broad periods: pre-World War II until the early 1970s, massive resettlement of local communities into HDB public housing estates in the 1970s and 1980s, and rapid urbanization and globalization since the early 1990s. I examine the *kopitiam*'s evolution of its social-cultural distinctiveness and diversity through its foods, peoples, community and heritage.[1] I show how the *kopitiam* evolved from a monocultural into the multicultural community site[2] as part of a migration-diversity story which continues to dynamically unfold, and examine some interconnected dimensions of its history, heritage and multiculturalism.

Migration and Globalization, Local-Global Nexus

This paper is mainly empirical in substance, with several thematic foci broadly framing its discussion and its anthropological focus: a historical perspective on migration, local-global nexus, the significance of migration to the cultural and social life of local community, and the social and cultural dimensions of multiculturalism constructed historically through migration, settlement and adaptation.

In the Singapore context, a *longue durée* historical perspective on migration necessarily looks at mobility and settlement over the last 700 years in different eras of globalization (Tan, Heng and Kwa 2009). This paper however focuses on the two periods of mass migration throughout the nineteenth and early twentieth centuries of British imperialism and since the 1980s. British colonialism brought diverse peoples, mainly from China, India and the Malay Archipelago, to Singapore and Malaya to work and live in the ports, mines, plantations and emergent villages and towns. As Singapore received massive waves of immigrants, it grew rapidly from an entrepot trading port to a settlement with rich hinterlands in Malaya and Southeast Asia. These immigration flows stopped only just before the Second World War.

Migration to Singapore since the mid-1980s takes place in a new era of post-colonial economic globalization. Coming in more varied forms and levels of skills, immigrant settlers and transient workers now originate from varied Asian sources such as China, India and Southeast Asian countries such as the Philippines, Thailand, Indonesia, Malaysia and Myanmar, and from countries and regions further afar, such as Australia, Europe and North America. These workers occupy jobs at all levels in various industries and fields in the manufacturing, services, construction and communications sectors that have fuelled Singapore's post-colonial economic growth.

Against this historical background of labour migration, "immigrant" society, roots and cultures are foundational or common themes in various narratives on Singapore. In scholarly works on various colonial and post-colonial nation-building state and social projects, the place of immigration and its multivaried dimensions appear either as explicit subjects or assume implicit presence. My focus is on how migration flows and settlements, through diverse groups and their cultural inputs and interactions, have historically and socially shaped the *kopitiam*'s evolution.

The *kopitiam*'s migration-diversity story also tells much about the local-global nexus which characterize how spaces, places and communities are drawn into the processes of globalization. In Singapore, the *kopitiam* stands out as a unique institution with its particular local-global nexus of economic, social and cultural ingredients and infusions, through the generations of diverse peoples who inhabit it and through the foods (Mintz 2009) and activities that they bring and partake of. This uniqueness and its neighbourhood location and public-ness provide multifaceted insights into the local through its everyday life which tends to be taken for granted. Everyday life can be conceived as "reality par excellence" in which tension and demand on an individual's consciousness is highest (Berger and Luckmann 1966). It is the arena that provides the actual context for the meanings and experiences of culture and community (Geertz 1975; Cohen 1982). Put another way, everyday life is the "habitable reality" in which people appropriate, individualize and give meaning to various elements of mass culture such as language (de Certeau, 1984). Furthermore, it is in everyday life that modes of interaction, negotiations of similarities and differences (Cohen 1982; Heller 1984); and civil and moral orders (Suttles 1968; Whyte 1993; Lai 1995) are established.

THE *KOPITIAM* IN HISTORY

In Early Settlements during the Colonial Period

The *kopitiam* had humble origins as a small-scale economic enterprise. Found in early settlements of plantation, workplace, village, street or neighbourhood in nineteenth and early twentieth century colonial Singapore, they sold cheap drinks and sometimes meals to poor male immigrant workers, and were run by individuals or small teams of immigrant men and, later, families. Known as *han*, *tong* and *than* in Chinese dialects and *gerai* in Malay, most were no more than carts or makeshift structures, often with itinerant hawkers operating alongside. In the pepper and gambier *kangkar* (plantation) settlements, the forerunner of the *kopitiam* was probably set up alongside the liquor, provision and pawnshops run by the *kongsi* (company). As populations and demands grew, some of these expanded into modest-sized "eating houses" in the main street and centres of emergent villages, enclaves and small towns and near workplaces. Proprietors sold both drinks and food or only drinks and teamed up with/rented out stall space to food operators — this formula worked well and persists till today.

The early *kopitiam* and food stalls assumed a strong ethnic dimension in their spatial distribution and cuisine, as they "followed" immigrant workers and met their desires for culturally familiar foods. By 1900, the Chinese had become the majority population in Singapore, and Chinese "eating" stalls were thus numerous. They typically sold noodles and pre-cooked "economy rice" — affordable combinations of rice with dishes like salted eggs, fish, vegetables and meats cooked in their distinct versions by place origin. Some eateries offered common *tze-char* (cook-fry) cook-to-order dishes which approximated home-cooked meals. In the enclaves settled by Indians and Indian Muslims, similar *kedai makan Mamak* (Indian Muslim food shop in Malay; *Mamak* refers to Indian Muslims) sold breads (*prata, thosai*) and various combinations of rice with curries and meats for meals, while *sarabat* stalls sold coffee, teas and nibbles. Similarly, those *kedai-kedai* (shops) and *gerai-gerai* (stalls) in areas settled by Javanese, Sumatrans, Boyanese, Bugis and Madurese sold various *nasi* (rice) dishes such as *padang, rawan, jenganan, lemak* and *sambal*, spicy meats and vegetables, and various cakes and cuisines from their homelands. Such ethnic food stalls found in the pluralistic areas and edges of town, such as the old Esplanade, also catered to the diversifying taste buds of residents and visitors.

With the sale of food and drink, the *kopitiam* naturally and gradually became a social centre among the largely male immigrants. Among the Chinese, its early forms were probably their only alternative to the brothels and alcohol, opium and gambling dens. When gambling dens were outlawed in 1829 by the colonial government, some *kopitiams* served as a front for betting and gambling operations. Some also served as meeting place for secret society members to discuss deals and for negotiations. But in the main, most *kopitiams* were simple eateries where, besides food, customers sought simple rest, company and recreation. It was also a place for men, as women immigrants were few and were also expected to remain at home or in women's quarters. Among women, usually only hawkers, workers and servants were found in workplaces, markets or *kopitiams*; women did not chat or idle in *kopitiams*.

As a social centre, the *kopitiam* was the place to gather for news, chats, stories and to play chess or cards, its strategic location in the street, village or neighbourhood at the same time providing a view of people and the world passing by.[3] News of the outside world — on immigrants' homelands, Singapore, Malaya, and elsewhere — came via vernacular newspapers subscribed by the *kopitiam* and from which reports were read, alone or aloud to others many of whom were illiterate. When Rediffusion (the first commercial and cable-transmitted radio station in Singapore) started broadcasting services in various Chinese dialects and languages in 1949, many *kopitiams* subscribed to it to attract customers. Rediffusion not only offered daily news but also stories, songs and music of various linguistic and cultural traditions, from the classical to contemporary pop, and provided many hours of free entertainment and favourite programmes to customers. Similarly, the first televisions were installed by some kopitiams for customers when they became available and affordable in the 1960s and 1970s, gradually replacing Rediffusion.

The Hainanese Kopitiam

The *kopitiam*'s early history is incomplete without understanding the significant part played by the Hainanese *kopitiam*. Among the Chinese, the dominance of the Hainanese in the *kopitiam* business is an interesting tale of the latecomer and minority immigrant group whose survival skills later gave them an unexpected edge. Mostly men arriving later than the other dialect groups that had already built up various occupational niches backed by exclusivist clan associations, the numerically smaller and marginalized Hainanese found employment in despised or difficult work as farmers, rubber-tappers, seamen, cooks, waiters and servants. Throughout the nineteenth and early twentieth centuries, those who worked as cooks and domestics in European or Peranakan households built up a reputation as loyal and reliable "houseboys" and "cookboys", and came to be in great demand for the maintenance of colonial and rich lifestyles.

Changing economic and political conditions during the turbulent pre- and post-war periods, however, saw the gradual demise of the Hylam domestic workers. Their growing demands for better work conditions and competition from well-organized Cantonese single women immigrants (the *ma-tsae*) from the 1920s onwards greatly reduced their appeal, their decline in this sector culminating in the exodus of the British in the immediate pre-war, post-war and pre-independence periods (Lee 2009, p. 13). Many were forced to enter new occupations, and they turned to what they knew best — foods, beverages and services. Striking out on their own individually or in small teams of relatives or friends, Hainanese men tapped on their culinary, housekeeping, service and management skills cultivated from working in European households to set up *kopitiams*, bakeries, eateries, canteens and related food and beverage businesses such as coffee processing and food catering. Others found waged employment as cooks and waiters in Western-style hotels, clubs, restaurants and cafes, while yet others started their own inns and small hotels. They were also joined by Hainanese rubber-tappers displaced from work during the 1930s Great Depression (Lee 2009, p. 14). Other Hainanese immigrants entered the *kopitiam* trade directly, picking up trade and related skills. Their endeavours were further strengthened by the ideal common among Chinese immigrants to get out of arduous waged labour into *ka-ki-kang* (self-employment) and, better still, to be a successful entrepreneur through hard work.

As such, the 1920s–50s became a period of growth and thrive during which the Hainanese carved out and consolidated their distinct *kopitiam* business niche (Lee 2009, pp. 14–15). The now famous Killiney Kopitiam chain, for example, had a humble beginning as a shop set up in Killiney Road in 1919 by a Hainanese immigrant <http://www.killiney-kopitiam.com>. Similarly, the now famous family-run Ya Kun Toast began with fifteen-year-old Hainanese immigrant Loi Ah Koon who arrived in Singapore in 1926 and first worked as a coffeestall assistant before setting up his own shop <http://www.yakun.com>. Yet Con, Chin Chin and Swee Kee, all renowned for chicken rice and other Hainanese dishes, started operating in 1931, 1935 and 1949 respectively, while the famous Chin Mee Chin Confectionery in Katong was opened in 1925 by the Hainanese Mr Tang. Hainanese *kopitiams* numbered between twenty to thirty in the Hainan enclave in town, with the then Coffee King Lee Chang Er, owning seven kopitiams (Lee 2009, p. 18), while Hainanese *kopitiams* also sprang up in other locations.[4] The dominance of Hainanese in the food and beverages industry by the early 1930s led to the formation of the Kheng Keow Coffeeshop and Eating House Owners Association in 1934, later renamed the Kheng Keow Coffee Merchants Restaurants and Bar-Owners Association (新加坡琼侨咖啡酒餐商公会) in 1952 to reflect the expansion of the business and related trades during the 1950s which was considered the peak of the Hainanese *kopitiam* business.[5]

The core attraction of Hainanese *kopitiams* and eateries was their foods. Drawn from their culinary work backgrounds in European households, some distinct dishes were hybridized creations with Hainanese-Western roots, such as the breakfast of coffee[6] with kaya-butter toast and half-boiled eggs, pork chops and assorted confectionery (developed from the original British breakfast, Western pork chops and Western confectionery respectively). Other dishes were chicken rice, curried chicken and beef noodles. The early Hainanese *kopitiams* and eateries may thus be credited with introducing to the public Hainanese, Western and hybridized Hainanese-Western foods many of which have now become iconic or favourite Singapore foods. They may also be credited for being foundational in developing the *kopitiam* into a public institution and the strong public culture of eating and drinking by the 1950s. But where the *kopitiam* business became a successful niche among the Hainanese, it attracted other newcomers and competition. The numerically larger Foochows expanded so rapidly that they set up the Singapore Foochow Coffee Restaurant and Bar Merchants Association (新加坡福州咖啡酒餐商公会) with about 600 registered members by the 1950s (Lee 2009, p. 18).

The Indian and Malay Eateries

Paralleling the growth of Chinese *kopitiams* and eateries were those set up by Indians, Indian-Muslims and Malays which catered to demand for Indian and Malay ethnic foods by the expanding Indian and Malay immigrant populations. For example, Zam Zam which was opened in 1908 in Jalan Sultan sold Indian-Muslim foods such as *briyani*, *murtabak* and *prata* (with different curries and meats) and drinks such as coffee and varieties of tea. The first Indian vegetarian eatery Ananda Bhavan (now a chain across "Little India") was founded in 1924 by Indian immigrant Bhavan in Selegie near the Indian enclave of Serangoon <http://www.anandabhavan.com>, while vegetarian restaurant Komala's was opened in 1947 by immigrant Murugiah Rajoo and brothers from Tamil Nadu, India, after Rajoo had first worked as a waiter for ten years at Komala Vilas vegetarian restaurant in the Indian enclave <http://www.komalasweb.com>, <http://web.singnet.com.sg/~komala>. Such eateries sold Indian vegetarian foods such as *prata*, *thosai*, *vadai*, pancakes, and sweets in their diverse varieties. Sabar Menanti restaurant in the ethnic Kampung Glam and Kampung Jawa enclaves, famed for *nasi padang* and other Minangkabau dishes, was first set up around 1958 as a food stall by an immigrant from Sumatra (Omar 2005). Indeed, Indian-Muslim and Malay stalls and eateries, although smaller in numbers, have equally contributed to the making of the Singapore *kopitiam* as a public institution and to the public culture of eating and drinking.[7]

Resettlement into the HDB "Heartlands"

The *kopitiam* underwent much change in the immediate years of independence and nation-building, beginning from the mid-1960s until the mid-1980s and early 1990s. This was a period of massive urban renewal and rural resettlement, during which the HDB was tasked with meeting Singapore's land redevelopment needs and with resettling populations from often overcrowded or dilapidated urban areas, slums, squatter settlements and villages into HDB housing estates. Large plots of land with numerous settlements, farms and villages across Singapore were cleared for public housing and other schemes or for renewal, and their entire populations moved out into high-rise blocks of flats in new instant neighbourhoods. Along with these new public housing estates was born a new type of *kopitiam*.[8]

Designed as part of basic facilities in the HDB estate's town and neighbourhood centres, this new *kopitiam* was typically located at each end of a row of shops and close to the other facilities of hawker centre and market. Most of the new kopitiams' operators were likely former operators and others displaced by resettlement and offered cash compensations, priority HDB accommodation, and the option of relocation into or priority allocation of HDB business premises at concessionary resettlement rental rates (Lim and Lim 1985, pp. 311–16, 326–28). Others were individuals seeking new business opportunities. Similarly, the many itinerant hawkers and makeshift stallholders who found themselves compulsorily licensed and resettled as part of the government's town cleansing, public health, urban renewal and resettlement programmes, also found new stalls available in the new *kopitiams*, hawker centres and markets in the new HDB estates.

The new *kopitiam* in the new public housing estate was new in an unprecedented sense — its multiethnic and multicultural makeup. Where it was previously largely ethnic-based in location, cuisine and clientele, this new *kopitiam* was clearly multiethnic, mirroring the new multiethnic composition of the new estate whose populations were resettled from mainly ethnic-based settlements. This feature became an instant reality as the *kopitiam* naturally became one of the first public gathering sites for those disoriented by resettlement and for reorienting them. Through it, co-residents and neighbours from former communities were reunited with each other, strangers became recognizable as familiar faces, and yet others befriended as members of a new social network and co-residents of the new shared community.[9] The *kopitiam* operator quickly adapted to providing food and drink for an ethnically mixed clientele through the "sell drinks and rent foodstalls" formula in which he sold drinks and rented out several stalls selling a variety of ethnic foods. Residents then began to develop a cross-cultural taste for foods due to regular exposure in the *kopitiam*. "Multicultural" thus became the unwritten formula for the *kopitiam*'s survival, growth and success in the new multiethnic neighbourhood, and in doing so reinvented itself as a public place for the cultural confluence of cuisine, clientele and community in local everyday life that persists to this day.

THE HDB HEARTLAND KOPITIAM TODAY

The *kopitiam*'s migration-diversity story and manifestation as a public site of multiculturalism today is best understood by way of the kinds and flows of foods, people and activities passing through them.

Foods, Foods and More Foods

There is an enormous variety of foods sold in the HDB *kopitiam*. Culturally, food ranges from Chinese to Malay, Indian/Indian-Muslim and "Western", derived and hybridized from an earlier immigrant past. Individual items such as chicken rice, noodles, *prata* and *nasi padang*, once identified as ethnic and introduced by/for immigrants, are now iconic Singapore foods and readily available in most *kopitiam* as basic and popular everyday items. The Hainanese-Western breakfast set is now standard fare. The "economy rice" stall that once offered cheap food to poor Chinese immigrants retains its status as the *kopitiam*'s "anchor" stall while the *tze-char* kitchen is now in effect a small restaurant serving a wide range of cook-to-order dishes. The Indian/Indian-Muslim foodstall selling *prata*, *chapati* and meat dishes, the Malay stall selling *mee rebus* and meat dishes, and the "Western" stall offering local versions of Western foods (chops, steaks, grills, fries) are at least three other "must-haves" for a kopitiam to be "complete". Both traditional ethnic foods and hybridized and cross-cultural versions abound, such as noodles (Chinese dialect group, Indian and Malay, in dry, fried or soup versions); rice (Chinese, Malay and Indian, each with a range of meats and vegetables); curries (Chinese, Hainanese, Malay, Indian); breads and pancakes (Chinese, Malay, Indian and Western); and *rojak* (Chinese, Malay, Indian). A diversity of drinks match this food "fair" and are often ordered in their hybridized Singlish names, such as "milo dinosaur" (a cup of Milo with an extra spoonful of powdered undissolved Milo added). For individuals, most of whom have developed at least a moderately multicultural taste, it is now common practice to rotate different ethnic dishes among their meals at the *kopitiam*, and common for family members to be eating different ethnic dishes at the same time.

A *kopitiam*'s range of ethnic foods also varies by ownership, location and customer base. For example, stalls in Chinese-owned 128 Kopitiam, Bedok, besides offering common dishes, also serve distinctly traditional Chinese dishes such as teochew porridge, szechuan duck, black chicken, pig's innards and trotters, and frog legs and turtle soups. The stalls in nearby Mukmin Restaurant serve a range of Malay and Indian-Muslim foods and desserts, the classics being various kinds of rice with spicy meats and vegetables, breads and cakes as well as Malay and Indian hybridized versions of Western foods such as *rendang* burgers and roti John. Some HDB *kopitiams* and stalls have also attained fame for their foods within the estate or beyond, appearing on local food and heritage trails by word of mouth and through the Internet[10] and are sites sought out by eager "foodies" who travel all over Singapore to eat. Their claims to fame and sometimes creation of a particular dish are based on "first" setup, originality, authenticity, heritage and tradition, special skills, styles and ingredients mostly traceable to immigrant roots.

Since the 1990s, the foods that have shaped and substantiated Singapore's diverse culinary landscape (Chua and Raja 1997, p. 1) are being further infused with new ingredients and inputs by locals and new immigrants. In Marine Parade and Bedok *kopitiams* for example, the traditional "Western" food stall now additionally serves burgers, pizzas and spaghetti besides chops and steaks; Indonesian *ayam penyet* and Thai *tom yam* are popular in Malay cuisine; the Korean and Chinese noodles stall in MP59 Kopitiam is well patronized; while Japanese and fusion foods (e.g. XO brand fried rice) were offered by the fusion food stall Asia.Com in VStar. While some dishes and stalls may "die" in the highly competitive culinary environment of Singapore (fusion food Asia.Com stall and Botak Jones (Marine Parade outlet) serving American foods closed after a year), what is firmly established is the concept of "multicultural" in the kopitiam itself — it has to offer a wide range of ethnic, hybridized and now-considered "national" foods that meet the ethnic, multicultural and adventurous palates of customers and at affordable prices. In turn, it is the strong public culture of eating, first initiated through meeting immigrant needs and now expanded to include eating a diverse range of foods, which sustains the multicultural *kopitiam*'s survival and success.

Kopitiam People

Owners, Stallholders and Workers

The *kopitiam*'s immigrant sole proprietor making coffee is a sight of the past. Today's HDB *kopitiam* owner is more likely an absentee capitalist landlord who owns several *kopitiams* in various parts of Singapore. This is a consequence of intense competition and capital movements in this lucrative business, in which older founding proprietors unable to keep up with competition or wishing to retire have sold their shops to new and aggressive players.[11] Additionally, *kopitiam* owners' children are often reluctant to inherit their parents' trade because of its long hours, hard work and low status.[12] All five *kopitiams* observed have changed hands at least thrice since the late 1990s, with the exception of Mukmin Restaurant now run by the founder's son. It was rumoured that the new *kopitiam* owners are rich new citizens from China and Malaysia.

Kopitiam stalls tell a complex story of sole proprietor or small family businesses and adjustments to inter-generational mobility and economic pressures of costs and competition. Like the children of *kopitiam* owners, stallholders' children are also reluctant to take over their parents' trades because of long hours, hard work and low status and the wide range of alternative occupations for those upwardly mobile. As a result there has been some loss of culinary skills, standards and secrets and some stalls have closed when their operators retired (Huang 2008; Yen 2008). Additionally, since the late 1990s, rising costs and competition have led stalls to close for good or to relocate, sometimes several times, to less competitive areas.

Thus for example, the father-sons team of popular Hainanese Chin Swee Chicken Rice stall moved out of Marine Parade because of rising rents; Lao Feng Turtle Soup's stallholder in Bedok intends to retire after several decades due to spiralling rents and costs of ingredients and also because his "highly educated" son never had any interest in the trade. For family-run stalls in Mukmin Restaurant, younger generation members hold full-time jobs and only assist after work or during the peak Ramadan season.

Hard work, long hours and low wages in the *kopitiam* and foodstall trades — constant features since their early immigrant days — have led to the current shortage of workers. The solution has been the hiring of cheap foreign workers, sometimes illegally. Under the law, the services sector must employ a minimum of nine Singaporeans or permanent residents before they can hire foreign workers, while only Singaporeans and permanent residents are allowed to work in food stalls, including *tze-char* stalls.[13] Foreign workers are hired mainly as assistants, servers and cleaners and are mainly from China (men and women) and East Malaysia (men); while *tze-char* kitchen staff are mainly from Malaysia and increasingly from China and "beer ladies" are from Malaysia and China. On the whole, there is a perceived influx of workers from China in hawker foodstalls and *kopitiams*, while other nationalities are also entering the scene, such as Filipinos (Othman 2008). The scene of workers in many *kopitiams* today is a mix of locals and foreigners. Locals tend to be older men and women who are the identifiable "aunties" or "uncles"; the cooks tend to be younger Chinese men from Malaysian small towns, while the servers and assistants tend to be young men and women from China and who work for short periods before being replaced by another batch of Chinese workers.

The hiring of foreign workers has in turn kept local wages low and led to competition between local and foreign workers for jobs,[14] as well as spawned some mutual stereotyping. Locals are characterized as choosy and unwilling to work long hours, while Chinese workers are variously seen as *xiao long nu* (little dragon ladies), potential husband-stealers and poor cooks. As one customer put it: "they don't contribute to the cooking culture, they are just cheap labour; they don't know how to cook local dishes, only *ban mian* (flat noodles) and dumplings".

Customers and Community

In contrast to an earlier time in immigrant history when the *kopitiam* was a male domain, the *kopitiam*'s customers today are families, schoolchildren, social groups of men, women and youths, and individuals who are mainly the local neighbourhood's residents and who frequent it according to their everyday life schedules and needs. It is the place where individuals, groups, working couples and families eat, socialize and idle. Now a taken-for-granted scene, women eat and drink in the *kopitiam* in same-sex or mixed groups or on their own. "Latchkey" school children with parents at work can also safely eat there alone. This is the public home ground of the *Ah Laus, Pakciks* and *Makciks* (references to the elderly in Chinese and Malay) and *Ah Bengs, Ah Lians, Mats* and *Minahs* (references to the Chinese and Malay young).

The *kopitiam* that opens daily from dawn till midnight is at once a place of intense colours, sounds and activities. Customers queuing for food, stallholders shouting orders, cooks preparing foods, cleaners clearing tables, people eating and chatting, the television screening programmes — these are the everyday scenes of the multicultural public site that the *kopitiam* has evolved into in the local community. In recent years, some *kopitiams* have been bought over and turned into large foodcourts, but by and large, by virtue of its location, the heartland *kopitiam* is a place that provides a sense of social intimacy and sense of community for residents. And as if in a play about everyday life, they all make their appearances at different times to perform on the stage that the *kopitiam* is.

As a social centre, the multicultural *kopitiam* remains, as in the past, a window to the world through media access, only that cable television has replaced cable Rediffusion. There is always something to watch, including international news, soap operas, documentaries, local sitcoms and reality shows. Highlights are "live" sports competitions such as the Olympics and local and international soccer league games, when fathers and sons, couples, friends and foreign workers turn up to watch, and from which new Singlish terms are spawned, such as Pang Pow [firing cannon in Hokkien] for Arsenal and Tok Tok Ham for Tottenham Hotspurs soccer teams. Indeed, the *kopitiam* is one of the few public places where local languages are still heard and the multicultural Singlish language further developed, such as "palata" ("prata"), and "you sit I bring" (please be seated and I will bring your order). Here too, discussions about world events, local politics, jokes, stories, personal histories and various matters big and small continue to be conducted and heard abundantly in the true tradition of coffeeshop talk. The *kopitiam* is thus a site where "heartlanders" frequent irrespective of various age, ethnic, income and work backgrounds. The well-dressed office worker and the pyjama-clad elderly lady in her wheelchair, the retired old man and the school student — all may enter the *kopitiam* and share space at the same or adjacent tables. It is normal to ask "can I sit here?" and unthinkable to reply "no, you cannot". This is shared space that offers a sense of being open and equal to all (Chan 2003, pp. 132, 135), with social boundaries temporarily removed or well negotiated within an order of civility honed over time, since immigrant days.

The practices of religious diversity and negotiations of religious boundaries in the *kopitiam* highlight particularly well the developed codes of civility as well as the strength of its multiculturalism in its equality, tolerance and sense of community. Visually and symbolically, these are manifested by the peaceful coexistence of Muslim signboards, which typically display green and yellow icons of mosques, crescent moon and star and Arabic inscriptions about Allah, and Chinese *kopitiams'* and stalls' altars for the deities deemed important for peace and prosperity. Alongside the availability of diverse foods, religious boundaries mainly along lines of "halal" for Muslim food and "non-halal" for other foods are maintained. Stalls observe these boundaries in food preparation and service, such as with colour coded crockery. While Muslim stalls are easily patronized by non-Muslims, the Chinese-run stall may carry a "no pork no lard" sign to attract Muslim customers comfortable enough with this boundary. Customers demarcate eating spaces within an unspoken but well-understood code when eating halal/non-halal dishes at a shared table or common space. Religious events further highlight religious diversity and its negotiation and tolerance. During Ramadan, Muslim customers do not consume food during fasting time and Muslim stalls may operate at different hours and sell special food items for the breaking of fast. Mukmin Restaurant, for example, opens closer to breaking fast time when there is a frenzied sale of foods by the stalls and free food is offered by the owner to the poor and needy as a gesture of almsgiving. It is also a time for non-Muslim customers to savour the foods of the Ramadan season. For Chinese *kopitiams* and stalls, offerings are made daily and on auspicious occasions, such as during the Seventh Month Festival and Lunar New Year, while the *tze-char* stall offers special *lou hei* dishes and lion dance troupes perform for luck and prosperity during the latter season. In general, the code of civility for tolerating and accommodating religious needs, practices and taboos in the kopitiam are well developed and understood by stallholders and customers alike, honed through everyday practice over time.

A NEW CHAPTER IN THE KOPITIAM STORY

Kopitiams have entered a new era in their evolution since the early 1990s. There are growing competitive pressures, with original owners subletting or selling their shops and stall tenants moving in and out amidst a general trend of accelerating costs of food ingredients and rentals. The demise of most old *kopitiams* and stalls will probably go unremembered. What is being told and played out today are the success stories of those early immigrants' *kopitiams* and eateries that had a headstart and that are now run by subsequent generations of family through inheritance and intergenerational skills transfers, now characterized by rebranding, modernized management systems, new ideas of public eating culture and, of course, reinvented and hybridized dishes, such as the cases of Jack's Place, Han's, Killiney, Yakun (all Hainanese), Bhavan and Komala's (South Indian) and Sabar Menanti (Indonesian/Malay). There are also new "rags to riches" success stories akin to immigrant narratives, such as that of Pang Lim, the 13-year old kitchen helper who became Koufu foodcourt chain boss[15] and Lim Bee Huat, the nine-year old *kopi kia* (coffee boy) who became *kopi king* of the Kopitiam chain[16] and who dreams of "a *kopitiam* on every street" and hopes to "fill the street corners with coffee, kaya toast and eggs". At the same time, expanding markets and intense competition has led such enterprises to set up outlets throughout Singapore. Expansion has also gone international, such as with Komala's, Kopitiam, Han's and Yakun whose staff and family members are effectively a class of international "circulating migrant" entrepreneurs who undertake frequent travel and short stays abroad to manage their overseas operations.

Kopitiam Heritage Commoditized and Commercialized

In the relentless competition, elements of *kopitiam* tradition, culture and heritage are being invoked to maximize business claims and opportunities by *kopitiam* and food operators who consciously appeal to specific elements which play on memory, nostalgia and even pride. The *kopitiam* has undergone sufficiently long evolution to have built up history and tradition, and there is thus sufficient space for historicizing and recreating the past and invoking memory and nostalgia, while the appeal to social ties and heartland intimacy through its social role and location further lend a sense of historical and contemporary meanings. Thus for example, the Koufu chain claims to "reinvent the coffee shop traditions with a fusion of eastern and western techniques so that the company can evolve through modern management concepts and yet stay true to good old coffee shop traditions", and "to preserve the uniqueness of authentic Singapore hawker cuisines". It also claims to be able to personalize service with "friendliness and intimacy" because its shops are located in housing estates <http://www.koufu.com.sg/profilechampions.html>. The Killiney Kopitiams recreate the atmosphere of the old Hainanese coffeeshop with period furnishings, décor and historical memorabilia. Its mission statement is "to keep the '*Kopitiam*' tradition going for this generation and for the many generations to come", while its tagline is "Welcome to the good old days." Hainanese Ya Kun's branding lies in its belief that "a good toast binds kinship, friendship and partnership" and its mission includes "preserv[ing] its unique and rich heritage". Both Killiney Kopitiam and Ya Kun have received "heritage" as well "spirit of enterprise" awards in recent years. It is thus also not surprising that a legal case involving the use of the name "Kopitiam" took place in 1988 when the competition first began.[17]

In the claims of tradition, culture and heritage, the ethnic and multiethnic or multicultural elements are also played up through the history of each enterprise and through the foods sold, in which originality, authenticity and diversity are capitalized on. In this, the Hainanese operators' claim to both *kopitiam* and culinary heritage, already firmly established in the first half of the twentieth century by Hainanese immigrants, is an outstanding example by virtue of having been among the first to start and to contribute through their unique fusion foods. Indeed, the "Hainanese *kopitiam*" that have been foundational in "tradition" and "heritage" have become legendary and popularized within the now developed larger kopitiam culture.[18] At the same time, operators are aware that *kopitiams* and foodcourts must remain multiethnic and multicultural in their foods sold and in their appeal to customers. Thus, Kopitiam has set up the Banquet chain of *halal* foodcourts (which is in reality a halal multicultural *kopitiam*) and Han's runs several *halal* Hanis Café and Bakery outlets. For Koufu, it "... want[s] to nurture the inherent joy of sharing a meal or drink with family and friends, by providing friendliness and a spark of inspiration in the everyday life of people of all ages, social classes and ethnic backgrounds" <http://www.koufu.com.sg/profilehistory.html>, while Komala's restaurant claims that "it is the commitment to such values [quality, value-for-money authentic Indian food, commitment to cleanliness and hygiene] that earned Komala's popularity with the Indians, Malays, Chinese and tourists throughout its 50-year history in Singapore" <http://www.komalasweb.com/>.

Needless to say, foods and food cultures themselves are central to heritage. Food specialization, hybridization and fusion, clearly traceable to immigrant histories of various ethnic groups and their culinary contacts and inputs, continue to make food cultures a living heritage, sustained by and in turn sustaining and exciting the public culture of eating. Some new, reinvented, hybrids and further hybrids of food dishes have even triggered food crazes and the occasional culinary war between cooks and food operators, such as over laksa, chicken rice, beancurd, nasi padang and kaya toast.[19] Competing food heritage claims in the competitive local and tourism sectors have recently even threatened to take a regional dimension between countries in Southeast Asia such as Malaysia, Singapore and Indonesia where foods have followed migrations and developed into local versions, igniting even nationalist sentiments.

Whither the *kopitiam*'s customers and community amidst these rapid changes? *Kopitiam* culture is by now firmly established as part of an everyday lifestyle that cuts across class and ethnic backgrounds. There is now a huge variety of *kopitiams* and food outlets competing to keep up with customers' changing tastes as well as create new expectations of the coffeeshop and eating experience. Customers move about for choice and are not limited to neighbourhood ones unless they are locale-bound or cash-strapped. Still, for the heartland residents, the neighbourhood *kopitiam* remains a place of choice in everyday life. In the growing competition between local neighbourhood *kopitiams* and bigger players, the smaller ones are able to offer a sense of intimacy and community that the larger crowded ones may not.[20]

CONCLUSION

The story of the *kopitiam* in Singapore is deeply embedded within a larger historical and social narrative of migration and cultural diversity. Born out of the necessity for food and company among male immigrants of various ethnic backgrounds in colonial Singapore, the *kopitiam* served as a simple eating place and social centre, as well as became an economic niche for those with culinary and service skills or who had little choice but to work long hours at low wages in this low-status trade. Reflecting ethnic dimensions in terms of spatial locations, foods sold and customer bases, the *kopitiam* also evolved to become the social centre in the local community, serving as the focal point of everyday life and at the same time providing links to the outside world through media channels. Through resettlement into public housing heartlands and over time, the monocultural *kopitiam* evolved into a multicultural institution that is a confluence of cuisine, clientele and community. The multicultural heartland *kopitiam* today remains *the* institution of local community and everyday public life. Open equally to all, it loudly displays the public culture of eating, drinking and talking that is considered by some as the national pastime, and satisfies the need for replenishment, rest and recreation through culturally familiar foods, friends and fraternities.

The confluence of cuisine, clientele and community in the *kopitiam* makes it a significant site for providing glimpses into local-global connections and social diversities that migration and globalization can bring over time, particularly to an open and globalizing place like Singapore. The *kopitiam* confirms and richly illustrates at the local level the habitable reality of everyday life (de Certeau 1984) and as reality *par excellence* (Berger and Luckmann 1966), as well as meanings and experiences of culture and community (Geertz 1975; Cohen 1982). This includes some modes of interaction and negotiations of similarities and differences (Cohen 1982; Heller 1984), and the gradual construction of a social and civil order (Suttles 1968; Whyte 1993; Lai 1995). It further complicates these notions, through its migration-diversity narrative, with elements of pluralism and multiculturalism that are continuously evolving and also best appreciated in historically and socially specific contexts.

This multiculturalism is most captured through its food inputs, ingredients and infusions which have followed the diverse migratory peoples to Singapore and whose descendants now inhabit this space. Indeed, kopitiam cuisine is a richly illustrative case of the flows and contributions of non-Western and Asian cuisine to the world that Mintz (2009) notes as poorly recorded and recognized. *Kopitiam* cuisine (also that of hawker centres and restaurants), with its strong heritage of immigrant roots, diversity, hybridization and fusion, have been taken to new levels in recent years and popularized simultaneously as ethnic, national and multicultural. While some dishes may vanish and cooking secrets die out, there are enough intergenerational transfers of cuisine skills, recorded recipes and creative players to ensure continuity. Indeed, the thriving diversity and hybridization of foods with its seemingly endless possibilities attests to Singapore's global position as multicultural food capital and contributor to world cuisine. The *kopitiam* remains a prominent site that provides the social and popular setting for sustaining this heritage and its further development.

Clientele and community in the *kopitiam* similarly display multicultural dimensions and dynamics of the migration-diversity narrative in Singapore. The *kopitiam* continues to thrive as a site of social diversity through the meals and meetings it provides and enables in the lives of those who frequent it — old immigrants and their descendants, and new immigrants and transient workers — and who engage with each other through everyday modes of behaviour. Old immigrants and their descendants are more familiar with this pluralism and its negotiations for keeping civil and social order. In some areas such as the religious, accommodations are negotiated and borders maintained, while in others like ethnic cuisine, there are opportunities for pushing and crossing them. New immigrants in the neighbourhood and clientele at the kopitiam must familiarize themselves with and adapt to these established everyday modes of civility and interaction such as in the *kopitiam*.

Against a general backdrop of locals' reluctant acceptance and resentment of foreign workers who are perceived as economic competitors, limited social and cultural integration and strong mutual stereotyping, local-foreign divides and everyday politics assume a particular significance in the *kopitiam* context. Migrant workers in the *kopitiam* are a peculiar part of its pluralism and community — their presence is needed but their transience means that they are unable to partake substantially and over time in the community. This is particularly so for those from China who tend to be rotated, as compared with Malaysians who tend to remain working in the same stalls. Chinese workers and immigrants also tend to be more stereotyped by locals, and are often perceived to be inadequate in English and monocultural in orientation. Thus for example, the following reflects popular sentiments towards those from China in adapting to Singapore:

> First, acknowledge that Singapore is not China and that people are more Westernised. Second, learn English even if it is a coffeeshop version. Third, mix more with locals and see how they interact with each other. Fourth, believe that Singapore is a law-abiding place and that laws are strictly enforced without favour. Fifth, do not think that all Singaporeans are rich. Sixth, adapt to the local cuisine.[21]

Language and cultural orientation issues for foreign workers in the *kopitiam* are not as significant as their transience. Yet, transient workers count too, as they become a permanent feature even as individual workers may come and go, and need to be included in the established everyday civilities of *kopitiam* culture. Here, locals' treatment and expectation of transient foreign workers within the *kopitiam's* everyday multiculturalism is important, even as interaction is likely to be limited to co-existence and tolerance within what is mainly a transactional business relationship between customer and worker.

So how will the migration-diversity story of the *kopitiam* develop from here? So long as there are cultural flows and interaction, there will be a multicultural *kopitiam* that is the confluence of cuisine, culture and community. Even as the mobile now move about varied settings for food and company, it remains that the *kopitiam* culture is a way of everyday life and arguably makes the *kopitiam* a quintessential Singapore experience and a living heritage site. And so long as love of food and eating out remain strong, the multicultural *kopitiam's* cuisine, culture and community will continue to thrive and evolve. Arguably, the *kopitiam* is like a miniature society and metaphor for Singapore,[22] telling a story of its immigrant and social histories and that of ordinary people's lives, capturing their struggles for livelihood and the evolution of Singapore's multiculturalism from the ground. This story is not yet concluded; it continues to unfold with dramatic developments of a local-global nature before our very eyes today.

Notes

1. Research employed historical and anthropological approaches, with data drawn from archival and media documents and from primary fieldwork (July–Nov 2008) based on conversational interviews and observations at *kopitiams* in Marine Parade, Bedok and Eunos — "first generation" HDB estates built under resettlement schemes in the early 1970s. Their populations are socially mixed and multiethnic, comprising Chinese (majority in every case), Chinese Peranakan, Malays, Indians, Eurasians and various other backgrounds many of whom were first resettled from surrounding areas, and new immigrant populations since the late 1990s. I did not encounter any major problems with observations, mainly because of the openness of *kopitiams*. For access and interviews, I spoke several Chinese dialects, Malay and English and sometimes capitalized on my childhood background as a "kopi kia" (child) and as resident, familiar customer, and interested documenter of food cultures.
2. I move between *kopitiams* in general and those in public housing estates which cater to local residential communities.

3. Chua (1995) elaborates on the *kampung* (village) *kopitiam* as the location par excellence for collective idling by males.
4. Such as Telok Ayer, Siglap, Chai Chee, Thomson and Nee Soon, while in Seletar and Sembawang, Hainanese cafes served mainly British and Commonwealth troops and their families. Two other outstanding examples of Hainanese eateries are Jack's Place <http://www.jacksplace.com.sg> and Han's <http://www.hans.com.sg>.
5. Membership rose from 61 at its inception to 221 in 1940 and 505 in 1950 (Lee 2009, pp. 16–17).
6. Hainanese coffee merchants and *kopitiam* operators also developed their special recipes and distinctive forms of roasting coffee beans and brewing coffee.
7. The historical evolution and individual stories of Indian, Indian-Muslim, Malay and other eateries within the contexts of the social history of Singapore and their respective communities need to be researched and told alongside the Chinese ones, for a more complete and inclusive story of *kopitiams* and food heritages in Singapore's multiculturalism.
8. See Lim and Lim (1985) for details of resettlement policy, process and pact and Chua, Sim, and Low (1985) for a detailed longitudinal case study of resettling a village. Unfortunately, the latter study did not track the resettlement consequences for the village's one and only coffeeshop.
9. Personal communication with older residents resettled in Marine Parade.
10. See, for example <http://www.foodlane.sg>, <http://www.makansutra.com>, <http://www.hungrygowhere.com>, <http://www.makantime.com>, <http://soshiok.com>, <http://www.goodfood.sg>, <http://www.yebber.com>, <http://www.ieatishootipost.blogspot.com> and <http://lazyfoodies.blogspot.com/>.
11. Lim Bee Huat, founder of the Kopitiam chain (with about 70 outlets as at August 2009), bought his first kopitiam in Bishan housing estate with a "jaw-dropping" bid of S$2.01 million. The shop's value later rose to S$6 million (The Kopi Tiam King. <http://www.kopitiam.biz/content/showcontent.asp?section=success>. Accessed 22 Sept 2008).
12. The early Hainanese were known to invest in their children's education for upward economic mobility, as a result of which their well-educated children did not want to take over their *kopitiams*.
13. Both the Foochow Coffee Restaurant and Bar Merchants Association and Kheng Keow Coffee Merchants Restaurant and Bar Owners Association are jointly appealing for this no-foreigners rule to be relaxed. See *Straits Times* (2009d).
14. See various articles in the *Straits Times* (2007b; 2007a), and Lin and Au Yong (2008) and *Straits Times* (2009c).
15. Pang worked variously as kitchen helper, street hawker, fruit seller and coffee shop stallholder before opening his first coffeeshop in 1990 with his younger

brother and uncle. Pang's Koufu chain operates about thirty foodcourts, five coffee shops and five cafes, mainly in HDB heartlands <http://www.koufu.com.sg/profilehistory.html>.
16. Lim Bee Huat started as a coffee-stall assistant who harboured entrepreneurial ambitions and made acute observations about the trade along the way. He bought his first kopitiam in 1988 and moved swiftly to set up outlets which today number seventy <http://www.kopitiam.biz/content/showcontent.asp?section=success>.
17. The legal tussle between Kopitiam Singapore Restaurant and the Kopitiam Pte Ltd over the exclusive use of the name "Kopitiam" resulted in the latter's favour as it was ruled that the term *"kopitiam"* was generic and could be used by anyone.
18. A recent television sitcom revolves around the *kopitiam* and is titled "Hainan Kopi Tales".
19. Yakun makes and sells its own brand of Hainanese kaya (*Straits Times* 2009*b*), while Han's continues the Hainanese tradition of hybridizing dishes and confectionery. For examples of the kaya craze, kaya toast wars and food feuds, see *Straits Times* (1999), *Straits Times* (2005), and *Straits Times* (2009*a*).
20. The issues of competition, tradition, heritage and community also further raise complex issues of the interplay between policies and market forces which are beyond the scope of discussion here.
21. *Straits Times* (2009*e*).
22. Like the teahouse is for writer Lao She who, in his famous play *Teahouse*, wrote that "a big teahouse is like a miniature society" and can be read as a metaphor for China. The play spans fifty years of modern Chinese history, witnessing the disintegration of the Qing Empire and the beginning of the struggle to build a modern nation-state through the portrayal of *xiao renwu* — ordinary characters — from all walks of life who frequented the Chinese teahouse. Singapore playwright Kuo Pao Kun (Kuo 2001) attempted to do the same for Singapore with his play *Kopitiam* (1996).

References

Berger, P.L. and T. Luckmann. *The Social Construction of Reality: A Treatise in the Sociology of Knowledge*. Harmondsworth: Penguin Books, 1996.

Chan, S.C. "Consuming Food: Structuring Social Life and Creating Social Relationships". In *Past Times: A Social History of Singapore*, edited by K.B. Chan and C.K. Tong, pp. 123–35. Singapore: Times Editions, 2003.

Chua, B.H. "That Imagined Space: Nostalgia for Kampungs". In *Portraits of Places: History, Community and Identity in Singapore*, edited by B.S.A. Yeoh and L. Kong, pp. 222–41. Singapore: Times Editions, 1995.

——— and A. Raja. "Hybridity, Ethnicity and Food in Singapore". Unpublished academic work. Singapore: Department of Sociology, National University of Singapore, 1997.

———, J. Sim, and C.W. Low. "Resettling Soon Hock Village: A Longitudinal Study". In *Housing a Nation: 25 years of Public Housing in Singapore*, edited by A.K. Wong and S.H.K. Yeh, pp. 335–74. Singapore: Maruzen Asia for Housing and Development Board, 1985.

Cohen, A.P. "Belonging: The Experience of Culture". In *Belonging: Identity and Social Organization in British Rural Cultures*, edited by A.P. Cohen, pp. 1–18. Manchester: Manchester University Press, 1982.

de Certeau, M. *The Practice of Everyday Life*. Steven Rendall (Trans.). Berkeley: University of California Press, 1984.

Geertz, C. *Local Knowledge*. New York: Basic Books, 1975.

Heller, A. *Everyday Life*. London: Routledge and Kegan Paul, 1984.

Huang, L. "Going, Going Gone?". *Sunday Times*, 3 August 2008, p. 24.

Kuo, P.K. "Kopitiam". In *Images at the Margins: A Collection of Kuo Pao Kun's Plays*. Singapore: Times Books International, 2001.

Lai, A.E. *Meanings of Multiethnicity: A Case Study of Ethnicity and Ethnic Relations in Singapore*. Kuala Lumpur: Oxford University Press, 1995.

———. "A Neighbourhood in Singapore: Ordinary People's Lives 'Downstairs'". In "Future Asian Space: Projecting the Urban Space of New Asia", edited by Hee Limin, Boontham Davisi and Erwin Viray, pp. 115–37. Singapore: National University of Singapore Press, 2011.

Lee, M.S. "Hainanese Gobidiams in the 1930s–1950s: Food Heritage in Singapore". Unpublished paper submitted for the Independent Study Module. Singapore: Department of History, Faculty of Arts and Social Sciences, National University of Singapore, 2009.

Lim, H.Y. and K.H. Lim. "Resettlement: Policy, Process and Impact". In *Housing a Nation: 25 Years of Public Housing in Singapore*, edited by A.K. Wong and S.H.K. Yeh, pp. 305–34. Singapore: Maruzen Asia for Housing and Development Board, 1985.

Lin, K. and J. Au Yong. "The Coffee Shop Divide". *Straits Times*, 27 April 2008. <http://business.asiaone.com/Business/Story/A1Story20080425-61897.html>. Accessed 7 August 2008.

National Environment Council. "Clean Toilets in our Garden City". News Release no.082/1999, Date of issue: 11 August 1999. In *National Environment Report*, 7 February 2004, <http://www.env.gov.sg/info/press/ENV>. Accessed 1 September 2009.

Mintz, S. W. "Asia's Contributions to World Cuisine". *The Asia-Pacific Journal*, Vol. 18-2-09, 1 May 2009.

Omar, M. *Sabar Menanti Restaurant*. Singapore: National Library Board, 2006.

Othman, D. "Filipinos are your New Servers". *Straits Times*, 14 July 2008. <http://www.straitstimes.com/Free/Story/STIStory_257417.html>. Accessed 1 September 2009.

Straits Times. "Spread Some Love Around". 5 December 1999.

———. "Now Who's the Toast of the Town?". 22 May 2005. <http://www.smu.edu.sg/news_room/smu_in_the_news/2005/sources/ST_20050522_1.pdf>. Accessed 25 August 2009.

———. "Language Problems in Service". 12 December 2007*a*.

———. "Taking Jobs away from Locals". 12 December 2007*b*.

———. "Famous Food Feuds". 11 January 2009*a*.

———. "Toast to Sweet Success". 9 March 2009*b*.

———. "Are Locals Shunning Jobs at Tze Char Stalls?". 5 July 2009*c*.

———. "Tze Char Stalls Need Foreign Workers". 5 July 2009*d*.

———. "Your Insights". 16 October 2009*e*, p. A25.

Suttles, G. *The Social Order of the Slum: Ethnicity and Territory in the Inner City*. London: University of Chicago Press, 1968.

Tan, T. "From Illegal Hawker to Food Chain Boss". *Straits Times*, 14 April 2007. <http://wineanddine.asiaone.com/Wine%252CDine%2B%2526%2BUnwind/Features/Topics/Story/A1Story20070622-14990.html>. Accessed 25 August 2009.

Tan, T.Y., D. Heng, and C.G. Kwa. *A 700-year History: From Early Emporium to World City*. Singapore: National Archives of Singapore, 2009.

The Kopi Tiam King. In "S-Files: Stories Behind their Success". Singapore: Success Resources Pte Ltd. <http://www.kopitiam.biz/content/showcontent.asp?section=success>. Accessed 22 September 2008.

Whyte, W.F. *Street Corner Society: The Social Structure of an Italian Slum*, 4th ed. Chicago: University of Chicago Press, 1993.

Yen F. "Makan Mashup". *Straits Times National Day Special*, 9 August 2008, p. 17.

9
SPATIAL PROCESS AND CULTURAL TERRITORY OF ISLAMIC FOOD RESTAURANTS IN ITAEWON, SEOUL

Doyoung SONG

INTRODUCTION: NEW CULTURAL TERRITORY IN SEOUL

Considering its population size of 10 million, Seoul has a relatively low level of cultural and ethnic diversity not only in numerical terms (Choe 2003, p. 24) but also in terms of dominant ideas of ethnic unity, influenced at least in part by the historical experience of colonialism. However, a new trend appeared at the end of the 1980s, becoming much clearer in the 2000s: the advent of what has been called "diaspora foreigners' space" (Kim 2005, p. 25) or "ethnic villages" (Kim and Kang 2007) in several areas of Seoul. In some of these places, a legacy of foreign coercive occupation still affects their spatial formation. Nevertheless, a more remarkable phenomenon is the emergence of new cultural players. These new cultural players, often new ethnic groups, are widening a kind of liminal space installed by previous occupants. They transform these spaces into their own cultural territory.

In this chapter, I discuss the advent of an "Islamic area" in Itaewon where the number of Islamic restaurants and *halal* grocery stores is growing.

Islamic restaurants and Islamic food shops presuppose the presence of Muslim consumers who observe the food restrictions of Islamic religion. The process of their expansion, and the perceptions of Koreans and foreign Muslims on the food and spaces of Islamic food consumption such as these restaurants will be observed and analysed. Based on this analysis, I demonstrate how the consumption and interpretations of "Islamic food" in Korea unfolds in non-uniform ways. For the Muslim consumers, these shops offer not only tastes from their homeland but also the possibility of keeping their religious identity. For Korean consumers and other non-Muslim clients, Islamic restaurants and grocery stores represent a form of "exotic dining experience". This "special experience" is, for them, labelled according to the food's regional and national identification, but usually without consideration of the religious signification of the food. In this respect, this chapter speaks to both the literature on diasporic and transnational food consumption (Cwiertika 2002; Collins 2008; Gabbacia 1998) and the ways in which food consumption constitutes an engagement with emergent "others" within society (Hage 1997; Hooks 1992). Through a focus on the foreign district of Itaewon in Seoul the chapter illustrates that it is particular urban spaces that facilitate the co-constitution of new food cultures and the multiple engagements with difference (Bak 2005; Duruz 2005; Crang, Dwyer and Jackson 2003). At the end of this chapter, it will be shown that the consumption of foods can be interpreted as an expression of the desire for cultural diversity amongst urban inhabitants in Seoul.

ITAEWON: FOREIGNERS' TERRITORY IN SEOUL

Itaewon district is located in Yongsan-gu, a geographically central area of the city of Seoul. Positioned next to the U.S. Army camp, it is a retail strip composed of a busy main street and many small alleyways where shops and residences are mixed together. The name Itaewon started to appear in historical records of the sixteenth century as a connection point of Seoul with the southern region of Korea. It was then located just outside of the ancient city of Seoul which had less than half of the surface of today's Seoul city. At the end of the nineteenth century, the Itaewon area was occupied by the Chinese army and, later, by the Japanese army until 1945. At the end of the Second World War in 1945, U.S. army camp occupied a large part of Yongsan. Located just at the outskirts of the Yongsan army camp,

Itaewon became a commercial district supporting the U.S. forces. Since the 1950s, shops and clubs in Itaewon have functioned as a recreational area for U.S. army personnel. Itaewon also played a role as a "resource place" offering alternative cultural products for Koreans. Itaewon became a gate through which American and other foreign cultures were introduced to Korean residents.

The Seoul Olympic Games in 1988 and the associated exposure to external influences contributed to notable changes in the characteristics of Itaewon. In particular, Western and Japanese tourists started to frequent Itaewon as an area where they could shop without language problems because the main languages on the streets of Itaewon were English and Japanese. Such a case was unique in Seoul at the time, and remains so today. More recently, movements of human capital and knowledge into Korea have significantly diversified, particularly the increase in non-Western and non-Japanese visitors. Being the only urban place open to foreigners, Itaewon has become the place that foreigners frequent. In this way, Itaewon has become a kind of "international zone" with a certain degree of cultural diversity. Foreign food offered by Itaewon restaurants represents an important expression of this newly developing cultural diversity and its territoriality in Seoul.

Foreign food restaurants in Itaewon were established with the expectation of serving foreign customers among the rapidly growing number of foreign tourists and business people, diplomats, and other visitors who wanted familiar food in Korea.[1] Catering to Korean local customers was not the primary concern for these restaurants, and was considered unnecessary and not even advisable in this extra-territorial zone. Even Korean visitors to this district expected to experience an "authentic foreign taste".

Some restaurants targeting "cosmopolitan" businesspeople as their clients were established that focused on providing "international standard" Western food. However, it was the newly arrived small snack corners and fast food places that claimed to offer "real home-made food" — meaning, they offered the atmosphere and tastes of a particular "local" culture, "just like home". Young English teachers from North America, the United Kingdom and Australasia, and migrant labourers from South and Southeast Asia and other parts of the world were taking the place of U.S. army personnel in the Itaewon neighbourhood (Kim 2004, p. 41). Koreans' growing travel experiences since the end of 1980s also contributed to the growing pool of new customers for these small "ethnic food" restaurants.

After having "first hand" experiences abroad, an increasing number of Koreans desired either tastes that reminded them of their time abroad or the taste of "something new". What they wanted was the "original" "local" flavour of each particular region of the world. Indeed, foods that are considered a "difficult taste for Koreans" can serve as an effective advertisement for foreigners and Koreans alike who are seeking the "authentic strangeness" of "traditional ethnic" food.[2] In this regard, the character of "extra-territoriality" in Itaewon began changing. This resulted in the setup of restaurants with more diverse cultural, class, and regional backgrounds. Consumers started to have more choices with increasingly diversified menus from different cultures. Significant changes happened, however, with the massive introduction of migrant labourers from South and Southeast Asian regions in the 1990s.

ISLAMIC FOOD PLACES IN THE ENVIRONMENTS OF KOREAN FOOD CULTURE

Since the early 1990s, migrant workers from several developing countries, including China, Indonesia, Pakistan and Bangladesh, began to enter South Korea. Even though their status as migrants was initially not formally recognized by the state, their presence was not just a temporary phenomenon (Seol 1997, p. 13). The number of migrant labourers has since grown considerably, among them large proportion of Muslims, especially from South Asia and Southeast Asia (Ministry of Justice 2007, p. 43). Contemporaneously, there has also been a general increase in business people, tourists, and other kinds of visitors from Islamic cultural regions.

Although the Muslim communities in Seoul are dispersed under different employment conditions and residency statuses, many of them frequent the Itaewon district in Seoul for their religious practices as it is where the Islamic Central Masjid of Korea is located. However, new visitors to this district are not limited to Muslims. Other foreign nationals of different origins also frequent the area, adding cultural diversity to Itaewon's landscape. As the number of foreign migrants considerably grew once again at the beginning of the 2000s, a new food market has emerged in and around the Itaewon district. As noted above, this district was previously dominated by American culture (Choe 2003, pp. 3–4), and has often been perceived as an "international zone" characterized by cultural diversity

(Kim and Kang 2007: 66; Kim 2005, p. 12) that is incomparable with any other district in Seoul. Restaurants represent 'typical' food elements in this newly developing landscape of cultural diversity. Pronounced among them are restaurants specializing in Islamic food.

It is well known that there is a relationship between food and cultural values (Gabbacia 1998). Korean food culture is not an exception: Koreans incessantly connect the taste and image of specific food items with certain concepts of their cultural identity (Han 1994, p. 51; Kwon 2005, p. 6). Foods used in Korean rituals often provide a significant cultural reference for the interpretation and validation of foods in everyday life (Ju 2000, p. 17). In an environment of increasing global flows, food is also interpreted in the context of identity, from a cross-cultural perspective. With rapid modernization and globalization, Korean food culture also has undergone considerable change. A most remarkable change in that process was the introduction of Chinese and Japanese food (Park 1994, p. 96), and later, the Westernization of food culture in general. The constant growth of meat consumption, for one, is a reflection of the Westernization of Korean food (Walraven 2002). But the most direct clash of foods and the need for food adaptation surges in one of the most direct cultural encounters: the migration of people (Slocum 2011).

In South and Southeast Asia, food regulation has been perceived in connection to religious or ethnic group identity. For Hindus, the concept of pollution related to food is one of the most crucial notions about the order of the world (Dumont 1981, p. 32). For Muslims, food restriction is also important. Islam adopts a kind of distinction system employing concepts of permission (*halal*) and prohibition (*haram*) in many domains of everyday life (Choe 1997, pp. 206–07). The consumption of pork is not permitted, but the treatment of food is also a delicate matter: meat that did not undergo the "correct" religious treatment is not considered "proper". A specific way of slaughter should be used for the preparation of meat (Sakr 1996, p. 24; Kim 2002, p. 173). Another specific element of prohibition among Muslims is alcohol consumption.

In the modern history of Islamism in Korea since the Korean War in the 1950s, most Korean Muslims have had serious difficulty in observing Islamic food restrictions in their ordinary daily lives. This is because of the fact that for most Koreans, pork and alcohol are indispensable culinary elements that are ingrained in all aspects of social life.[3] After the 1970s, the growing number of Middle Eastern Muslim visitors to Korea enlarged the

Muslim population in Seoul, while the Korean Central Masjid was built in Itaewon in 1976 to meet the growing need for Muslim religious worship. However, these developments were not influential enough in changing the food environment of Korean Muslims. The market for *halal* meat was not mature enough — a reflection that there were not enough (foreign) Muslims looking for *halal* food in Korea at that time. Furthermore, the preparation of *halal* food is more demanding and time-consuming than the actual cooking of the food (Lewis 2001, p. 47), and the supply system of *halal* food material was lacking in Korea. Clearly, then, the particular food environment in Korea posed a serious challenge for the adaptation of South and Southeast Asian Muslim workers in Korea (Ministry of Culture and Tourism 2007, p. 243).

From the viewpoint of Korean food culture, the introduction of Islamic (*halal*) food in Korea is a kind of culture shock due to its strong restriction and denouncement of alcohol and certain meat consumption. Meat consumption in Korea has steadily grown with the influx of Western influence, and has since acquired diverse, if not sometimes contradictory, symbolic values. The consumption of alcohol was never discouraged in Korean culture, and Chinese and Japanese influence, in which alcoholic drinks are an indispensable aspect of food culture, has reinforced the place and meaning of alcohol consumption in Korean food culture. Thus, for Koreans, Islamic food is not only unfamiliar; it also set up a challenge because its very characteristics are opposed to important symbolic aspects of local food cultures.

Restaurants providing *halal* food first appeared in Seoul at the beginning of the 1990s, in the Itaewon district near the Central Masjid of Islam. The 1990s was a period of rapid influx of migrant workers from South and Southeast Asia (Seol 1999, p. 78). Several factors of globalization emerged in this period in Korea. The general restriction on Koreans' tourism to foreign countries was entirely lifted at the end of the 1980s. Visits of foreign tourists to Korea also increased following the 1986 Asian Games and the 1988 Olympic Games. Both factors have meant that ordinary Koreans have become increasingly exposed to foreign social and cultural practices. The growing number of tourists and South and Southeast Asian migrant workers have played a significant role in the transformation of the food landscape of Itaewon (Jeong 2000, p. 72). Restaurants abiding by the restrictions of *halal* food started to open one by one as a result of this growth. *Halal* food restaurants began to stand out among some Indian food restaurants. Originally known for "specializing in Indian food", these restaurants also began to explicitly associate themselves with Islamic cuisine through the use of signboards that advertised "Islamic food" or "*halal* food". In the early 1990s, *halal* food was served mainly in some of the Indian and Pakistani restaurants managed by Muslims. After several years, a few Turkish restaurants opened serving *halal* food. Only after 2000 did some Middle Eastern restaurants open, offering a menu catering to different nationalities that consume *halal* food. The majority of these restaurants' clients in earlier days were Westerners including diplomats, business people and tourists mainly from United States or European countries. Some visitors from Middle Eastern countries and some Koreans who were dining with their foreign partners also frequented these restaurants. In this manner, these earlier *halal* food restaurants took their place among other relatively tourist restaurants (Ya 1997, p. 13). However, the majority of Muslims frequenting Itaewon were not diplomats or business people. They were migrant labourers mainly from South and Southeast Asia, more specifically from Bangladesh, Pakistan and Indonesia. For these migrants, the prices in most Islamic food restaurants in Itaewon were too high; simple grocery stores were more important for South and Southeast Asian migrant labourers. From these stores, they could purchase materials with which they could prepare their meals according to religious and regional specificities (Yi 2007, p. 34). More affordable Islamic restaurants started to appear around 2000 in Ansan,[4] Gwangju[5] and Itaewon. These restaurants serve "Indian food" or "Pakistani food", along with specifically "Islamic food". Access to these restaurants was, at the same time, more or less "closed" to outsiders from other religious or ethnic groups. Situated in the narrow backstreets, it is difficult for the uninitiated to discover them off the main tourist streets of the district.

ISLAMIC RESTAURANTS FROM THE INDIAN SUBCONTINENT[6]

Islamic restaurants or *halal* restaurants can be categorized by nationality or region of origin, the period it opened, and management type. In Itaewon, it should be noted that the price of food tends to be influenced by the nationality of clients (Kim 2004, pp. 42–44). In the year 2007–08, for instance, the price of food for one meal per person cost around 30,000 won[7] for tourist restaurants in Itaewon. A few of the first Islamic restaurants in Seoul that opened in the 1980s in Itaewon fall into this category of tourist restaurants, with the majority of their clients being Westerners. In the middle of the

1990s, mid-level priced Indo-Pakistani and Middle Eastern restaurants opened. With their entrance to the market, clients for *halal* restaurants had more choice in terms of the price and range of menu, along with regional diversity. It was now possible to taste and express national character, social class, values for religious and regional significations for more diversified clients. During fieldwork in 2006, I found many Bangladeshi cooks and servers employed in "Indian" or "Pakistani" food restaurants. At the same time, most South and Southeast Asian *halal* restaurants emphasized that they offer "authentic Indian food". Usage of adjectives such as "Indian" and "Pakistani" reflects the "national" connotation of food. India, Pakistan and Bangladesh are neighbouring countries with a tumultuous history of conflict after liberation from British colonialism. In the case of India, the religion of the majority is not Islam but Hinduism. How and why then, do most "Islamic food restaurants" in Korea advertise themselves as "Indian" food restaurants while they are actually Pakistani or Bangladeshi?

Both differences and commonalities over food exist between Hinduism and Islam. There has been a serious conflict around food taboos between the two religions for a long time in the Indian subcontinent, especially concerning beef (Gupta 1981, p. 132). Some Hindus profess vegetarianism. For Muslims, meat has symbolic value: mutton consumption is even an indispensable part in Islamic rituals like *Aid-el-Kabir* and *Aid-el-Fitur* (Azmi 2003, p. 29). On the other hand, there are also many common practices between Hindus and Muslims of South Asia and Southeast Asia with regard to food consumption. Pork is absolutely forbidden for all of them. Chicken is permitted for some Hindus and most Muslims. Removal of blood from the beast, regardless of the kind of animal, is a common way of slaughtering for both. Both groups use strong spices like curries and *masala*. "Naan" bread, yoghurt, salads and other vegetable dishes are also a common menu for them. When the *halal* food restaurants first appeared in Seoul, most of them employed adjectives like "Indian food", including those restaurants managed by Pakistanis and Bangladeshis, as their main clients were Western tourists and business people. However, as time went by, the economic relationship between Islamic cultural regions and Korea has also grown and, as a result, there are greater numbers of Muslim merchants and business people coming from the Middle East, South Asia and Southeast Asia to Korea, as well as migrant workers from South and Southeast Asia. These groups have contributed to the diversity of Muslim ethnic groups and social classes within Korea. In this new context, some

"Indian food" restaurants have started to introduce *halal* food openly as their main specialty. In the following section, I introduce two divergent cases of how Islamic food restaurants operate in Korea.

THE FLEXIBLE IDENTITY OF A HALAL FOOD PLACE: THE CASE OF A-RESTAURANT

Despite the strictures of Islamic food culture there is considerable diversity in the types and forms of food production and consumption in *halal* restaurants in the Itaewon area. A-Restaurant, which was opened in Itaewon in 2002, offers a useful example.[8] This restaurant advertised itself as a place that served *halal* food from the time it opened. Mr A, the eldest of the brothers who run A-restaurant, had first acquired Korean nationality and invited his two younger brothers to Korea. Together they opened an "Indo-Pakistani" and *halal* food restaurant. Considering the growing number of Bangladeshi and Pakistani migrants in Korea, Mr A then expanded his business in a new direction, collaborating with two Bangladesh merchants to open a new grocery shop selling condiments and other food materials, including *halal* meat, in Itaewon in the autumn of 2007. Mr A is now expanding his business to carpets and other handicraft goods imported from Northern India and Pakistan.

The prices and menu of A-restaurant is strategically positioned. It is neither a very classic "Indian royal food" restaurant nor a cheap snack bar. This strategy aims to capture larger categories of possible clients. Five Pakistani waiters and a Korean waitress who serves Korean-speaking clients were working at A-Restaurant in 2007. More than half of A-Restaurant's clients are Westerners, including tourists and business people. According to the manager, among the Westerners, British clients who are already familiar with South Asian cuisine strongly implanted in the United Kingdom (Buettner 2008, p. 865) frequent the restaurant more than others.

To promote its position as one of the main *halal* food providers, A-Restaurant has been active in catering for parties and special occasions organized by embassies and corporate branches from Islamic regions such as Malaysia, Pakistan, and some Middle Eastern countries. They also offer catering services for *halal* food consumers from other Islamic regions. To reassure Muslim clients, they emphasize that their materials are "directly imported" from South Asia and Southeast Asia or are supplied by *halal*-

certified food producers. In fact, most of their food materials are purchased from *halal* grocery shops where Australian *halal*-certificated mutton is displayed side by side with Vietnamese sauces.

A-Restaurant is also pursuing a "localization" strategy in their menu. According to its manager, Koreans comprised approximately one-third of their clients in 2007. While many Koreans like hot and spicy food, most have had difficulties adapting to "original" masala and curries from India and Pakistan because of the strength of the spices. A-Restaurant's strategy was thus to prepare different kinds of masala and curry plates: mild ones and original strong ones. In principle, servers do not inform Korean clients that their curries are toned down to become mild because they are aware that most Korean clients come to the restaurant to taste the "original food" of an exotic foreign country. Sometimes they have some Korean clients who demand "real strong and spicy masala" instead of the mild versions. These are likely to be clients who have travel experiences or have been ex-residents in the Indian subcontinent. Other interesting cases of adaptation in A-Restaurant's menu are "fried chicken" and "chicken salad" under the category of "Chinese Food". This is mainly for Korean children who are uncomfortable with tandoori chicken and spicy curries. Fried chicken and chicken salad are popular enough in India and Pakistan and it would seem unnecessary to indicate them as "Chinese food". However, the category of "Chinese food" in an "authentic *halal* food restaurant"[9] of "Pakistani authenticity" is designated an exceptional food category. While this seems a paradox, it does not seem to bother the clientele. Diversity and flexibility of the menu work well, making this an acceptable "mid-level family restaurant for everyone" (including Muslims).

AN ISLAMIC RESTAURANT FOR KOREAN CUSTOMERS: THE CASE OF B-RESTAURANT

B-Restaurant was opened in 1990 by Mr C, a Korean Muslim who had lived for about ten years in Delhi, India. Opened and maintained by the Korean owner himself, it has cooks and servers from Bangladesh and Pakistan. The location of B-Restaurant is en route to Seoul's Central Masjid of Islam on the main street of Itaewon. It started as an "Indian" restaurant catering mainly to Korean customers. Interestingly, in the advertisements and some magazine articles about this restaurant, there is no mention of Pakistan or Bangladesh. In a magazine article published in 1995, the dishes of B-Restaurant was described as having a relatively mild taste compared to typical Indian foods "because the spice is less strong, the taste of its food is acceptable for Koreans' palate" (Park 1995, p. 117). The fact that this restaurant has "Kimchi Briyani" in its menu also shows that this restaurant has Korean customers in mind. An informant told me that Mr C had originally opened a lodging house for South and Southeast Asian Muslims, using his own Muslim network in the late 1980s. Later, he conceived the idea of opening an "Indian food restaurant". It is not clear whether Mr C himself learnt Indian food cooking or whether some South Asian migrants worked as cooks for Mr C. It must be noted that at that time, the employment of migrant workers in his restaurant was illegal. Indeed, there are many cases of illegal employment of migrant workers in the restaurant business, and it is often difficult to verify details of employment for restaurants' staff members.

Cultural categorization of food in B-Restaurant is not clear, especially for their regional characteristics. For example, several paradoxes appear in the magazine articles about this restaurant. One article says that, according to Mr C, B-Restaurant is offering "Middle Eastern and Indian food" without clear distinction because there is "no significant difference between Middle Eastern food and Indian food" (Kim 1995, p. 143). While such a generalization probably indicates Mr C's desire for a larger clientele, his statement is neither correct nor a suitable advertisement to attract Muslim clients.

More paradoxes exist around nationality and religious or ethnic identity of food in this article about B-Restaurant. For one, the religious character of Islam, as emphasized in the article, is not clearly associated with the general image of India. It must also be pointed out that "Indian food" is a generalized term which fails to take into account the vast diversity and complexity of Indian culture. Using descriptions such as "Indian" food and "Middle Eastern" food alongside "Islamic food" can be risky and sometimes insensitive, depending on the religious and ethnic background of the clientele. Regardless, B-Restaurant still introduces itself both as a "typical Indian restaurant" and a "typical Islamic restaurant". At the end of the 1990s, it even used expressions like "typical Arabic food restaurant". In this respect the management of B-Restaurant is weighing several categorizations for more successful marketing. While it emphasizes the "traditional Indian food" for Korean and Western clients, it also presents the significance of *halal* regulation in Islamic religious practices for South Asian and Southeast Asian Muslims, as well as Middle Eastern Muslims. For the latter, the restaurant often employs several symbols of the Middle

East and Islam for the restaurant's decor. Concerning Korean customers, B-Restaurant's manager knows that Koreans do not take *halal* seriously, and B-Restaurant is perceived just as an "Indian food" restaurant with reasonable prices, and that consuming Indian food can be good for special occasions. Furthermore, B-Restaurant offers a non-vegetarian menu because it is not a "general Indian food" restaurant but a Muslim restaurant. Between Hindu-vegetarian food and Muslim-non-vegetarian food, the latter has the advantage of enticing Korean customers most of whom prefer to have meat on their table. In fact, many Korean customers do not even question the difference between "Hindu Indian food" and "Muslim Indian food". The significance of this difference is most often lost on Koreans. As more Korean clients frequent B-Restaurant, its menu has also been continually adapted to suit their tastes. As in the case of A-Restaurant, B-Restaurant's cooks develop new menus based on the responses of the different client groups. For example, B-Restaurant prepares two kinds of rice: Korean-type sticky rice, and South Asian or Southeast Asian long-grained rice. Many Korean customers prefer Korean cooked rice in their meal. However, there are also some Koreans who demand "foreign looking" rice because they want to eat something new or eat what they had experienced during their stay or travel in India and Pakistan.[10] For the latter case, clients demand not only exotic or delicious food, but also the "original hot taste of the Indian local food" — a referent for cultural authenticity. B-Restaurant's cooks also prepare three different levels of intensity for their spicy sauces, with the mildest one normally preferred for the buffet menu which is the most common choice of Korean customers. Even alcoholic beverage is served at B-Restaurant. It is said that "only some beer" was offered until 1999, but it started to offer wine, whiskey, and other alcoholic beverages since 2002. Mr C had his own *halal* meat shop but it closed three years ago, after several grocery stores owned and managed by Bangladeshi merchants opened. Now, B-Restaurant purchases its food materials there.

SHIFTING GEOGRAPHIES OF FOOD AND CULTURE

For more than three decades, Itaewon was dominated by American culture. It is now in the process of becoming a more culturally diverse area. Restaurants specializing in foods from different cultural regions reflect this trend. Nevertheless, the growing cultural diversity does not mean equality of treatment of each culture. In the case of ethnic food restaurants, there are different "levels" of status attached to them by the customers. The perceived status of a restaurant is based on the price of food, and recognition with respect among the clients and restaurateurs themselves.

European and Korean clients appear to interpret the relative position of food through reference to the more general cultural and economic position of the country it originates from. In Itaewon, some European restaurants enjoy the highest status level. On par with these European restaurants are the Indo-Pakistani restaurants M Restaurant and A Restaurant, whose main clients are diplomats, business people, Western tourists and Koreans looking for a "different taste". These restaurants are located in the same neighbourhood and are usually part of the itinerary of more or less the same kind of clientele. Many "Indian" restaurants employ Pakistani or Bangladeshi cooks and servers. However, since they are conscious of clients' hierarchical perception of national foods (Kim 2004, p. 38), only a few restaurants represent themselves as "Pakistani" or "Bangladeshi". It means that the restaurant owners themselves are adapting themselves to Koreans' general perception of hierarchy among nations of South Asian countries where India is on a higher level than Pakistan or Bangladesh.

South Asian and Southeast Asian Muslim clients' perceptions of food and understanding of Islamic restaurants are notably different from that of both Korean and Western clients. Cultural and religious beliefs are crucial in their choice of food and the place of consumption. A Hindu Indian, for example, would never attempt to enter a *halal* restaurant or "Indo-Pakistan food" restaurant in Korea, just as he would not in India. For him, this poses a serious risk of pollution, even an occasion of self-negation. Additionally, because of the history of conflict among the different ethnic groups (Amir 2000, pp. 23–24), members belonging to a particular group would not dare cross spaces that are usually identified with another group. In this way, for South Asian and Southeast Asian Muslims in Korea, the restaurant where they choose to eat is a kind of exclusive territory for the particular group that they identify with. Each ethnic and religious group has its own place of food consumption which is distinguishable from the other groups'. This exclusion is not easily grasped by outsiders like Korean customers who are just hoping to taste some "Indian food" regardless of the religion or ethnicity that it is associated with.

On the other hand, giving weight to the *halal* certification of the food can be an advertisement towards a wider clientele from Islamic regions like the Middle East. If the "Indian food" signage is mainly for Europeans and Korean customers, the *"halal* food" signage is mainly for religious Muslims.

Offering *halal* food widens the scope of the restaurant's clientele to Muslim communities in general. This is the reason why many Indo-Pakistani restaurants have emphasized that they offer *"halal"* menus — they want to consider not only the Pakistani business people, but also Malaysian or Middle Eastern Muslims as their potential clients.

With globalization, more Koreans have become curious about "alternative menus" from "other" cultures. This has been discussed in previous research as the strategy of distinction (Seo 1992), that can be interpreted as a kind of cultural capital. In this context, the main menus that Koreans have sought to experience are Italian, French, or other Western European food. More recently, however, there has been a diversification in Koreans' foreign food consumption in a way such that the experience and knowledge of South Asian and Southeast Asian foods has also become a kind of cultural capital among Koreans.

With the development of new media like the Internet, the significance of individuals as information suppliers in the area of consumer culture has increased (Mathews 2000, p. 46). Equipped with new and highly accessible media tools, ordinary consumers become amateur writers, reviewers and critics. They take an active part in web communities, and share first-hand experience of other people's cultures. This ability of ordinary individuals to disseminate information to a wide audience was not usually possible in traditional media. In effect, these "power users" of new media are partially replacing the role of traditional cultural gate-keepers such as professional culture critics, journalists and academics (Wright and Hinson 2008).

For information on cultural experience, weekly magazines, newspapers and television programmes used to play a powerful role in disseminating and influencing the public. Today, however, Internet blogs and website communities are flourishing with first-hand tasting reports on "exotic" foods. They are also frequently updated. The supply of speedy and fresh information gives individuals new possibilities of the power to influence. Some blogs are even taking on the role of a verifier and countercheck food critiques of information found in newspapers and magazines. Most of the latter are themselves also adapting to changing lifestyles due to the increasingly common five-day work week in Korea. This is most apparent in the increasing number of "weekend" and "culture" sections in newspapers.

These altered forms of traditional media have also contributed to the promotion of *halal* food restaurants since the 1990s. In the 2000s, some weekly magazines and Internet media were changing their search from "nice" and "classical" foreign restaurants to a focus on "authentic atmosphere of traditional foreign cultures". Sometimes even shabby or humble decorations were praised as an expression of the "original culture" because "high culture" can be perceived as being "touristy" and having been "distorted for exhibitionism". Drab and humble decors were probably influential in offering some imagined flavour of "tradition" (Alsayyad 2001, p. 39). Here, unfamiliarity can serve as an opportunity for exploration of "culturally diversified consumption". A humble, small snack corner or stall offering food from the "narrow backstreet" of a certain developing country's dirty and bustling city, would be praised as the authentic bearer of "a real hot taste". This kind of "snack corner" can sometimes compete with some high-class Western restaurants. The capacity to try food offered by this kind of humble-looking but good-tasting food place would be recognized as a marker of cultural capital by consumers who are tired of articles on "chic and stylish" things. It is also notable how online networks affected offline geographies. Offline experiences, such as the increase in international travel and migration, and direct contact with foreign food cultures by individuals from a range of social classes and interpretations on their own experiences, are all elements that feedback into online interaction.

There appears to be a tendency towards diversification of foods in Itaewon. However, this is not just a simple diversification of existing elements. Rather, the established boundaries of food culture in Itaewon are markedly diminishing, in which fusion and hybridization strategies (Canclini 1995, p. 114) of food have given birth to "Americanized Indian food" or "French style Arabic food". From the consumer's viewpoint, one can enjoy a "humble" snack corner of Islamic food and consume high class food in a chic Italian restaurant in the same area without any sense of identity confusion. This also applies to the supplier: the same person can own and manage a French home style food restaurant and a Spanish barbecue house. In this way, he can play with categories or cultural identities of food he or she offers, for his own benefit.

CONCLUSION

Globalization has provoked a certain anxiety about the influence of global forms and homogenization of culture (Martin 1997). What this chapter has illustrated in terms of the realm of Islamic food restaurants in Itaewon, however, suggests an equally significant process of diversification. In the landscape of Itaewon, the once-dominant influence of American food culture has been diminishing with the increasing influence of globalizing processes in Korea. Diversity of cultures has clearly grown along with the international movements of peoples and cultures. In the case of Islamic restaurants in Itaewon, the reason for this growing diversity in the urban cultural landscape is the evolution of communication tools and that of migration. Increased contact with foreigners and with foreign cultures in South Korea sets the background for this trend. This trend is also attributable to Korea's new immigration policy, especially since 2004, that permits easier naturalization and the acquisition of Korean nationality and easier access to business ownership for certain categories of foreigners. It is also related to the growing number of migrant workers of Islamic background. These in turn mean the expansion of business opportunities for suppliers of Islamic food in Korea.

In the past, supply and demand of Islamic food in Korea was limited but the growing number of migrant workers had significant effects on the labour and food markets, including the number of suppliers. In this process, the increase in one factor creates the diversification of another factor, namely, the presence of different kinds of food providers. Islamic food consumers now also have more choice. The expansion of the *halal* food market in Korea is offering a more diversified dining experience to Korean consumers. It facilitates, for example, cultural consumption by individuals who have experienced Islamic foods through their travels abroad and their demand for Islamic foods in Korea. Perceptions and interpretations about the meaning of Islamic foods also diversify in this context.

For Muslims and other non-Koreans with specific food needs, more alternatives have emerged in the form of new *halal* and vegetarian restaurants and grocery shops. Food market development also provides more business opportunities to Muslim migrants. Growing flows and frequency of information through different kinds of media, including Internet and short weekly journals, also play a crucial role in the expansion of cultural spaces where foreigners in Seoul can find objects of their necessity in easier ways. We can describe this transformation of the environment of cultural consumption as a kind of "globalized cultural supermarket" (Mathews 2000, p. 104). As the space of this supermarket grows, the number and categories of merchandise grows in direct relation to diversification (Micklethwait and Wooldridge 2003, p. 24).

The result of these migration, food supply, and consumption processes has been the metamorphosis of Itaewon's urban landscape. A remarkable transformation of street corners is taking place where new "Indian" or "Islamic" restaurants replace old bars and clubs frequented by U.S. army personnel. Foreigners and Koreans are mixed together in "foreign" grocery stores where they purchase "exotic" or "home country's" spices without difficulty. Islamic bookshops and travel agencies specializing in destinations like Bangladesh, Jordan and Uzbekistan are being established in the area surrounding the Central Masjid of Korea. More recently, Indonesians have their own grocery stores where they can meet their compatriots and eat not only *halal* dishes but Indonesian specialities like *nasi goreng*. Nigerian migrants have their own barbershops and restaurants in Itaewon too. Here in Itaewon, food is playing a key role as a trans-border agent and the provocateur of a new process of territorialization that incorporates different cultures and social networks as an integral part of this globalizing urban district in Seoul.

Notes

1. There is now an extensive literature on food in the social sciences and humanities that focuses on consumption amongst diasporic and transnational groups that highlights the reproduction of familiarity in the sensual and social dimensions of culinary consumption (Bell and Valentine 1998; Collins 2008; Slocum 2011).
2. As Bell Hooks (1991) argues, much of these practices are part of a kind of touristic engagement with the other (see also Hage 1997), but they also represent opportunities, however small, for engagement with the other (Duruz 2005; Lai this volume.)
3. Several interviews suggested that only small numbers of Korean Muslims practise Islamic food restriction on a daily basis. This handicap may be one of the reasons for the weakening legitimacy of leadership of Korean Muslims in the Muslim community of Korea, where foreign Muslims are a majority.
4. Ansan is a city in the Southwest of Seoul, approximately 40 km from the centre of the city and connected via Subway line 4. It was established as a city in 1986, when several towns of the Hwaseong county were incorporated. Mainly built as an industrial zone of the Seoul National Capital Area, Ansan had about 40,000 companies with approximately 250,000 employees in 2007, for the total population of 734,000. Among the employees in its industrial companies, as many as 36,000 foreign labourers were counted in 2007, including migrant workers from some Muslim countries.
5. Gwangju is a city in Southeast of Seoul, about 35 km on the highway from

Seoul to the southern parts of Korea. The area of Gwangju was mostly rural, populated with farmers until the beginning of 1990s. Since the 1990s, small and medium-sized industrial companies started to develop in the area and Gwangju became an independent city in 2001. In 2007, approximately 42,400 employees, among whom some important number of foreign migrant labourers, were working for 13,550 companies,

6. Cases of Islamic restaurants used in this article are also analysed in my previous work on Itaewon district (Song 2006).
7. This was about US$28 at the time.
8. Restaurants and their owners' names have not been used to maintain anonymity.
9. For the discourse of "authenticity of food" related with "national character" in Korea, Han's paper (1994) offers good reference.
10. India is one of the favourite tourist destinations for Koreans since the 1990s.

References

Alsayyad, N. *Consuming Tradition, Manufacturing Heritage: Global Norms and Urban Forms in the Age of Tourism*. London: Routledge, 2001.

Amir, S. *Muslim Nationhood in India*. New Delhi: Kanishka Publishers, 2000.

Azmi, J. *Halal Food, Kuala Lumpur: A Guide to Good Eating*. Kuala Lumpur: Kasehdia Sdn. Bhd, 2003.

Bak, S. "From Strange Bitter Concoction to Romantic Necessity: The Social History of Coffee Drinking in South Korea". *Korea Journal* 45, no. 2 (2005): 37–59.

Buettner, E. "'Going for an Indian': South Asian Restaurants and the Limits of Multiculturalism in Britain". *The Journal of Modern History* 80, no. 4 (2008): 865–901.

Canclini, N.G. *Hybrid Cultures: Stages for Entering and Leaving Modernity*. Minneapolis: University of Minnesota Press, 1995.

Choe J-I. "Itaewon gonggane natanan 'Americanization'e gwanhan yeongu" [A study on the Americanisation of the space of Itaewon district]. M.A. thesis, Seoul National University, 2003.

Choe Y-G. *Islam munhwaui ihae* [Understanding Islamic culture]. Seoul: Sinjipyeong, 1997.

Collins, F.L. "Of *Kimchi* and Coffee: Globalisation, Transnationalism and Familiarity in Culinary Consumption". *Social and Cultural Geography* 9, no. 2 (2008): 151–69.

Cwiertka, K.J. "Eating the Homeland". In *Asian Food: The Global and the Local*, edited by K.J. Cwiertka and B.C.A. Walraven. Richmond: Curzon, 2002.

Dumont, L. *Homo Hierarchicus: The Caste System and its Implications*. Chicago: University of Chicago Press, 1981.

Duruz, J. "Eating at the Borders: Culinary Journeys". *Environment and Planning D: Society and Space* 23, no. 1 (2005): 51–69.

Gabbacia, D.R. *We Are What We Eat: Ethnic Food and the Making of Americans.* Cambridge: Harvard University Press, 1998.

Gupta, N. *Delhi between Two Empires 1803–1931.* Delhi: Oxford University Press, 1981.

Hage, G. "At Home in the Entrails of the West: Multiculturalism, 'Ethnic Food' and Migrant Home Building". In *Home/World: Space, Community and Marginality in Sydney's West*, edited by H. Grace, G. Hage, L. Johnson, J. Langsworth, and M. Symonds. Annandal, NSW: Pluto Press, 1997.

Han, K-K. "Eotteon eumsikeun saenggakhagie jota: Kimchiwa hanguk minjokseongui jeongsu" [Some food is good to think: Kimchi and authenticity of Korean national character]. *Hangukmunhwainryuhak (Korean Cultural Anthropology)* 26 (1994): 51–68.

Hooks, B. *Black Looks: Race and Representation.* Boston: South End Press. 1992.

"Introduction to Korea Muslim Federation". <http://www.koreaislam.org/intro/intro01.jsp>. Accessed 1 April 2008.

Jeong, H-J. "Itaewon sangupgaro maeryeokyoso bunseoke gwanhan yeongu" [A study on the attraction factors of Itaewon street]. Ph.D. thesis. Seoul National University, 2000.

Ju, Y-H. *Eumsikjeonjaeng munhwajeonjaeng* [Food war, cultural war]. Seoul: Sagyejeol, 2000.

Kim, E.M. and J.S. Kang. "Seoul as a Global City with Ethnic Villages". *Korea Journal* 47, no. 4 (2007): 64–99.

Kim, E-S. "Jiguhwasidae geundaeui talyeongtohwadoen gongganeuroseoui itaewone daehan minjokjijeok yeongu" [An ethnographic study of Itaewon as deterritorialized space]. In *Byeonhwahaneun yeoseongmunhwa umjikineun jiguchon* [Changing women's culture, transforming global village], edited by E-S. Kim et al. Seoul: Pureunsasang, 2004.

Kim, H.M. *Global sidaeui munhwa beonyeok* [Cultural interpretations of global age]. Seoul: Ttohanauimunhwa.books, 2005.

Kim, I-S. "New Foreign Restaurants in Itaewon". *Figaro*, no. 5 (1995). Seoul: Gyeonghyangsinmunsa.

Kim, Y-S., ed. *Al-Quran.* Seoul: Myeongmundang, 2002.

Kwon, S-I. (Gwon, Suk-in) "Hyeonjihwa, jeonghyeonghwa, jiguhwa: Jae Mexico/Ilbon haninui minjokeumsik munhwa" [Localization, typification, globalization: Ethnic food among the Koreans in Japan and Korean-Mexicans], *Bigyomunhwayeongu (Cross Cultural Studies)* 11, no. 2 (2005): 5–34.

Lewis, B. *Islam in History: Ideas, People, and Events in the Middle East.* Illinois: Open Court Publishing Co, 2001.

Martin, H.-P. and H. Schumann. *The Global Trap: Globalization and the Assault on Prosperity and Democracy.* London: St. Martin's Press, 1997.

Mathews, G. *Global Culture/Individual Identity Searching for Home in the Cultural Supermarket*. London: Routledge, 2000.

Micklethwait, J. and A. Wooldridge. *A Future Perfect: The Challenge and Promise of Globalization*. New York: Random House, 2003.

Ministry of Culture and Tourism. *Ijumin gongdongcheui munhwadayangseonge daehan josayeongu: damunhwa jidojejak* [A Study on the cultural diversity of migrants' community: Cultural map of multiculture]. Seoul: Ministry of Culture and Tourism, 2007.

Ministry of Justice. *Gugnae cheryu ofhuhin deungroktong-gye* [Statistics of foreign residents' registration in Korea]. Seoul: Ministry of Justice, 2007.

Park, E-K. (Bak, Eun-gyeong). "Junggukeumsikui yeoksajeok uimi" [Historical meaning of Chinese food in Korea]. *Hangukmunhwainryuhak (Korean Cultural Anthropology)* 26 (1994): 95–116.

Park K-H. "Looking for Some Different Taste?". *Feel*, No. 4 (1995). Seoul: Josunilbosa.

Sakr, A.H. *Understanding Halal Foods Fallacies and Facts*. Kuala Lumpur: Foundation for Islamic Knowledge, 1996.

Seo, H-J. "Sangpum sobiui munhwajeok gyuchik mit sangjingjeok uimie gwanhan yeongu" [Cultural logic and symbolic meaning of consumption: A case study of restaurant specializing in Italian food]. M.A. thesis. Seoul National University, 1992.

Seol, D-H. "Oegukin nodongjawa hanguksahoeui sanghojakyong" [Interaction between Foreign Migrant Labourers and Korean Society]. *Nodongmunjenonjip (Journal of Labour Problem)* 13, no. 1 (1997): 131–58.

———. *Foreign Migrant Laborers and Korean Society*. Seoul: Seoul National University Press, 1999.

Slocum, R. "Race in the Study of Food". *Progress in Human Geography* 35, no. 3 (2011): 303–27.

Song, D. "Jonggyowa eumsikeul tonghan dosigongganui munhwajeok netweok" [Religion, Food and Formation of Cultural Network in Urban Space: Halal Restaurants of Itaewon Area, Seoul]. *Bigyomunhwayeongu (Cross-Cultural Studies)* 13, no. 1 (2006): 98–136.

Walraven, B.C.A. "Bardot Soup and Confucians' Meat". In *Asian Food: The Global and the Local*, edited by K.J. Cwiertika and B.C.A. Walraven, Richmond: Curzon, 2002.

Wright, D.K. and M.D. Hinson. "How Blogs and Social Media are Changing Public Relations and the Way it is Practiced". *Public Relations Journal* 2, no. 2 (2008): 1–21.

Ya, E-S. "Gwangwangteukgu yejeongjiroseo Itaewon jiyeokui gwangwangoisiksanup jinheungjeonchaek yeongu (A study on the promotion policy of tourist food industry in Itaewon area, a special district for tourism]. Ph.D. Thesis, Suwon: Kyunggi University, 1997.

Yi, S-Y. "Guknae geoju Islam gyodoui sikseupgwan bunseok" [Analysis on the daily food consumption of Muslim residents in Korea]. M.A. thesis. Sukmyeong Women's University, 2007.

10

COMPETITION AND CONSTRUCTEDNESS
Sports, Migration and Diversity in Singapore

Robbie B.H. GOH

INTRODUCTION: SPORTS, (IM)MIGRATION AND NATIONAL IDENTITY IN SINGAPORE

Sports migration is fast becoming a significant dimension of transnational studies. Up to about the latter part of the 1990s, the most significant sports migration moves were probably confined to soccer (one of the most popular and monied sports in the world), and even these were largely intra-continental (and occasionally trans-Atlantic) movements into the English Premier League and the Serie A. From the late 1990s onwards however, a number of select but highly publicized moves of East Asian players to European clubs — including Japan's Hidetoshi Nakata who started playing for Italian club Perugia in 1998, and Shunsuke Nakamura who moved to Reggina in 2002, China's Li Tie who moved to Everton in 2002, South Korea's Park Ji-Sung who moved to Holland's PSV Eindhoven in 2003, and others — marked the beginning of a more open era of sports migrations and their impact on fandom, merchandising, tourism, media and related industries.[1] Unlike players from earlier eras, who might have moved to another country for reasons other than sports (education, family/personal factors, political reasons) and had longer periods of acculturation and naturalization before often going on to play for their adopted country, the sports migrations of the late 1990s onwards were often specifically for employment and career development, could be for a short duration only, and often only involved club representation, resulting in somewhat divided loyalties and club-nation conflicts. The late 1990s also saw the professionalization of Rugby Union, and the movement of many Pacific Rim players to Europe to play for clubs in England, Ireland, France and Italy. Other Asian athletes who made well-publicized moves to Western teams include Japanese baseball players Hideo Nomo, who moved to the Los Angeles Dodgers in 1995, and Ichiro Suzuki who moved to the Seattle Mariners in 2001, as well as Chinese basketballer Yao Ming, who moved to the Houston Rockets in the 2002 draft pick.

Sports migration is a very interesting phenomenon within global migration for a number of reasons. In the first place, migrant sportsmen run a huge socio-economic gamut: it is the top performers and top earners who garner the most public attention when they change clubs and move transnationally, while in almost all sports there are much lower-ranked professionals who barely earn their keep and are not dissimilar to other "abject cosmopolitans" (Nyers 2003). Like migrant labourers and domestic helpers, "abject" sportsmen may lack many of the rights and protections — health care and insurance, labour rights, rights of entry and domicile for their immediate family — that are enjoyed by cosmopolitan professionals and top sports migrants. Unlike the big names who are protected by signing bonuses, endorsement revenues and powerful lawyers and agents, athletes on various forms of trial or probationary basis are much more vulnerable to repatriation or falling through the socio-economic cracks (through unexpected events like injury or relegation in ranking) than even lower management positions. Sports migration is thus an inherently destabilizing phenomenon, not only for the athletes themselves, but also for the public who have to contend with the dualism of "star" and "journeyman", talented asset and abject foreigner, in the figure of the transnational athlete.

Secondly, athletes can play a peculiar role in the visceral and affective life of a city, region or nation, by featuring prominently in the particular community's representative sports teams and becoming bearers of the community's feelings of pride. This is due to the highly symbolic and ritualistic nature of spectator sports, which structures and interpellates supporters and audiences into "tribal" identifications, and (in the case of the more combative contact sports) also play a role in "male socialization" and inculcating cultures such as masculine "toughness" (Voigt 1980, pp. 128, 132; Mrozek 1980; Chick and Loy 2001). The sheer reach and accessibility of sports stand to foster "greater national cohesion" (as Lechner [2007, p. 108] argues in the context of soccer in the Netherlands), especially when this synchronic trans-social reach is reinforced diachronically over a long national history of the game. In addition, sports present themselves as a particularly "benign" way to construct national and community identity, seemingly with nothing (or less) at stake in terms of "territory ... or ideology or religion" or "the serious business of the nation", while at the same time offering a considerable amount of flexibility and diversity in terms of its "imaginative construction of an ongoing tradition". Since there is "no single Dutch soccer experience", for example, this permits different teams and supporters to negotiate and construct particular strands of the larger collective imaginary (Cronin and Mayall 1998, p. 2; Lechner 2007, pp. 108–109). Historically, the examples of other nations show how sports offer opportunities for interactions between immigrant and mainstream groups, and for that matter between immigrant groups, creating a "plasticity" of identity that works against the more obdurate racial-communal boundaries in politics, employment, housing, and other socio-economic areas (Hay 1998, p. 63; Burdsey 2007, pp. 35–38). In addition, in an age of globalization, sports and sport-related industries (media coverage, merchandising, tourism) play a very significant role in connecting people, groups and communities across national boundaries, space and time.

At the same time, it is also true that global sports are beset with a complex "power geometry" between groups and nations, and between the global and the local (Maguire 2005, p. 4). The globalizing forces in sports, and their ability to forge markets which unify various consumers (clubs, players, media companies, fans), still run against various local points of resistance in terms of the peculiar features, rituals, history and traditions of a community's sporting culture, as shown in Andrews and Ritzer's (2007, p. 39) study of Australian Rugby League club Souths and its relationship with the Sydney working-class community of Redfern, or in Collins' (1998, p. 156) study of "cosmopolitan" teams in Northern English communities/clubs like Wigan. Such studies suggest too that the particular sport in question does matter: the unique economy, ecology, tradition as well as rules and performative characteristics of a particular sport engage with local and global forces in different ways. Thus, as Jones (2004, p. 59) points out, soccer for example relies more on "team strategies and game tactics" and less on individual skills compared to several other sports such as swimming, boxing or badminton. This has implications for race, migration and diversity, as the later discussion will show.

Sports migration is thus on the one hand a kind of ideal cosmopolitanism, fuelled by a buoyant economy and the powerful visceral and affective forces of fandom in many professional sports, as well as the athletes' symbolic power to represent a particular community or territory. On the other hand, this ideal is intersected by the particular contours of local community responses to sports migrants, and the differentiated niches that athletes in different sports may find (or fail to find) in the community. Furthermore, the wide socio-economic range occupied by sports migrants, the thin line that often divides successful and beloved athletes from unsuccessful and abject ones, also means that athletes often provoke ambivalent attitudes in the public, in one moment (and in certain athletes) invoking attitudes appropriate to desirable foreign talent, and in other moments (in the same or different athletes) invoking the rejection usually associated with migrant labourers or refugees.

FOREIGN LABOUR, FOREIGN TALENT, AND THE CRISIS OF ASIAN MULTI-CULTURAL MODERNITY

The case of Singapore aptly illustrates the complexities of sports migration as it plays out against the context of national policy, and the particular desires and anxieties of the local community. Much has been written about Singapore's racial landscape and its managed multiculturalism, and for the present purposes it is sufficient to refer only to the most salient points. Singapore's colonial history, during which large numbers of Chinese and Indian merchants, indentured labourers and other settlers arrived, left it with the legacy of a highly multiracial society. With decolonization in the 1950s and independence in 1965, a number of social problems arising along racial lines — including Chinese schools infiltrated by Communism and agitating for increased government support for Chinese education, and incidents of racial clashes between Malays and Chinese (Turnbull 1977, p. 248; Wong 2002, p. 63) — indicated the clear and fragile racial fault-lines in this multiracial society. The government's response has been to tightly govern the four official racial categories (Chinese, Malay, Indian and Others) through language and education policies, public housing, laws policing religious harmony, and other measures. The result of this heavy emphasis on and scrutiny of racial categories and boundaries is a multicultural policy that works through "a process of simplification and symbolic representation", in which race becomes "highly politicized" as an essential ideological category (Chua 1998, p. 190; Clammer 1998, p. 49).

However, from the 1990s onwards, Singapore's labour requirements and its recruitment of well-qualified foreign professionals as part of its push to compete as a global city has led to an influx of foreigners living and working in Singapore, from a wide variety of nations and of varied skills and socio-economic backgrounds. Today there are some 1.32 million foreigners in Singapore, forming about 27 per cent of the total population (Singapore Police Force figures, cited in Othman 2008, p. 2). As can be imagined, the introduction of significant numbers of immigrant ethnic others brings with it various anxieties about the violation of these racial boundaries and balances. Despite the wide range of backgrounds of these foreigners, the public response to them has tended to polarize at the two extreme ends: unskilled "foreign workers", and highly-skilled "foreign talent". These classifications are built into the Ministry of Manpower's (MOM) categories of employment permits. "Employment passes" are for "skilled" foreigners who have "recognized qualifications" and seek "professional, managerial and executive or specialist jobs" (MOM 2008*a*), and there are even built-in salary criteria and checks on qualifications, varying according to the different categories of employment passes — above $7,000 for the P1 pass, between $3,500 and $7,000 for the P2, and more than $2,500 for the Q pass. In contrast, work permits are for "unskilled" foreign workers, most of whom fall into the two biggest groups: foreign domestic workers and workers mainly in the construction, services and manufacturing sectors. Qualifying requirements for work permit holders and for their Singaporean employers have been tightened considerably in the past few years due to a spate of incidents of abuse and ill-treatment of workers. Nevertheless, such employment permits are primarily given to those with only very basic education: no stipulation of educational qualifications for basic jobs like "dispatch and delivery services", and a "minimum of 8 years of formal education" for domestic workers (MOM 2008*b*; 2008*c*). The MOM also has an "S Pass", which essentially fills in the intermediate space between the two main categories of "employment pass" and "work permits".

The influx of "foreign workers" has led to fairly predictable anxieties about their large numbers in the context of a small country like Singapore, the public nuisance posed by the congregation of these workers in certain areas (Little India, Beach Road, parts of Orchard Road), and the perceived increase in dirt and crime that they bring (Othman 2008, p. 1; Yeoh and Huang 1998, pp. 593, 597; Quek and Tan 2008, p. A4; Goh 2008, p. A30). This general response of fear and repulsion is quite different from that evoked by the highly paid and high-profile "foreign talent" that has been brought in to occupy key positions in local banks, government-linked investment agencies and other important organizations. The appointments in the late 1990s and early 2000s include American John Olds as CEO of the Development Bank of Singapore, Alex Au (a Hong Kong resident) as CEO of the Overseas-Chinese Banking Corporation, and Briton Chris Matten as Managing Director for Corporate Stewardship of Temasek Holdings (Leong 2002, p. 4).

The appointments of these and other well-paid foreign professionals has consistently led to public discussion about the merits of such foreign appointments relative to the hiring of Singaporeans, Singapore's over-reliance on foreigners, whether they actually add value to their organizations and the nation, and other related concerns. Indeed, since the median monthly income for the Singapore labour force is $1,875 (2001 figures; MOM 2002), foreign employment pass holders (who must earn at least $2,500, and in the case of the P1 class pass-holders, at least $7,000 to qualify) have significantly greater earning power than the average Singaporean, and arguably represent a "levelling upwards" of socio-economic standing. Foreign talent has attracted other negative comments, including Singaporeans' views that the so-called "foreign talent" are in fact overpaid and under-talented, most talented at "over-representing themselves" to gullible Singaporeans, ultimately "no better than us", and creating an "embarrassment" to the nation — Seah Chiang Nee's commentary on the website "Little Speck" is a representative view (Seah 2002).

Such has been the extent of public concern that the government has actively defended and justified its policy of hiring foreign talent: no less an authoritative voice than Lee Kuan Yew has put this recruitment process in context by asking the rhetorical question, "If we did not have foreign talent, do you think you would have this Singapore?" (cited in Divyanathan 2001, p. S10). The Minister for Transport Raymond Lim has acknowledged that "foreign does not always equal talent", and that "politically, [it] makes sense" that the government should recruit from Singaporeans first, and only recruit foreign talent when there is no equivalent Singaporean talent, although he also feels that "economically", this it is beyond the government's ability to judge and ascertain prevailing skill levels to that degree of accuracy (Lim 2001, p. 40).

Apart from the obvious polarization of Singapore's management of and attitudes to foreigners, together with its inescapable cultural polarization of undesirable "third world" Asians and more-or-less desirable Westerners, one of the most interesting features of Singaporean society is its very anxiety about foreignness. As an obviously and avowedly multiracial and multicultural society and a young nation, the bulk of whose population was itself migrant in origin not too long ago, Singapore's pronounced anxieties about foreigners — especially those from other countries in Asia, including China itself from which the majority of Singaporeans themselves originated — may reflect over-determined causes, including its small size, its highly regulated structures and normative-homogenizing culture and value systems such as competitiveness, and the government's own careful management and control of foreigners.

THE DEVELOPMENT OF SINGAPORE'S FOREIGN SPORTS TALENT (FST) SCHEME

What makes foreign sports people constitute a unique group is not only their escape from the polarization and dichotomy ("unskilled"-"talent"), which characterizes foreign workers in general, but also their ability to provoke questions that other forms of labour generally do not do. While in both cases the presence of foreigners raises all kinds of socio-economic questions, the responses they provoke tend to invoke deep questions about "what it means to be Singaporean" — precisely the questions of national identity which tend to be invoked in the periodic debates about foreign sports people. While public debates and anxieties about "dirty" foreign workers and "overpaid" foreign executives arguably play out close to the surface of their essentially social and economic planes, sports displaces debate and anxiety from its apparent plane (athletic ability and competition) onto deeper and more primal (but also more inchoate and visceral) levels of social meaning, where foreign sports people represent and thus call into question the very notion of Singaporean identity and pride. In so doing, sports arguably constitutes a peculiar thrust within the issues of migration and diversity, one which moves debates and responses from the level of "need" and "tolerance", to the level of a core, foundational national identity expressed in the "language of the local" (Andrews and Ritzer 2007, p. 32) — in this case, what it means to be "Singaporean".

In Singapore, with its ambitions to be a transnational hub of various sorts — the "cultural capital of Asia" according to MITA's Renaissance City Report, the "biomedical hub", and of course broader ambitions to be a transportation, finance and tourism hub of Asia (Goh 2005, pp. 189–96) — sports have a role to play in making globalization tangible and manifest in everyday, practical ways. Less lofty and abstract, more accessible to the Singaporean man on the street, more a part of everyday conversation and experience, sports in Singapore has the potential to be "a powerful tool to bring people of different races and socio-economic levels together to cheer a common cause" — in the words of the Ministry of Community Development, Youth and Sports (MCYS) (2008) — while avoiding the economic and political minefields of foreign labour and global capital.

Singapore's attempts to develop a sports culture and to introduce foreign talents into that sports scene arose in tandem with its global orientation and aspiration from the 1990s onwards. On the one hand, Singapore's treatment of foreign sports people replicates many of the strategies and structures of its general policy towards foreigners. On the other hand, some of the characteristics of sports — its ability to accommodate a variety of groups, its inherently communal-tribal nature, the ability of certain sports people to capture the imagination of and represent a community — may also usefully interrogate and offer suggestions forward for Singapore's wider treatment of foreigners.

In 1993, Singapore began actively recruiting foreign sports talent (FST) to live and train in Singapore, with the prospect of becoming Singapore citizens and representing Singapore in their particular sport. The scheme, initially called "Project Rainbow" was launched by the Singapore Sports Council, and the first recruit was China-born table tennis player Jing Junhong (REACH "Shaping Up", undated). It was implemented in conjunction with a general "Sports Excellence" (SPEX) scheme, where "elite athletes [regardless of their national origins] were identified and groomed to win medals" (Ministry of Community Development and Sports (MCDS) 2001, p. 4). Over the years the scheme was refined, and a 2003 press release from the then MCDS (now Ministry of Community Development, Youth and Sports) spelt out the essential features and goals of the scheme which remains today: recruitment is carried out by the various National Sports Associations (NSAs), who have to have a long-term strategic plan covering "the number of athletes, the gaps to be filled by FSTs, the development paths and post-career plans for all their athletes and the integration plans for FSTs" (MCDS 2003). MCDS's press release takes the following three points as a given:

(a) FSTs have played a role in raising Singapore's sports standard and enhanced our image as a sporting nation.
(b) FSTs complement our sports development. However, in the longer term, we need to develop a sizeable pool of local athletes who can do well in major international competitions.
(c) There should be plans to help FSTs integrate into our society and prepare them to be self-reliant citizens after their competitive years are over (MCDS 2003).

The press release affirms Singapore's commitment to the FST scheme as well as the impact and importance of the scheme to Singapore sports, while also thinking of the FSTs as long-term citizens rather than just as short-term assets or commodities.

The goal of integrating FSTs was fostered by the establishment of the Singapore Sports School in April 2004. The school's nine core sports — badminton, bowling, football, golf, netball, sailing, swimming, table tennis, and track and field — reflect Singapore's strategic sports, the ones in which it feels the most confident about making an international impact (Singapore Sports School 2008). In addition to providing both academic and sports training to promising young Singaporeans, the school's remit is to support the NSAs by providing their FSTs with "accommodation, education and training", and give them "an opportunity to integrate with their Singaporean peers and build life-long friendships", in the words of MCYS Minister Vivian Balakrishnan (Balakrishnan 2005). Here and elsewhere, attention is also paid to the complementary goal of having the FSTs help inspire, influence and otherwise spur Singaporean athletes towards excellence, as part of an even larger goal of a "sporting Singapore", characterized by the "3 pillars" of "sports for everyone, sporting excellence, and a serious sport industry" (MCDS 2001, p. 4).

At one level, the scheme is clearly a success, as the relevant agencies and government bodies were quick to point out: the REACH report on

"Shaping Up" mentions the following: in 1999 "Singapore sportsmen who were born overseas brought in six gold medals at the Southeast Asian (SEA) Games' table tennis events, the Republic's best haul in the sport at the Games"; in 2001, "foreign-born athletes contributed twelve of the ninety-five medals won by Singapore at the SEA Games" and in 2002 helped Singapore to its "best ever achievement in the Commonwealth Games" — twelve medals, four of which were gold. The culmination of the scheme to-date must surely be the 2008 Beijing Olympics, where Singapore's China-born table tennis players Li Jiawei, Feng Tianwei and Wang Yuegu won the silver medal in the team event — Singapore's best all-round medal showing at an Olympic games since weightlifter Tan Howe Liang's Silver at the 1960 games. All three table tennis players were products of the FST scheme: Li recruited in her early teens and coming to live and train in Singapore in 1996, becoming a Singapore citizen at the age of eighteen, while Wang came to Singapore in 2004. Feng, the latest recruit of the three, only came to Singapore in 2007, and became a citizen in early 2008.

In the finals of the 2008 Olympics, the Singapore team lost to China, causing a number of wags to call the finals "China A versus China B".[2] This phrase appears repeatedly in street conversation and webposts immediately following the event. This kind of popular response was not the exclusive one — many letters to the press expressed the writers' pride in their compatriots' achievements,[3] and many turned up at the airport and celebratory parade to wish them well — but it does capture something of the significant scepticism that continues to be attached to the FST (not just in the aftermath of the Beijing Olympics, but throughout the time span of the FST scheme), despite the obvious and incontrovertible benefits it has had on Singapore's international sporting achievements. Some of these negative views have to do with FST recruits who just have not lived up to their promise: one such athlete is China-born shot-putter Zhang Guirong, who took on Singaporean citizenship in 2003. She is the current holder of the national shot-put record, which she achieved with a second-place showing in the 2005 Asian Championships. However, at the 2008 Olympics she finished 29th out of a qualifying field of thirty-three, and her best throw was well below her national record. She has fallen out with the Singapore Athletic Association and refused to sign a contract "due to disagreements over training and allowances", and is currently based in Shenyang, China. Her entire career as a "Singaporean" sportswoman has now been called into question, with remarks like "wasted talent" and a "slide into oblivion" (together with the not-too-subtle hint about wanting more money) targeted at her (Thomas 2008, p. 56).

Even with successful sports people (like the Beijing Table Tennis silver medallists), questions have been raised about their longer term value and commitment to Singapore, and whether they are worth the opportunity cost (of training and nurturing more Singaporean athletes). Sports discussion site "Red Sports" carried a post-Beijing story about Li Jiawei's possible plans to give up full-time sports in order to study at Peking University and play for the University team. Although the post stressed that Li has yet to make up her mind, the announcement of her plans — which is called a "bombshell" — clearly evokes a sense of betrayal of the country which recruited and nurtured her, and which has helped her win many titles and "close to a million dollars in awards and winnings" (*Red Sports* 2008). The winning trio of Li, Feng and Wang received S$750,000 as an incentive award for their silver-medal feat, and this generous grant (and the financial security this and other earnings promise) casts a shadow over Li's comments that this may be her last Olympics, despite being only twenty-seven years old. Li was the flag-bearer of the Singapore contingent at the opening ceremony, and carried the flag at an angle and altitude which appeared to allow the edge of the flag to drag on the ground, immediately prompting a number of blog criticisms questioning her patriotism and the seriousness with which she was taking her duties as national athlete and flag-bearer. Some of these bloggers alluded to basic army lore about the respect that must be shown in the handling of the Singapore flag, drummed in during the compulsory military National Service that all able-bodied Singapore men must perform; this National Service lore thus becomes yet another defining point of a "Singaporeanness" which Li and other recent Singaporeans are seen as lacking. Other blog comments have been quick to find fault with the performance of the paddlers in the individual events at the Olympics and at previous games, where their less-than-spectacular performances have raised questions about their talent and determination.

Thus despite the ability of some of the more successful foreign sporting talent to win fans and evoke national pride among their fellow Singaporeans (in contrast to foreign talent in the business world), they have also inevitably stirred up anxieties which resemble those evoked by foreign CEOs. One blogger on the "Singapore News Alternative" site explicitly conflates foreign sporting talents with other foreign talents, and this view is worth quoting at some length, as a fairly representative view on the matter:

> Frankly, I might have an opinion about foreign talents in this nation, and I have probably blogged a few times about them too — mostly on whether some of them are really talented or my disbelief that those jobs cannot be filled by Singaporeans. Otherwise, my unhappiness is with foreigners whose CVs look impressive but can't work for nuts, or those who think they should be treated like kings as if we owed them a living. I am quite sure some of you would agree with me here as you have run into them at work, or read about foreign athletes quitting on us after we spent a lot of money nurturing them. And these are the black sheep — the fallen talents — which have given them all a bad name. (Nowhere.per.sg 2008)

The success of the silver medal-winning table tennis team at the Beijing Olympics, in stirring up both patriotic endorsement and sceptical criticism, has served to highlight a fundamental resistance to newly-minted Singaporean athletes, whatever their success (or lack thereof) on the international stage. Sports, and prominent successes in the same, have some ability to transcend the resentment, envy and scepticism which attaches to foreign talent imported in the business sphere. However, they do not totally or even largely remove the sense that sporting talents are still foreigners whose successes are not entirely Singaporean successes, and who take opportunities and resources away from some Singaporeans who might have similar levels of talent. The case of China-born paddlers like Li, Feng and Wang, shot-putter Zhang, swimmer Tao Li, and others, show that it is not race and overt racial markers which perpetuate their foreignness (unlike perhaps the case of foreign workers like the Thais, Filipinos, South Indians and others who are more clearly racially marked in the context of Singapore), since it would be difficult to single them out from the majority Chinese Singaporeans by appearance alone. The example of Singapore sports seems to reinforce the point made by Andrews and Ritzer (2007, p. 30) that even in sports (with its apparently global influence and flows), "the local persists in the glocal and globalizing forces can never be totally triumphant over the glocal". This is even more true of popular sports like soccer, which inspire considerable community involvement, show the persistence of "the vocabularies of the nation-state (Hiroki 2004, p. 172) and the "languages of the local" (Andrews and Ritzer 2007, p. 34), and nationalize discourses and even stereotypes (Maguire and Burrows 2005, p. 133), even as the sport is characterized by globalization, corporatization and intense competitive pressure. Local resistances to the import of sports talent sketch a vaguely defined but nevertheless affectively powerful vision of a "Singaporean" cultural and national identity which continues to resist easy accommodation of outside elements, even where the racial type, formal conditions of citizenship, and international successes of the foreign sports talent seem to beg that accommodation.[4]

THE "BEAUTIFUL GAME": CONSTRUCTING COSMOPOLITANISM, MIRRORING MULTICULTURALISM

One possible structural problem with the prominent FST athletes is that they have tended to feature in sports where individual ability rather than a high degree of teamwork is the key. Although the Singapore paddlers won their medal in the team rather than individual events, table tennis, in general, is a sport in which individual skill levels, and often an individual's singles-contest with her opponent, are the chief features. It did not help, from the point of view of the foreign talent debate, that all three paddlers were recruited relatively recently from China, without a single Singapore-born player (or one who had taken citizenship much earlier) on the team. This is in contrast to sports like soccer and rugby where individual talents matter much less within the all-important coherence and teamwork of a large body of players (Jones 2004, p. 59). If one of the aims of the FST scheme is to be "sparring partners for our local ... athletes" and help in the bigger picture of developing "a sizeable pool of local sports people who can do well in major international competitions", then the success of Singapore's table tennis team can only be deemed a partial and shorter term success (MCDS 2003; Balakrishnan 2005).

The case of soccer is quite different. In addition to being very much a team sport where individual talent can be entirely negated by poor teamwork, the "beautiful game", as it is often called, has the worldwide following, corporate interest, local support base (of players and fans) and other factors to stimulate a national sporting project. It is potentially large enough (in every sense) to be able to incorporate foreign players without entirely sacrificing local identity, culture and players. There are certainly precedents of successful national soccer teams which have featured multiracial players drawn from immigrant roots, as with the 1998 French World-Cup winning team, nicknamed the "black blanc beur" (black, white, Arab) team.

Yet football's cosmopolitanism also has to work within local conditions. Singapore has a long soccer history, beginning with games involving Europeans and locals in early colonial times, and has had its share of regional successes, including a number of Malaysia Cup victories over Malaysia State rivals, and a fourth-place showing at the 1966 Asian Games (Football Association of Singapore 2008a). This has led to a considerable body of fan sentiments and lore, including references to the "Kallang Roar" (referring to the game-time atmosphere in the Kallang Stadium, a venue with considerable sentimental associations, a "topophilia" that Maguire and Possamai [2005, pp. 42–43] attribute to football stadiums in particular), as well as the immortalization of local heroes like Quah Kim Song, Dollah Kassim and Fandi Ahmad. In 1995, the Football Association of Singapore (FAS) made the decision to leave the Malaysia Cup in order to foster a more competitive and internationally geared domestic competition, which became the S. League. Typically, this was a major move involving considerable government input (the S. League council was chaired by then Senior Minister of State for Law and Home Affairs Ho Peng Kee, and its advisor was then Minister for National Development Mah Bow Tan) and with a vision and timing which aligned it with Singapore's other sports internationalization measures in the mid-1990s (S. League 2008).

The shift from the Malaysia Cup league to the S. League was never intended as a withdrawal into the domestic, but rather as a transformation of the domestic into an internationally competitive arena. FAS has no less a goal than "Singapore in the World Cup" (FAS 2008b), and to this end, began recruiting foreign teams into the S. League — in effect, applying an adapted form of the FST scheme, except that it was entire teams and their managements which were being recruited, rather than individual players. At the same time, the ultimate goal was that some of the more outstanding players would be recruited, given citizenship and ultimately play for Singapore.

There is thus a dualism in the "foreign" element of the S. League system: on the one hand, at the level of teams, foreignness is marked and perpetuated, the foreign teams remaining very much foreign, with little mixing with the Singapore teams other than direct competition for the championship. Each of the Singapore teams is allowed to have a number of foreign players (a minimum of three, and a maximum of four) on their roster; foreign teams by S. League laws are allowed to register local players, but by and large, their rosters are composed of foreigners (FAS 2008c, p. 51).

In fact, all of the foreign teams currently in the S. League — China's Dalian Shide, Japan's Albirex Niigata and South Korea's Super Reds — have filled their rosters entirely with players from their home nations, with the only exception of Albirex's South Korean player Park Myung Eun.

Several regulations help to preserve these national boundaries: Singapore teams are subject to a salary cap of S$85,000 for the entire team, while foreign teams do not have a salary cap imposed on them, which effectively means two different kinds of economies at work in Singaporean and non-Singaporean teams. Very strict regulations forbid a club from "directly or indirectly inducing a Registered Player/Coach of another club to leave for any purpose whatsoever the club with which he is registered", at pain of severe penalties (FAS 2008c, p. 66); transfers can thus only take place through the official channels between clubs, and strictly during the official transfer period. This strictly regulated nature is in contrast to the much more competitive and dynamic transfer practices in bigger and more monied leagues like the EPL. It also seems reasonable to surmise that foreign clubs see it as expedient to help fulfil the strategic aims of their host country and league, while also fulfilling their own national agendas — in most cases, the foreign teams are developmental clubs for their own senior teams in their home countries.

The foreign clubs also tend to have very strong links to their respective expatriate communities and corporate interests in Singapore: Albirex is a good example, with very strong support from the Japanese community in Singapore, and with a sponsorship list that reads like a directory of major Japanese corporate interests locally (including main sponsor Sanyo, and other sponsors Toyota, Mitsubishi, Citizen, Nippon Express, and others). South Korean club Super Reds likewise have a strong Korean corporate presence among their sponsors (which include Semitech and TES), and strong ties with the Korean community in Singapore. While the club's main webpage <http://www.superredsfc.org> and some of its sub-pages have English versions or content in English, its fan club pages are entirely in Korean, and one of its pages entitled "Korea Contents World" contains links to various Korean media pages.

The Football Association of Singapore has succeeded in recruiting a number of foreign players — including current national players British-born John Wilkinson and Daniel Bennett (although Bennett had spent time in Singapore as a child, with his family), Nigerian-born Precious Emuejeraye, Serbian-born Mustafic Fahrudin, and Chinese-born Shi Jia Yi.

Five foreign-born players in the current squad of twenty-two is not a very high percentage, certainly not when compared to Singapore's table tennis or even its badminton team. Japan's team for the 2002 World Cup had a comparable ratio of four out of twenty-three players of foreign origins, which did not stop its fans from making a considerable show of support especially for the games played on Japanese soil (Yoshio and Horne 2004, p. 69). Yet even this is enough to rile a number of Singapore soccer fans, who make the familiar disparaging remarks about foreign "rubbish" with over-inflated reputations, "not local" or "Singaporean" (or "true-born Singaporean") and thus not worthy of support whatever their success.[5] Adding fuel to the fire of anti-foreign sentiments are the controversies and scandals that have been attached to foreign teams and players in the history of the S. League, including allegations of ill-treatment of players by clubs, foreign players breaching contractual obligations, and cases of financial misconduct — the most spectacular case being the arrest and conviction in early 2008 of six players from the former Chinese S. League club Liaoning Guangyuan for accepting bribes to fix matches (Chong 2008, p. 4).

Although S. League rules incorporate the possibility of disqualification, de-registration and rotation of its foreign teams, there does seem to have been quite a significant degree of transience and rapid turnover in the league's relatively brief twelve-year history: Liaoning and another club, Sporting Afrique, each only participated for one year, while another former S. League club Sinchi FC only lasted three years. Current clubs Albirex, Dalian and Super Reds have only been involved in the S. League for a few years. No foreign club has yet to come close to winning the championship, and although the Super Reds are leading the 2008 league table, the overall performances of foreign teams in the S. League is mixed, at best. This shorter term and splotchy involvement of foreign teams is certainly contrasted, in the minds of many supporters, with the much longer history of Singapore's involvement in leagues like the Malaysia Cup, and with the patriotic intensity and passion that that league competition provoked. Even today, more than a decade after Singapore's exit from the Malaysia Cup, and with so many more recent soccer developments to write about, it is fairly common to see fans writing about memorable moments involving Singapore's Malaysia Cup contests, and the atmosphere in the "grand old lady" of the National Stadium.[6]

What is interesting about the S. League project, compared to other sports in Singapore such as table tennis, is the cautious and tightly regulated invocation of foreignness by the FAS. The S. League regulations and the Association's practice effectively creates temporary and controlled zones of foreignness, with (apart from the actual competition between teams) only limited possibilities of crossing, as manifested in the relatively limited number of foreign players who have made it to the current national team. This is a very different strategy from the Singapore Table Tennis Association's approach, and may well reflect the more team-oriented nature of soccer compared to table tennis, but also the longer history and more local flavour of Singapore soccer.

Paradoxically, the most international and global game, soccer in the Singapore context has manifested itself as a rather cautious and guarded foreign recruitment or involvement policy, which appears to reinforce theories of sports which insist on the perpetuation of local or glocal cultural forces in the face of the global or grobal (Andrews and Ritzer 2007). In its carefully-regulated version of internationalization and sports immigration, Singapore soccer implicitly respects and nurtures a deeper sense of history and national identity than is merely represented by formal citizenship, while nevertheless conforming to the general processes and goals of the FST scheme. Soccer in Singapore — with its longer and emotionally charged history, bigger fan base and more team-oriented structure than many of the other key sports — suggests the limits of sport migration, and the contours of sporting nationalism in Singapore's present social condition. It may well be that sport in Singapore will one day "be represented by people of multiple races and cultures that co-exist and recognise each other through their 'routes' rather than their 'roots'" (Hiroki 2004, p. 167); but if so, it seems likely that the gradualist and communal approach of soccer is going to be the way, rather than the more fast-track and spectacular processes of agencies like the Table Tennis Association. The nuances of different sports is also shown by the contrast provided by the Singapore Sailing Federation, which has consistently resisted the impulse to recruit any foreign sporting talent (although it does have foreign coaches — a much less visible and less contentious move, in the light of sporting nationalism). Sailing has been a highly successful sport for Singapore, consistently bringing in medals at SEA games and Asian games levels (at the 2006 Asian games, Singapore won five gold medals, making this one of the most successful sports for the nation [Singapore Sailing Federation 2008]). The emphasis on training and strategy, the relative unimportance of physical size and strength in this sport, and the relatively calm seas surrounding Singapore, all make this a strategic sport in which the recruitment of foreign sporting talent need not feature prominently, and where a stricter notion of "national" representation can be pursued.

CONCLUSION: SPORTS AS INDEX/SYMBOL OF GLOBALIZATION AND DIVERSITY

This overview of "foreign talent" in the context of Singapore sports, and within the larger context of the "foreign worker" and "foreign talent" discourses in Singapore, suggests the ways in which sports both embodies symbolic capital and is also an index to the strength of local sentiments. Thus, on one hand, the evident support for and pride in the accomplishments of Singapore sports people shows the potential for sports to escape the stricter local-foreign binary which dominates public debates on the presence of unskilled foreign workers and highly-paid expatriate professionals and managers in Singapore. The Singapore Government's FST scheme, with its goal not only of short-term achievements on the international arena, but also of raising the overall sporting climate and competitiveness in Singapore, recognizes and capitalizes on this symbolic capital.

However, the abstract and abstracting quality of symbolic capital — its ability to capture the imagination of individuals and at least temporarily transcend individual and communal boundaries — is its weakness as well as its strength. In the present stage of Singapore's evolution as a sporting nation and society, that abstract quality does not always succeed in the face of a lived, popular and insistent notion of "Singaporeanness": one which may not have a strict definition (for instance, in terms of how long, exactly, one has formally held citizenship) to rely on, but which nevertheless manifests itself in the dogged assertion of a kind of local authenticity which the majority of foreign-born and recently recruited athletes are seen as lacking. Since the value of sports lies in large part in its ability to win fans and fire the imagination of a community, these individual and collective demurrals are actually significant, as a sign of the existing boundary of an "imagined community" called "the Singaporean". In the case of Singapore sports, that "national" construction inevitably includes (together with sporting memory and pride) even the racial and cultural prejudices which, at least for now, continue to define "Singaporeanness". In the face of this persistently local or glocal (the latter acknowledging Singapore's own multiracial identity and its immigrant history) quality, a globalized diversity is still a highly fragile condition, tolerated so long as it does not push the buttons of (the question of) a "real Singaporean" identity and pride.

In revealing the particular negotiations of the local and the global in the phenomenon of sports migration, the Singapore example also reveals the ever-constructed and ever-contingent nature of cosmopolitan diversity. While it is tempting to exempt cosmopolitan elites in fields like business, finance, IT, and R&D from both the abject condition of migrant workers and the more variable and even fickle cosmopolitanism of transnational athletes, the fact is that all cosmopolitanisms are contingent, constructed by their interplay with local conditions. Financial and business cosmopolitans are constructed by economic conditions and opportunities, as the exodus of Asian finance and other related professionals from the United States and back to many Asian countries after the sub-prime crisis of 2007 indicates. Sports migrants, in their duality of affective power and competitive vulnerability, are a constant reminder of the role of local policy, affects and industry conditions on which cosmopolitan elitism is ultimately based.

Even more than that, sports migrants show the importance and also the ambivalence of the powerful affective forces underlying cosmopolitanism. If athletes invoke more of the community's affects than other forms of migrants, due to their role as representative symbols of the community, this affective factor is also in operation in other forms of cosmopolitanism. Whether it is fear of "dirty" foreign workers loitering in public places or resentment of highly paid foreign talents, fondness for the cultural "colour" that migrants bring and pride at the nation's or city's ability to attract celebrity migrants, deep-seated visceral and affective factors play a significant role in setting the limits of cosmopolitanism and diversity. In the final analysis, cosmopolitanism is part of the projection of local identity, community belonging, and community pride, and must take into account and negotiate with the community's history, culture and aspirations. Nowhere is this more evident than in the complex positions of sports migrants in the highly competitive and highly transnational world of professional sports.

Notes

1. There were earlier inducements for Japanese players to play overseas, although the main "fruits" of Japanese soccer migration (itself the most prominent example in Asia) date from 1998 with the move of players like Nakata. For a history of Japan's football migrations, see Yoshio and Horne (2004).

2. See, for example, a *Straits Times* online discussion thread for 18 August 2008, in particular the comments by "Silaterangy" and "Pushkin62". <http://comment.straitstimes.com/showthread.php?t=13050&page=2>. Accessed 19 September 2008.
3. Fairly representative are the letters written by Ryan Huang and Michael Loh, which appeared in the "Voices" section of *Today*, 21 August 2008, p. 34. Huang's letter called the paddlers "catalysts" for "creating a sustainable pool of local talent," while Loh's letter simply dismisses the "griping" about the paddlers' place of birth, emphasizing instead that "it is the record [of Singapore's silver medal] that counts."
4. This local resistance is not unique to Singapore, and was echoed by a Malaysian blogger who, in arguing against importing and relying on foreign-born athletes for Malaysia, criticized the Singapore model. Unlike countries like the United States which attracted many people in search of a better life (some of whom then incidentally became national athletes), Singapore's practice is to "tempt the foreign athletes to crossover". The writer urges Malaysia to a different strategy, to "stay local for now and build from the bottom" (man@mom 2008).
5. Judging by posts on "Singapore Soccer" dated 16 May 2007 <http://sgfootballfans.blogspot.com/search/label/foreign%20talent%20scheme>, on "Singapore Olympic Team" at the "SGforums" site dated 2 and 3 August 2008 <http://sgforums.com/forums/3/topics/326105>, and on "Singapore Soccer" dated 25 June 2008 <http://rebeldiamonds.wordpress.com/2008/06/25/singapore-soccer-and-the-2010-dream/> — representative of a large number of other such comments.
6. See, for example, several posts by "PC" on "Singapore Soccer" dated 30 April, 1 May and 8 July 2007 <http://sgfootballfans.blogspot.com/search?q=malaysia+cup>, and by "kopiosatu", "borgkiller", "windjammer", "baseline" and "sohguanh" (all posted 25 July 2003) on "SGforums" <http://sgforums.com/forums/8/topics/53108>.

References

Andrews, D.L. and G. Ritzer. "The Grobal in the Sporting Glocal". In *Globalization and Sport*, edited by R. Giulianotti and R. Robertson, pp. 28–45. Malden, MA: Blackwell, 2007.

Attorney-General's Chambers. "Maintenance of Religious Harmony Act". Singapore Statutes Online. <http://statutes.agc.gov.sg/>. Accessed 25 July 2007.

Balakrishnan, V. "Speech delivered at Singapore Sports School Open House", 23 July 2005. <http://app.mcys.gov.sg/web/corp_speech_story.asp?szMod=corp&szSubMod=speech&qid=2063>. Accessed 19 September 2008.

Burdsey, D. *British Asians and Football: Culture, Identity, Exclusion*. London: Routledge, 2007.

Chick, G. and J.W. Loy. "Making Men of Them: Male Socialization for Warfare and Combative Sports". *World Cultures* 12, no. 1 (2001): 2–17.

Chong, E. "Six Match-Fixing Liaoning Soccer Players Jailed". *Straits Times*, 23 April 2008, p. 4.

Chua, B.H. "Culture, Multiracialism, and National Identity in Singapore". In *Trajectories: Inter-Asia Cultural Studies*, edited by K.H. Chen, pp. 186–205. New York: Routledge, 1998.

Clammer, J. *Race and State in Independent Singapore 1965–1990: The Cultural Politics of Pluralism in a Multiethnic Society*. Aldershot: Ashgate, 1998.

Collins, T. "Racial Minorities in a Marginalized Sport: Race, Discrimination and Integration in British Rugby League Football". In *Sporting Nationalisms: Identity, Ethnicity, Immigration and Assimilation*, edited by M. Cronin and D. Mayall, pp. 151–69. London: Frank Cass, 1998.

Cronin, M. and D. Mayall. "Sport and Ethnicity: Some Introductory Remarks". In *Sporting Nationalisms: Identity, Ethnicity, Immigration and Assimilation*, edited by M. Cronin and D. Mayall, pp. 1–13. London: Frank Cass, 1998.

Divyanathan, D. "Foreigners Boosted Economy by 37%". *Straits Times*, 1 November 2001, p. S10.

Football Association of Singapore. "History". http://www.fas.org.sg/default.asp?V_DOC_ID=830>. Accessed 22 September 2008*a*.

———. "Roadmap". <http://www.fas.org.sg/default.asp?V_DOC_ID=888>. Accessed 22 September 2008*b*.

———. *Official Handbook 2008*. Singapore: Football Association of Singapore, 2008*c*.

Goh, C.L. "Serangoon Gardens Dormitory Debate". *Straits Times*, 6 September 2008, p. A30.

Goh, R.B.H. *Contours of Culture: Space and Social Difference in Singapore*. Hong Kong: Hong Kong University Press, 2005.

Hay, R. "Croatia: Community, Conflict and Culture: The Role of Soccer Clubs in Migrant Identity". In *Sporting Nationalisms: Identity, Ethnicity, Immigration and Assimilation*, edited by M. Cronin and D. Mayall, pp. 49–66. London: Frank Cass, 1998.

Hiroki, O. "The Banality of Football: 'Race', Nativity, and How Japanese Football Critics Failed to Digest the Planetary Spectacle". In *Football Goes East: Business, Culture and the People's Game in China, Japan and South Korea*, edited by W. Manzenreiter and J. Horne, pp. 165–79. New York: Routledge, 2004.

Jones, R. "Football in the People's Republic of China". In *Football Goes East: Business, Culture and the People's Game in China, Japan and South Korea*, edited by W. Manzenreiter and J. Horne, pp. 54–66. New York: Routledge, 2004.

Lechner, F. "Imagined Communities in the Global Game: Soccer and the Development of Dutch National Identity". In *Globalization and Sport*, edited by R. Giulianotti and R. Robertson, pp. 107–21. Malden, MA: Blackwell, 2007.

Leong, C.T. "Ho Ching is Temasek Executive Director". *Straits Times*, 21 May 2002, p. 4.

Lim, R. "External Challenges Facing the Economy". In *Singapore in the New Millennium: Challenges Facing the City-State*, edited by D. Da Cunha, pp. 26–49. Singapore: Institute of Southeast Asian Studies, 2001.

Maguire, J. "Introduction: Power and Global Sport". In *Power and Global Sport: Zones of Prestige, Emulation and Resistance*, edited by J. Maguire, pp. 1–20. Abingdon: Routledge, 2005.

──── and M. Burrows. "'Not the Germans Again': Soccer, Identity Politics and the Media". In *Power and Global Sport: Zones of Prestige, Emulation and Resistance*, edited by J. Maguire, pp. 130–42. Abingdon: Routledge, 2005.

──── and C. Possamai. "'Back to the Valley': Local Responses to the Changing Culture of Football". In *Power and Global Sport: Zones of Prestige, Emulation and Resistance*, edited by J. Maguire, 41–60. Abingdon: Routledge, 2005.

man@mom. "Relying on Foreign Athletes is not a Solution". NST, 28 August 2008. <http://thebeijing2008.blogspot.com/2008/08/relying-on-foreign-athletes-is-not.html>. Accessed 21 September 2008.

MCDS. "Report on the Committee on Sporting Singapore (summary version)". 2001. <http://www.mcys.gov.sg/MCDSFiles/download/Sporting%20Singapore%20Report%20(Summary%20Version).pdf>. Accessed 19 September 2008.

────. "Foreign talent remains part of sports scene". Press Release of 26 December 2003. <http://app.mcys.gov.sg/web/corp_press_story.asp?szMod=corp&szSubMod=press&qid=232>. Accessed 19 September 2008.

MCYS. "Ministry of Community Development, Youth and Sports: Introduction". 2008. <http://app.mcys.gov.sg/web/sprt_main.asp>. Accessed 18 September 2008.

MOM. "About the Pass". <http://www.mom.gov.sg/publish/momportal/en/communities/work_pass/employment_pass/about_the_pass.html>. Accessed 20 September 2008*a*.

────. "Entry Requirements for First-Time Foreign Domestic Workers". <http://www.mom.gov.sg/publish/momportal/en/communities/work_pass/foreign_domestic_workers/application0/requirements/first-time_foreign.html>. Accessed 20 September 2008*b*.

────. "Requirements: Services Sector". <http://www.mom.gov.sg/publish/momportal/en/communities/work_pass/work_permit/application/requirements/Services_Sector.html>. Accessed 20 September 2008*c*.

────. "Key Labour Indicators". 2002. <http://www4.gov.sg/mom/manpower/manrs/lforce/ki.pdf>. Accessed 9 April 2002.

Mrozek, D.J. "The Cult and Ritual of Toughness in Cold War America". In *Rituals and Ceremonies in Popular Culture*, edited by R.B. Browne, pp. 178–91. Bowling Green: Bowling Green University Popular Press, 1980.

Nowhere.per.sg. "Bashing Foreign Talents". Singapore News Alternative, 17 August 2008. <http://singaporenewsalternative.blogspot.com/2008/08/bashing-foreign-talents.html>. Accessed 21 September 2008.

Nyers, P. "Abject Cosmopolitanism: The Politics of Protection in the Anti-Deportation Movement". *Third World Quarterly* 24, no. 6 (2003): 1069–93.

Othman, Z. "Unjustified Fears?". *Today*, 15 September 2008, pp. 1–2.

Quek, C. and A. Tan. "Two Dead with Multiple Wounds". *Straits Times*, 20 September 2008, pp. A3–A4.

REACH (Reaching Everyone for Active Citizenry @ Home) (n.d.). "Shaping Up: Feedback on Health and Sports." <http://app.reach.gov.sg/reach/Portals/0/doc/Shaping%20our%20Home/Shaping%20up.pdf>. Accessed 18 September 2008.

Red Sports. "Li Jiawei to Play for and Study at Peking University Next Year?". 24 August 2008. <http://redsports.sg/2008/08/24/jiawei-study-peking/>. Accessed 21 September 2008.

Seah, C.N. "Foreign Talent". *Little Speck*, 30 April 2002. <http://www.littlespeck.com/content/economy/CTrendsEconomy-020430.html>. Accessed 19 September 2008.

Singapore Sailing Federation. "History". <http://www.sailing.org.sg/aboutus/history.php>. Accessed 10 August 2008.

Singapore Sports School. "About". http://www.sportsschool.edu.sg/infolinks.aspx?id=1. Accessed 19 September 2008.

S. League. "About S. League". <http://www.sleague.com/Web/main.aspx?ID=8704a261-98eb-4b3e-a432-a7ddd625eacf,,&TargetPageID=>. Accessed 22 September 2008.

Thomas, L. Still Waiting for Zhang". *Today*, 21 August 2008, p. 56.

Today. "Voices" section, 21 August 2008, p. 34.

Turnbull, C.M. *A History of Singapore 1819–1975*. Singapore: Oxford University Press, 1977.

Voigt, D.Q. "American Sporting Rituals". In *Rituals and Ceremonies in Popular Culture*, edited by R. B. Browne, pp. 125–40. Bowling Green: Bowling Green University Popular Press, 1980.

Wong, T-H. *Hegemonies Compared: State Formation and Chinese School Politics in Postwar Singapore and Hong Kong*. New York: RoutledgeFalmer, 2002.

Yeoh, B.S.A. and S. Huang. "Negotiating Public Space: Strategies and Styles of Migrant Female Domestic Workers in Singapore". *Urban Studies* 35, no. 3 (1998): 583–602.

Yoshio, T. and J. Horne. "Japanese Football Players and the Sport Talent Migration Business". In *Football Goes East: Business, Culture and the People's Game in China, Japan and South Korea*, edited by W. Manzenreiter and J. Horne, pp. 69–86. New York: Routledge, 2004.

INDEX

A
"abject cosmopolitans", 255
active citizenship, 33
Adachi ward, Tokyo, 17
  basic plan of, 62–63
  comparative chart of Shinjuku wards and, 70–71
  cultural and interactive integration in, 72
  foreign population in, 66, 68
  foreign residents, 66
  initiatives, 63
  integration reforms in, 73
  international marriages in, 67–69, 77
  rights of migrants, 65
  specific measures undertaken by, 64–65
  structural and identificational integration reforms, 78
  towards belonging and local citizenship, 73–74
alcohol consumption in Korea, 237, 238
Alien's Land Act, 1961, 117
Alliance for Human Rights Legislation for Immigrants and Migrants (AHRLIM), 137, 142–43, 144
  discriminatory policies and laws against, 141
  immigration policy, 145
  protest for marriage migrants, 147

Amerasians, 120, 121
American culture in Itaewon, 236, 244
American food culture in Itaewon, 248
Ansan, 249n4
Arabo, 203n4
ASEAN. *See* Association of Southeast Asian Nations (ASEAN)
Asian countries
  citizenship in, 36–41, 49n1
  citizenship to migrants, 41–43
  diversity in, *see* Diversity in Asia
  dual citizenship legislation of, 39–40
  feminization of human mobility, 4
  human rights movements in, 9
  human rights tradition in, 38
  intermarriages in, 42
  international and internal migration in, 8
  labour migration in, 4, 9
  migration in, *see* migration in Asia
  migratory movement types in, 38
  nationality laws in, 49n1
  population movements in, 4
  rate of naturalization in, 47
Asian multi-cultural modernity, crisis of, 257–60
Asia-Pacific countries, sex-trafficking into, 8

assimilation, 60
  by immigrants, 108, 112, 113
  non-intervention to, 119–23
Association of Southeast Asian
    Nations (ASEAN), 41
  countries, human rights
      mechanism, 9
Australia, multicultural policy in, 35

B
Balakrishnan, Vivian, 262
Bangladesh migrants, 96, 97
Barth, Frederik, 187
Beijing Olympics, 263, 265
Berry, J.W., 60
black people, 165
Breivik, Anders Behring, 130, 131
British
  colonial administrators, 12
  colonialism, 210, 240
  imperialism, 210
brokerage agencies, 6
Buck, Pearl S., 120
bumbay stereotype, 195–96
bumbayin, 203n4
Burmese migrants, 51n24

C
Canada, multicultural policy in, 35
caste identity in India, 191
Chen Shui-Bien, 140
China
  Dalian Shide in, 268, 269
  internal migrants in, 7–8
  international migration systems
      of, 14
  migration in, 2, 3
  Chinese "eating" stalls in Singapore,
      212
  food items in, 218
Chinese literacy programme, 136–37,
    147
Chinese-Malay-Indian-Others (CMIO)
    model, 87, 89, 92

  of multiculturalism, 12
  multiracialism, 93, 99
  racial arithmetic of, 88
Chinese migrants, 2
Chinese Residents Association (CRA),
    118
Chinito, 203n4
citizenship, 32
  active, 33
  Adachi, 73–74
  in Asian countries, 36–41
  concept of, 33, 44, 45, 48
  dual, *see* dual citizenship
  era of globalization, 132–37
  European Union, 155n2
  gender biases in, 42
  global, 84
  globally-oriented, 85
  intermarriages in Asia, 42
  in Japan, 37, 44
  Japanese, 33
  laws, 37
  marriage, 47
  in migrant integration, 35
  to migrants in Asian countries,
      41–43
  migration and approaches to, 15
  national-based, 65
  naturalization, 47
  passive and active, 33
  from perspectives of social
      movements, 152–54
  radical modes of, 17
  rights and duties for, 33
  in Singapore, 37, 90, 91
  in Taiwan, 17, 137–39
civic rights, 74, 133
class identifications
  ascriptions by others, 195
  media as agents, 198–201
  racialized and pathological bodies,
      195–98
  self ascriptions of, 191–95
Clifford, James, 186–87

Index

CMIO model. *See* Chinese-Malay-Indian-Others (CMIO) model
colonial administration
　in Malaya, 11
　in Singapore, 11
colonialism
　British, 210, 240
　Japanese, 3, 15
　in Seoul, 233
colonial policy, 88
colonization, migration as, 186
Commission for Women's Rights and Welfare, 138
communalism in Malaysia, 11
community
　in *kopitiam*, 220–22
　rights, 60
Constitution Amendment, 133
contemporary migration, 1, 16
contract labour systems, 5
Copenhagen Declaration on Social Development, 60
cosmopolitan
　city, 83, 86
　democracy, 85
cosmopolitanism, 10, 83
　academic discussions of, 84
　application of, 84
　city-planning issues, 85
　concept of, 84
　constructing, 266–71
　forms of, 272
　intellectual discussions of, 84
　manifestation of, 86
　minimal requirement of, 100
　moral and cultural, 85
　of Singapore, 93
　state visions of, 87
　variants of, 85
Council for Cultural Affairs, 141, 148, 155n8
Council for Hakka Affairs, 140, 146
Council of Labor Affairs, 144
cross-border minorities, 10

cross-border movements, 32
cultural groups in mixed-ethnic people, 165
cultural identities, 134, 182, 187, 237, 247
cultural integration, 58, 61
　reforms of, 71–72
　in Shinjuku and Adachi wards, 69–71
cultural pluralism, 35
cultural rights, 33
cultural territory in Seoul, 233–34
culture in Itaewon, shifting geographies of, 244–47
customers in *kopitiam*, 220–22

D

Dalian Shide in China, 268, 269
David, Randy, 185
Declaration of Cultural Citizenship, 141
degree of animosity, 91
democracy, cosmopolitan, 85
democratic multiculturalism, 9
Democratic Progressive Party (DPP), 140, 141, 145
democratization, Taiwan's, 137
diaspora
　Indian. *See* Indian diaspora
　media role in, 182–84
"diaspora foreigners' space", 233
diaspora populations, 32, 39
　benefits of, 46
diasporic identities, 187
diversification
　of foods in Itaewon, 247
　in Koreans' foreign food consumption, 246
diversionary tactics of government, 149–52
diversity
　in Asia, 2, 10
　of cultures, Itaewon, 248
　in East Asia, 20

ethnic, *see* ethnic diversity
  policy, 19
  in Singapore, 209–10, 271–72
  in Southeast Asia, 20
  unity in, 10, 16
diversity in Asia
  dimensions of, 7, 20
  forms of, 13
  migration and experiences of, 14
  of migration-related issues, 9
  and multiculturalism, 12
  in pre-colonial eras, 15
  scholarship on, 10
  social and cultural, 10, 12
  temporal and spatial dimensions of, 1
  in Western contexts, 19
divorce
  foreign mothers, 168, 169
  inter-ethnic couples, 166–67
DPP. *See* Democratic Progressive Party (DPP)
dual citizenship
  legislation of Asian countries, 39–40
  in Philippines, 39
  voting rights, 32, 39
dual nationality, 39–40
  children, 68, 69

E

East Asia
  multiculturalism in, 136
  social and cultural diversity in, 20
economic growth in Taiwan, 137
economic integration, 39
education, 63, 67
  human rights, 71
  Japanese language, 69
  multicultural awareness, 71
  subsidies, 75
employment passes, categories of, 258

Employment Permit System (EPS), 115, 116
  in South Korea, 38
English-medium programmes, 150
Esser's social integration dimensions, 61
ethnic boundary maintenance, 188
ethnic Chinese
  incorporation policies, 118
  policy, 118
  residents, incorporation of, 118–19
  schools, 119
  settlers (Huaqiao), 116–19
ethnic diversity, 63, 76, 233
  of Metro Manila, 184
  sources of, 108
ethnic food restaurants in Itaewon, 235, 244
ethnic groups, 141, 155n9
  in diaspora, 186, 188, 192, 194
  theory of, 187–88
ethnic homogeneity
  idea of, 114
  in Korea, 15, 116
  maintenance of, 115
  myth of, 114
ethnic identity, 183. *See also* multi-ethnic identity
  ascriptions by others, 195
  media as agents, 198–201
  of mixed-ethnic children, 165
  racialized and pathological bodies, 195–98
  self ascriptions of, 191–95
ethnic Korean migrants, 17
ethnic minorities in South Korea, 108
ethnic power relations, 169
  effects of, 175–77
  on mixed-ethnic children, 175–77
  reflected in behaviour of foreign mothers, 172–73
  reflected in choice of school, 173–75

Index

ethnicity
  Japanese, 170, 171, 178
  non-Western, 178
  and race, 164
  single, 170–71
  Thai, 171
  Western, 170, 178
Europe
  colonies development in, 2
  Filipino mail-order brides in, 3
  liberalized policies and laws in, 136
European Union (EU) citizenship, 155n2

F

family reunification, 32, 38, 41, 115
female marriage migrants, 5
female migration, 4, 5
feminization
  of Asian migration, 3, 6
  human mobility within Asia, 5
Filipino mail-order brides in Europe, 3
Filipino migrants, 47
Filipinos
  class identity, 191, 202n4, 203n6
  in Metro Manila, 184, 198
five-six stereotype, 186, 192, 193, 195, 196
FLEA. *See* Foreign Residents' Local Election Rights Act (FLEA)
food
  costs of, 223
  cross-cultural taste for, 217
  culture, 225
  culture in Itaewon, 247
  Hainanese *kopitiams*, 215
  halal, 222
  HDB *kopitiam*, 217
  heritages in Singapore, 229n7
  Indian and Malay eateries, 215–16
  Indonesian, 218
  in Itaewon, shifting geographies of, 244–47
  multicultural taste, 218
  regulation in South and Southeast Asia, 237
  restriction for Muslims, 237
Football Association of Singapore (FAS), 267, 268
  foreign-born players in, 269
foreign brides, 137–38, 147, 155n4
foreign children, difficulties in school, 69
foreign food restaurants in Itaewon, 235
foreign labour, 257–60
foreign nationals in Japan, 56–57
Foreign Resident Advisory Board, 73
foreign residents
  business activities in, 71
  cost of health care coverage, 66
  cultural and interactive integration reforms, 71–72
  employment of, 65
  financial realities and criminalization of, 66–67
Foreign Residents' Local Election Rights Act (FLEA), 117
  motivation for, 118
Foreign Sports Talent (FST) scheme, 260–66
foreign talent, 7, 257–60
foreign workers, 59
  in Japan, 56
  kopitiam in Singapore, 220
  language and cultural orientation issues for, 227–28
  multiculturalism, 228
Foreigner Advisory Committee, 73
"foreigner-related crime", 67
foreigners' territory in Seoul, 234–36
France, cultural differences in, 35

French Revolution, Jacobin phase of, 33

G
gambling dens in Singapore, 212
gender identification
    ascriptions by others, 195
    media as agents, 198–201
    racialized and pathological bodies, 195–98
    self ascriptions of, 191–95
Gillespie, Marie, 183
global citizenship, philosophy of, 84
globalization, 2, 33, 246, 256, 261
    cosmopolitan democracy, 85
    demands of, 88
    eras of, 133, 210
    factors of, 238
    migration and, 226
    modernization and, 237
    processes of, 211
    realities of, 50n13
    Singapore, 209
Goh Chok Tong, 86, 89
governance in Asia, 20–21
government, diversionary tactics of, 149–52
guestworkers, 108, 110, 112, 116, 117, 119, 122, 123, 133, 134
    advocacy NGOs, 121
    policies, 115, 118
Gwangju, 249n5

H
Hainanese coffee merchants, 229n6
Hainanese *kopitiam*
    Chinese immigrants, 214
    employment in, 213
    Western foods, 215
halal certification of food, 245
halal food
    in Itaewon, 18, 241–42
    in Korea, 238, 239
    in Seoul, 239, 240
    in Singapore, 222, 224
Hall, Stuart, 187, 188, 202n3
HDB. *See* Housing and Development Board (HDB)
"high quality" immigrants, 139
Hindu Punjabis in London, 191
Hinduism, 240
Hong Kong
    extension of work contracts, 43
    visa-free arrangement, 50n17
honorary citizen in Singapore, 90, 91
Housing and Development Board (HDB), 209
Humanitarian Organization for Migration economics (HOME), 51n26
human mobility within Asia, 5
human rights, 133
    in Asia, 38
    democracy issues, 145
    education, 71
    movements in Asia, 9
    principle of, 34
human trafficking, 8, 94, 121
Hylam domestic workers, 213

I
identificational integration, 58, 61
    reform in Adachi, 73–74
    reform in Shinjuku, 74–77
identity
    ethnic, *see* ethnic identity
    formation, 20
    of mixed-ethnic children, 164–65
immigrant incorporation policies, 107
    development in South Korea, 113–23
    in South Korea, 109, 110–11
    in Western European countries, 109

immigrant movement in Taiwan, 132, 136
  development of, 142–43
immigrants
  assimilation by, 108
  characteristics of, 111
  Hainanese, 214
  modes of incorporation, 112–13
  policies, idiosyncracy of, 124
  potential, 114
  rhetoric of incorporation, 113
  spheres of incorporation, 111–12
immigration
  citizenship rights, 35
  laws in Malaysia, 43
  to Singapore, 210
  in Taiwan, 153
Immigration Act, 138, 143, 155n3
immigration policies, 132
  AHRLIM, 145
  in Taiwan, 137–39, 153
imperialism
  British, 210
  Japanese, 114
India
  caste identity in, 191
  Citizenship (Amendment) Bill, 2003, 39
  migration in, 2
  naturalization, 37
  partition of, 3
  rural regions of, 95–96
Indian diaspora in Metro Manila, 184–87
  data gathering, 189–90
  media as agents, 198–201
  race and media, 195
  racialized and pathological bodies, 195–98
  self ascriptions, 191–95
  theoretical approaches and research questions, 187–89

Indian eateries in Singapore, 215–16
  food items in, 217–18
  hybridized versions of Western foods, 218
Indian subcontinent, Islamic restaurants from, 239–41
Indian women
  on global television, 200–01
  in Miss Universe and Miss World pageant, 199–200
Indigenous Peoples' rights of political participation, 140
Indo-Caribbean
  girls in New York City, 199
  youths in New York City, 183, 202
Indonesia
  naturalization, 37
  unauthorized migrants, 43
  unity in diversity of, 16
Indonesian
  domestic workers in Singapore, 3
  migrants, 43, 47
Industrial Trainee System, 115
interactive integration, 62
  in Adachi and Shinjuku wards, 61, 70–71
  cultural and, 69–72
  social integration metrics of, 58
inter-ethnic couples
  divorce among, 166–67
  in Japan, 166
  social image of, 166
intermarriages, 179n3
  in Asia, 42
  with Japanese nationals, 45
  and mixed-ethnic children, 166
  trends in, 42
internal migration in Asia, 8
internal migratory trends, 7
international community, 132
international human rights standards, 65

inter-nationalism, 48
Internationalization Strategy and
    Foreign Talent Policy, 87
international marriage, 58
  in Adachi, 67–69
  migration, contemporary modes
      of, 6
  rates, 76
international migrants, 34
  population, 32, 34
  UN recommended definition of,
      49n5
International Migrants' Day, 44
international migration
  in Asia, 8, 10
  of China, 14
  measurement of, 32–33
  source of data on, 49n4
  statistics on, 32
international mobility, dominant
    state-sanctioned forms of, 7
interviews in research methodology,
    170
Ishihara, Shintaro, 67
Islamic food culture, 241
Islamic (halal) food in Korea, 238, 239
Islamic restaurants, 239
  from Indian subcontinent, 239–41
  in Itaewon, 248
  in Korea, 241–44
  for Korean customers, 242–44
  in Seoul, 239, 240
Islamism in Korea, 237
Itaewon
  American culture in, 236, 244
  American food culture in, 248
  diversification of foods in, 247
  diversity of cultures in, 248
  ethnic food restaurants in, 235, 244
  food culture in, 247
  foreigners' territory in, 234–36

foreign food restaurants in, 235
foreign migrants in, 236
halal eateries, 18, 241–42
Islamic restaurants in, 248
restaurants, 235
Italy, scholars and politicians in,
    51n28

J
Jacobin phase of French Revolution,
    33
Japan
  colonization of Korea, 44
  cultural and language barriers in,
      61, 72
  democratic process in, 44
  foreign nationals in, 56–57
  foreign resident in, 44–45
  foreign workers, 56
  ideological homogenization of, 16
  Immigration Control Report, 2007,
      56, 57
  intermarriages in, 42
  internationalization programme, 45
  living together in, 45
  migrant communities in, 44
  migration policy, 41
  mixed-ethnic children in, see
      mixed-ethnic children in
      Japan
  nationality law, 37
  naturalization rate, 44
  residents of Shinjuku, 76
  sex workers in, 3
Japanese
  citizenship, 37, 44
  ethnicity, 170, 171, 178
  imperialism, 114
  migrants, 2
  in Singapore, 268
  soccer migration, 272n1

Japanese colonialism, 15
  Koreans movement under, 3
Japanese language, 66, 71, 75, 176
  education, 69
Joint Committee of Foreign Migrant Workers in Korea (JCMK), 116
Jung Dae Chol, 117
Jurong West, 94
  foreign workers in, 96
jus sanguinis, 137, 139, 142, 153

K

Kant, Immanuel, 84, 85
kayumanggi, 203n4
Kim Dae Jung, 118, 125n4
KMT. *See* Kuomintang or Chinese Nationalist Party (KMT)
kopitiam in Singapore, 18
  customers and community, 220–22
  early settlements during colonial period, 211–13
  food, 217–19
  Hainanese, 213–15
  Indian and Malay eateries, 215–16
  migrant workers in, 217–19
  migration and globalization, 210–11
  migration and social-cultural diversity, 209
  owners, stallholders and workers, 219–20
  public eating culture, 223
  resettlement into HDB, 216–17
  shops and stall tenants, 223
  social-cultural distinctiveness and diversity, 209–10
  tradition, culture and heritage, 223–24
Korea
  alcohol consumption in, 237, 238
  ethnic homogeneity, 15
  globalization factors in, 238
  halal food in, 238, 239, 248
  immigration policy, 248
  Islamic food restaurants in, 234, 241–44, 248
  Japan's colonization of, 44
  meat consumption in, 237, 238
  Nationality Law, 37
Korean
  consumers, 234
  foods in rituals, 237
  migrants, ethnic, 17
  mixed-race, 119–23
  movement under Japanese colonialism, 3
  in Singapore, 268
Korean customers, Islamic restaurant for, 242–44
Korean-dominated foreign community, 77
Korean food culture, Islamic food places in, 236–39
Korean immigrant incorporation policies, 124–25
Korean Immigration Bureau, 119
Korean Muslims, 237, 249n3
Korean National Human Rights Commission (KNHAR), 116
Korean War, 237
"kosians", 121
Kuomintang or Chinese Nationalist Party (KMT), 140, 145

L

labour immigration, 99
labour migrants, 42
  contemporary populations of, 16
  support and assistance, 51n21
labour migration, 3, 8, 38
  in Asian countries, 4, 9
  growth of, 5
  policy in Malaysia, 43

in Singapore, 210–11
   temporary, 49n2
labour shortages
   in Asia, 5
   in Japan, 56
Lee Hsien Loong, 86, 93
legislation, rationale of, 117–18
Legislative Yuan, 142–43
liberal-democratic principles, 136
Little India
   foreign worker population, 96
   weekend enclave in, 95, 96
living together, in Japan society, 45
local-global nexus, in Singapore, 210–11
London, Hindu Punjabis in, 191
"low quality" immigrants, 139

M

mainland brides, 138
mainland China, marriage migrants from, 139, 147, 155n6
Malay food shops in Singapore, 215–16
   food items in, 212, 217–18
   hybridized versions of Western foods, 218
Malaya
   anti-colonial Communist movement in, 11
   colonial administration in, 11
Malaysia
   citizenship law, 51n21
   communalism in, 11
   history of migration, 43
   immigration laws in, 43
   labour migrants, 4
   multiculturalism, 35
   women's groups in, 51n22
"male socialization," 256
Manchuria, internal migrations within, 3

Manila, Indian immigrants in, 185, 194, 196
marriage migrants, 5, 6, 17, 42
   demanding requirements, 125n7
   incorporation policies for, 122
   from mainland China, 139, 147, 155n6
   mixed-race Koreans and, 119–23
   from Southeast Asia, 139
   support and assistance, 51n21
marriage migration, 16, 38, 136–37, 138, 155n4
   migrant workers comparing to, 153
   organized by TASAT, 146, 148
Marshall, T.H., 33
meat consumption, in Korea, 237, 238, 240
media
   as agents of inclusion and exclusion, 198–201
   role in diaspora, 182–84, 188, 189
Metro Manila
   Indian diaspora in, *see* Indian diaspora in Metro Manila
   Miss Universe pageant in, 199–200
migrants
   Bangladesh, 96, 97
   Burmese, 51n24
   Chinese, 2
   communities in Japan, 44
   ethnic Korean, 17
   female marriage, 5
   Filipino, 47
   Indian, 185
   Indonesian, 43, 47
   integration of, 35
   international, *see* international migrants
   marriage, *see* marriage migrants
   non-naturalization by, 44
   rights of, 36

Index   287

transnationalism, 36
two-tiered system in, 38
Migrants Trade Union (MTU), 116
migrant workers, 131, 141, 153
   from Bangladesh/India, 96
   cosmopolitan sensibilities, 96
   hostel for, 94
   intermarriages with nationals, 42
   in Jurong West, 94
   in *kopitiam*, 227
   "race" and nationality, 95–96
   registration of, 38
   rights, 39
   in Singapore, 93, 95
   substantial gatherings of, 95
migration citizenship, in Asian
      countries, 36–41
migration in Asia
   in colonial societies, 11
   complex dimensions of, 20
   contemporary forms of, 13, 14
   feminization of, 3, 6
   gendering of, 6
   migration patterns, 5
   scholarship, 2
   skilled migrants, 4
   temporal and spatial dimensions
      of, 1
migration information system, 49n3
migration policy, in Japan, 41
migratory movement, types of, 38
Ministry of Community
      Development and Sports
      (MCDS), 261
Ministry of Community
      Development, Youth and Sports
      (MCYS), 261
Ministry of Education, 138
Ministry of Interior (MOI), 138, 139,
      150
Ministry of Manpower (MOM), 258
minority groups, 13, 188

minority rights
   in East Asia, 136
   theory of, 134
mixed-ethnic children in Japan
   of divorced foreign mothers, 168,
      169
   empirical data from, 163, 165
   ethnic identity of, 164, 165
   ethnic power relations on, 175–77
   foreign mothers of, 172–73
   intermarriage and, 166
   local council schools for, 173–75
   racial identity of, 164, 165
   raised by single foreign mothers,
      167
   raised by single Thai mothers, 177
   research methodology types in, 170
   research objectives in, 169
   sociological perspective on, 164–65
mixed-race Koreans, 17, 119–23
money-lending scheme, of Punjabis,
      186, 192, 193
monocultural society, 131
multicultural awareness education, 71
multicultural citizenship, 134, 135, 154
multicultural coexistence policies
   in Adachi ward, *see* Adachi ward,
      Tokyo
   cultural and interactive integration,
      69–72
   identificational integration reform,
      72–77
   in Shinjuku ward, *see* Shinjuku
      ward
   structural integration, 61–69
Multicultural Coexistence Promotion
      Committee, 69
multicultural elements, *kopitiam*, 224
Multicultural Family Support Act,
      109
multicultural participation
      programmes, 151

multicultural policy, 35
Multicultural Promotion Committee, 73
multicultural Singlish language, 221
multiculturalism, 10, 35, 107, 109, 112, 122, 123, 228
  in Asia, 20–21, 42
  assimilation to, 60
  CMIO model of, 12
  conservative and progressive critiques of, 19
  crisis of, 35
  democratic, 9
  in East Asia, 136
  elements of, 226
  of human rights, 17
  in Japanese society, 47
  kopitiam, see kopitiam in Singapore
  in Malaysia, 16
  mirroring, 266–71
  models of, 15
  modes of, 19
  in Singapore, 16, 257
  social and cultural dimensions of, 210
multiculturalism in Taiwan, 134, 140–42, 154
  demonstrating values of, 146–49
  development of immigrant movement, 142–43
  and multicultural citizenship, 154
  national anxiety, 130–32
  radicalizing existent values and rhetoric, 143–46
multi-ethnic identity, 164, 165, 169, 177, 178
  of children, 171–72
multi-ethnic municipalities, 58
multilingual advisory services, 71
multi-racial society, in Singapore, 101n2

multiracialism, 88, 93
  CMIO model of, 93, 99
  ideology of, 84, 88
  nation-state's version of, 89
  Singapore's project of, 88–89
Muslims
  communities, in Seoul, 236
  consumers, 234
  food restriction for, 237
  Korean, 237, 249n3
  migrants, business opportunities to, 248
  population in Seoul, 238

N

national citizenship, 133
national diversity policy, 19
National Election Commission, motivation for FLEA, 118
national elections, in Philippines, 39
national identity, 88, 270
  cultural and, 266
  in Singapore, 254–57
National Immigration Agency (NIA), 131, 138, 142–43, 151, 155n12
National Sports Associations (NSAs), 262
Nationality Act in 1999, 137
nationality laws, 37, 49n1
naturalization, 68
  of Koreans, 45
  for migrants, 7
  permanent residence, 47
  preconditions for, 41
  rate in Japan, 44
  requirements for, 37
  rules, 107
  in South Korea, 125n7
  of spouses of Japanese nationals, 69
Negro, 203n4
Netherlands Minorities Policy, 135

Index

Network for Migrants' Rights (NMR), 116
New York City, Indo-Caribbean youths in, 183
Nigerian migrants, in Itaewon, 249
Niigata, Albirex, 268, 269
non-governmental organizations (NGOs), 3, 45, 151, 152
non-halal food, 222
non-profit organizations (NPOs), 72
non-Taiwanese, 132, 149
non-Western ethnicity, 178
non-Western mothers, in Japan, 172, 173
non-white societies, 163, 165

O
old comers, 59
Olympics
　in Beijing, 263
　in Seoul, 235
Organic Act of National Immigration Agency, 138
Overseas Certificate of India (OCI), 39

P
pan-Indian identity, 182
passive citizenship, 33
peaceful cosmopolitan order, 84
peoples of Indian origin (PIOs), 183
People's Republic of China (PRC), 96, 141
permanent migrants, 34
Permanent Residence Act (PRA), 117, 118
permanent resident
　in Singapore, 90, 91
　workers, 220
Philippines, 5–6
　Indian diaspora in, 183, 184
political and voting rights, 39
Punjabi immigrants in, 194
Sindhis in, 194
unauthorized migrants, 43
plural society thesis, 11
pluralism, 90, 112, 114, 227
　cultural, 35
　differential exclusion to, 116–19
　elements of, 226
　religious, 35
political accommodation, in Malaysia, 11
political participation, Indigenous Peoples' rights of, 140
political rhetoric, 145
political rights, 35, 133
population
　ethnic Koreans, 67
　international students, 67
　Japan's foreign resident, 56–57
　problem in South Korea, 125n8
　in Tokyo, 59
postcolonialism, 20
post-national citizenship, 134
P-pass holder, in Singapore, 90, 91
professional migrants, 38
"Project Rainbow", 261
Punjabi immigrants, class and ethnic identity, 191–95

Q
Q-pass holder, in Singapore, 90, 91

R
race-based colonial policies, 11
racial harmony, 89
racial identity, of mixed-ethnic children, 164, 165
racial landscape, of Singapore, 257
racism, 196
Rediffusion, 213

religious harmony, 89
religious pluralism, 35
Republic of China (ROC), 137, 140, 144
reunification, family, 32, 38, 41, 115
R-pass holder, in Singapore, 90, 91
Rugby Union, professionalization of, 255

S
"S Pass," in Singapore, 258
scholarship for migration, 2, 5, 14, 36
   and diversity in Asia, 2, 10
   international mobility, 7
Seoul
   colonialism in, 233
   cultural territory in, 233–34
   foreigners' territory in, 234–36
   halal food restaurants in, 239, 240
   Islamic restaurants in, 239
   Muslim communities in, 236
   Muslim population in, 238
   Olympic Games in, 235
sex-trafficking, 8
sex workers, in Japan, 3
Shinjuku ward
   comparative chart of Adachi ward and, 70–71
   cultural and interactive integration in, 72
   financial realities, 66
   foreign children in, 69
   foreign resident population, 63, 66–67
   integration reforms in, 73
   Japanese residents of, 76
   list of specific measures undertaken by, 64–65
   parallel societies, 74–77
   structural barriers, 63
   in Tokyo, 17

Silverstone, Roger, 182–83, 188
Sindhi immigrants
   class and ethnic identity, 191–95
   in Manila, 185–86, 191, 192
Singapore
   arts and culture in, 86
   broadcasting services in, 213
   citizenship, 37, 50n10, 90
   colonial administration in, 11
   competitive culinary environment of, 219
   cosmopolitan discourses, 99
   cosmopolitan diversity in, 272
   cosmopolitanization of, 84, 86–87, 93
   culture and community, 211
   development of FST scheme, 260–66
   eating houses in, 212
   employment passes in, 41, 258
   ethnic distribution in, 100n1
   extension of work contracts, 43
   food heritages in, 229n7
   foreign clubs in, 268
   foreign workers, 87
   gambling dens in, 212
   halal foodcourts in, 222, 224
   immigrants to, 93
   Indonesian domestic workers in, 3
   Japanese community in, 268
   kopitiam in, *see kopitiam* in Singapore
   Korean community in, 268
   labour requirements in, 258
   local-global nexus in, 210–11
   migrant workers in, 93
   migration to, 210
   multicultural public housing setting in, 18
   multiculturalism in, 257, 266–71
   multi-racial society in, 101n2

Index   291

national identity in, 254–57
paddlers, 266, 273n3
permanent residents in, 91
post-colonial economic growth, 210
PRC-Chinese in, 91, 92
project of multiracialism, 88
public sociability of, 95
race relations in, 93
racial landscape of, 257
socio-cultural thickness, 92
South Asian male migrant workers, 87
S-pass holders, 41, 258
sporting nationalism in, 270
sports migration in, 254–57
as symbol of diversity, 271–72
table tennis team in, 263, 266
Singapore National Olympic Council, 86
Singapore News Alternative, 264
Singapore Sailing Federation, 270
Singapore soccer, 254, 269, 270, 273n5, 273n6
Singapore Sports School, 262
single ethnicity, choosing, 170–71
single foreign mothers, multi-ethnic children raised by, 171–72
skilled migrants, 4, 6, 7, 38, 46, 47
skilled migrant workers, 36, 38, 50n12
S. League, 267, 269, 270
social-democratic citizenship, 33
social integration
    of foreign residents, 63
    between locals and foreign talents, 87
    metrics, 58
    policies, 60–61
    types and associated specific measures, 62
social movements, citizenship from perspectives of, 152–54

social reproduction, significant mode of, 6
social rights, 33, 133
social welfare programmes, 68
sociocultural texture, 83
South Asia
    food regulation in, 237
    foreign workers, 95
    international migration systems of, 14
South Korea
    age-specific fertility rates, 125n6
    ethnic minorities in, 108
    ethnic purity in, 114
    ideological homogenization of, 16
    immigrant incorporation policies in, 110–13
    immigrant incorporation policy development, 113–23, 124–25
    intermarriages in, 42
    legislation for migrant incorporation, 109
    naturalization in, 125n7
    population problem in, 125n8
    tangible policy changes in, 109
Southeast Asia
    food regulation in, 237
    growth of refugees in, 3
    marriage migrants from, 139, 146, 147, 153
    social and cultural diversity in, 20
    women immigrating to Taiwan, 136
Southeast Asian (SEA) Games, 263
Sports Excellence (SPEX) scheme, 261
sports in Singapore
    globalizing forces in, 256
    salary cap in, 268
    as symbol of globalization and diversity, 271–72

sports migration, 272
  limits of, 270
  in Singapore, 254–57
state's cosmopolitan project, 86–87
Statistics and Information Department, Minister's Secretariat, Ministry of Health, Labour and Welfare (SID-MHLW), 179n5
structural integration, 61–69
  reforms, 73, 74
  social integration metrics of, 58
Sun Yat-Sen, 137
Super Reds, in South Korea, 268, 269
Swedish multiculturalism, 135
symbolic capital, 270

T

Taipei City Government, 148
Taipei, marriage migrants in, 146
Taiwan
  citizenship, 17, 137–39
  development of immigrant movement in, 142–43
  economic growth in, 137
  extension of work contracts, 43
  government, 132, 137, 139
  immigration policies in, 137–39
  intermarriages in, 42
  migration, 38
  multiculturalism in, 134, 140–42, 146–49
  National immigration Agency, 42–43
temporary labour migration, 38, 49n2
temporary migrants, 34, 47
temporary migration, 39
territorialization, 249
Thai domestic workers, in Singapore, 3
Thai ethnicity, 171
Thai food items, 218–19

Thai mothers, mixed-ethnic children raised by, 164, 171, 172, 175–77
Thailand, 5–6
  Burmese migrants in, 51n24
  Chinese diasporic presence in, 16
  labour migrants, 4
  levels of unauthorized migration, 38
Tokyo Metropolis
  cost of living, 68
  foreign population in, 59
  foreign residents, 59
  local governments in, 59
  public safety in, 79
traders, in pre-colonial era, 185
traditional ethnic food, authentic strangeness of, 236
TransAsia Sisters Association in Taiwan (TASAT), 137
  marriage migrants organized by, 146, 147
transnational citizenship, concept of, 36
transnational marriages, 13
transnational migration, 83, 92
twice migration, 194

U

unauthorized migrants, 43, 46
unity in diversity, 10
Universal Declaration of Human Rights, 144
UN Trafficking Protocol in 2003, 9
urbanization, 209

V

violent criminals, in Shinjuku, 67
voting rights, 34
  in Philippines, 39

W

Wang Yuegu, 263

Western European countries, 109
Western food, in Seoul, 235
Westernization of Korean food, 237
Western mothers, in Japan, 172, 173
whiteness, 163, 178
white suburbs, 165
work permits, for unskilled foreign workers, 258
World Summit for Social Development, 60

Y
Yang, Philip, 130–31
young people
    from Indian diaspora, 188
    in Manila, 189–90

Z
zero-immigration policies, 114
Zhang Guirong, 263

Printed in the USA
CPSIA information can be obtained
at www.ICGtesting.com
LVHW010432090724
784965LV00001B/28

9 789814 380478